10/90

50
Strange Stories
of the
Supernatural

EDITED BY
JOHN CANNING

Bell Publishing Company
New York

Contents

Editor's Note

To many, especially in the West, increasing affluence seems to have been accompanied by a growing lack of meaning in their lives. They have come to see that a greatly improved standard of living does not of itself bring happiness or fulfilment; and this realization has brought a disenchantment with science and a yearning for a new dimension in experience which will help them to regain a sense of direction.

To these people it seems evident that science cannot explain everything or solve all problems. For modern technology, despite its blessings, has created a polluted planet; and science cannot throw much light on experiences such as love or the sense of beauty—perhaps the most important things in life.

Already alienated from organized religion—science had made deep inroads among the faithful—men and women have recently been showing a quickening interest in psychic phenomena. If there are really such powers as precognition, telepathy, clairvoyance and psychokinesis, then perhaps these may provide a means for contact with a reality not available through the five senses.

Even since the creation of the British Society for Psychical Research in 1882, there have always been men of science who have interested themselves in parapsychology. Among early members of the SPR were the physicists Sir William Barrett, Oliver Lodge and William Crookes, the astronomer Camille Flammarion, and the psychologist William James. But they were a small minority among their sceptical colleagues.

Now even within the scientific world attitudes are changing, with

9

the United States leading the way. The Stanford Institute has run tests on Uri Geller; and at the Menninger Foundation in Topeka, Kansas, researchers have been impressed with the skills of a middle-aged man named Jack Schwarz, who appears to have similar powers over his bodily processes to those of Tahra Bey, whose exploits are described in this book.

The U.S. Government itself is now prepared to support psychic research. The National Institute of Mental Health has recently granted Maimonides Medical Centre in Brooklyn funds for tests in extra-sensory perception; and the National Aeronautics and Space Administration has financed a Stanford Research Institute programme to teach ESP skills to NASA personnel.

All this is a very long way indeed from J. B. Rhine's card-guessing experiments at Duke University in the 1930s, and a strong indication that parapsychology and the occult will be a major field of research in the future. But these subjects are also completely fascinating for the general reader.

At the level purely of entertainment (though inevitably there is information too for those who would know more), I have endeavoured to bring together here some of the strange and startling events from the realms of the occult. These range in time from the Middle Ages to the present day, and in character from folk myths and hauntings to seemingly supernormal powers displayed under near-clinical conditions.

In several of the chapters, where the events recounted might have caused pain or embarrassment to surviving relatives, I have changed names and geographical locations. The essential facts, however, remain true. In the case of folk-legends, the contributors have endeavoured to reconstruct the stories as convincingly as possible within the framework of ascertainable historical fact.

JOHN CANNING

The Mysterious Orient

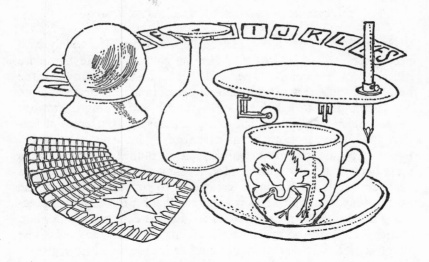

MADAME BLAVATSKY
AND THE MAHATMAS

Madame Helena Petrovna Blavatsky was a truly remarkable woman. Her forceful, colourful, vital character fascinated people, made her many friends but often alienated them. Although she was proved to the satisfaction of almost everybody to be a fraud in some things, her teaching has survived to this day. It is impossible not to concede that she possessed remarkable powers, nor to admire her courage, perseverance and enthusiasm, even in the face of ridicule and hardship.

She was born in Ekaterinslav, Russia, in 1831. Her father, a German in the service of the Tsar and governor of the district, was of noble blood; and on her mother's side she was the granddaughter of Princess Helene Dolgorouky, whose ancestors were closely connected with the reigning family.

Helena was a premature baby, sickly and weak. For this reason her baptism was quickly arranged, a priest and witnesses summoned. As the priest pronounced on her behalf the Renunciation of the Devil, his robes caught fire, and several people were badly burned.

This was considered in the locality to be an evil omen, and nobody was surprised when the child seemed to be bewitched. Nymphs and goblins were her constant companions, at least in her own mind, and her imaginings so affected the household that she was constantly being sprinkled with holy water in an effort to exorcize the spirits.

13

For a while, in her teens, Helena Petrovna travelled widely with her father. This broadening of her outlook only made her more independent, and served to persuade her much-tried family that the best way to suppress her unhealthy interest in spirits, death and the occult would be to marry her off. A match was arranged between the seventeen-year-old girl and General Blavatsky, Governor of Erivan. This unfortunate man was described by his wife as being between sixty and seventy years old and a "plumeless raven". It is more likely that he was under fifty, for he was still alive thirty years later, and certainly he had a great deal to put up with from the lively, independent girl. It is well known that for those women practising the occult sciences a state of virginity is extremely important. Whether or not the marriage was consummated (and Madame Blavatsky strongly denied it through her life) it lasted a very short time. After repeated quarrels the young wife left and set out on her travels.

Later HPB (as she was called for most of her life) told her friends that from Russia she went to Cairo, where she became a pupil of an old Copt possessing magic powers; and thence to Paris where she met Daniel Dunglas Home, the noted spiritualist, who wished to train her as a medium. It is possible that HPB learned a great deal from him, although years later she was at pains to refute spiritualism and to adopt a completely different motive for producing her marvels.

Her travels continued. In Quebec she sought out Indian tribes in the search for knowledge, and in New Orleans learnt much of voodoo, that necromantic cult about which, at that time, few white people knew anything.

At this time HPB's philosophy, later to be taught to so many, was already forming in her receptive and imaginative mind. The vision of an Indian, tall, dignified and stern, whom she recognized as a messenger from Tibetan adepts in the occult, had appeared to her once or twice in her youth. Now she determined to visit Tibet and seek out the masters who could initiate her into the true knowledge. Although she said later that she had taken the full seven years' initiation, the time she spent there was certainly only as many months. Her means, supplied irregularly by her father, were not sufficient to allow her to travel indefinitely and in 1858, after ten years' wandering, she returned home to Russia.

From her arrival she was a *succès fou*. Those who remembered her as a child were now adults, and only too anxious to learn their futures and to hear from their dead friends. Madame Blavatsky was able to oblige them to the extent of rapped or written replies to mental questions, to provide prescriptions, cures and manifestations. That she had considerable sense of humour is shown by her revenge on a lady who doubted her powers. When this person asked her to name the best conductor for these occult rappings from the spirits she received the word "gold". At the same instant she rose to her feet, hand to mouth. The gold fillings in her teeth had been firmly rapped.

Another phenomenon which HPB at that time demonstrated was a change in weight of either inanimate or animate objects. On one occasion, merely by fixing it with a concentrated gaze, she succeeded in making a small chess-table so heavy that several people were quite unable to lift it. After a number of attempts had been made HPB carelessly waved her hand and looked away; the table again became its normal weight.

Perhaps her most difficult convert at that time was her father. He was not only indifferent to her marvels, but pronounced them "bosh". One day however he let himself be persuaded by two old friends to go into another room and write one word, unknown to anyone, on a piece of paper. He returned saying that if his daughter could persuade her spirits to rap out what he had written he would be forced at last to believe her—and consider himself also as a proper subject for incarceration in a lunatic asylum.

Without touching the plate which was the sounding-board for the raps, HPB watched with amusement while the answer was received. On seeing the transcription her father trembled and became very pale. It was the word he had written, and such an odd one—the name of a favourite horse—that there was no possibility of guess-work. This served to convert him to belief in his daughter's powers, and thereafter he was proud of her successes and supported her until his death a few years later.

After a while HPB's wanderlust overtook her again. Eventually she settled in Cairo where she founded the *Société Spirite*, and earned her living for a time as a medium. This period is notable only for the fact that she made a friend of Madame Coulomb, who provided both money and hospitality, but who later in her life became her chief detractor, bringing down like a card-house the reputation HPB had worked for so many years to achieve.

These earlier chapters of Madame Blavatsky's life are only partly authenticated, and it is from the time of her arrival in America in the early 1870s, and her meeting with Colonel Henry Olcott, that her known story begins. Olcott, her chronicler had a great regard for the truth, and although he may have given her the benefit of the doubt in many instances, he was also a journalist, a man of inquiring mind and no fool. Madame Blavatsky was the spring from which the Theosophical Society fed, but the Colonel was an administrator as well as a believer. Although their relationship could at times be stormy, this combination of talents created a belief which continues, admittedly among only a small minority, to this day.

Colonel Olcott always had a considerable interest in spiritualism, and in October, 1847, was present at a demonstration by two mediums, the Eddy brothers, when a colourful and compelling sight caught his attention. At this time HPB, dressed in a bright red shirt, may not have been so corpulent as she afterwards became, but her figure and personality dominated any room she occupied. She herself, with characteristic lack of physical vanity, described her appearance as "Kalmucko–Buddhisto–Tartaric". Her broad flat face and ungraceful figure were redeemed by fine, narrow hands, bedecked with rings, and by her large, expressive, compelling, grey-blue eyes. All this was topped by light brown hair, very thick, centrally parted and as crinkled as sheep's wool.

The elegant hands were stained brown from the cigarettes which she constantly smoked, rolling them herself (and in those days it was a strange habit for a woman). Her speech was polyglot and strewn with oaths. Nevertheless, before that first evening ended Colonel Olcott was fascinated by her. Moreover he noticed that the Eddy brothers and other mediums enjoyed greater success when HPB was present at a séance; for it ensured that only genuine spirits were called up. Not only this, but these other mediums were controlled by their spirits while HPB, in similar circumstances, was commanding the spirits to do her will, in full awareness.

As a result of Colonel Olcott's interest and complimentary articles in the newspapers, HPB achieved a formidable reputation in America. She took an apartment in New York which she called the "Lamasery" and which she filled with a motley collection of stuffed creatures—snakes, monkeys, owls; even a lion's head glared down from the walls. Buddhas, cuckoo-clocks and canaries crowded the little Japanese cabinets. And in the midst of this HPB held court, chain-smoking, wrapped in her favourite garment, a greasy, red-flannel dressing-gown. The effect would have seemed ludicrous, but such was her enthusiasm and magnetism that she gathered round her the élite of all those aspirants to occult knowledge with which America at that time abounded.

In 1875 came the turning point in her life. From spiritualism

Madame Blavatsky decided to turn to the Masters who, she had long thought, would guide her to the discovery and diffusion of the knowledge of the laws governing the universe. To that end she, Colonel Olcott and W. Q. Judge, a devoted occultist, founded the Theosophical Society. The aim of the Society was to supersede or control the forces of nature through the Adepts, those masters of lore, living in Tibet, who through long initiation have attained the astral plane. These Masters, or Mahatmas, could materialize themselves and other natural objects where they wished, see past and future, and prolong their own lives at will. They could use their powers for evil and indeed there were, according to HPB, some who did, but the Society was interested only in the good.

Although the Society became fairly well established, HPB and the Colonel soon ran into financial difficulties and there was not enough money to expand the Society. So it was with relief that HPB and the Colonel welcomed into their circle the old, infirm and apparently rich Baron de Palm. Soon after becoming one of the initiates this gentleman made a will leaving everything he possessed to Olcott, for the use of the Society, then almost immediately died. The Society received many congratulations on their inheritance, but alas for their hopes the Baron's vaunted riches and lands proved entirely imaginary. He had lived for years at others' expense and this was his last joke.

Worse was to follow. Already made to look ridiculous, the Society was brought into further disrepute by a very injudicious act on the part of HPB herself. For a reason which no one can explain (and bigamously since General Blavatsky was still alive), she married a coarse Armenian, many years younger than herself. Perhaps she believed him to be rich. At any rate she never allowed the marriage to be consummated, and after a few months, during which time she discovered he had no money after all, she left him.

About this time her first book, *Isis Unveiled*, was published. It was a remarkable work, a hotchpotch of beliefs, religions and legends from all times and places. Olcott, who was with her as she wrote, testified that he was completely convinced that at times the author was not HPB but a Mahatma inhabiting her body temporarily. Certainly such differences of style, literacy and language in one work are hard to explain. The book went some way towards redeeming HPB's reputation, but she now decided that for a while she wished to study rather than teach, and she and Olcott determined to go to India. A society called the Arya Samaj had recently been formed there to revive the ancient and mystic principles of the Hindu religion, and its leader had corresponded for some time with Olcott. In answer to an invitation to visit Indian and exchange ideas, the Colonel and HPB embarked.

. On their arrival at Bombay in 1879 the Colonel made an instantly favourable impression by stooping and kissing the ground. The Arya Samaj welcomed them lavishly, although their motives were not entirely pure. They were delighted that an American organization, the Theosophical Society, was favourable to Indian hopes of self-government; and indeed HPB perhaps carried her enthusiasm for Indian aspirations too far, since for quite a time after her arrival she was shadowed by the police.

Madame Blavatsky realized that she could not totally ignore the European community if she were successfully to establish the Society. A.P. Sinnett, the editor of the *Pioneer*, an important English-language newspaper, had written to her on her arrival. As an enthusiastic occultist he was prepared to give her his support, and she must eventually do all she could to win his confidence and allegiance. However until she could meet him she and the Colonel travelled to many places in India, questioning ascetics, fakirs and swamis in the search for knowledge.

A few months after their arrival in India, HPB and Olcott produced the first copy there of the Theosophical Magazine. Apart from fascinating articles on western occultism and other subjects on which she could be supposed to be informed, oriental philosophy, the Vedas (Hindu sacred writings) and similar matters were discussed vivaciously and accurately. The magazine was a great success and did much to establish HPB's reputation in India.

Eventually she and Colonel Olcott were invited to Allahabad to stay with A. P. Sinnett and his wife. Disconcerted at first by her rough manners and strange appearance, Sinnett found to his relief that his friends considered her a fascinating eccentric. She was invited to many houses, principally, one imagines, for the marvels—well publicized by the ever-busy Olcott—which she could perform. At this time, however, HPB was disinclined to perform any "monkey tricks" as she insisted on calling them, claiming that her Masters were against the casual showing of phenomena, and that knowledge should not be used in this way. Later, in order to prove the existence of these same Adepts, she was to relax this rule time and time again.

Sinnett and the others of the growing band of Indian Theosophists were in no doubt at all that, despite her tantrums when requested to produce marvels, HPB had been chosen by the Masters to be their representative, although they were disappointed that they themselves could not receive a message from or manifestation of, these supreme beings.

The arrival of her old friends the Coulombs in India delighted HPB. Also it must be admitted that HPB was no sort of house-keeper, and was grateful for this work to be taken over by her friend. Her household also included Damodar, a tubercular and pathetic youth who had severed connections with his well-to-do family in order to join HPB.

With her household thus in safe keeping, HPB travelled to Ceylon with Olcott at the invitation of Buddhist high priests. Their welcome on this island far outdid any previously encountered, and they felt themselves so attuned to the Buddhist religion that they immediately became initiated into it. Although several branches of the Theo-sophical Society were established in Ceylon, their success among the Buddhists did them no service with their associates of the Hindu society Arya Samaj. On the return to India of HPB and Olcott, the leader of this society suggested that they should dissolve their partnership. This was agreed, but after a while the Arya Samaj went further, denigrating the Theosophists, giving publicity to their lack of an exact dogma and even their lack of funds. Happily it did little harm to Madame Blavatsky. She was very busy building a new and more dramatic doctrine.

When Sinnett again invited her to stay, Madame Blavatsky announced that she had at last the direct guidance of an Adept, Mahatma Koot Hoomi. No longer was she a tyro, unfit to produce proof of the existence of the initiates. On the contrary she was happy to communicate their wishes, gifts and opinions to those deserving of them.

At any dinner party or gathering, messages would be distributed from the astral plane, etheric music heard and objects moved by an unseen agency. Two notable marvels took place, both in broad day-light. Mrs Sinnett, while out for a walk, confided in HPB that what she really needed to confirm her belief in the Mahatmas was a materialized and personal note from one of them. HPB wrote upon a piece of paper, crumpled it in her hand and, without moving away, indicated a tree near by. Impaled on a twig was a similar note with the message, "I believe I was requested to leave a note here. What do you want with me?" The signature was in Tibetan characters. Mrs Sinnett was sure that this could only have happened through a supernatural agency—and indeed it greatly enhanced Madame Blavatsky's reputation. The next sensational episode took place in the presence of impartial strangers and had even more impact.

HPB, Colonel Olcott and the Sinnetts arranged a picnic with another lady and a Major Henderson, not a Theosophist. Their baskets were packed, and on their way they were joined by an English judge who asked to come with them. On their arrival at the picnic spot it was realized that there were only six cups and saucers for seven people, and it was suggested to HPB that she should produce some convenient materialization. After looking about her for a few minutes, she pointed to a place in a small mound and asked Major Henderson to dig there with a knife. He took only a few moments to unearth a cup and saucer, matching those in the picnic basket.

One more phenomenon deserves mention. At a dinner in the house of a friend, Mr Hume, HPB told Mrs Hume that she would find any article for her that she particularly wanted, of course with the help of Koot Hoomi. Mrs Hume asked for a pearl brooch, given away some time before. A little later HPB told the company to search a particular flower bed—and there was the brooch wrapped in paper.

After these remarkable feats, HPB was pressed by Hume, Sinnett and others to produce a miracle of universal appeal. Perhaps she would cause a copy of the London *Times* to appear at Simla on the day of publication in England? Sinnett found a reply from the Master in his office a few days later. It explained that if such a miracle, easy enough to accomplish, should become known to the masses, it would cause world-wide disturbance, mobbing and disruption, the only way to make everyone believe in the eternal truths was by a process of gradual enlightenment. Sinnett was flattered by the further advice: "One witness of well-known character outweighs the evidence of ten strangers—work on the material you already have and you will receive further proof."

Despite these encouraging words and a perfect flood of correspondence between Koot Hoomi and Sinnett, it proved impossible for either that gentleman or Mr Hume to communicate with the Master without HPB as an intermediary. Indeed at the Sinnetts' suggestion to Koot Hoomi that the advancement of the Society would perhaps be better in his own hands, Koot Hoomi replied in no uncertain terms that ingratitude for the unceasing efforts of the two founders could form no part of the Theosophical philosophy.

All these messages arrived in mysterious fashion, either falling to the floor from apparently thin air in front of the recipient or pressed into their hands by no perceptible means, or perhaps merely throughout the long exchange of letters between the Mahatma and

Sinnett the latter, though determined to use his normally considerable critical faculties, never doubted their provenance. The letters came to him, first in one handwriting, then in another—and some HPB freely admitted to having written herself under her Master's control. Perhaps Sinnett's admiration of her whole-hearted absorption in the work of spreading Theosophical knowledge, her courage in continuing her course despite difficulties, her capacity for hard and continuous concentration on her writing—all these things prevented his doubting her integrity.

Over the next year or so HPB was mainly concerned with her magazine and her writing. She also travelled throughout India, raising funds, producing phenomena and learning from a variety of people. She became seriously ill with Brights disease, accompanied by boils and ulcers. Although in a very low state of health she made a long journey alone to Darjeeling, and then crossed into Sikkim. Once there, she said, she met her Masters, and was quickly cured.

Perhaps the most important incidents to take place after this were those in which at last Koot Hoomi showed himself in his physical body to those Theosophists who had despaired of ever seeing their spiritual masters. On several occasions a white-clad, dignified and turbanned Indian appeared, gliding to and fro, and remaining for several minutes before vanishing. There were many eye-witnesses to these longed-for manifestations, and the standing of the Theosophical Society had never been so high.

At the Society's headquarters in Adyar, HPB had constructed a shrine, or small cupboard, containing portraits of the Masters. This became famous as the spot in which messages from the Mahatmas were usually left, even in HPB's absence. On one occasion when she was away visiting friends, General Morgan, a man of unimpeachable character called at her house in Adyar to see the shrine. As it was opened a small dish fell out and shattered, much to the distress of Madame Coulomb. She picked up the shards, wrapped them in cloth, put them back inside the shrine and shut the doors, all the while lamenting the accident. The general, a little bored with all the fuss, said that if it was so important the Mahatma had better mend it. At this the consumptive young Damodar opened the doors to find not only a message from Koot Hoomi, but the dish, completely intact.

Though this incident had a great effect on both Europeans and Indians, it heralded the decline of HPB's golden years. The English branch of the Society disapproved of the Buddhist influence, and there were charges of plagiarism and fraud to be answered. It appeared that Koot Hoomi had repeated in one of his messages a long extract from a speech made by an American spiritualist three years before. Koot Hoomi was righteously indignant at this *lèse-majesté*, but he was calm compared with the ebullient HPB. She flew into a royal rage, as she always did when her Mahatma was doubted. Another reason which decided her to return to England was that the Committee of the Society for Psychical Research was anxious to interview her. Since Colonel Olcott was to accompany her, the Coulombs were to stay on as caretakers. With these arrangements, which were to prove so disastrous, completed HPB embarked again.

Her meeting with the SPR did not go entirely smoothly. Sinnett also had come to England, and with him acting as liaison officer it did not prove entirely disastrous. HPB gave full permission for a member of the committee to visit the Indian branches of the Theosophical Society and to make whatever investigations he thought proper.

She was travelling in Europe when the blow fell. Her trusted friend, Madame Coulomb, feeling herself likely to be ousted in HPB's absence by other members of the Society and turned out to starve, resorted to blackmail. Abetted by her husband, she demanded a large sum of money for keeping their mouths shut about the frauds they alleged HPB had perpetrated with their assistance. This money was refused and the Coulombs immediately went to a missionary, a bitter enemy of HPB, and planned her ruin.

Soon the Christian College magazine of Madras commenced publication of the "Coulomb Letters". If true they were damning. They explained in full the broken dish of General Morgan, the manifestations of the Mahatma, and so on through all HPB's apparent marvels. All the letters, the Coulombs claimed, which had so convinced Sinnett and others had been written by HPB and her associates and released by threads from roof beams, or by mechanical means. The materialized Mahatma was none other than one of the Coulombs, wearing a stuffed cotton mask which they had made themselves to represent Koot Hoomi.

Olcott and HPB hurried back to India to refute these charges. If HPB could have brought a libel action against the Christian College magazine and her erstwhile friend she might well have won. Handwriting experts were not unanimous, and the Coulombs not reputable people. However, Olcott thought it unwise, and perhaps he was right, to put so unstable and excitable a woman as HPB in the witness-box. But HPB had another disaster to face.

The investigator for the Society for Psychical Research produced his interim report. Despite the freedom he had been given to interrogate Theosophical Society members, the hospitality he had received and the facilities given to him to examine the shrine and HPB's house, his report was annihilating. He denounced Madame Blavatsky as a complete impostor. Cruelly and unnecessarily he also accused her of coming to India as a Russian spy.

Whatever was discovered of HPB's deceptions, whether her powers were less and her ingenuity greater than her followers wished to think, no other of her detractors ever believed this last accusation: but to HPB it was almost a death-blow. Yet another tragic effect of the investigator's visit to Adyar was the death of the pathetic Damodar. He had done his utmost to uphold HPB against questioning, but had broken down and, seriously ill, he left Madras to travel north. Leaving Darjeeling to try to reach his Masters, he froze to death on the road.

Broken in health, Madame Blavatsky returned to England. As always, her courage and energy soon had her back at her writing, denouncing the SPR, supplying Sinnett with all kinds of dramatic information for the biography of herself on which he was then engaged, and making new friends. Happily the publication of her new book *The Secret Doctrine* now had an all-important effect on the future of the Theosophical Society, for it was read by a brilliant woman who was to become the Society's inspiration and expand its activities throughout the world. This was Mrs. Annie Besant, who immediately adopted the tenets and teachings of Madame Blavatsky.

The two women became inseparable, but for HPB life was nearing its end. Annie Besant was obliged to travel abroad, and at once HPB declined in health. She had been an invalid for some years, but suddenly the energy and courage which had sustained her obese and diseased body drained away. She died, in the arms of her friends, on 8 May, 1891.

Whether Helena Petrovna Blavatsky was the fraud her enemies claimed, or whether she was genuinely able to control psychic phenomena and command spirits has never been proved. What is certain is that she was a woman of remarkable mesmeric powers which, combined with boundless enthusiasm, wide occult knowledge and a true belief in the possibility of attaining an understanding of the after-life, converted many intelligent people to her philosophy.

MIRACLE-MAKING IN BENARES

Benares, or Varanasi as it is widely known today, is reputed to be one of the most ancient cities in the world. It is located fairly centrally in northern India on the River Ganges, and is regarded as the holiest of the Seven Hindu sacred cities. It has survived the ravages of time and invaders; in 1194 it was sacked by Muslims, most of the temples being razed to the ground and replaced by mosques, and was ceded to the British in 1775. Each year a million or more pilgrims visit the city to bathe in the holy water of the Ganges and, since it is believed that those who die in Benares proceed direct to heaven, the burning-ghats on the river, where the dead are cremated, are kept busy.

Paul Brunton's first reaction on entering India's holiest city was that it possessed "a most unholy smell". This arose from the fact that the roads were paved with a mixture of cow-dung and earth, added to which an old moat surrounding the city had been used for generations as a refuse dump and drain. Nevertheless, it was a sacred city and therfore an inevitable target for Brunton's questing mind, which was not concerned with tourism but with the higher realms of mysticism and philosophy.

Brunton's extensive wanderings throughout the East are recorded in his books, which he started to write during the 'thirties. At that time he was a relatively young man, armed with a knowledge of shorthand, a stock of notebooks and a folding Kodak camera. In addition to his travel books, however, he also wrote two books on mysticism and Yoga (*The Secret Path* and *The Quest for the Over-self**) which, though aimed at the western reader, proved to be a remarkable distillation of the essence of Oriental mysticism both in practical and philosophical terms. They underline Brunton's true motivation as a man in search of esoteric knowledge, prepared to travel thousands of miles to find it, record it, analyse it and finally present it in an intelligible and logical form to the western mind. To what end? Perhaps in response to some inner compulsion which certainly, on the evidence available, dominated many years of his active life.

So it was not by accident that Brunton came to the holy city of Benares. In his pocket was a piece of paper bearing the name and address of a Yogi miracle worker, one of whose disciples he had previously met in Bombay. The name of the Yogi was Vishudhananda. As he had no formal letter of introduction, Brunton could not know what kind of reception to expect, but he was determined to meet his man if at all possible.

To locate the address he explored the narrow winding streets of Benares on foot, which was not without its hazards as he was aware of a generally hostile attitude towards a lone European wandering through the holy city; indeed, on one occasion a threat to shoot him was hissed behind his back, though on turning round he saw no sign of a fanatical face in the crowded street. Soon he came to a district where the houses were larger and more prosperous in appearance, with spacious and well-kept compounds. It was here that he eventually found his destination—a gate with the name Vishudhananda inscribed on one of the posts.

To arrive at the house was one thing; to enter it another. The veranda was guarded by a young man who created the impression, perhaps deliberately, of uncomprehending stupidity. Brunton's requests to see the Yogi teacher got him nowhere—the young guardian merely shook his head. No such person was known there. Brunton's impression was that perhaps the young man genuinely believed that no European could possibly have any business with his Yogi master and that the address he had been given was in error. Determined not to be put off and relying on Hindu hospitality, Brunton brushed aside all objections and simply walked into the house, leaving the young man at his post on the veranda.

In one of the inner rooms he came upon his objective—a bearded old man of venerable appearance reclining upon a couch while around him on the floor squatted a group of well-dressed Indians.

* Published by Rider.

Their surprise at Brunton's unexpected and unannounced intrusion can well be imagined. Brunton made the conventional salutation, saying, with palms touching, "Peace, master", and set out to explain his presence. He was, he explained, a writer and student of Indian native philosophy and wisdom, and well understood that holy teachers never made public exhibition of their powers. Nevertheless, in view of his deep interest in their ancient wisdom he begged indulgence to be treated as an exception.

The students squatting on the floor stared in astonishment at each other and then at their teacher, Vishudhananda. The latter, a man of over seventy, had large deeply pouched eyes and a short nose above his long grey beard. Around his neck hung the sacred thread of a Brahmin. His eyes, not unexpectedly, fixed coldly upon the European visitor. Brunton recorded a "strange force" pervading the room which made him feel uneasy.

At length Vishudhananda announced in Bengali via a disciple that no audience could be granted unless Brunton were accompanied by Pundit Kavirj, the Principal of the Government Sanskrit College, to act as interpreter. The pundit was a long-standing disciple of the Yogi and had a perfect command of English. An appointment was made for four o'clock the following afternoon.

The next step, after Brunton had expressed his thanks and made his departure, was to find Pundit Kavirj, but this time he hired a passing carriage to take him to the Sanskrit College. The Principal had gone home. Undeterred, he drove on for another half hour to a tall ancient house where the Pundit lived, and this time he was lucky. He found his man sitting on the floor of a top room, surrounded by books and documents, a Brahmin in appearance, with a refined, scholarly face of light complexion. Brunton explained his mission and after some hesitation the Pundit agreed to the next day's appointment.

Having arranged his programme satisfactorily Brunton could now relax for a while. He took a carriage to the bank of the Ganges and wandered along the terraced stone steps which had been built originally for the benefit of the bathing pilgrims but now, after many centuries of use, the steps were worn and uneven. Even so, pilgrims and priests swarmed everywhere. His chief impression was one of untidiness and irregularity: in his own words "temples tumble into the water; glistening domes are neighbours to squat, square decorated palaces which rise to varying heights; while the whole hotch-potch of buildings mingles the ancient and the modern indiscriminately".

The next day, as arranged, Pundit Kavirj and Brunton arrived at Vishudhananda's house at exactly four o'clock. This time there was no problem about entering. The teacher was in his room as before, surrounded by about six other disciples, and Brunton was invited to squat down a few feet away from the couch upon which he lay.

Vishudhananda immediately asked Brunton if he wished to see one of his wonders and when Brunton, pleased and surprised, deferentially replied: "If the master wishes to grant this favour," he was asked for a handkerchief—preferably a silk one. "I will create for you any scent you wish," said Vishudhananda, "using only a lens and the rays of the sun."

Fortunately Brunton did have a silk handkerchief, which he handed to the teacher, who then produced a small lens with which he intended to concentrate the sun's rays. At that time of day the sun was not shining directly into the sheltered room, but Vishudhananda overcame the problem by sending a disciple out into the courtyard with a small mirror, by means of which he reflected the sun's rays into the room.

"Now," said Vishudhananda, "I will create a scent for you out of the air. You have only to choose which."

Brunton asked for white jasmine, a strong and familiar scent.

The teacher then picked up the handkerchief in one hand, held the burning lens above it and for about two seconds a brilliant spot of sunlight glowed on the silk. When he handed the handkerchief back to Brunton it smelt as though it had been drenched in the fragrant scent of white jasmine.

Brunton looked carefully at the handkerchief. There was no sign of moisture or of any stain to indicate that liquid might have been dropped on it, nor any scorching of the fibres from the lens.

Brunton's bewilderment was so apparent that Vishudhananda offered to repeat the demonstration, and on the second occasion Brunton chose the scent of attar of roses. This time he watched carefully every move that the master made, closely examining his hands and his spotless white robe, but could see nothing that was not perfectly straightforward. The procedure was repeated, using another corner of the handkerchief, which this time smelt strongly of attar of roses.

Mystified, Brunton begged him to repeat the feat yet again, and Vishudhananda obligingly produced the scent of violets, while Brunton watched as carefully and with as little result as before, while in contrast to Brunton's eagerness and astonishment the

27

teacher remained imperturbable. To him this was an everyday event, of no particular remark.

"Now I shall create the scent," he told Brunton, "of a flower which grows only in Tibet."

Once more Vishudhananda concentrated the sunlight, on the fourth corner of the handkerchief, and then handed it to Brunton. This time the subtle scent was one which he failed to recognize.

Still filled with doubt, Brunton put the handkerchief back in his pocket. Had he witnessed a true "wonder", or had Vishudhananda somehow contrived to hide the perfumes in the folds of his robe? This explanation was hardly possible for it would have meant that the master would have had to carry upon him a stock as large as that of a Paris *parfumier* to allow for the random choice that Brunton might make. Moreover, during the whole procedure his hands had been always in view.

Brunton looked carefully at the lens, but it was an ordinary magnifying glass set in a wire frame, with a wire handle, of the kind Brunton himself had used as a child. There was nothing in the least suspicious about it, and Brunton had noticed that the disciples—all of whom he had been told were men of good reputation and education—showed no sign of assuming that the master's recent demonstration had been anything but genuine magic. The only possibility left was that Brunton had somehow been hypnotized—but when he got back to his quarters later on he showed the handkerchief to three other people, each one of whom confirmed that it bore strong traces of the various scents.

As he rose to take his leave Vishudhananda told Brunton that he would like to show him another marvel, but that it required the full light of the sun. However if Brunton would come again at midday later on in the week Vishudhananda would show him a feat that he rarely performed, that of restoring life to the dead. Naturally Brunton accepted eagerly, but with some scepticism. Raising the dead was a rather different matter to producing scents from the air and he felt sure that some trickery would be involved.

On the appointed day Brunton returned to the house of the Yogi, again in the company of Pundit Kaviry. Explaining that he could only perform this marvel on small animals, and then only restore them to life temporarily, Vishudhananda told one of his disciples to strangle a sparrow. The bird was then left for an hour to ensure that it was indeed dead.

Brunton examined it closely. The small bundle of feathers was stiff and cold, the eyes staring. He could detect no sign of life whatever.

At the end of the hour the master took his magnifying glass and concentrated the rays of the sun, now at its noonday height, on to one of the eyes of the bird. Motionless Vishudhananda sat hunched over the bird, his large brilliant eyes fixed unwinkingly on it, his face betraying no emotion.

After a few minutes Vishudhananda suddenly began a weird crooning chant in a language unknown to Brunton. A few moments later the bird's legs began to twitch, the feathers fluttered slightly and within a few minutes the sparrow was on its feet, hopping a little uncertainly around the floor. However it soon gathered enough strength to spread its wings, and for half an hour it flew around the room, occasionally finding somewhere to perch.

Brunton was speechless with astonishment. So incredible seemed the incident that he was obliged to make a real effort of will to pull his wits together and assure himself that what was happening was real and not some strange dream or hallucination. The atmosphere was tense, but as he searched the faces of the Pundit and of the Yogi's disciples, Brunton saw nothing but absorbed interest as they watched the little bird.

Suddenly the spell was broken. Without warning the bird fell from the air and dropped to the floor where it lay without moving. Once again Brunton carefully examined it and once again it was obviously quite dead.

Brunton told Pundit Kavirj to ask the master whether he could have kept the bird alive any longer. Vishudhananda replied that with further experiment he hoped to do greater things, but that that was the most he could do at present. Kavirj added, independently, that what Brunton had already seen should satisfy him; he could not expect the master to continue to perform marvels as though he were a street magician, but he added that Vishudhananda could produce grapes and sweetmeats from the air, and restore a faded flower to full bloom.

Brunton then asked Vishudhananda the story of his life and learned he had been born in Bengal. At the age of thirteen he was bitten by a poisonous insect which made him so ill that his mother despaired of his life and took him down to the banks of the Ganges to die. Watched by the relations who had come to observe the funeral rites, his mother lowered the body of her son into the water. But the holy river refused to receive the dying boy. As he was lowered into the water it receded, and as he was raised up it rose again to its former level.

A Yogi sitting near by observed this and came over to the boy's family. He predicted that the child was intended to live: his life was reserved for great things and he would become a famous Yogi himself. He then rubbed some herbs on the poisoned wound and told the parents to take the child home. Seven days later the Yogi arrived to tell the parents that their son was completely cured. This was true, but in that week the entire personality and character of the child had changed: he was no longer content to remain at home with his family but wished instead to become a wandering Yogi.

When he was eventually given permission to leave he went in search of the adepts of Yoga and made his way to Tibet. There, among the hermits who lived in the caves of the snow-covered, windswept mountains he searched for the master who, according to the beliefs of the aspirant to the the mysteries of Yoga, must become his personal teacher.

He returned disappointed to his home, but his determination remained and on a second visit to southern Tibet he at last found the right man. He was, Vishudhananda said, 1200 years old (and he said it as calmly as if he had said 50), and he had initiated Vishudhananda into the principles of Yoga body control and into the art of what he called "solar science".

Vishudhananda continued his training in the bleak mountains for twelve years and was then sent back to India where, in due course, he himself became a teacher of Yoga in Puri, in the bay of Bengal, where he still had a large house. Among his disciples, all high-class Hindus, were rich merchants and landowners, government officials and even a Rajah.

"How do you perform the wonders that you have shown me?" asked Brunton.

The Yogi folded his plump hands. "What you have been shown," he said, "is not the result of Yoga practice, it is the result of the knowledge of solar science. Yoga is the development of will power and mental concentration, but solar science is merely a collection of secrets and no special training is needed to make use of them. It can be studied just as any of the western material sciences can be studied. It is nothing new and was well known to the great Yogis of ancient times. Now, except for a rare few, the knowledge has almost been lost to this country. There are life-giving elements in the sun's rays and if you knew how to select and separate those elements you too could do wonders. There are etheric forces in sunlight which can be controlled and which give a magic power."

Brunton asked Vishudhananda if he were teaching these secrets to his disciples and was told that certain of the disciples would be chosen, when they were ready, and the secrets given to them. He was taken to see the laboratory which had been built for the purposes of study, demonstration and experiment. It was a modern, red brick building, several storeys high, its windows still awaiting the huge sheets of glass—red, blue, green, yellow and clear—through which the sunlight could be reflected.

Brunton returned to sit before the master, brooding on the fact that, as a westerner, he would never understand the mysteries of oriental magic. As though he had read Brunton's thoughts, Vishudhananda said: "I could not initiate you as my pupil unless I secure permission beforehand from my Tibetan master. That is a condition under which I have to work."

Although he was sure that such a request would not be granted, Brunton asked how Vishudhananda could communicate with his master if he were in Tibet.

"We are in perfect touch upon the inner planes," replied Vishudhananda, and once again Brunton was aware that he had not understood the Yogi's meaning.

"Unless you practise Yoga you cannot obtain enlightenment," the teacher said, "and when you are ready you will be able to find a teacher, if not in the flesh, in the inward eye of the seeker." Meanwhile he told Brunton how he could begin to practise the Yoga of Body Control, by showing him the Lotus position which is, to Europeans, such a contortion.

"Just as every human being both thinks and acts, so there must be training for both sides of our nature," said Vishudhananda. "The body acts on the mind and the mind interacts on the body; they cannot be separated in practical development." He fell silent and Brunton became aware that, suddenly, the Yogi had had enough; it was time for him to leave. But there was one last, irresistible question.

"Have you discovered whether there is any purpose, any goal in life?"

The pupils smiled at Brunton's simplicity: only a westerner would ask such a question, and the teacher did not even bother to answer.

It was Kavirj who finally explained. "Certainly there is a purpose. We have to attain spiritual perfection, to unite with God."

Brunton strolled home through the teeming narrow alleys of the city and paused to sit for a while beside the holy river, pondering upon what he had heard and seen. How could Vishudhananda have produced the scents? He had heard of two others in western India who had been able to do so, but both were now dead. And was the concentration of sunlight merely a blind for something else? How had he revived the dead bird, and what could explain the longevity some Yogis attained?

The old Indian philosophy that the universe is but phantom-like in its real nature drifted into B⁓nton's mind. Reality seemed distant; no experience too strange, but as he eventually made his way back to his quarters and the everyday world it was with the knowledge that he would never truly comprehend the secrets of this ancient land.

THE INDIAN ROPE TRICK

"Anyone," a retired Indian Army officer said to me once, "who has lived in India for twenty years as I have, and who can still claim that he does not believe in magic is either a fool or a liar."

For India is a land steeped in magic as ancient as any that can be found in the world. It is the birthplace of mysteries which have attracted seekers after truth from all over the globe. It is also the birthplace of Yoga, whose followers range from the housewives of suburbia to the high priests of knowledge.

The marvels that some of these men of magic are reputed to have performed are truly remarkable. But there is one which is perhaps the most baffling of all, not only in its actual performance, but also in the fact that, while it is said to have been seen in many places by thousands of people—including such eminent men as Beebe, the naturalist, and Gorki the novelist—there are others who have been unable to find anyone who can perform it, and who say it does not exist or is merely a hallucination.

It is, of course, the famous Indian Rope Trick, a gruesome and extraordinary feat which has not only been performed and written about for centuries, but which has also been the subject of many heated arguments. Let us begin, however, by describing the trick. For this we shall use the eye-witness account of Sheikh Abu Abdullah Mohammed, a native of Tangier, and one of the earliest travellers through the Orient.

In the fourteenth century he was the guest of the ruling Khan, in

Hangchow and, in his book of travels, *Ibn Battuta,* he says that one evening he was guest of honour at a sumptuous banquet which was attended by many Mohammedan merchants and princes. The banquet took place in one of the many courts of the Khan's palace, where fountains and scented plants cooled the air, and where, as usual, troupes of dancers and jugglers entertained the guests to a succession of tableaux, dances, acrobatics, juggling feats and magical delights. As the day drew towards evening one of the jugglers, a heavily built, surly-looking fellow, stepped into the centre of the courtyard. The music stopped and the other entertainers backed away, leaving him alone.

Like the other members of the troupe he wore a loose-fitting shirt and wide baggy trousers which would not impede his movements. Unlike the others he carried over his shoulders the most magnificent cloak Sheikh Abu had ever seen. It was made of thousands of irridescent feathers, threads of silver and gold, and brilliant gems. It shimmered like the throat of a great bird, flickering with turquoise, blue, purple and a liquid red that flowed like volcanic fire along its folds. Around its edges ran a border of huge yellow-green eyes, like those in a peacock's tail.

In his hand this imposing man held a wooden ball. A strip of leather, woven like a rope, hung out of a hole in the sphere. He stretched his arms out wide, holding the ball at arm's length, and began to turn, faster and faster. His cloak, now spread out upon the air, seemed a sun-lighted whirlpool of brilliant water spiralling inwards to the juggler's dark head at its centre. Faster and faster he whirled and then suddenly stopped and, with a quick twist of his body, sent the wooden ball soaring into the sky.

Whether the sphere flew so high as to go out of sight, or just disappeared into thin air, the Sheikh could not say—but it vanished in the twinkling of an eye. The magician, however, was still holding the leather rope, which had unwound from inside the ball and now rose vertically into the blue sky. How high it went it was impossible to say. There seemed no reason to doubt that it was still attached to the invisible wooden ball, and in some way suspended.

The juggler paused while the Sheikh marvelled at what he had seen so far. Then he turned slowly and searched the crowd of entertainers lining the sides of the court. All cowered before his gaze save for one small boy who burst from the crowd and began running for an archway. The juggler pointed and a dozen arms stretched out to trap the boy who was brought, struggling, to the magician. Suddenly his struggles ceased and, seeming to accept his fate, he walked quietly and with resignation up to the leather rope. The juggler pointed to the sky and the boy began to climb. He was not a strong boy; the first few feet of the climb obviously cost him a great effort and it took him quite a few minutes to reach the height of the palace's domed roofs. Then he seemed to lose all weight and to climb at an incredible speed, his size diminishing at every second until, in no time at all, he was out of sight.

For a while there was silence. The crowd stared upwards and the magician waited, apparently expecting something. Then he began to show signs of growing impatience. He tugged at the leather thong several times, and when nothing happened he called. There was no answer, and he shouted again and again. With each minute that passed he became more irate. Finally, in a terrifying rage, he threw off his cloak, unsheathed a curved sword which was lying near by, gripped the sword in his teeth and began to climb the rope.

The Sheikh was astounded. In not more than two or three seconds the magician also was lost to sight, so fast did he climb. For a few minutes there was silence, the crowd gazing upwards towards the point where the leather rope disappeared in the arch of the sky.

Suddenly the air above the palace courtyard was rent with anguished screams. The Sheikh felt his blood freeze; they were the high-pitched screams of a young boy in terror of his life. The Sheikh leapt up, spurred by the instinct to save the child, and ran to the foot of the rope. But there was nothing to be seen. The thin, twisted rope stretched upwards to disappear into the heavens, and yet the terrible screams continued.

Suddenly they stopped as suddenly as they had begun, and then a tiny dot appeared in the sky, falling rapidly, growing larger. It thumped to earth at the foot of the leather rope before the Sheikh— the hand and forearm of a young boy, still bleeding where it had been viciously hacked from the body.

The Sheikh retreated, horrified, but more dots were appearing in the sky—the boy's other arm, and part of his thigh. Then a hail of pieces fell; a mutilated foot, a leg cut short below the knee, a part of a foot with the toes still attached, the poor, skinny torso chopped into quarters. Eventually, with a force that spattered the Sheikh with blood, the head of the boy, terror written across its face, landed on the loathsome pile.

The Sheikh fell to his knees, weeping, and as he knelt he saw the magician, black and evil against the sky, slithering down the leathern rope, using it only to break his fall as he landed beside his victim.

Quickly the magician threw his splendid cloak over the remains. In

35

what seemed a devilish dance of triumph he jumped repeatedly upon the dismembered body. Finally, suddenly exhausted by his efforts, he turned, picked up his bloody sword, slowly wiped it and put it back in its scabbard. Then, with all the aplomb of a dancer, he whirled his cloak up from the ground, spun it twice about his head and allowed it to drop, shimmering, upon his shoulders. In the same instant the boy appeared at the magician's right hand, caught the wooden ball as it fell from the sky and, unconcernedly, began winding in the rope. The sad pile of butchered limbs had vanished.

At this point the Sheikh believes he fainted, for when he came to other guests were supporting him and the Khan was giving him water. Everyone was astonished by his description of what had happened. They assured him that they had seen no rope, no boy climbing into the sky, no dismemberment, nothing more than an athletic dance and an acrobatic act performed by a man in a cloak and a young boy.

What, in fact, had hapened? Had the Sheikh really seen the Rope Trick or had he been in some kind of trance, or subject to hypnotic suggestion? Why had he been the only one out of all the guests to have seen what he believed had taken place?

These same questions can be asked of practically every account of the Indian Rope Trick. The descriptions are often incoherent, vague and without supporting evidence; and witnesses have admitted that they did not, later, discuss it with anyone else or even mention it to those close to them. The accounts are so consistently strange, and yet have been so persistently repeated over the centuries, that in 1934 an extensive investigation was made by the Occult Committee of the Magic Circle, whose president at that time was Lord Ampthill, once Viceroy of India.

The Committee decided, after taking the evidence of a great many people, that there could be no such thing as the Indian Rope Trick. There were two main reasons for this, the first being that the accounts were all vague, unsubstantiated and unacceptable. The second reason was that they believed that to simulate the Indian Rope Trick the apparatus needed would be so expensive as to be outside the reach of the average poor Indian. Moreover, the complexity of the apparatus required would make it impossible for the illusion to be created with little organization in any convenient spot— which was how most of the accounts described it. Therefore the Committee, having ruled out *real* magic, and having decided that hypnotism or drugs could not account for the reports, decided that the Indian Rope Trick did not exist and the people who said they had seen it were not telling the whole truth.

However the report of the Committee's deliberations gave rise to a long correspondence in *The Listener* and induced the Magic Circle to offer a reward of 500 guineas, a considerable sum in 1934, to anyone who could perform the Indian Rope Trick. This brought forth a juggler named Karachi, whose claims interested Harry Price, then Honorary Secretary of the University of London Council of Psychical Research, who invited Karachi to London to perform the trick. Karachi, however, rejected the site chosen for him—a Hampstead garden—and said he preferred to work in a wide open space. Karachi (whose real name was Arthur Claude Derby) was allowed to choose his own site, a field near Wheathampstead in Hertfordshire, and allowed access to the site for several days to prepare the trick.

The trick was eventually performed on 7 January, 1935, and a report with photographs was published in *The Listener* of 16 January, 1935. The team of witnesses, having fortified themselves against the winter cold in the local pub, gathered in the muddy English field on a drizzly day, to watch the famous trick being performed by an Englishman and his son with blacking on their faces. As a warming-up session, Karachi performed a few balancing acts before the major illusion began. Karachi threw a rope to his witnesses—an ordinary rope about six feet long. Karachi then took the rope behind a multi-coloured cloth of velvet set up as a screen. The rope appeared to rise from behind the cloth as if it were pushed up from below. Quite stiff the rope (if it was *the* rope) ascended to a height of five feet, then slowly sank back below the cloth.

Karachi then threw another, ordinary, loosely woven rope to his audience. The second rope was passed back and placed beneath the cloth. Once more an end appeared and edged upwards, this time to a height of eight feet. At this point Karachi stopped and ordered his son to climb it. Quickly the boy did so. Then he came down again—and that was the end of the demonstration.

In the bar of the local pub Karachi offered to explain how the trick was done, but Harry Price wasn't interested. He also claimed that he knew how to make the boy disappear and undergo all the traditional misfortunes, but that would take a great deal of preparation.

The demonstration had been filmed but, not surprisingly, when the account of the event and the film were submitted to the Occult Committee it refused to award the 500-guinea prize. In reply Karachi issued a challenge to the Committee offering to perform the trick under a set of very reasonable conditions chosen by himself. The challenge, however, was never taken up.

Twenty years later another seeker after truth, a determined and adventurous young journalist named John Keel, who thought he had learned the secret, had as little success with *his* demonstration. His speciality, as he says in his book *Jadoo*, is magic, the forbidden arts, and his favourite hunting grounds are the hills of Africa and the plains of India. In pursuit of his thirst for knowledge, Keel found himself in Secunderabad, where he learned of a faith healer who had some unique talents.

Keel set out to find this man, following some rather sketchy directions, and with no success. Finally, at the top of a hill, he sat down to rest in a small white-domed structure equipped with benches for the convenience of climbers. The only other person there was an old man. To his surprise the man, dressed in a *dhoti* and with a small cap on his head, addressed him by name. He appeared to know many things about Keel, and even gave him advice about a story he had been working on the night before, and which wasn't going well.

Keel was astonished but, the old man realized, also sceptical. Amused, he told Keel that many things he believed impossible were possible and that he could, for example, tell him how the Indian rope trick was performed. At the same time, however, he said that Keel had great inner resources which he had not yet discovered, and that if he reached for these untapped resources he would find the answers to what he was looking for and more besides.

The old man would say no more, nor allow Keel to accompany him when he decided to go home. He left Keel dazed with the realization that he had at last learned the secret of the great Rope Trick that had for so long baffled the western world. And according to Keel it is as simple as this.

"The secret does not lie in the ground or in the rope, but in the air. Wires hold the rope up. In ancient times magicians used a length of thin strong line made from black hairs woven together. Remember, this trick was introduced when 'invisible' wires, now a standard magician's gimmick, were completely unknown. And it was always performed at dusk, at the conclusion of the jugglers' performance because the hair ropes weren't totally invisible."

But how were the ropes supported? Keel maintains that the rope trick was usually done in mountainous regions, never in desert country, in a valley between two hills or rocky knolls.

"The invisible wire," he says, "was stretched from the summit of one hill, across the valley, to the summit of the other hill. With higher hills in the background even ordinary wire is invisible ... With the added advantages of dusk there is little chance that the wire could be seen because it's human nature to think the rope's support must be vertical, not horizontal!"

There is also a simple explanation for those cases where the boy is reported to have climbed into the sky until he disappears from view. Torches or lanterns, Keel says, made the spectators night-blind when they looked up into the dark sky.

The rope was lifted up to the suspension wire in the following way. A thinner rope or thread was previously dangled over the wire, with one end trailing to a concealed spot where an assistant could pull it. A small hook at the other end hung near the magician. The rope itself was unprepared except for the wooden ball, which had two purposes—it gave weight to the end of the rope to make it easier to throw it up and it had holes in it in which the hooks could be inserted.

Thus, at the beginning of the trick the magician would throw the rope up once or twice and allow it to fall back inert, until finally he would connect the hook on the end of the fine "ascension" wire to one of the holes in the ball. The next time he threw the ball up the assistant had only to haul on the thread and the rope would begin to rise until it reached the wire. The magician would then call his boy and order him to climb. The rope, held by the ascension wire, would bear the weight of the small boy and, when he reached the top, he would pull a hook from his pocket and fasten the ball more securely to the wire so that it would bear the magician's weight.

When the magician also reached the top of the rope he would pull from various parts of his clothing pieces of a freshly butchered animal, usually a large monkey, wrapped in cloth similar to that which the boy was wearing. He would drop these one at a time while the boy screamed agonizingly, until finally a head, wrapped in a turban, would strike the ground.

While assistants fussed around below assembling the parts into a large basket the magician would hurry the boy into a special harness he wore inside his own baggy clothes and then slide down the rope. It was easy enough then for the boy to emerge from the master's clothing while the attention of the audience was directed to something else, and reappear whole and in one piece, while the bloody bits of body were hidden under a cloak or spirited away by assistants.

If you read this account of the secret in connection with the tale told by Sheikh Abu, you will see that many things can be explained by it. The wires could have been stretched from wall to wall of the courtyard; the iridescent cloak could have hidden much and distracted considerably; the dismembered corpse is not so implausible. On the other hand Sheikh Abu states that the performance took place after all the other jugglers and dancers, but he also says the sky was blue, and one must assume therefore that it was not dusk—though doubtful light appears to be a prerequisite of the trick.

However this all explains quite a lot, very satisfactorily. And John Keel decided to give his own demonstration of the trick in New Delhi, intending to perform just a part of it. He sent out invitations, bought a long rope and found an intelligent boy to act as his assistant. A grove of trees on a golf course, close to a picturesque old temple, provided an ideal spot, and Keel rigged a network of black threads across the clearing in such a way that the rope would rise about fifty feet into the air. He could not find a boy to climb it, but he thought it would be a convincing demonstration.

As usual the weather was sunny and cloudless on the day of the demonstration and about fifty reporters turned up to watch the show. And then, at the last minute, a storm blew up, a high wind rose and a monsoon cloudburst crashed around them. It was the first and last storm Keel experienced during his entire stay in New Delhi, and in a few minutes it was all over. But it had wrecked the careful set-up. The threads were tangled in the bushes and the boy had fled from his hiding place. Distraught and nervous Keel fumbled about with the threads and managed to get the rope about four feet off the ground. Eventually he gave up. The newspaper reports, he says, were all very kind and fair. Their friendliness and concern helped soothe the embarrassment and pain of his failure.

The famous trick has still not been performed successfully in front of an audience even though the "secret" has now been published. The Magic Circle's offer remains unclaimed, and the mystery stays unsolved. Apparently it was a freak storm that ruined Keel's demonstration. Or was it India, jealously guarding her ancient secrets?

THE PRINCESS AND THE PEKINESE

For years the snub-nosed, long-haired (and some might say gro-
tesque) little animal, the Pekinese, was the royal dog of China.
Hence, of course, its name, for it was bred in the royal kennels of
Peking, and only the Emperor was allowed to possess such a beast.

So it was indeed the greatest of honours when the Emperor, near
the middle of the sixteenth century, decided to send not just one
Pekinese, but two, to England's Queen Elizabeth I. It would be a
mark of friendship and respect: accordingly one of the finest dogs
and one of the finest bitches in the Royal Peking Kennel were
selected.

Then came the complicated arrangement whereby these two would
make their journey to the distant land of England, by land and sea.
Much study was devoted to the matter and eventually it was decided
on a route; this would be by caravan across China and the steppes
of Asia to the start of the maritime part of the trip. And during the
journey they would be housed in an exquisitely wrought, hand-
carved, ivory box. It was a large box, for in view of the length of
the journey it was likely that the English queen would get a bonus
in the shape of a litter of Pekinese puppies.

And no ordinary kennel-maid could be sent with a gift so
precious. One of the royal Princesses, a beautiful, almond-eyed girl of
seventeen, was chosen to travel and supervise the feeding and clean-
ing of the animals, however many of them there would turn out to

41

be. For this menial task she had a servant, of course, but it was her responsibility to make sure the dogs all arrived clean, plump and well at the English Court.

So long was the overland trip from Peking to the Black Sea, that it would not have been surprising if the little Pekinese bitch had produced several litters by this time. But in fact she produced only one, of five fine healthy pups. (And the unexpected rigours of the sea journey would make sure neither she nor her mate ever thought of such a thing again.)

A sumptuous craft had been built at a Black Sea port, to the Emperor's own design. The party embarked with delight, for now they were bidding farewell to the dust and heat of Asia; setting sail amid balmy breezes, in a wide, flat, gilded vessel which gave everyone plenty of room to move around, even the well-grown pups who could chase each other round the decks while servants cleaned their ivory cage.

The trip along the Black Sea was a joy. There was sufficient wind to keep the square Chinese sails stretched tight, but insufficient to produce more than a ripple on the bright blue water. The Bosphorus was thrilling, the Mediterranean a new world.

But as the Chinese vessel approached the Pillars of Hercules—Gibraltar—the temperature dropped sharply, the wind rose and what had been a wonderful summer cruise became, dramatically and very sickeningly, a hideous, stormy, ordeal. By the time they had cleared the Pillars of Hercules and were heading north for the Bay of Biscay, it was very obvious that the craft on which the Emperor had lavished so much loving care was quite unseaworthy in these northern, western, waters.

When they reached the Bay their flat-bottomed, lovely ship was three parts wreck. The gilt and red lacquer which had made her so beautiful when the Princess and her companions embarked had all but chipped away, or been obliterated by salt spray. One mast had snapped in two, the huge Chinese rudder took ten men to hold it in these seas, and the Chinese captain had little trouble in persuading his Princess that they must put in to a French port. Repairs would of course be possible, but somehow, said the captain, it might be wiser to charter a more suitably designed ship for the last, nasty bit of water to England. Even with a new mast the Chinese vessel would be a disgrace to the Royal Court of Peking: her planned triumphal progress up the River Thames would be like an old ship's last sad journey, to the breakers.

If a new ship were chartered, with a French crew, the Chinese crew and their captain could stay and supervise repairs, so that in a week or two the Princess and her servants could be brought back and re-embarked for the journey home.

So they put in to Brest. A French ship was found, but the French captain had to be well paid for his services. For some reason he seemed most reluctant to load up the seven little dogs, with their strange demeanour. Even the beautiful Princess, with her unfamiliar oriental features, seemed to fill him and his crew with dread. The captain demanded his enormous fare in advance, and even though he swiftly divided a part of it among his crew there was angry muttering as the ship sailed.

The Chinese courtiers did their best to make the Princess comfortable and happy in this sturdy but utilitarian vessel. Yet it was such a terrible come-down from the stately Chinese junk they had brought from the Crimea that the Princess had a sense of shame mounting to panic as she realized how the Chinese Emperor, greatest man on earth, would now be represented to an English Queen. She hoped the Queen would like her dogs. At least they were still plump, healthy and numerous.

For the first few hours out of Brest the Atlantic Ocean behaved itself. But even during these calm hours there was a sinister and threatening attitude among the crew, who were convinced that this devilish septet of baby dragons would bring bad luck. The presence of the slant-eyed oriental lady and her followers only reinforced this foreboding.

The crossing was to be straight across from Brest to Land's End, then a cautious clinging to the English south coast until the mouth of the Thames was reached. But as ill luck would have it, they ran into a vicious storm sweeping in from the western Atlantic just as they sighted Land's End. A moment later Land's End had vanished in an explosive sea far more terrifying than anything the Princess and her party could possibly have imagined. In this crisis the French captain was quite incapable of exercising discipline or steadying the vessel as he ran to and fro, screaming hysterical instructions. The crew, ignoring him, tried to take in sail.

A mast snapped—just as it had done on the ornate Chinese junk, but perhaps with more justification. In a moment a vast shroud of canvas was covering the deck, muffling the screams and curses of the angry, frightened crew.

The canvas was somehow got overboard. And then the Princess, who understood not a word of French—or English for that matter— understood quite suddenly what design the crew of this hateful vessel

43

had on her, her courtiers, and above all, her seven beautiful Pekinese. She let out a scream which momentarily silenced the wind as two burly crew members picked up the ivory box with its precious little dogs, and flung it into the boiling sea.

And now the Princess knew that she had no wish to live; honour demanded that she die rather than arrive without her precious charges.

Clinging perilously to a spar, she saw that her fears for her companions had been correct. Two crewmen each picked up a Chinese girl from among the ladies-in-waiting and hurled them overboard. A few moments later the only male member of her entourage, an elderly Mandarin, had been flung screaming into the water.

Two men approached her across the crazily tilting deck, and through the deluges of sea-water sweeping over the side. Whatever happened, she said to herself, these ruffians would never have the satisfaction of throwing a Princess of the Imperial Court into this barbarian ocean. They advanced inexorably upon her in a fantastic form of slow motion, for the ship was pitching so that one minute they were yards below her, the next, yards above.

She flung herself over the side.

The beautiful girl disappeared almost immediately, and the baleful ship bored and corkscrewed swiftly away into the storm. Yet it was the brutish crew who felt themselves relieved of a malevolent influence. For the dragons and their keepers had been committed safely to the deep.

★　★　★

On board the French ship it seemed as if captain and crew had been right in their theories, for within minutes the storm died away. Within half an hour the sun was shining, the wind was a gentle zephyr and the whole episode seemed to have been a hideous nightmare. Only the snapped mast and its missing canvas gave proof of anything untoward.

As for those orientals—had they existed at all?

Yes, they had. A seaman had been quite badly bitten by one of the dogs as he allowed a grimy finger to pass between the exquisite ivory bars of the cage. He had screamed with pain as he helped fling the lot into the sea, and however much the affair might seem a bad dream his badly lacerated finger was evidence that it had been something more real.

There was no point in going on. The captain had received his huge payment in advance and now, with nothing to deliver, the only thing was to get back to France and re-fit.

And spend the money.

The ship limped home, its crew sworn to secrecy and heavily bribed. It avoided Brest, changed its name with a pot of paint, and arrived at Le Havre "from Scandinavian waters".

The Chinese captain, still making good his own vessel (indeed, he had hardly begun) learnt from England that the French ship had foundered with the loss of all on board. In some strange way it seemed that only Chinese bodies had been found on the English coast, not too far from Land's End; but this was probably because the arrival of English, French and other European bodies on that treacherous coast was so common an occurrence that no one bothered to report it.

The tragedy was duly reported to his Imperial Majesty in Peking.

At Le Havre, where a damaged French vessel had taken refuge to be re-masted after a storm in Scandinavian waters, a sailor with a damaged hand, bitten by some *sal chien* they had stupidly taken on as a mascot, died from his minor wound.

This, at Le Havre, was not all that startling. Everyone knew that a dog bite, from a mad dog (and sometimes it was hard to tell whether the thing was mad or just hungry) could be fatal. Death sometimes took place months after the bite, and it was the most horrifying death any devil could invent. The victim went screaming mad and died of thirst while refusing even the sight of water. Today we call the disease "hydrophobia", which means hatred-of-water; another name for it is "rabies", or canine madness.

We do know, however, that one or more members of the crew talked about the events on board ship that fateful day. It was almost inevitable, for it is seldom a whole crew can keep a secret. And eventually the story became quite widely known in French maritime areas.

No attempt, however, seems to have been made to bring the men concerned to justice. The French authorities, distracted by the convulsions of the bloody Wars of Religion which were racking the country at the time, were too preoccupied with the more major issues.

One final sixteenth-century episode remains, however.

The news of the Chinese bodies near Land's End was provided in the first instance by the village idiot, a genial, harmless, young man called Peter. He had been wandering about, as he always did at low tide, in search of shellfish, or pretty stones, when he saw an ivory box half buried in the sand. Peter had never heard of ivory, but it was a really beautiful box, about the size of a coffin. A coffin with bars.

Inside the barred coffin were seven dead animals. They were just about the most extraordinary Peter had seen. The box was quite easy to open, even for simple Peter, and he lovingly squeezed all the little animals to get out the water, but not a one recovered.

Sadly, he dragged the box and the seven dead Pekinese away from the approaching tide.

To his even greater distress Peter now came upon several human bodies. They were not yet bloated in death, and to Peter they were all strangely beautiful. He felt angry about the storm which had delivered yet another cargo of death to his own private seacoast. In all, Peter found seven beautiful girls, one of them more beautiful than the rest and exquisitely bejewelled. He also found one old man. Peter did not touch the jewels, just dragged all the bodies up the sand so the tide would not remove them. Then he ran to the nearest fisherman's cottage.

Soon there was a band of men with spades. After removing all the jewellery and some of the clothes from the Chinese bodies, the good fisherfolk buried them and the strange little dogs (minus their box) in the sand just above high tide.

Peter spent a long time collecting flowers, and eventually he had amassed a great armful which he placed on the huge grave.

One of the fishermen had scratched his wrist on the ivory box. He wasn't quite sure how it had happened, but when the digging was over he saw the blood oozing slowly down his hand. It was a trivial injury, and he, like a number of others, had done very well out of the day. He forgot about the scratch, which healed quite quickly.

Three months later he was dead.

At first, no one drew any connection between the scratch and the dreadful death. Then, as at Le Havre, people put two and two together. From that day on, no one would go near that stretch of rock-strewn beach.

Only simple Peter, who regularly brought flowers.

Memories are long in that part of the world and for years no one —but Peter—would go near that stretch of coast. In any case it was distant, unattractive, inhospitable. But every week, for years, Peter would collect his little bunch of flowers and place it near where the Chinese and their dogs were buried.

Eventually Peter—sixteenth-century Peter, for we must not forget that these events happened four hundred years ago—died. For anyone else it would not have been "just a simple death", but Peter had long been prone to epileptic fits, and the unusually nasty and frightening one he had, when he frothed at the mouth for hours and then seemed to fling himself over a precipice (for that was where he died, not far from his beloved grave) went almost unremarked. Peter was little mourned and not long remembered.

The years went by, lengthened to decades, to centuries. Three hundred years passed, and only the fisherman's tales kept the details alive—as they do today. No longer was there a virgin English queen who had only just established her country as a leading power; now there was a cantankerous widow whose subjects, long accustomed to power, claimed both west and east (with a few unimportant exceptions) and who was most unlikely to be sent anything but scorpions from China. Victoria's reign was proud and prosperous, with an ever-increasing urban population. As a result, and for those who could afford such a thing, the "picnic" became popular. Then, on one day out of the seven, a family might take out cold foods and wine, beer or ginger-beer to enjoy in the countryside. Or at the seaside.

The seaside had its own peculiar charm in that one could keep one's beverage, whatever it was, nice and chilly in a rock pool, until one was ready to drink it. The family played cricket, or rounders, in bare feet on the sand. And at the end of the day, everyone was happily tired with a surfeit of salt water, if not always of sun.

It was in August, 1850, that one such Victorian family, a quite prosperous one, went down to the sea, to a remote area not too far from Land's End. It was Sunday, and a picnic day. Their name was Carmichael, and they had been holidaying at a little village called Mousehole. The family seem to have included mother and father, four children and grandmother. Three of the children were girls. The youngest was a little boy of about seven. His name was Peter.

The picnic basket was large and overflowing; its leather strap was really doing its duty as they lugged it from the pony-cart to this unspoiled, unknown, part of the coast. It was in fact, not a very pretty bit of coast—but at least they would be alone.

Games were duly played, everyone, even grandma, paddled with shoes off; skirts or trousers were rolled discreetly up. Then came the time for lunch. Both wine and ginger-beer had been brought, and it was all now retrieved from the rock pool where it had been cooling since the pony-trap arrived at half past ten.

A large meal was consumed, the drinks were finished. The grown-ups lay down on the sand, kerchiefs over their faces against the sun, and fell happily to sleep. The three girls and their little brother went exploring.

Half an hour and the children were back. "Oh, but surely you can see Mother and I, and your Grandmother, are having a nap? *Surely* there must be something else to explore. Why, this is real pirate country—who knows what you may find?"

"Yes, Father. And we're awfully sorry. But Peter's found this really lovely bit of coral for you—and he cut his foot with it. That's how he found it, you see, by standing on it, sort of. It's awfully pretty—and it's terribly sharp."

Thus galvanized, our Victorian family sat up and took note. Tincture of Iodine was produced, and a roll of quite unsuitable bandage. The iodine was painfully applied.

"That's quite a nasty gash," said Mr Carmichael, "almost as if you'd been bitten by some animal. You weren't, were you?"

"No. 'Course I wasn't."

Grandmother was holding the beautiful coral which had caused the accident. "Oh, it is lovely," she said. "But it almost *does* look like a dog's tooth."

In three months, little Peter was dead.

Everyone had forgotten the episode with the coral. And rabies has always been a rare disease in England: few doctors have seen a case.

It was his grandmother, only a few hours before the little boy's agonizing death, who brought out the tooth-shaped coral. As senior member of that ill-fated outing, she had been given the pretty thing. Now, vague, partly rational doubts assailed her, and with eyes staring and damp with tears, she handed it to Peter's father.

Mr Carmichael hastened to the doctor with the tooth. After all, it seemed the only way the boy could have received an infection in the past months.

The doctor reached for a bulky medical book and nervously thumbing through the pages. "What an extraordinary thing!" he said. "These are the classic symptoms of rabies—hydrophobia—and it can only be given, let's see, 'is usually transmitted by the bite of a rabid dog'. Isn't that extraordinary!"

A MAGICIAN IN EGYPT

Paul Brunton's long and extensive travels through India in search of mystical and spiritual truths were duly followed by a somewhat similar pilgrimage to Egypt, ostensibly as a journalist, which he was, but in reality motivated by the same urge to uncover the ancient philosophies and disciplines followed by the devout and to some extent by the apparent miracle workers and fakirs. Egypt, representing the Near East rather than the Far East, possessed a different cultural background, and much of the mystical lore was linked to what we know as Ancient Egypt with its various symbolic gods. His quest, in its own way, proved successful, none the less, and the following encounter with an adept fakir is of particular interest.

Tahra Bey is described by Brunton, perhaps not without justification, as Egypt's most famous fakir. He was not, as might have been the case in India, a poor man rejecting worldly possessions and relying on charity for food; on the contrary, he was prosperous, well known in certain royal circles, and occupied a modern luxury flat of the type then springing up in the European suburbs of Cairo. Nevertheless, his "magical" accomplishments appeared to be considerable.

He was born in 1897 at Tanta in the Nile delta; his mother died in childbirth. His father was a Copt. Due to political problems they went to live in Turkey, where they settled in Constantinople. The youth received a good modern education, studied medicine and eventually qualified as a doctor. In due course he opened a clinic in

Greece, and it was there that he performed what he regarded as his most remarkable feat in allowing himself to be buried alive for no less than 28 days, despite opposition from a number of religious dignitaries who considered the feat as a menace to their religions and doctrines, but the government approved on the grounds that as Tahra Bey was a doctor he had the right to be buried as he wished.

Visits to Serbia, Bulgaria and Italy followed. In the latter country he permitted tests by well-known scientists who put him in a lead coffin which was then nailed down and submerged in a swimming bath, but after about half an hour the police interfered and stopped the demonstration. Nevertheless, it was successful. Later, in France, the experiment was repeated and extended for 24 hours. Tahra Bey said that he was glad to undergo this test because so many critics claimed to have exposed the performance of Indian fakirs in being buried alive in that they have secret air channels dug into the earth to enable them to continue to breathe (no doubt this did occur in the case of some pseudo-fakirs). It was for this reason that Tahra Bey performed his feat under water where everything could be observed and controlled by scientists and critics alike. His fame became such that he received invitations from King Fuad of Egypt, King Carol of Rumania and King Victor Emanuel of Italy—and he was also received several times at Chigi Palace by Benito Mussolini.

Brunton's quest, however, lay in witnessing some of these feats for himself under controlled conditions rather than listen to historical detail, and, as usual, he was able to persuade his host to perform. Bey himself was a short, distinguished looking man with black hair and olive skin. His face was bearded and peaceful. He could wear Arab garments or well cut European clothes with equal elegance. His eyes had a piercing quality, with strong white irises lending depth and mystery to the jet black pupils. His manner was soft and gentle, and he was as courteous and polished as all the better class Egyptians. He murmured his sentences so quietly and so humbly that no one might guess that he was a man with some of the most mysterious forces of nature under his command and control. His air of self-possession was notable, and he smoked innumerable cigarettes in the course of a day.

In his luxury flat Tahra Bey made the following positive statement on the subject of his powers: "We must begin by recognizing within ourselves the great possibilities we all possess, and until we do this we must remain bound hand and foot to unnecessary limitations that prevent us from exercising our marvellous psychic and material powers. People, when confronted with the phenomena which I can produce, think it some kind of conjuring or else something entirely supernatural. In both cases they are wrong. They do not seem to grasp the fact that these things are perfectly scientific, obeying the laws of nature herself. It is true that I am using psychic laws which are little understood, but nevertheless they are *laws*. Nothing that I do is arbitrary, supernatural or against such laws.

"As for those who imagine I am a kind of stage illusionist—a conjurer—I must pity their narrow minds, their inability to envisage any higher possibility for mankind and the limited experience which has fallen to their lot."

For the actual demonstration, which took place in Tahra Bey's flat, Brunton collected a small group of doctors and other professional men whose interest he had engaged in this heterodox subject. They were privileged to watch a series of astonishing if gruesome demonstrations which Tahra Bey performed with an ease and swiftness that was astounding. (Unfortunately Brunton does not name or identify any of these witnesses, which is a pity in view of the dramatic events which were to follow.)

Tahra Bey had changed his European clothes for a long robe of white linen. An Arab burnous was tied around his head with double blue and gold cords. A five-pointed gold star, the emblem of the Order into which he had been initiated, hung suspended from a neck chain. Around his waist was a golden girdle. He stood with arms folded upon his chest, calmly awaiting the moment to begin.

On the floor were a number of objects which were minutely examined by those present. These included a table loaded with daggers, hatpins, needles, skewers, bits of glass, and on another table rested a plank, studded with the points of long sharp nails, a block of heavy stone, a weighing machine and a large hammer, a white fowl and a grey rabbit, both tied by the feet and lying in a basket. There were also two gleaming scythe blades, a pair of trestles, a long coffin, a still longer and larger box, a heap of red sand and a pair of spades, plus a few hand towels with some cotton wool and other odds and ends.

Two young men acted as assistants in the demonstration. It began as follows. The fakir touched the back of his neck and pressed the skin just above the nape firmly with his fingers, while with the other hand he pressed the temples of his forehead. He then sucked abruptly into his mouth so that for a moment his throat was agitated. Within a minute his eyes closed and he was entranced, uttering a sudden peculiar cry, and entered a state of catalepsy so rigid that he would have fallen like a dead man if his assistants had not caught him in their arms. His body was now as stiff as a piece of wood.

One of his assistants then stripped him bare to the waist while the other fixed the scythe blades to the top of the trestle table. Tahra Bey's body was then lifted on to the scythe blades, one under his shoulders and one under his ankles. At this point a doctor present measured his pulse beat and was surprised to find that it was as high as 130—nearly double the normal. The large block of stone was then brought forward and put on the scale; it weighed 90 kilograms, or around 200 lb—the weight of a heavily built man. The block appeared to be made of solid rock granite.

The assistants placed the stone on Tahra Bey's bare stomach, and then struck it vigorously, blow after blow, with a blacksmith's hammer. The body remained taut and rigid, as if made of iron, until eventually the stone split into two pieces which fell to the floor. The fakir was then lifted up, placed on his feet and supported. Apparently he was quite unconscious of what had happened and had not suffered any pain. The doctors examined him with interest and discovered that the scythe blade edges had not left the slightest marks on his skin, although the block of granite had produced a red mark over his abdomen.

Tahra Bey was then placed on the nail-studded wooden plank, where an assistant stood on him, one foot on his chest and the other on his abdomen, and jumped up and down. A physical inspection of his bare back showed not the slightest mark of penetration by the spikes. His pulse rate was now 132. He was again lifted to his feet, whereupon his eyes slowly opened and his eyeballs rolled like someone just emerging from a dream and still very far away. For the next half hour those eyes remained uncannily fixed as, little by little, he returned to life. He made a violent effort to inhale air, opening his mouth so wide that his audience saw his tongue was curled back into his throat. After breathing for a moment, he used a finger to restore his tongue to its normal position, and now appeared to be his normal conscious self once more.

However, he rested for only a minute or two before submitting to further tests. Doctors were asked to pierce his jaws with a pair of hatpins, which one of them promptly did, running a hatpin through each cheek, and then thick skewers were used. Tahra Bey remained awake, fully realizing what was happening. He did not seem to feel the slightest pain. Even more startling was when he allowed a doctor to plunge a dagger into his throat in front of the larynx, the point reappearing when the dagger had passed through about one inch of flesh. One or two of the doctors somewhat sceptically watched the pupils of his eyes to see whether they were contracted or dilated, thus perhaps indicating the use of drugs, but his eyes were quite normal.

What perhaps astonished the doctors most of all was the total absence of blood on Tahra Bey's skin. They experimented by cutting his face with pieces of glass and sticking needles and knives into his shoulders and chest, but always with the same bloodless result. One of the doctors asked the fakir if he could produce blood from the wounds, and immediately blood began to flow until it covered his chest, at which point he stopped it again by the mere exercise of will power. Within a few minutes the wounds had practically healed.

Next a flaming torch was passed up and down one of Tahra Bey's legs by an assistant until the flesh could be heard to crackle in the heat, but his face remained serene and undisturbed. One of the doctors, still not satisfied about the use of a powerful pain relieving drug, checked the heart rate and made other medical tests while the flame was being applied, but there was no sign of abnormality.

After sundry other feats with needles and knives, Tahra Bey then gave a demonstration of his power over animals by hypnotizing the rabbit and hen. He pressed a nerve centre at the back of their necks and made a few passes with his hands, after which they became totally inert and would remain in whatever position he placed them. When the experiment was over they jumped up, quite alert and none the worse for their experience. Tahra Bey then informed us that his body was no longer insensitive to pain, as this period lasted only some 20 to 25 minutes after his first entrancement, and he was now completely normal.

Finally came the most spectacular demonstration of the evening— that of being buried alive. This feat was carried out under stringent test conditions which did not admit of the slightest doubt as to its genuineness. It began with Tahra Bey predicting the exact hour and minute when he would emerge from the trance into which he would throw himself. He told his audience to give him one and a half hours, as he would arrange his awakening for five minutes after that time.

After the floor of the apartment had been carefully examined, the coffin was brought into the centre of the room. The floor, incidentally, was composed of mosaic tiles in the Egyptian fashion and had nothing below it but the ceiling of the room underneath. The possibility of secret trapdoors or piping was dismissed, and in any case a rug was laid across the floor on which the coffin was placed. Tahra

Bey then went through the same process as before, putting himself in a state of total catalepsy. Supported by the assistants, his body was then examined by the doctors who found that both breathing and heartbeats had stopped. The body of the "living corpse" was now laid in the coffin, nostrils and mouth stuffed with cotton wool, and completely covered by the assistants with soft red sand. The wooden lid was then fitted and nailed down.

Next the long wooden trough was put on the carpet and the coffin lifted carefully into it. Now the trough was filled with sand to the top, completely covering the coffin. That done, the doctors and observers settled down to one and a half hours of waiting, satisfied that everything used in this feat had been carefully examined, that there was no possibility of fraud and that everything had been controlled. If Tahra Bey survived this test they would be forced to pay tribute to his extraordinary powers.

At the end of the allotted time period the sand was unshovelled and thrown aside; the coffin was disinterred and the lid opened. There beneath the remaining sand lay the body of the fakir, as stiff as a corpse, his skin now a dull grey colour. He was taken out of the coffin, whereupon the rigidity eased and he was placed in a chair. After a few minutes there were signs of quiet breathing and his eyelids flickered. Gradually the body became reanimated until after about ten minutes he was his normal self once more and was able to sit and talk about his strange experience.

Thus: "My sleep was so profound that I know nothing of what you have done to me. I recall only that I closed my eyes in this room and that, by the mysterious process of post-suggestion, I have awakened in this room again at the exact moment I set myself."

Brunton's feelings as he finally left the apartment contained the sentiment, ironic in retrospect, that "the tottering figure of materialism would be brought to the execution block before the end of this century". A few days later, Brunton was to visit Tahra Bey in his flat once again, this time for a discussion and interview.

Referring to his critics (rather wistfully, as though he would prefer them as friends rather than enemies), Tahra Bey said: "They think, for instance, that when I run hatpins through my jaws then it is just a matter of forcing my will to resist the pain; yet, if that were true, why are there not scars on my body after I have been so badly wounded and cut? The fact is that they cannot get away from their accustomed ways of thinking. They cannot grasp the possibility of the truth of my own explanations. Let them try to stick knives and skewers into their own throats and faces—they will soon see the difference. They may keep on saying to themselves that they do not feel it and they may try their utmost not to, but they certainly will do so."

Then, by way of explanation, Tahra Bey continued: "Two secrets—hardly the correct term, but it will suffice—enable me to perform all my feats. They are pressure on certain nerve centres of the body and ability to enter into the cataleptic coma. Anyone who is suited and is prepared to undergo the long training which I had to undergo in order to master the application of these two secrets may perform the same feats. Without such application I could not claim to have the courage to resist the pain of these feats. I am not built like those Indian fakirs you have seen who voluptuously seek to torture themselves and endure voluntarily terrible sufferings dictated by the doctrines of their asceticism. The only things I share with them are, on the ascetic side, to live inwardly detached in spirit —and, on the side of practices, the swallowing backwards of the tongue and the entry into catalepsy."

Tahra Bey amplified his explanation that as the nerves are conductors of pain, finger pressure can draw the blood away from the brain on selected nerve centres so that they are struck with anaesthesia. One should not practise this without long and proper training. When this is accompanied by the complete swallowing backwards of the tongue and inhalation of air, rigid cataleptic coma is sure to follow, and the flesh becomes totally insensitive to pain, however intense. The nerve centres on which pressure is exercised are the carotid arteries serving the head, the hypnotic centres of the temples and the pneumo-gastric nerves—but these are not to be played with.

On the question of tongue swallowing Tahra Bey said that even when he was four months old his father began to turn his tongue back with his finger, resulting in a kind of convulsive fit. Today "I can swallow my tongue backward with ease and sometimes experience difficulty in returning it to its normal position". This seals the windpipe and also prevents the entrance of dangerous insects and germs while the body is lying helpless underground.

Before entering catalepsy, yogis always prefix the moment of their awakening by means of auto-suggestion, just as one can go to sleep at night having decided the time of waking the following morning. This is proof that the subconscious mind never sleeps; it is only the conscious mind that undergoes such a lapse. It also explains why sleep walkers often perform quite intelligent actions without remembering afterwards what they did.

The beginning of a cataleptic trance, Tahra Bey went on, brings about the cessation of two vital functions, namely, breathing and blood circulation. Most people would declare that death must inevitably supervene, but he declined to argue the point as Brunton had already witnessed catalepsy in India. The point is that the whole rhythm of life is suspended. This is not the kind of catalepsy that is sometimes obtained in hypnotic experiments on other persons, in which the circulation of blood is intensified because the methods used are quite different and totally unrelated.

Insensibility against pain lasts about 25 minutes after awakening from the second degree of trance. No such period marks the case of merely hypnotized subjects, although it is true that the latter can be rendered insensible to pain. To remain insensible to pain after the state has passed is another thing altogether.

As to why Tahra Bey's body remained unscarred after the many stabs and wounds he had received during the course of his career, two things had to be done. One was to accelerate temporarily the blood circulation (the doctors found that the pulse rate rose to 130 during the actual demonstration), the swiftness of blood flow helping to heal the wound with amazing rapidity. The other was to raise the blood temperature to fever heat in order to disinfect the wounds of germs which may have been introduced. There is never any suppuration and the wounds generally heal within a few minutes or, in more serious cases, in a few hours.

Being buried alive as a practice was commonplace in Ancient Egypt, as in India. In those days there was virtually no materialism; everyone believed in the soul, and therefore such experiences were understood. "The danger of modern habits of thinking is that it deprives men of that incalculable force, the power of the soul. By means of cataleptic entrancement physical life is suspended, but the unseen life of the soul nevertheless continues to function. To demonstrate this demands long and severe training which is usually begun at a very early age."

There are certain parallels in the animal kingdom. Many amphibia, for instance, though breathing air, can remain under water without air for many hours, and winter hibernation, when breathing and blood flow is virtually suspended (or in some cases totally suspended, as in certain species of bats) is a well-known phenomenon. Such animals are able to enter into a state of catalepsy—"and if animals can do it, why not human beings, who after all possess animal bodies?" Tahra Bey pointed out that were he not in a state of catalepsy during the experiment of being buried alive, he would suffocate within ten minutes.

Brunton asked if, when buried alive, the soul is detached from the body and enters the "Beyond", and what experiences can be remembered from that sphere? Tahra Bey said he could tell nothing, as he did not wish to pose as a man knowing the secrets of the Beyond. "There are still mysterious depths which we have as yet been unable to penetrate. The trouble is that we enter a state similar to that of sleep walkers—when we return to normal life we are unable to remember anything of our apparently supernatural adventure. Perhaps we have explored the region of the world of spirits, but as we do not remember our experiences we can say nothing of that world."

He added: "We must accept the facts as we find them. However, I believe that I returned as in real death to unite my soul with the Universal Soul—the Unknown Force. In that sense I believe we are immortal."

Although the interview continued for a while, it dealt mainly with the historical aspects of being buried alive and its effects on the body over relatively short periods. For Brunton the demonstration had been dramatic in the extreme, while the philosophy behind its success always returned to the same basic tenets as he had encountered before: the overriding importance of the soul, the long and severe training and discipline required to perform such apparently miraculous feats, and, as always, the presence of an immortal Universal Force or Spirit which manifests itself through the souls of individual bodies.

The latter concept is, of course, the fundamental of Eastern religions and mysticism generally, but it also applies in a different way to Western religious beliefs. For Brunton, the interlude with Tahra Bey was one of the most telling and sensational of his long quest through the East for the ultimate truth, and perhaps, in his own persistent way, he eventually found it.

A Coven of Witches

CANEWDON

There are still wild and lonely areas of Essex where the marshy ground makes civilized living difficult or impossible, and where the winds whistle unchecked over the Thames estuary. Many roads lead only to lonely villages and no further, and although Essex has been saved from the sea of concrete which would have surrounded the proposed Maplin airport urban development has smothered, like a parasitic creeper, many of the smaller villages. It is difficult now to imagine how isolated and inward-looking they were only a century ago, how remote from the bustling cities, the advances of technology, and the advent of the age of reason.

The part of south-east Essex which is bordered on the east by the North Sea, on the south by the River Thames and on the north by the Crouch is still known as Witch Country. For hundreds of years the tradition of witchcraft flourished in this area; it was the scene of many notable witch-hunts and trials which reached their peak in the sixteenth century, and of a remarkable belief in witches that persisted into the twentieth.

This belief in witches is as old as time. It appears again and again in legends of prehistory and in the oldest records of man. It is based on superstition and fear and lack of understanding, and much of the powers ascribed to the witches of the past who ended their lives miserably on the scaffold can be attributed in a perfectly straightforward fashion to natural facts since proven by science.

In 1486, however, a definitive work, the famous *Malleus Male-*

ficarum (Hammer of the Witches) was written by two Dominican monks. It was, in effect, a handbook for witch-hunters, and it sets out quite clearly the manner in which witches collaborate with the Devil—their pact being essentially a willing one—and how their existence is maintained by the activities of succubi and incubi. It explains that celestial bodies play a large part in the casting of spells, and that the vast majority of spells are connected with sexual activities since women are naturally more lascivious than men.

The book then discusses the powers of witches and how they may be counteracted, and describes the rituals which witches carry out. Finally the authors advise the reader as to how to discover and try witches, describing the kinds of evidence that can safely be accepted as proof of a witch's guilt.

Malleus Maleficarum remained the authoritative book on witches for over two hundred years during which period three Witchcraft Acts were passed in England. The last case of witchcraft to be tried in England took place in Leicestershire in 1717. The prisoners— a woman and her son and daughter—underwent the usual tests for witchcraft but were set free. In 1735 the statute against witchcraft was repealed; those who persecuted witches were in danger themselves, but throughout the century there were occasional cases of local people attempting to revenge themselves on women they believed were witches.

The "age of reason", born during the century through the writings of Thomas Paine and other liberal philosophers, reached the cities of the following century, but it failed to affect much of the countryside where the uneducated men and women continued to believe in magic and witchcraft and in the traditional ways of countering it. In 1880 two men were convicted of trying to submit a woman to the "swimming" ordeal because she had bewitched their bed, which rocked and swayed at night. In 1945 a murder which took place in Warwickshire was believed to have been a ritual witch murder and associated with another murder of a man believed to have been a witch which took place in 1875. The scene of this murder, Long Compton, has a traditional association with witchcraft; an ancient saying claims that: "There are enough witches in Long Compton to push a wagon load of hay up Long Compton Hill."

This brief glimpse into the history of, and the persistence of belief in, witchcraft, makes the story of Canewdon appear a little less incredible, although some of the stories connected with the village have over the centuries become distorted beyond credulity.

Canewdon lies about six miles north of Southend, in the flat marshy country close to the River Crouch. It is in the heart of the Witch Country and tradition says that as long as the church tower stands there must always be six witches in Canewdon, "three in silk and three in cotton", and of these six one must traditionally be the parson's wife, one the butcher's wife and one the baker's wife. When the last witch dies the church tower is doomed to fall—or if the tower falls the witches will die. Canewdon church tower stands squat and strong among the encroaching houses of the townsfolk who have moved into Canewdon, and the legend still persists along with Canewdon's reputation for evil.

Although Canewdon is rapidly becoming urbanized, this is a comparatively recent change and until quite recently children danced seven times round the church as a precaution against witchcraft. There are still villagers who prefer not to go near the churchyard, nor to pass near a certain crossroads at night. There is a good reason for this fear, for a witch who long ago paid the penalty for her wickedness was buried at the crossroads with a stake through her heart. Now her ghost emerges as a shadowy cloud from the church-yard and makes its way, always following the same route, towards the river and is only to be seen at certain fixed points on the road. The spectre disappears some fifty yards before the river bank, for ghosts cannot cross water.

A visitor to Canewdon reported this ghost some twenty years ago, but the details were different. He said he met what appeared to be a woman, wearing a crinoline and poke bonnet, on the road leading to the river. She was moving apparently at abnormal speed and floating above the ground. As she drew near, some mysterious force lifted the terrified visitor from his feet and flung him down, and he saw that the figure had no face beneath the bonnet.

Despite the fact that ghosts cannot cross water, this same woman has more recently been seen in the lounge of the Old Ferry House, on the far side of the river, and minus both bonnet and head. The ghost does no harm, occasionally opening and shutting windows, hovering on the stair or beside the fireplace in the lounge, and some-times creeping into empty beds and breathing heavily. Things being as they are the ghost is now regarded by the owner of the house as a social asset, but the local inhabitants are still convinced that it is the ghost of the executed witch.

Another headless spectre, however, has been reported in Canew-don, which could be the crinolined lady. The story is told by Charles Needham, a London barrister who, in 1895, recuperating from an illness rented a small cottage on the edge of the quiet and charming village. The servants whom he hired to look after him during the day seemed concerned by the fact that he was willing to sleep alone in the house, but for some nights he was undisturbed.

Then one night he was startled to see that someone seemed to be trying the latch of the back door. Charles Needham hurried to the front door which was unbolted, and as he slid the bolts he saw that latch rise and fall too. Undaunted, Needham opened the door but there was nobody there.

Thinking he was the victim of children's pranks, Needham said nothing. But one night, after he had been playing chess with the village doctor, his host offered to drive him back to his cottage. The horse reached the entrance to the lane leading to the cottage and obstinately refused to go any farther and so Needham, unwilling to trouble his friend, walked the rest of the way alone. As he came up the lane he saw a small light ahead of him and at one side of the road, and thinking it was some other person also alone in this lonely spot at midnight he hurried to catch him up. Close to his cottage a figure stepped out into the moonlight, remained quite still for a few moments and then turned towards him.

Horrified, Needham saw that it was a woman without a head. He ran all the way to the pub where he was greeted without surprise by the villagers who told him that the ghost was a familiar one—it was that of a woman whose husband, believing her to be a witch, had murdered and decapitated her many years ago.

Another of Canewdon's legends—and one which is remarkably persistent despite its fantastic nature—is the story of the witch who stole the church bell and then rowed across the river in it, using feathers for oars. The bell capsized and the witch was drowned, and on stormy days the bell may occasionally be heard tolling beneath the water.

The witch's body was recovered and buried beside the river at a spot where an area of barren ground was known as the Witches' Field. Here, it is said, the witches could be seen meeting to renew their powers after flying to their rendezvous on the river bank.

Canewdon was not only one of the last places in which the traditional belief in witches survived, but also the home of one of the last Masters of Witches. (Canewdon legend maintains that their witches have a master.) This old man, George Pickingale, died in 1909 aged ninety-three. Pickingale was both a black and white magician, and while he was much feared by the villagers who dared not disobey him for fear of what he might do in reprisal, he would also charm their warts and was sometimes called in to settle their disputes. He used his reputation to exploit the villagers, who were convinced that he had the power to summon the local witches by means of a wooden whistle and that he could bewitch the threshing machinery if he felt so inclined. On the other hand, if he did choose to work he could summon up a whole bevy of imps who would do it all for him while he sat in the shade smoking his pipe.

When George Pickingale died it was said that he passed his power on to his son—but since nothing has been heard of him it must be assumed that he no longer exercises it. This need to pass on the power is one to which Canewdon witches were continually subject, as was the familiar peculiar to them—the white mouse—and their unique ability to immobilize wheels.

Stories are told of Canewdon witches who could not die until someone accepted the power which they had to pass on. The witches' familiars were often the repositories of this and, as the belief in witchcraft began to decline, it is said that one old woman, lying in agony and unable to leave the power which held her bound to this earth, finally gave a low whistle at which a number of white mice appeared from a box. The old woman then died, but the mice refused to leave the body of the witch and had to be buried with her. Sometimes the witches' familiars had to be burned to prevent the power being passed on to their children willy-nilly.

Canewdon witches were also able to enchant wheels of carts and wagons, and a tradition persisted well into the twentieth century that it was unlucky to take a bicycle into Canewdon for it would surely suffer a puncture. A Mr Witcutt, late rector of Foulness island, told the story of a wagoner who had refused to buy some beer for a Canewdon woman. Afterwards he found that his horses couldn't move, and that however much he whipped them they were unable to get the wagon rolling. The wagoner's mate, however, was a local man and knew his witches. So he told the wagoner it was no use hitting the horses—try hitting the wheels. The wagoner did so and the Canewdon witch emerged screaming, the marks of the whip on her face.

The belief that witches could transform themselves into wheels was fairly widespread, but it was perhaps only the villagers of a place like Canewdon who became adept in dealing with witches. There is a strong tradition of witches having been ducked in the village pond, and the local people soon learnt the rudiments of white magic and knew that the best way to keep witches out of the house was to put a knife or a pair of scissors under the doormat.

Another remedy against witchcraft was the "witch bottle", and this may be said to be the speciality of a white magician, Cunning Murrell, who lived in Hadleigh, close to Canewdon. Murrell was well known as an astrologer, had considerable skill with simples and what might now be called faith healing, and by means of a magic mirror could trace lost property or find missing people. It was said he could also foresee the future, but he was a kindly man and when one of his clients asked him to foretell the next ten years he persuaded her he could not see that far. He foretold accurately her life for eight years, and in the ninth year she died.

Cunning Murrell was often called in to help when witchcraft was suspected. During the 1850s a young girl fell foul of an old gipsy woman whom she had treated brusquely. Soon afterwards the girl was attacked by fits which followed all the traditional signs of a bewitchment—she ran about on all fours, had convulsions, barked like a dog and so on.

Cunning Murrell confirmed that this was a case of witchcraft and prepared one of his witch bottles, iron bottles made for him by the village blacksmith which were filled with a mixture consisting of the blood and urine of the victim, together with some hair, herbs and pins. This was then boiled on the cottage fire at midnight in order to draw the witch to the scene of her crime. Soon footsteps were heard outside and the voice of an old woman crying out in agony, "For God's sake stop, you're killing me". At that moment the bottle exploded (they usually did, sometimes causing a good deal of damage to property) and the voice outside ceased. From that time on the girl began to recover, while some days later the body of an old gipsy woman, badly burned, was discovered some miles away.

Cunning Murrell dealt with another witch by telling her victim to follow her to her home, thrusting a knife into the witch's footprints. The woman hopped all the way home in agony, cursing her assailant. Murrell's success in such matters was such that he was credited with being a Master of Witches such as Pickingale, with the powers to command the women to obey. It is said that he once demonstrated his power by taking part in a contest with a witch of Canewdon. For some time neither party seemed to be gaining the upper hand until at last Murrell commanded the witch to die. Which she promptly did.

In 1860 Cunning Murrell died, one of the last of the Cunning men of England. In true witch tradition—white or black—he tried to pass his power on to his son who was, however, quite unworthy, his father having so sadly neglected properly to bring him up to be his heir that he could not even read. Cunning Murrell left behind him a quantity of books on astronomy and astrology, methods of preparing amulets and so on. All these books actually survived until 1956 when, save one, they were destroyed as being worthless.

The first documented witch of Canewdon was Rose Pye, who was tried in 1580 and acquitted. The last six witches to have been documented lived around the 1880s, and were described by those who remembered them only some twenty years ago. One of them was well known to bewitch wagon wheels and to possess imps. Another inflicted plagues of lice on those who annoyed her. A third fixed people with glaring eyes and prevented them from entering the church. A fourth was a cripple who cast spells and was loathed for her venomous temper. Another was not unkind, but occasionally terrified her neighbours by materializing at their bedside and peering fiercely at them from beneath her poke bonnet, while the sixth betrayed herself as a witch by refusing to step over a doormat beneath which a steel knife was hidden.

It is said that by the turn of the century the situation had so deteriorated (or improved) that jam-jars of urine had replaced the complicated brew and the iron witch-bottles used by Cunning Murrell. And certainly, today, the witches of Canewdon are as hard to find as is the old village. The remains of Pickingale's cottage—which eventually fell down since nobody would live in it after his death—have long since been swept away, and the inhabitants scoff or become irritated, or exploit the old tales according to their own interests.

Modern witchcraft would find little sympathy with the old witchcraft of Canewdon, and the modern Satanists are a different cult again. Reason seems at last to have driven the witches out of Canewdon; but there is perhaps just enough of the inexplicably supernormal to make one think.

At Canewdon the persistence of the tales and the "ghost" stories is interesting, despite the urbanization. And I know that when I came out of Canewdon church after having had a look at the carved witches' cat and the old altar tomb where it is said the children used to listen to the Devil rattling his chains—I found that my car had its first puncture for over five years.

THE SHIP THAT WAS CURSED

They made a macabre outline against the sky and the sea, the three wild-haired women, the child and the big black dog. A man watched them from a distance. They held strange objects in their hands, little images of men and of a ship, all made of clay.

One of the women screamed out a series of curses and the images were flung into the water. A sudden storm blew up. The water seemed to turn red for an instant. And a real ship, many miles away, was doomed.

Leader of the women was Margaret Barclay, who sought revenge against John Dein, her brother-in-law, and his friend, Provost Tran. They were both aboard that ship. She wished them dead.

The year was 1618, and her anger against them had started some months back. John Dein and his wife had accused Margaret of theft and Provost Tran had supported them. So she had them up for slander in the church court of the district of Irvine, Ayrshire, where they all lived. The court ordered a reconciliation. Margaret was commanded to shake hands with her sister-in-law before the assembled company.

She obeyed, but declared afterwards: "I only shook hands with her because the court said I must. I haven't forgiven her or her husband and I never shall."

John Dein was a ship's captain. His vessel, with full complement of sailors, was due to sail for France on a commercial venture. Provost Tran was going with him, to handle the business side of things when they reached France. Two other merchants were accompanying them.

Margaret said, before witnesses: "A curse upon that ship! I pray God that it will sink to the bottom of the sea and all on board be eaten up by crabs!" Then she set her mind to the business of making sure that the ship did sink. Secretly, in the hope that she would never be found out, she began to experiment in magic.

The ship sailed. Time passed. There was no news. Then a rumour began to circulate. It was started by a roving juggler and conjuror who made a precarious living by performing magic tricks. His name was John Stewart. He visited Mrs Tran and they chatted about her husband, the Provost. "I am so looking forward to his return," she said.

"Are you so sure that he will return?" asked Stewart.

"Of course. He's been on voyages before."

"There's always a last voyage, Mrs Tran."

"What do you mean? Tell me. As the Provost's wife I have the right to know."

"The Provost's wife? The Provost's widow, more like," said Stewart.

Frightened, Mrs Tran made further inquiries, and Stewart's prophesy turned out to be true. Two sailors who had sailed on the ship came back. They said that she had been wrecked on the English coast near Padstow and they were the only survivors. All the others had been drowned.

Now people thought back to Margaret's curse on the ship and wondered if she'd had anything to do with it. Then there was John Stewart with his warnings. Had those two been in league together and sunk the ship by witchcraft?

The city magistrates and ministers came to question Stewart.

"What dealings have you had with Margaret Barclay?"

"No dealings. She came to me for advice, that's all."

"What sort of advice?"

"She wanted me to teach her how to work magic, to make her wishes come true."

"And what were her wishes?"

"She wished for revenge on those who'd wronged her, but I told her I had no magic arts, so I couldn't help her."

After further questioning, and with some torture involved, he changed his story: "I knew Margaret Barclay well. Shortly after the ship sailed, I went to her house. I found her there with two other women. They were making clay figures."

"Did the figures resemble anyone?"

"One of them was fair and handsome like Provost Tran. Also they moulded a ship out of clay. While they were doing it, the Devil came to keep them company. He came in the shape of a big black dog."

"And then what happened?"

"When the clay ship and figures were ready, the three women and the Devil-dog went to an empty house near the seaport." He took them to the shore and pointed out the house.

"They gathered there, then they all went down to the water's edge, called out curses, and flung the figures of ship and men into the sea. I watched them. As soon as the figures sank, the sea stormed and raged and the water turned red—red as juice in a dyer's cauldron."

Now the magistrates lined up a number of Margaret's women friends, for an identity parade.

"John Stewart, you said there were two women with Margaret Barclay. Are they here?"

He studied the line of frightened women, then pointed an accusing finger. "She's one."

The woman, Isobel Insh, screamed in protest: "No, it's a lie! I've never seen that man in my life before!" But the inquisitors did not believe her. They dragged her away and shut her up in the church belfry, then turned their attention to her daughter. This was a little girl of eight years old who lived in Margaret's house as a servant and helped her to look after her baby. She was asked if she had seen the clay figures being made.

"Yes, I was there," said the child.

"Was you mother, Isobel Insh, there too?"

"She was."

"Who else?"

"A girl. I don't know her name. She lives in the town. We went to the house by the shore, then down to the water and threw the clay images into it."

They asked her about the black dog.

"Oh, yes, a dog came with us. A great black dog with flashes of light coming out of its nose and mouth. It gave us light while the spell was being cast, to make the ship sink and all aboard her drown."

"All this is very wicked and terrible," the men told her. "Why didn't you speak of it before?"

"I promised Margaret Barclay that I wouldn't. She said that if I kept quiet she'd give me a new pair of shoes."

The magistrates returned to John Stewart. Why hadn't he mentioned the presence of the child?

"I didn't think to," he said, "but the little snatchet was there all right."

Meantime the "little snatchet's" mother was still shut up in the belfry tower, and she was in a state of panic. She knew what happened to those accused of witchcraft. When the magistrates came to question her, at first she denied everything. Then she realized that her daughter had given her away, and admitted that she had been there. "But I was only a bystander," she said. "I didn't ill-wish anyone."

"Isobel Insh, do you have supernatural powers?"

She hesitated. If she said "No", they wouldn't believe her. If she said "Yes", she would be admitting that she was a witch. She thought of a way to get round them, or so she hoped. She looked at one of her inquisitors who was a sailor and said: "I have supernatural powers. If you let me go free, you will never have a bad voyage in all your life to come. My powers will keep you safe."

This statement quietened them, for although she was afraid of them and they had worldly power, they were also afraid of her and all her kind, because of whatever secret powers she might possess.

"We will return tomorrow," they said at last, "to hear your full confession of sorcery. Promise that tomorrow you will confess."

"I promise," said Isobel.

They left her alone again. She brooded over tomorrow. If she broke her promise and refused to confess, they could keep her prisoner here for years—a living death. If she did confess, she would be executed as a witch. She had to escape.

She was heavily fettered. A normal person would have been unable to move under the weight of those chains, even though they were unattached to the walls. But Isobel, with superhuman strength, managed to climb out of a back window in the tower and on to the roof. Open sky and solitude gave her an illusion of freedom. Brief illusion. She was soon seen by people below. Gazing up at her, they gathered, murmuring, about the church. She was as trapped in space as surely as she had been trapped in the tower room.

She dragged herself from one side of the roof to the other, missed her footing, tumbled, rolled, nearer and nearer to the edge of the roof—and finally she crashed to the ground.

The crowd converged on her helpless figure. They carried her to a bed. No friends came. They were all afraid of being involved with her now. But the magistrates came to her bedside with more questions. Badly hurt and in pain, she not only refused to confess fully but withdrew her previous admission. "I am innocent," she declared. "Leave me alone!"

On the fifth day after her fall, she died. It was believed that she had obtained poison somehow and poisoned herself. So Isobel Insh was free, but Margaret Barclay and John Stewart remained to face the music. A day was fixed for their trial for witchcraft.

Stewart was imprisoned in solitary confinement. Half an hour before the trial was due to begin, the magistrates and ministers came to urge him to beg God for mercy, to release him from his bonds to the Devil. Stewart gave in and did as they asked. He was suffering from the weight of chains on him. "I am so heavily fettered that I can't raise my hand to my head or bread to my mouth," he said.

They left him, apparently unable to move hand or foot, but when his guards returned they found that he had hanged himself from a hook on the door. He had used a string either from his head-wear or his garter. The hook was not high and his feet dangled only a little above floor level. How he had managed to do it, chained as he was, no one knew.

The guards cut the string, laid him on the floor and tried to revive him. They were too late. John Stewart had cheated his executioners and juggled his way to freedom by dying.

Now only Margaret Barclay was left to stand trial for sinking the ship. They determined to get a confession out of her so put her to torture, using what was known as the "safe and gentle torture".

She had to put her bare legs in the stocks, and one by one iron bars were placed on them until the weight became unbearable. For each admission of witchcraft that she made, a bar would be removed; for each denial, a bar would be added.

As the pain in her legs became excruciating, she cried out: "Take them off! Take them off! I'll tell you everything."

The bars were removed. "I have nothing to tell," she said now. "I am innocent."

The bars were replaced. Again she screamed that she would tell all if they were lifted. "If you'll clear the court, I'll confess only to the justices themselves," she said. "I will confess truly before God." So the court was cleared of all but the justices and the torture ceased. Margaret confessed: "I pray for the mercy of God and the destruction of the Devil, my old Master. I did destroy John Dein's ship. I hoped to kill only John Dein himself and Provost Tran—but not the rest of the crew." Then she added: "But it was Isobel Crawford's doing as much as mine."

Isobel Crawford. A new name in the proceedings. This was the third woman, whose identity had been secret so far.

The trial was delayed while Isobel Crawford was found and questioned. She said that she was guilty of the crime of witchcraft, but that Margaret Barclay had been the ringleader. She herself had been no more than an accomplice.

With this new evidence to hand, Margaret's trial continued. Until this moment, her husband had kept well out of it, but now he must have felt some smattering of loyalty towards his wife, for he turned up in court for the first time and brought a lawyer to act on her behalf.

This revived hope in Margaret.

"Do you wish to be defended by a lawyer?" she was asked.

"As you please," she said, adding spiritedly: "My confession was made in an agony of torture. Before God, all that I said under torture was false and untrue. I am innocent!"

She turned to her husband and cried: "You have been too long in coming."

The jury now had to decide whether her confession had been true, or whether it had been an untruth forced from her by torture. They were sure that she was guilty, yet it was true that she had been tortured. They got round this difficulty by saying that, at the moment of her confession the iron bars had not actually been lying on her legs, so she did not confess "under torture" at all.

Therefore she was brought in guilty of witchcraft and condemned to death.

Margaret had fought hard to save her own life, but now that the battle was lost she no longer protested her innocence. She said that her previous confession had been true, that she had been a servant of the Devil for a long time, and that she had caused the ship to sink by making the clay images, casting a spell and flinging them into the water.

"I was responsible for it all," she admitted, in her last hours, "and Isobel Crawford is innocent. I beg you to set her free."

She died a witch's death, being strangled at the stake, and her body afterwards being burned to ashes.

Her dying wish, however, was ignored. Isobel Crawford was not set free. A confession was demanded of her and she suffered the same torture as Margaret. For although she had admitted some guilt when first arrested, now she was declaring her innocence.

Isobel Crawford proved to have an immense capacity for enduring pain. She received thirty stone of weight on her legs without crying out for mercy. Her torturers began to wonder if she would ever give in. These witches were made of stern stuff. The Devil aided them perhaps.

Then, instead of adding more weight to her legs, they shifted the bars to another position, so that they rested on a different part of her legs.

A new searing agony was awakened, and it broke her.

"Take them off! Take them off! I'll confess!"

The cruel weights were removed. She confessed that she had been in league with Margaret Barclay, the witch, and a servant of the Devil for years. She was sentenced to death.

At this point she behaved quite differently from Margaret. Whereas the latter had fully admitted her witchcraft once her life was forfeit and she had nothing to lose, Isobel denied her confession, extorted from her in such pain. She remained defiant up to the moment of her execution. When she stood at the stake and the minister was praying for her soul, she interrupted him: "I am innocent. You judges are the guilty ones."

It was the custom for a person condemned to death to pardon the executioner. This Isobel Crawford refused to do. "Pardon you? Never. *I* am innocent. *You* are guilty."

Shortly afterwards, innocent or guilty, she was no more than a handful of ashes and a stench of burning in the air.

Thus the four people who had conspired to sink a ship by their black magic arts were all terribly punished, and they all died by violence, two by suicide, two by strangulation and burning.

Margaret Barclay was the most powerful of the four and deeply aware of her own powers, as she showed by her final confession. She had wanted to destroy, and had succeeded. She had the knack of getting other people to do as she wished, for all her accomplices knew what a dangerous game they were playing and the dreadful penalty if they were caught. They were murderers-from-a-distance, using a method of murder which, because it is so nebulous and inexplicable, is even more terrifying than the human brutality of a blow, a shot or a stab. Human brutality showed clearly enough among those who accused, tortured and executed the witches. Fear of those dark powers made them cruel. They believed that they were fighting against the power of the Devil and his servants on earth. Ironically, as in all wars, they did evil things in their battle against evil.

So in that litle Ayrshire town, the Devil had a victory either way, for as his old servants were destroyed he soon found new ones among the destroyers.

As for the big black dog which had kept the witches company in the house and on the seashore, there is no record of it being seen again in those parts.

THE BROTHERS AND THE WITCH

So many of the well-confirmed tales of the supernatural have as their setting either the extreme north or the extreme south of the British Isles that one is inclined towards the theory that occult and supernatural beings prefer the wilder coastal settings. Be that as it may, the following events have been told so often and are so firmly established in local lore that many Cornishmen believe in their reality as firmly as they do in the historical reality of, say, the Duke of Wellington—who, it just so happens, was achieving high fame at the time.

It was an autumn evening in the year 1810; and the town was Helston, where the Lizard peninsula can be said to begin. The peninsula leads down the Lizard Point, the most southerly feature of England's mainland. Helston is the home of the famous Flora dance and was later in the century to claim as one of its sons the boxer, Bob Fitzsimmons.

Two apprentice saddlers, Charlie and Jim Williams, were in their attic bedroom in one of the roads off the steep high street, rather uncomfortably perched on stools. "But what's wrong, Charlie?"

"Nothing. It's nothing at all .Just that I'm not tired. I don't see why, just because we're apprentices, we have to be in bed by nine. I could stay up for hours. We could have a game of cards, now, couldn't we?"

Jim, the elder brother, all of thirteen years, but a strapping lad, almost a man, looked at his eleven-year-old younger brother. Why, if ever a boy needed eight hours between the blankets, it was little Charlie Williams. There were great black shadows under each eye, the complexion was pale, almost grey.

"Never mind, Charlie. I think Mr and Mrs Carver know what's best for us. And in a year or two, we'll be our own masters, able to get to bed when we want."

"I suppose so. But I still don't want to go to bed. Not here—in the Carvers' house. I—I have terrible dreams, Jim——"

"That's because you eat too much last thing at night. A huge great slab of Mrs Carver's bread and cheese isn't the thing to dream on. And washed down with her ale. You're too young for that. Just try cutting down on the grub."

"Oh—all right." Young Charlie threw the last bit of bread and cheese into the fireplace.

It had taken the boys a month or so to get used to the Carvers. Helston was quite some distance from their home at Marazion and Mr Carver had at first seemed gruff, almost hostile, and definitely so when the boys made stupid mistakes. "Saddler can't suffer fools gladly, lad. It's more than the business is worth, having shoddy work turned out."

But a moment later Mr Carver was all smiles. "I'm sorry, lads. I get a bit gruff, sometimes. But I like the pair of you. Sure you're getting enough to eat?"

"Oh yes, sir. And thank you, Mrs Carver, it was a beautiful supper, really it was."

The cosy Mrs Carver, roughly as wide as she was high, would then embrace the boys in turn.

So it was a happy enough life. But this new hatred of going to bed which was being shown by young Charlie Williams worried his elder brother. He would lie in the next bed, unable to sleep himself while the younger brother seemed to fight the onslaught of sleep. Usually Jim was asleep before the muttering and the rolling in the next bed had stopped.

The next morning he was, for the first time, horrified at his younger brother's appearance. The boy was ashen and his lips were trembling so that he could hardly speak.

"Now Charlie, you must tell me. What are these dreams you're having?"

"It's nothing. Tonight—well, I won't have any supper at all, not a morsel. And if I have the same dream, I'll tell you about it——"

"The same dream? Why, d'you always have the same one?"

"Yes."

"But you've got to tell me now. The dreams are exactly the same?"

"Not exactly. But almost. And they're—they're awful——"

To the older boy's dismay, young Charlie burst into tears and cried as if his heart would break. Jim held him tight, and eventually the weeping stopped. "I'm sorry. Just being a cry-baby."

"No, you're not. We all get to cry a little, now and then. But you mark my words, if you're like this tomorrow morning, I'm getting Mr Carver to fetch the doctor. He'll give you some physic, and that'll put you right."

"Very well. Tell you about it tomorrow, if it happens again."

The day passed fairly uneventfully, except that the dog-tired Charlie made more mistakes than usual and Mr Carver was obviously holding himself in rein. Jim took him aside. "It'll be all right, Mr Carver, sir. Charlie just hasn't been sleeping. And if it's the same tonight, I'll ask you if you'd be getting the physician to see him."

"Physician? But don't you think, Jim my lad, that it's maybe just homesickness? I could always send him home to your parents for a few days, there's a stage-coach or diligence leaves quite often——"

'I don't think it's homesickness, Mr Carver.'

Mr Carver was concerned. Perhaps the boy was not getting enough to eat and drink, and that would be a terrible disgrace. Mrs Carver would make sure he got a really good supper from now on. And though he didn't approve of young lads having much ale at the best of times, maybe a mug or two more of it might give the lad a good night's sleep. Certainly did for him: an extra quart and he slept as if he'd been hit with a blacksmith's hammer. That is, until he had to get up and run some of it off, of course.

He intimated these thoughts to Jim.

"We'll see, sir. I think maybe tonight he ought to have a very light supper, just as a try-out, you might say. And then I'll tell you about it in the morning."

That night the two brothers went to bed at the usual hour, both of them rather hungry. For at least half an hour Jim Williams stayed awake, hoping to hear the peaceful breathing of a younger brother being welcomed into the arms of Morpheus. But he was tired from his own exertions in the saddler's workshop and he fell asleep, leaving Charlie still tossing and turning.

In the morning he was again shocked at his brother's appearance. Without wasting time, even before they got out of their little wooden beds, he demanded the full story. "Come on. I'm going to hear all about this dream, every bit."

"You wouldn't believe it——"

"That's for me to judge."

"All right, then. Well, it happens just the same way every night. Don't even know whether I'm awake or asleep when it happens——"

"When *what* happens?"

"You see this bed of mine's nearer the door than yours is. Every night a horrible old woman comes in that door, makes straight for my bed——"

"What's she look like? Like Mrs Carver?" To Jim's delight, he managed to draw a pale smile over the other's features.

"No, but she *is* fat. She seems to be dressed in brown or black, though it's hard to see, really. And her long, sort of grey-black, hair, it's piled on her head like a bun. Reminds me of *someone* round these parts, but, well, I just can't remember exactly. But she's terrible strong, grabs me by the neck. I can't possibly call out or do anything. And yet she weighs—she hardly weighs anything at all. She gets to fix a bridle, right over my head. I think it must be one of Mr Carver's——"

"Slips a *bridle* over your head?"

"Yes. And a bit between my teeth. Jim, she's so strong I can't possibly stop her; and she gets on my back and kicks me on either side. Just like you kick a horse. Then she makes me carry her round the end of your bed and out through the window; and though we're way up in the air, she seems to get me flying, turns me into a sort of flying horse. And out we go, her riding on my back——"

Under Jim's insistent questioning the rest of the story came out. They rode great distances, but Charlie could not say exactly where. He had a vague idea it was north of the Helford River in the direction of St Mawes.

After about an hour's galloping flight they arrived at the witch's destination—her coven—for there were other witches there. It was a very bleak foreshore between two giant rocks. Here she tied him up to a rotting post, and then started to babble with the other witches. Something foul was always being cooked.

"*You* never get any of it?"

"Oh no! I should be sick."

"And then what happens?"

"Then she unties me from the post, gets on my back, kicks me in the ribs and we head back here to Helston again. We sail down the high street, and straight in through the window. She gets off and very quietly leads me past the end of your bed, drags me into my own, and takes off my bridle. And then——"

"Yes?"

"Then she kisses me. I think this is the worst part of all. She kisses me and she goes out—out through the closed door. Oh, Jim, it's horrible, it really is."

And indeed it must be. Jim knew the ring of truth in his brother's voice and he could feel his own heart beat fast at the horror of it.

There was only one thing to do. "Charlie," he announced quietly, "we shall change beds tonight."

Charlie demurred, for he was fond of his elder brother, and hated the idea of his having the same ghastly experience. However, the rejoinder was firm.

"Remember I'm two years older than you and everyone says I'm big and strong for my age. So I'd like to have a tussle with this witch of yours."

"But don't you think, now we both know about it, we ought to tell Mr and Mrs Carver?"

"Maybe. But not until after tonight."

That day the brothers worked especially hard and Mr Carver noted that although the younger one was still pale and sickly looking, they both whistled from time to time as they worked. And their work was fine and accurate, too. He felt constrained to congratulate them. "You're doing a fine job, lads. I think you'll make good saddlers, the pair of you."

The boys mumbled their thanks and went on with the work of stitching two bridles. Jim found himself looking at all the bridles on the wall and wondering if any of these had been used by the witch. But no, they were all brand-new, beautiful bridles, and they could never have been taken down from their hooks.

That evening, sharp at the usual time, they went up to their room. Charlie had been prevailed upon to have a large supper, thick soup with a large pasty, and also almost a quart of beer. Jim, unsmiling, partook of hardly anything, and the Carvers watched with interest as the two of them went up the narrow winding stairs from the kitchen.

"They're a rum pair, those two," said Mr Carver.

"Oh, they're just boys," said his wife. "We mustn't worry about them. Did you see how much the little one tucked away tonight? I was proper delighted."

"And the big one had hardly anything. Strange——"

As arranged, the boys swopped beds, Charlie Williams tonight climbing into the one farthest from the door. And to his older brother's satisfaction he was soon fast asleep.

He was unaware what time he himself dropped off, and never was really clear later on just how long he had slept.

But he suddenly awoke with a feeling of great oppression upon him. He looked up and saw the old woman, bending over his bed—and there really *was* a bridle in her hand. Her grey face was lit by the moon streaming in through the bedroom window, and he could see that she was indeed rather fat, had her hair piled up in a ramshackle bun and was more or less entirely covered by a hideous, shapeless, black or brown dress of a coarse material, with a little black cloak about her shoulders. Her round face was not really malevolent, and she did, as Charlie had hinted, remind one of somebody, somebody one had seen, maybe in Helston.

He let the bridle be slipped over his head and he even took the bit between his teeth. Obedient to the rider's signals, he lifted her towards the window, feeling her calloused heels dig deep into his ribs. Charlie had been right, and despite her shape and strength, she was weightless.

Jim already had his plan. He would wait, though, until they had flitted out through the attic window: there'd be no point in waking up poor Charlie. Let him get a decent night's sleep tonight, and Jim would make sure he got one every night from now on.

Out of the window they floated. It was rather like swimming, through the night air, and Jim Williams found that his limbs took up the motion naturally as if he'd been carrying weightless witches all his life. In a way, until the fat old thing gave a vicious tweak to the reins, which hurt his mouth, it was quite pleasant, just swimming through that moon-bright autumn air with something weightless on his back. Weightless—and so fat!

Then, when they were well away from the house, he did it.

There was a terrible scream from the old hag as he dragged her down off his back with one hand and took the bit from between his teeth with the other. But she was so light, even though she had strength, that he had no difficulty in getting her off his back, changing places with her. The bit fitted well in her jaws.

"Get moving," he shouted in triumph. "Tonight it's my turn to ride, and I want to go fast. We've a long journey. First to Porthleven, then off to Mullion Cove. After that down the coast past Kynance to the Lizard Point. And we'll come back up the other side over Cadgwith and St Keverne. Across the Goonhillie Downs— they should be fine and misty and wonderful tonight—back here to Helston. And if you don't go fast enough, I'll just kick you till you do."

He did, and there was a grunt of pain.

"Come on, now. I want to be back in my bed by dawn."

He could see where they were and after describing an aerial arc around Porthleven, to his surprise the old woman descended the few feet to ground level, was actually galloping, like a horse, down the Lizard road.

And as they galloped on, she slowly began to take on the shape of a real horse. First her strange hair divided on the top of her head and became horse's ears. And the short cloak in front of him changed slowly into a long black mane. If he looked down he could see the short fat fingers, the shapeless shoes, becoming pairs of horse's hooves.

Surely no racehorse in history had travelled so far. The sound of its hooves was like the rattle of a drum roll, and it grew faster.

They were already in mist, the strange fascinating sea mist of the Predannack downs, where a rider's head can be above it and the rest of him and his horse quite hidden. Occasionally the top of a tree, one of the very few trees in that barren land, or the roof of a house, appeared above it and shot by. At Ruan Minor they turned off to Mullion, had a fine view from the cove of the grey, slow-breaking sea across to Mounts Bay; then stormed on past Kynance to the Lizard itself. The moon gave an eerie polish to everything and he had the strange feeling of riding on the blanket of mist.

He was singing with the exhilaration of the night air and the speed, when he suddenly noticed his steed was limping.

The galloping eased to a limping canter, then a walk. Jim dismounted carefully, holding tight to the reins, to inspect.

It was as he had thought. The shoes were worn almost through and one of them was hanging by only a pair of nails. He owed the witch no kindness, God knew, but common sense told him he must wake up some blacksmith and get a new set of shoes put on. Already there was a pale glow in the east, and if he didn't make haste, he and his horse-witch would not be back by dawn.

As luck would have it, he found an early-risen smith working at his bellows in St Keverne. He stopped his steed and watched as the puffing and huffing blew life into the embers by the anvil. Then he dismounted, still holding the animal firmly by its reins.

"Excuse me," he said nervously, suddenly feeling a thirteen-year-old boy again, not a champion rider, a tamer of witches.

'Yes?" said the smith.

"Could you—would you—shoe my horse for me? We've come a long way and she's lame."

Jim had not had occasion to ascertain the sex of his steed, but presumably it would be a mare.

"Aye, I'll do that for you," said the smith.

"Thank you very much. It's very kind of you, at this hour of the morning."

"Oh, that's all right. Money's money, whether the sun shines or the moon. You have got money, have you? To me, you look as if you'd just scrambled out of bed in your nightdress."

Jim had a moment of panic, then remembered. "This is the way I *like* to ride at night, in these clothes. More freedom. They're not really nightclothes, of course. And I have money, in this leathern bag around my neck."

He took out some silver coins from the bag he always wore this way day and night, and they glistened in the red light from the glow· ing coals.

The smith got to work. "My, these shoes have worn a fair way. You'd not get much farther with the likes of these. I've never seen such shoes, not even slippers, they aren't——" The man laughed at his little joke and Jim nervously laughed with him.

The four new shoes were fitted, the nails hammered home, and Jim paid the obliging smith, who took rather less than the youth had imagined the job was worth. "Good luck," he said. "Good luck, young fellow. And get safely home—before your folks see what you've been doing. I must say, though, I admire a lad with spirit——"

Jim mounted his horse-witch and galloped away, as the genial smith waved his farewell. The beast was running beautifully now, which was just as well, for the sky was becoming quite light.

They reached the Carvers' house in the side street.

"Right," said Jim. "I want you to change back into a witch—or I'll kick you real hard—and jump back into that attic window. And not a sound, understand?"

Obediently, the ears became hair again—a bun—and the rest of the horse became the rest of an old woman. One bound and they were through the window, Jim clinging on for dear life.

"And now get out," hissed Jim at the woman, "Get out, and *never* come back." The woman paused for a moment, then turned and slowly went out through the closed door.

Charlie woke, stretched himself. Jim had already slithered into the next bed.

"Oh Jim, I had a wonderful night's sleep. Not a nightmare, not even a dream, nothing. It was fine."

"Good. I had a pleasant night, too." Jim had decided not to tell the younger boy what had happened, lest it upset him and he start having dreams of a different nature. "No, I didn't dream either. But I think we'll stay in these beds from now on."

Helston was beginning to stir to a new day, and they could hear the Carvers busying themselves below, making breakfast, starting work. And then, in the distance, came a scream.

It grew louder and louder and they heard Mr Carver put down something heavy in his workshop and go out at the double, up Helston's precipitous high street. The screaming went on.

By the time he got back to the house the boys were up and dressed, and it was their master's turn to look haggard and distraught.

"What is it? What is it, John Carver?" asked his wife. "You look as if you'd seen a ghost——"

"My God, perhaps worse. There's been a fat old woman hanging around the top of the high street for some weeks now. Nobody seemed to know where she came from, even where she stays. Quite a friendly body, they say, but, well, there's something a bit uncanny, unpleasant about her."

"Oh, come to the point, John Carver."

"Well, believe me or believe me not, this old hag's sitting there on the ground, screaming her head off in agony. And small wonder. There's a brand-new horse-shoe nailed tight on to each hand and foot."

THE WITCHES AND THE KING

Ten miles east of Edinburgh, on the main road to Dunbar, lies the little town of Tranent, population 6,000 plus a few hundred.

In 1590, it was about a quarter of this size, and its deputy bailie —a municipal officer, something akin to the English deputy mayor —was a certain David Seaton.

Maid to David Seaton's household was Geillis Duncan, a kindly woman loved by all, who was always ready to help those in trouble, particularly men and women "greeved with any kinde of sicknes or infirmitie", for she possessed, it was generally recognized, remarkable powers of healing. Had she lived in England, Geillis would have been known as a Cunning Woman, or White Witch. As it was, having performed "manye matters most miraculous, which thinges forasmuch as she began to doe them upon a sodaine, having never doon the like before", she was the cause of, and suspected of having been deeply involved in, the case of the North Berwick Witches, one of the most famous of British cases of malevolent witchcraft.

That Geillis Duncan had no intention of unmasking the North Berwick witches, is certain. What happened was this.

Geillis was in the habit of not sleeping in the bed provided for her in his house by Deputy Bailie Seaton, and this became known to him. Since masters were responsible under the law for the behaviour of all the members of their household, Seaton decided to investigate where Geillis went and what she did on her secret nocturnal expeditions. Though admitting that the maid did indeed possess remarkable powers of healing, which powers she could derive from only one of two sources—God or the Devil—it occurred to the bailie that her nightly absences might indicate the latter rather than the former. Perturbed, he called to his house a number of Tranent's leading citizens, so that they might assist at his interrogation of the maid.

"The better to finde out the trueth", comments a contemporary account, Bailie Seaton first tormented her "with the torture of the pilliwinks upon her fingers". Geillis remained silent under the considerable pain caused by this vice-like instrument, so Seaton had her thrawed, i.e., a rope was placed round her forehead and tightened as is done with a tourniquet. Thrawing is even more painful than the pilliwinks, but still Geillis said nothing.

Seaton, however, was completely unconvinced by her silence that she was innocent, and ordered that she be searched for the Devil's mark.*

The searchers of Geillis Duncan presently declared that they had found such a mark on the "forepart of her throat". At the discovery the woman's composure forsook her and she confessed that "all her dooings was done by the wicked allurements and enticements of the Divell, and that she did them by witchcraft".

By first torturing Geillis and then having her searched for the Devil's mark, Bailie Seaton was acting contrary to accepted practice throughout Europe. But this was by no means an uncommon occurrence in Scotland, where the Scots appeared determined to take no risk where a man's or a woman's soul was concerned.

Geillis, like so many of her countrywomen, realized that silence or denial was useless once a mark had been found, even though she might be entirely innocent. On her confession, Seaton at once handed her over to the civic authorities, charging her with witchcraft. Under further interrogation, she incriminated Agnes Sampson of Hadding-

---

* The Devil's mark was acquired by the witch at her initiation into the Devil's service. Satan put his mark on her as a token of his authority over her. Any blemish on the skin, such as a birthmark, scar or unnatural pigmentation, was regarded as a possible Devil's mark. It was always on a part of the body hidden by clothes, and sometimes, according to Ludovico Sinistraro, the last of the great demonologists, "It is imprinted on the most secret parts of the body; with men under the eyelids or perhaps in the armpits, or on the lips or shoulders, or the anus, or elsewhere; with women it is generally under the breasts or on the private parts." Anyone suspected of being a witch or warlock was, therefore, first stripped naked—generally before a large crowd—and all the body-hair was "shaved off to the skin". If no mark was then visible, the most intimate orifices were searched. The discovery of a mark was inevitably followed by torture to extract confessions.

ton, seventeen miles from Edinburgh, Agnes Thompson of Edinburgh, Dr John Fian, "alias John Cunningham, Maister of the Schoole at Saltpans, in Lothian", Mistress George Mott of Saltpans, Robert Grierson, a ship's captain, Jennet Bandilandis, the smith at the Bridge of Hallis, and the wife of Seaton's porter.

On the following days, Geillis incriminated many others. Among the prominent citizens she denounced was Ewphame Macalyan Moscrop, a daughter of Lord Cliftenhall, and wife of Patrick Moscrop, a wealthy and influential man. Mistress Moscrop, Geillis claimed, "had conspired and performed the death of her Godfather, and who used her art upon a gentleman being one of the Lords and Justices of the Session, for bearing goodwill to her daughter". Another prominent woman was Barbara Napier, sister-in-law of the Laird of Carshogill, "who had bewitched to death Archibalde, last Earle of Angus".

Not only did Geillis specify the nature of their acts of witchcraft, but gave a full account of their activities, and it was this account that attracted the attention of King James VI. So much so, in fact, that he decided to take a personal part in the interrogation of the accused.

Agnes Sampson, who was the oldest of all those arrested, was the first to be taken to Holyrood House. She was "of a rank and comprehension above the vulgar, grave and settled in her answers". She refused point blank to confess, and no blandishment or threat of the King or Privy Councillors, who sat with him, could move her.

Eventually losing patience, James ordered her to be shaved and searched for the Devil's mark. During the search she was thrawn, but old as she was, she endured the pain with stoic silence. Then, after an hour of searching, the mark was found on "Here privie parts. Then she immediately confessed whatsoever was demaunded of her, and justifying those persons aforesaid to be notorious witches." She now made a full confession to the King.

On All Hallows Eve, she told James, she and all the accused together with a company of witches, had put to sea, each in a riddle or sieve, "and went in the same very substantially with Flaggons of wine making merrie and drinking by the waye in the same Riddles or Cives, until they came to North Berwick Church", where they disembarked, and joining hands, danced a reel as they sang

> Commer goe ye before, commer goe ye,
> Gif ye will not goe before, commer let me.

Leading the dance, she said, was Geillis Duncan, playing upon "a small trump, called a Jewes Trump", and so they entered Berwick church.

James at once sent for Geillis and commanded her to play the tune of *Commer goe ye before* on a "Jewes Trump", which she did to his clear delight.

When Geillis had finished, Agnes continued her confession. The Devil* in the form of a man, she said, was waiting for them in the church. Apparently they had taken too long over their singing and dancing, and had kept him waiting, so in penance he ordered each one to render him the *osculum infame*, that is, to kiss his naked posterior, as a "signe of dutie to him". He sat on the edge of the pulpit as the company filed by to present their duty.

This ceremony completed, the Devil had then treated them to an harangue "wherein he did greatlye enveighe against the King of Scotland". Some of those present had been bold enough to ask why he hated the King so vehemently, and he had said because James was his greatest enemy on earth. He had then demanded that they renew their oath to him, and when this was done they all returned home.

The next day, when Agnes Sampson was again brought before the King, the official account states that she "confessed before the King's Majestie sundrye things which were so miraculous and strange as that his Majestie saide they were all extreame lyars, whereat she answered, she would not wish his Majestie to suppose her woords to be false, but rather to believe them, in that she would discover such matter unto him as his Majestie should not in any way doubt of". And she was as good as her word.

The year before, James had married Anne of Denmark in Oslo, which was then under Danish rule. Agnes Sampson now took the King on one side and, speaking to him in a low voice, "declared unto him the verye woords which passed betweene the King's Majestie and his Queene in Upslo (Oslo) in Norway on the first night of their marriage, with their answere each to other". She was sufficiently right to amaze James who "swore by the living God, that he believed that all the Divels in hell could not have discovered the same: acknowledging her woords to be most true, and therefore gave the more credit to the rest which is before declared".

This incident convinced James that the old woman was possessed of supernatural powers, so when she went on to disclose that to-

---

* All groups of witches, large or small, had their leader, invariably male, who claimed to be, and was accepted as, the Devil. The Devil always took pains to keep himself completely aloof from his followers, except during the ceremonies of the Sabbat, as witches' meetings were called.

gether with others she had set out to encompass the King's death by witchcraft he believed all she said.

She had, she told James, taken a black toad and hung it up by the heels for three days. The venom which dripped from its jaws, she had collected in an oyster shell. Some of it she had kept in a sealed pot until such time as she could obtain from John Kers, one of the King's attendants and a friend of hers, an article of soiled linen used by James. Unhappily for the success of her plan, Kers had refused to co-operate. But for his refusal, she would have bewitched James to death "and put him to such extraordinary paines, as if he had been lying upon sharp thornes and endes of Needles".

Upon the failure of this plan, while James was in Norway, she and some other women had christened a cat, and had then bound each part of it to "the cheefest partes of a dead man, and severall joyntes of his body". On the following night, she and her confederates had sailed to Leith in their sieves, and there deposited the cat. At once a storm greater than any within living memory, had wrecked a ship sailing from Brunt Island to Leith carrying jewels and rich gifts for James's Queen when she arrived in Leith.

The same cat, she claimed, had been responsible for an inexplicable incident that had occurred when James was returning from Scandinavia. His ship, and only his, of all the flotilla accompanying him, had run into a head wind. All the others had had a fair wind.

By the standards of the day, James was a well-educated man, but like so many educated men at that time, he was very susceptible to any hint of the supernatural, the main embodiment of which was the witchcraft that had reached a new peak throughout Europe towards the end of the sixteenth century. As for the witches themselves, they seemed hell-bent on fostering the belief in their supernatural powers, which could only eventually encompass their deaths.

Though the tortures inflicted on Geillis Duncan by Bailie Seaton and on Agnes Sampson by her interrogators were horrible in their sadism, they were nothing compared to the sufferings inflicted on John Fian, alias Cunningham.

First, by thrawing of his head with a roape, whereat he would confess nothing.

Second, he was persuaded by faire means to confesse his follies, but that would revaile as little.

Lastly, he was put to the most severe and cruell paine in the world, called the bootes, who after he had received three strokes, being enquired if he would confess his damnable acts and wicked life, his tung would not serve him to speak, in respect whereof the rest of the witches

willed to search his tung, under which was found two pinnes thrust up
unto the head, whereupon the Witches did laye, *Now is the Charm
stinted*, and showed that those charmed Pinnes were the cause he could
not confesse any thing: then he was immediately released of the bootes,
brought before the King, his confession was taken, and his owne hand
willingly set ther-unto, which contained as followeth.

He declared that he was always present at the general meetings
of the witches, describing himself as the "clerk to all those that were
in subjection to the Devil's service". He administered to them the
oath of service, and recorded for them the orders which the Devil
gave him.

As much as any of the women, Fian was an ardent believer in the
supernatural powers bestowed by witchcraft, and indeed often had
recourse to them for his own ends. For example, he claimed that he
had bewitched a man living near Saltpans, because he was in love
with a young woman loved by himself. The bewitching caused the
man to go temporarily insane once every twenty-four hours, and
each fit lasted one hour. He suggested to James that the man should
be summoned so that he could demonstrate the truth of his claim.
Naturally, James agreed and the man was summoned to Holyrood
House on 24 December, 1590.

"And when he was brought to his Majesties Chamber, suddenly
he gave a great scritch and fell into a madness, sometime bending
himself, and sometime capering so directly up, that his head did
touch the seeling of the Chamber, to the great admiration of his
Majestie and others there present." The gentlemen there were quite
unable to hold him down until they had sent for assistance. Then
they bound him hand and foot and made him lie down until his
fit had passed. About an hour later he came to, and James asked him
what he saw and did in his fit; to which he replied that he slept
soundly all the time."

Fian also declared that he had used witchcraft to attract the young
woman to him. Unhappily, the attempt had no success, though its
results were somewhat hilarious.

Fian, who was the Saltpans schoolmaster, taught the girl's young
brother, and by artful questioning of the boy, discovered that he
shared a bed with his sister. On learning this, Fian promised to teach
the boy "without stripes" if he would bring him three hairs from
the young woman's pubes. Naturally the boy agreed, whereupon
Fian gave him a piece of "conjured" paper in which to wrap the
hairs.

However, what the boy had thought would be a simple procedure turned out to be very difficult. He made several attempts to obtain the hairs after his sister had gone to sleep, but each time she moved in her sleep. Then one night, just as it seemed that he was going to be successful, the girl suddenly sat up in bed, and called out to her mother what the boy was trying to do.

The mother was also knowledgeable about charms, and though the boy tried to remain loyal to Fian, she "beat him with sundry stripes" until he told the complete story. Whereupon she plucked three hairs from the cow's udder, wrapped them in the conjured paper and ordered the boy to give them to the schoolmaster.

Delighted that he would now have his way with the girl, Fian hurried at once to the church "and wrought his arte upon the haires". Within minutes, the cow appeared at the church doors, trotted up the aisle to Fian, "leaping and dauncing upon him". To escape the cow's attentions, the schoolmaster fled from the church, but wherever he went, the cow followed him "to the great admiration of all the townes men of Saltpans and many others who did behold the same".

The incident became widely known, and since it was believed that the schoolmaster had put a spell on the cow with the Devil's help "thereupon the name of the said Dr Fian (who was but a very young man) began to grow so common among the people of Scotland, that he was secretly nominated for a notable Conjurer". This reputation and his demonstration of bewitching the girl's lover had played a large part in landing him in his present predicament.

When he had signed his depositions, he was placed in solitary confinement. By lulling his gaolers into a sense of false security with a display of impressive piety, within a day or two he obtained possession of the key to his cell, and escaped during the night. He was quickly recaptured and taken again before the King. Under royal interrogation he declared that all he had formerly confessed was false. James questioned him in great depth, and formed the opinion that "in the time of his absence hee had entered into a new conference and league with the devill his master, and that hee had beene agayne newly marked".

A new mark could not be found, however, so James devised "a most straunge torment" to make him confess. Fian's nails were pulled out with pincers, and where the nails had been two needles were driven in up to their heads. The pain must have been insupportable, but Fian remained firm in his denials, so he was condemned to the boots once more. But though under this ghastly torture his "legges were crushte and beaten togeather as small as might bee, and the bones and flesh so brused ... whereby they were made unserviceable for ever", Fian would not admit to having made a new pact with the Devil.

James, seeing at last that nothing would make the young man speak, ordered Fian to be tried and sentenced to the penalties prescribed by law. Accordingly, on the last Saturday of January, 1591, Fian was thrown into a cart and taken to Castle Hill in Edinburgh. There he was strangled, before a huge crowd, and his body was thrown into the fire already prepared for the purpose.

Geillis Duncan and Agnes Sampson had already paid the penalty.

Little is known about the others who had been arrested with them except Barbara Napier, sister-in-law of the Laird of Carshogill, and Dame Ewphame Macalyan Moscrop, daughter of Lord Cliftenhall.

The jury, having heard the case against Mistress Napier, had the temerity to find her Not Guilty. On hearing the verdict, James flew into a rage, and recalling the Court, ordered the judge to sentence her to be burned at the stake, having first been strangled, her property to be forfeited to the Crown. He also had the jury tried for "wilful error on assize, acquitting a witch". Mistress Napier pleaded pregnancy, and after a time, "nobody insisting in pursuit of her, she was set at liberty".

Dame Ewphame's trial was also not without incident. The foreman of the jury refused to condemn her, so he was dismissed and a new juryman, who had not sat on the trial jury, was brought in and a unanimous verdict was then returned. Perhaps because she was a Roman Catholic, James ordered that she be "burned in ashes to the death", that is, without the merciful strangling that almost invariably preceded burning at the stake in such cases. The sentence was carried out on 25 July, 1591.

The remainder of the defendants were strangled and burned during February, 1592.

The acquittal of Barbara Napier, occasioned James's famous Tolbooth Speech (7 June, 1591) in which he set out his own firm belief in witchcraft. Six years later, the King published in Edinburgh his *Demonology*, written in the classical tradition of the European demonologists. Having come to the throne of England in 1602, and found that the laws against witches in his new realm were less fearsome than those north of the border, in 1604 he placed on the Statute Book a bill which provided for much harsher penalties for Englishmen found guilty of witchcraft than had been provided for by Elizabeth I's statute in 1563.

There is no doubt that it was James's personal involvement in the North Berwick case which confirmed him in his belief, as he said in the Tolbooth Speech, that witchcraft was "a most abominable sin ... We are taught by the laws of both God and man that this sin is most odious, and by God's law punishable by death: By man's law it is called *maleficium* or *veneficium*, an ill deed or a poisonable deed, and punishable likewise with death". He remained a staunch antagonist of witchcraft throughout his life.

Ghosts of Britain

THE GHOSTLY WHERRY OF
OULTON BROAD

We were fishing under a full moon near to midnight on Oulton
Broad, that lovely Suffolk lake which lies inland from Lowestoft.
The moon silvered the water. Grasshopper warblers, the "reeler
birds" of the old marshmen, reeled their tiny, unending song from
the acres of tall reeds which surround the Broad. Wild duck quacked
softly in reedy bays. Ashore a solitary light gleamed yellow from a
house across the dark waters of that bay which they call Borrows
Ham. A tawny owl hooted eerily from the dark, brooding pines on
a little knoll by the water's edge.

There, in the last century, on just such a night George Borrow,
that writer of resounding English, the man who wrote *Lavengro* and
The Romany Rye, the two greatest sagas of gypsy life in the English
language, lit a great bonfire under the trees and surrounded by the
dark faces of his gypsy friends, their eyes dancing in the firelight,
drank his wine, and roared the wild Romany songs to the stars.

Neighbours thought him mad. None dare say so for Borrow was
a man of strength and sinew, a great walker and, if tackled, a great
fighter. Did he not walk hundreds of miles through the sun-baked
mountains of Spain, a land of bandits and loneliness, simply to get
an atmosphere for that other classic of his *The Bible in Spain*?
There was the morning when he stepped out of the house, said to his
loving wife, who luckily understood him: "I'm going for a walk
my dear. Don't know when I shall be back." He was away three

months without a change of clothes. They say that he walked across England, right into Scotland, and then walked home again.

A friend of his said of this rough, Devil-may-care master of the English language: "He was very fond of ghost stories and believed in the supernatural."

Those words rang in my mind as I turned to Fred the boatman, and said: "Fred, we're fishing right off Mr Borrow's own bay within sight of his old wooden summer-house where he used to tell his ghost stories. Surely he must haunt the place. Have you ever seen him?"

"Not as I know on," said Fred, thoughtfully. "These here owd Broads are full of ghosts and rum owd tales. There's Black Shuck, the gret owd dog, big as a calf, with only one eye in his head what shines like a bike lamp. And there's a ghost, they say, of an owd monk in Burgh Castle ruins, but I don't think nawthen o' that. The heddest ghost in these here parts is the *Mayfly*. Ever hear o' she? She's due here to sail across this Broad half after midnight on June twenty-fower. Du (if) you see her you'll drop dead."

Vaguely I'd heard the story. Here and there it is whispered. Many laugh at it but the facts, such as they are, seem to point to truth.

The great white wherry, built of oak and teak, bluff bowed, built on the lines of ancient Egyptian river boats with the white "eye of Osiris" painted on either side of the bows sweeps across the broad under a mighty press of white sails, a great wave curling away on either side. Aboard the ghostly ship "Blood" Stevenson, the skipper, a giant of a man, wrestles with the slim terrified figure of a girl in a white nightdress, a ghastly gash in her neck, blood pouring down.

Suddenly the girl, screaming with terror, lunges her right hand upwards. The skipper, blood spurting from his throat, collapses on deck. A second later the girl, with a dying shudder, falls limp and lifeless across the body of the man who is known to have murdered at least three men in his time. And the white ship sweeps on.

Now all this began in the autumn of 1851 when a firm of maltsters at Beccles, that adorable little Suffolk town of history and beauty, which sits on the banks on that river of enchantment the Waveney, decided to send their champion wherry, the *Mayfly*, on a voyage which was to make one of the most horrifying, macabre chapters in the English lore of the supernatural.

First of all, what is a wherry? Only one or two are left in their unspoiled historic form on the Broads of Norfolk and Suffolk today. They are one of the oldest ship designs in the world. As such they deserve more than a passing mention, since this is possibly the only story of a haunted wherry in existence.

I described wherries thus in my *Portrait of the Broads* a few years ago.

"The Norfolk wherry is unique among boats. There was nothing quite like it in Holland. Nothing approached it in design or appearance upon the once-wide meres and great rivers of the Fens. That, in itself, is remarkable, for the wherry was primarily a trading ship in the not-far-off days when marsh-farmers and those whose land abutted on coastal creeks and estuaries, sent, perhaps, three-quarters of their produce by water. Roads were deep in mud for six months of the year. Farm roads were bottomless.

"Within my own lifetime wherries were an everyday sight. To see a wherry, long, low with broad-bosomed bows, sweeping huge and batlike down a river or through a reedy channel, with its great sail towering high above the marshland scene and touching the reeds was more than impressive—almost awe-inspiring. They were, in fine, the fresh-water equivalent of the great sailing barges of the Medway, the Thames, the Essex Blackwater and the Suffolk estuaries. Those were the greatest sailing ships in the world to be worked solely by a man and a boy. The wherry, of somewhat different construction, was their younger inland brother, although occasionally they took to salt water.

"The average wherry was long and shallow with a towering mast and a vast sail rigged on the principle of the old-fashioned Una rig, but with a boom. They were from seventy to twenty tons burden and crewed by two men and, occasionally, by one man only. They could sail very fast, extremely close to the wind and were so handy that they could be navigated among other craft in a narrow river reach, to within an inch or so without scraping paint. There was a tiny cabin in the stern. The steersman stood abaft of this against the tiller with the sheet working on the "horse" on the cabin roof in front of him. The mast moved on a fulcrum. The lower end was weighted so that one man, working the foresail, could easily lower it or raise it.

"I have been lucky enough to see, and occasionally sail with, some of the last of the wherries. Today what few trading wherries are left on the Broads have auxiliary motors. The old *Albion* which was saved by the Norfolk Wherry Trust is, I believe, the last one still propelled solely by sail."

Such then was this almost vanished type of sailing craft. Under full sail, and fully laden, a wherry could quite easily reach a speed of 7 to 8 m.p.h., almost the rate of a London taxi travelling through Hyde Park.

To return to our tale. Back to the autumn of 1851. The *Mayfly*, white-painted and shining, ship-shape from truck to keel, was lying at the staithe at Beccles. Her owners sent for the captain, a hairy, broad-shouldered, giant nicknamed "Blood" Stevenson. Immensely powerful, he was a redoubtable boxer at the time when bare-fist prize-fighting was the popular craze. Jem Mace and Tom Sayers were the heroes of the day. It was said that if "Blood Stevenson" had been properly trained and financially backed he could have been in a class fit almost to fight the bare-fist champion of England. Instead he had been at sea most of his life. He had a brutal temper and a murderous look in his eye when roused.

It was whispered that whilst in the merchant navy, where he served fifteen years before the mast, he fought five men aboard his ship single-handed, killed two of them and brutally injured the others. For this he went to jail for three years. When he came out he served aboard a Yankee hot-ship, got mixed up in another fight off the Florida coast and, with the police hot after him, "jumped his ship", and got a berth on another sailing immediately for England.

By this time he had such a bad reputation in the merchant service that he decided to find a job aboard one of the trading wherry fleets of the Norfolk and Suffolk rivers. Thus he came into the employ of the Beccles firm of maltsters.

One of the directors, a Mr Dormey, had a beautiful daughter in her early twenties. She was the belle of the town and admired by every man who saw her. "Blood" was one of her admirers. So was Jack, the mate of the *Mayfly*. Whereas "Blood" looked on this lovely and innocent girl with brutish animal lust, Jack, also a powerfully-built man, worshipped her shyly. Like most of the wherrymen he was a strong man, civil-spoken and a devout chapel-goer. Whenever the wherry berthed near a village on Sundays Jack put on his best "Sunday-go-to-meeting" dark suit and walked across the marshes to sing a hymn and say a prayer. Thus Mr Dormey's beautiful daughter, Millicent, had two very different types of admirers.

The only other member of the crew was a strong marsh-born youth of seventeen called Bert Entwhistle. Every dirty job aboard ship fell to Bert's lot, from scrubbing the decks to peeling the spuds. He never complained.

When "Blood" went ashore that September evening and was ushered into the owners' office at the maltings, Mr Dormey came straight to the point.

"Captain Stevenson, we have decided to entrust you with a highly important mission. A large chest containing gold coins has to be sent from here to our bank in Yarmouth. We have good reason to believe that if it goes by horse and cart along the dark roads, it will be held up and robbed. We are therefore sending a horse and cart with a large box aboard which will contain not gold, but two armed men. Whoever stops that vehicle will get a charge of shot instead of a box of gold.

"We have decided therefore that it will be safer to send this very precious cargo by water. You are a strong, powerful man. So is your mate Jack. A third deck-hand will be provided as an extra guard. You will be given shot-guns and a supply of cartridges. We feel, however, it is unlikely that anyone will think of intercepting the wherry—more especially as my daughter, Miss Millicent, will travel aboard as a passenger with the large box containing the gold, ostensibly as her luggage. We would like you to undertake this highly important and confidential job."

"I shall be honoured gentlemen," "Blood" replied. "May I be permitted to ask the value of the cargo?"

"Four hundred thousand pounds," said Mr Dormey coolly. "Blood" caught his breath. His eyes narrowed. "A very valuable cargo for inland waters, gentlemen," he observed. "Although, naturally as captain of trading ships abroad, I have been entrusted with far more valuable cargoes."

"That we fully expected, Captain Stevenson," was the reply. "And that is why we have decided to entrust you with the cargo. You will start at 10.30 tonight, half an hour after the cart leaves by road for Yarmouth and you will disembark Miss Millicent at Yarmouth, where her aunt will be waiting for her, and the box will be transferred to the ladies' carriage which will then drive direct to the bank. Is all clear?"

"All clear, gentlemen," said "Blood" smartly. He saluted and withdrew.

Millicent Dormey, tall, beautiful, flushed with excitement, thrilled at the idea of the trip, went aboard the *Mayfly*. A special cabin had been made for her in part of the extensive hold. Apart from the excitement of the trip, she was secretly elated to be travelling with "Blood", who, in her girlish eyes, was a sort of Greek hero, some kind of Achilles or Hercules. She had quite a passion for him in a strictly decorous way.

In due course the *Mayfly* cast off her warps and under a full-bellying mainsail swept down the river, a great white ghost ship stately under the moon. Fifteen miles to go and Millicent would be having breakfast with her aunt in their town-house in Yarmouth.

The wherry swept downstream past Worlingham, skirted Oulton Broad, headed north by Burgh St Peter and Somerleyton and, under the Roman ruins of Burgh Castle, burst suddenly upon the full tidal flood water of Breydon Water, a semi-salt-water lake of strong currents, covering more than a thousand acres which extends from the Castle Hill to the docks of Great Yarmouth. "Blood" Stevenson was at the wheel. It is a local legend that as a sea-going Captain, he had insisted on a wheel being fitted, instead of the long-handled tiller of the usual wherry.

As the great bluff-bowed ship hit the incoming tide, bucketted slightly, and threw up a sheet of spray, "Blood" turned suddenly to the third deck hand and said in a fierce undertone: "Are you with me or not on this trip? Are you for me or not?"

"Course I'm with you," said the deck-hand. "What do you mean 'for you' though?"

"I mean this," said "Blood" fiercely. "This ship and everything aboard of it is now mine. I'm the skipper. I own the lot. This ship goes where I say it will go. Now do you understand?"

"But you can't say it's your ship," the man retorted. "It belongs to the guvnor. You can't steal it. That's piracy. I'm no bloody pirate."

"Then you're bloody fish fodder," "Blood" retorted. He abandoned the wheel, swung his deadly right, caught the deck-hand full on the point of the jaw and knocked him senseless. He picked up the body and swung it overboard. An almighty splash and *Mayfly* surged on towards the lights of Yarmouth, a dead man bobbing in the long creamy wake astern.

The breeze freshened. The great ship stormed along, white and magnificent. She swooped past the docks and wharves, the quays and fishing boats of Yarmouth. She plunged her bows into the North Sea, stretching to infinity under the moon. The *Mayfly* dipped her bows, "took it green", slid and wallowed in the long roller of the sea. Soon the lights of Yarmouth were well astern. The ship's bows were pointed to Holland.

Down below Millicent Dormey was awakened by the sudden pitch and wallow of the ship. She came on deck to find out what was happening.

"Where are we, captain," she inquired. "Haven't we reached Yarmouth? I can't see any land."

"You won't see any sweetheart," "Blood" replied brusquely. "We've left Yarmouth behind. We're at sea."

"But why?" she asked. "We're supposed to stop at Yarmouth. My aunt will be waiting for me."

"You'll never see Yarmouth or your aunt again, my sweetie," came the brutal reply. "We're going where I decide to go. I'm captain of this ship. She goes where I says she'll go. Everything aboard, including the money, and *you*, my girl, belongs to me. You'll be my wedded wife, when we reach foreign parts. We've enough money to live like lords and ladies forever."

"But it's my father's money—my father's ship," she retorted, suddenly cold with fear.

"You'll never see your father either," "Blood" answered shortly. "Get down to your cabin. I've wanted you for a long time. Now you're mine. Jack! take the wheel."

Jack, the mate, stepped forward. He took the wheel, and gazed ahead with a face of stone. Millicent Dormey stood pale and defiant on deck. "Blood" picked her up with one powerful arm, dropped her down the companionway and followed.

Minutes later there came an agonized, horrifying scream from below. Millicent Dormey rushed up the companionway, bleeding from a gash in the neck. Her clothes were half torn off. "Blood" stumbled after her. He also was spattered with blood.

It was too much for Jack. He sprang at "Blood". The two giants grappled like tigers, lurched back and forth across the deck. They were pretty well matched. They fought, kicked, stumbled, fell, still locked together. Then suddenly "Blood" drew back that deadly right arm and hit Jack a sledge-hammer blow on the jaw which almost certainly broke his neck. As the ship wallowed in the North Sea, "Blood" hurled the body of Jack overboard.

Millicent bolted below. "Blood" followed.

Then as Bert, the boy, roused from his foc'sle slumber, stumbled on deck he saw "Blood" and the girl come up the companionway again. "Blood" attempted to grip her with his ape-like arms. Bert saw her swing her own delicate right arm. A sudden spurt of blood from the captain's throat and, coughing up his heart-blood, the murderer collapsed on deck. A moment later the girl, stabbed to the heart, fell across his dead body.

The boy, terrified out of his wits, stumbled into the dinghy astern, piled into it a keg of water, food, a bottle of rum, loaves of bread, a gun and cartridges. He cut the painter and was left bobbing, dead-scared and alone, in the North Sea, while the great white ship spattered in blood, with a dead man and a dead girl aboard, surged on its voyage alone into the unknown.

Days later the boy was rescued by a Dutch ship. He swore that while alone in that small boat, on the second or third dark night of terror the great white ship, sails full to the wind, had swept down on him, in a phosphorescent glow from stem to stern, and had circled him. Aboard the ship he saw the struggling figures of the girl in her torn nightdress, smothered in blood, and the giant "Blood" bleeding from the stab in the throat which killed him.

"Three years later," said Fred, my boatman, that night on Oulton Broad, "Mr Dormey was fishing right here with a boatman, same as we are tonight. Suddenly across the Broad, lit up in a glow, the *Mayfly*, white and ghostly, swept down upon them. Mr Dormey sat paralysed as the ship passed and the ghost of his daughter, fighting off 'Blood', screamed; 'Father, save me, save me.'

"Then the *Mayfly* vanished. You could smell sulphur on the air. There was a thud in the boat. Mr Dormey had dropped dead, his fishing-rod still in his hand."

THE LOST SOUL OF MRS LECKIE

"Father! Mother! Help! Grandmother is choking me!"

The child's screams rang through the house and ended with a hideous noise of choking. The parents rushed to her room. They found her dead in bed, with the marks of two fingers on her throat. She had been strangled.

This was the most horrific manifestation of the evil ghost of Mrs Leckie.

In life, she had been such a dear old lady, living in eighteenth-century Minehead, Somerset, with her son, daughter-in-law and grand-daughter. She was kindly, gentle, considerate and much beloved. Neighbours admired her saintly ways and told her son how lucky he was to have such a mother. One of her admirers said to her once: "You are such a wonderful person that the only tragedy is that you'll have to die one day and leave us all." For Mrs Leckie was getting on in years. Unexpectedly, she responded to this remark with: "You may like me now, but I'm afraid you won't enjoy seeing and speaking to me after my death."

"How could we ever see and speak to you then?"

"Wait and see," said Mrs. Leckie.

They waited. And they saw.

Mrs Leckie died. She had a grand funeral and lots of mourners. People wept, said what a darling she'd been, how much they'd miss her. "So terrible that we shall never see her again," they cried.

But many of them were to see her again quite soon, at different times and places; and she had turned into a real old devil, as if to make up for all the goodness and patience she'd shown in life. Perhaps she had been longing to break out for years and only death gave her the chance to show what she was really like behind her gentle façade.

A local doctor was one of the first people to see her ghost, although he didn't know who it was at the time. It was a lovely day and he was walking in the fields. He met an old lady, greeted her politely and helped her to climb over a stile. He realized there was something odd about her because when she spoke, her lips didn't seem to move, and her eyes stayed staring fixedly before her even when she turned her head. Her oddness made him feel uneasy, so he was glad to say goodbye to her and hurry across the next field. As he approached the stile on the other side, he saw to his astonishment that she was there, sitting on it.

No human being could possibly have got there ahead of him without moving very fast indeed—and indeed he'd have seen her run past him. He almost turned back the way he'd come, but told himself not to be foolish and went on towards the stile.

As he approached, she didn't move aside. She sat there, preventing him from climbing over.

"Excuse me, Madam, I want to get over here."

"Suppose I don't want you to."

"That's absurd—now, please——"

She laughed and sat firm, like a mischievous child.

"Let me help you over to the other side," he said.

And she: "I'm on the other side already."

Tired of argument, he climbed over, pushing her out of the way, and she gave him a vicious parting kick and shouted after him: "That'll teach you to show better manners to the next old lady you meet."

Later he described the old woman to friends and they said it was Mrs Leckie who had recently started to reappear. The events which the doctor described were fairly typical of her newly assumed unpleasantness. She turned up just anywhere and made a nuisance of herself.

One of her favourite tricks was to appear on the quay at Minehead and call for a boat! "Hey! A boat! Hey there, you lazy devils, I want a boat!" At first one boatman or another would go across to her, only to be cursed and sent away again. Then they began to ignore her, or try to, and she would stand there swearing and scaring everyone to death.

When she was alive, she had been angelic to her son. Nothing was too good for him. She had made sacrifices for him, waited on him, given him presents and seemed to worship the ground he trod on. But her returned spirit detested him and planned to ruin him. He was a prosperous man, a trader who did a lot of business with Ireland. Always he had several ships sailing between Ireland and England, carrying goods from one place to the other. The ghost of Mrs Leckie formed the grim plan of sinking his ships.

As one of Leckie's ships approached land, Mrs Leckie would appear standing at the mainmast and blow a whistle. However calm the weather, the sound of this whistle called up a violent storm, wrecking the ship and scattering the goods. Sometimes the seamen managed to swim ashore, but invariably everything else was lost. Ship after ship was destroyed in this way, and so was her son's prosperity. He grew desperate. All his own ships were lost and he could no longer afford to buy new ones. Even if he managed to hire a ship, he couldn't get any seamen to sail in her as they all knew the fate of the Leckie ships. Many of them had heard the weird sound of that whistle at the mainmast, seen and felt the violence of the magic storms, and had felt themselves lucky to escape with a fright and a wetting.

When she wasn't busy sinking his ships, she haunted her son's house, so that he could have no peace anywhere. She had a particularly sinister way of going about this, for she never let her son actually see her. She appeared to others in the house, reducing them to a state of hysterics, and this in turn distressed Leckie—but as he never saw her he couldn't do anything about it. Seeing a malevolent ghost is bad enough, but not to see one which those whom you love are seeing all the time is even worse. The son could detect her presence though the signs of fear his wife and daughter showed; but he was completely helpless to do anything about it.

For instance, his ghostly mother would come to his bedroom when he and his wife were in bed together. There would be poor Leckie trying to get some sleep and his wife would suddenly cry out: "Look! There's your mother, in the room with us."

Leckie would turn to the right, where his wife pointed, and see nothing.

"She's on the other side now," his wife would say.

Leckie would look left. Nothing. The wicked old ghost would manage to slip from place to place so that he always just missed seeing her. There was an element of the comic about these repeated bedroom scenes, except for the people involved. Leckie's wife was nearly going mad with the constant torment and Leckie himself was enraged with frustration. He felt so damned helpless. He'd never, never had any trouble at all with his beloved mother—but her ghost was quite beyond him.

Neighbours giggled sometimes when they heard of the goings-on at the house, and it was mortifying and embarrassing for the Leckies, especially with their business in ruins and their poverty increasing day by day.

Then came the shocking climax of their daughter's death. They had learnt to endure the ghost's persecution of themselves, but even they had not conceived that she would hurt their child. A dead little girl with the marks of two fingers on her throat—and her last cry: "Grandmother is choking me!"

It was the last straw. Everything had gone.

The child's funeral was a tragic affair. There were people who had envied Leckie's former prosperity and taken snide pleasure in seeing him ruined, and others who had laughed at the haunting of the marriage bed; but none could feel anything but horror at the death of the child. The ghost of Mrs Leckie had gone too far. She was hated now as much as she had once been loved.

Perhaps the force of people's emotions had some effect on her. Perhaps, like a child, in some terrible other-world second childhood, she had not entirely known what she was doing—had not been able to distinguish the crucial dividing line between mischief and murder. But the horror she had evoked reached her at last. She even came with a half-apology.

It was after the child's funeral. The bereaved young mother dragged herself to her bedroom and began listlessly to arrange her hair before the mirror. Suddenly she saw old Mrs Leckie's face reflected in it and peering over her shoulder. She turned, desperate with misery and quite beyond fear.

"For God's sake, Mother, why do you torture us?"

"Peace," Mrs Leckie said softly. "I shan't hurt you."

"What do you want of me?"

The ghost of Mrs Leckie didn't seem to know what she wanted. She had ruined her son and daughter-in-law and broken their hearts. Why? She didn't know. She was a lost soul.

Her acts of mischief became less virulent now, but of course it was too late for the damage she had done to be undone. Leckie and his wife lived out the rest of their lives poor and childless. But even after they were dead, the ghost of Mrs Leckie was not forgotten.

For many years afterwards it was said that the ghost still haunted the quay at Minehead, and seamen approaching land still listened for that unearthly whistle which presaged a storm. Perhaps they still do ...

A MOTHER-TO-BE'S REVENGE

It was a terrible night, with a cold rain slanting sideways in an even colder wind. The moon and stars were obscured by swirling, rain-filled clouds which were visible now and then for an instant as a flash of lightning lit what sky a man could see above the treetops.

This was a walk which James Graeme, the miller of Durham, did twice a day, once in each direction. At least once a week he asked himself why a reasonably prosperous miller of grain should choose to have his mill rather more than a mile away from his home, along a dark and wooded lane.

It was his wife's doing, of course, and there was no need for James to ask himself the question. It was she who objected to living over the mill, or in a cosy annexe built on to it, as so many other millers with more sense and less social pretension chose to live. For them, the problem of getting to or from work was merely that of slipping on, or off, a miller's apron and walking a few yards. Indoors. On a dreadful night like this, for example, he would have been home a full quarter of an hour ago, and bone dry. Instead, he was almost soaked to the skin, and likely to catch himself his death of cold.

It would serve her right if he did die. That would show her the foolish empty vanity of "not living over the shop".

A particularly vicious deluge of icy rain brought the matter home to him. Home!—and when would he get there? In another half-hour if he were lucky. Filling with self-pity as his clothes filled with water, he pictured himself lying ashen and with dimming eye, on his deathbed. His weeping wife bent over him, wringing hands in horrified distress. "Oh, but it is all my fault!" she would be wailing, and the miller almost heard the anguished words. "Oh, if only I'd not been so selfish as to demand a house away from your mill, James. Oh James, forgive me, I entreat you——"

So, with a weeping female face in his mind's eye, it was a startling sensation when another flash of lightning revealed another face. The hair soaked with what seemed rain, it was almost upon him.

The girl—for this she was, and not his wife—grasped his elbow and called out something to him above the sound of the rain. "Anne, my child," he stammered in dismay, peering at the dim features, "it is Anne Greenwood, is it not?"

He felt the girl's hand on his cheek now, and to his shock it was not just wet with rain like his own hands, but slimy, and as the next explosion in the sky revealed, slimy with blood. And the girl's dress was torn and bloody, her hair was bedraggled and soaked with rain, blood and mud.

"Aye, James Graeme, it is I. It *is* Anne Greenwood."

"But what in God's name has happened to you?"

"That is what I sought you out to tell you, James Graeme——"

"But you haven't been running, sore injured like this, just looking for me. Why, there are cottages where you should have gone, to have succour and treatment——"

"I needed you, James Graeme."

There was an awful solemnity about the five words, and somehow they jerked the miller to his senses. "Not a word more, my child, until I take you home, where my good wife and I will bandage your wounds and you can tell us then, not before, what dreadful things have befallen you."

"No. No, James Graeme." The slender young girl stayed, swaying slightly like a young silver birch but as if rooted in the ground. He seized an arm, was still more distressed to find it as slippery with blood as the hand of the other one, and tried to drag her with him through the rain. She would not budge, some superhuman strength holding her there.

"For God's sake, come quick, girl. You'll die if you don't. And that's Gospel truth, I've never seen anyone more in need of help than you are at this moment."

"*Look*, James Graeme. Merely look, and you will see why I cannot come with you." It was as if she had commanded the lightning this time, for a sheet of it seemed to light up the whole forest for five seconds or more.

As he obeyed and looked full at her, she tilted back her slender neck. For one all too brief moment it was merely as if she wanted to look up and observe the strange, turbulent skies. But at the end of that brief moment, James Graeme screamed.

Screamed as if wolves were after him. For Anne Greenwood's throat had been cut from ear to ear. Oh God—if she tilted her head back farther, it must surely fall off into the mud.

It was dark again, and her voice was calm. "You see now why I cannot come with you. Why in any case your good wife and yourself could not stop my dying."

He could say nothing. He wanted to scream again but could not.

"I cannot come, I will not come. No man can stop my dying, for I am dead already. Dead, James Graeme. And, as you can see— I have been murdered."

"Murdered? But how do you stand there, then, if you are dead? Oh, this is all some horrible dream and I will wake up tomorrow and run to your cottage and find you are well and living, and pretty as ever. I will, dear Anne, I will."

"You will not. And now listen to me, for my time is short. I am not here, not in the flesh, for I have been dead for many hours and my mortal remains lie where I will now tell you. And you must listen carefully——"

The cold and wet quite forgotten, and numb now only with horror, James Graeme listened.

"Those who killed me must be brought to justice: John Sharp and James Walker. And as time is running out, and my spectre will fade like a star in the sunrise, I will tell you why and how and where. And you must remember everything."

The miller nodded dumbly.

"I was with child by James Walker since he seduced me, not three months ago. It was the second day of December, the second day of the last month of last year—the Year of Our Lord, Sixteen Hundred and Eighty—that I so foolishly succumbed to his persuasions. I will not tell you how or why he succeeded, but the seed was sown and I was as much to blame. But then, when I told him I was carrying his child, James Walker's own child, he denied to me that anything had ever taken place. Told me off for a liar and a wicked girl. Warned me not to breathe a word to a soul. Even if I swore on the Holy Book as to what had happened, he would deny it and see to it that I was killed. He would kill me in any case, he said, before I spoke a word."

The rain ran off Graeme's nose and chin as he listened, transfixed.

"And of course I would not promise not to tell. For it was my child, too, and it needed a father. And because he was a coward, or perhaps because he retained some small measure of feeling for me, he paid another to kill me. One John Sharp——"

"John Sharp! That slippery, shifty, near-dwarf of a devil!"

"Today he killed me. Shortly after noon, and before this storm had broken out. It was cold, but I went for a stroll which I quite often take along this woodland lane; He sprang out at me from some undergrowth, and pulled out a long dagger, oh, a most fearsome thing. And he grasped me in his left hand with a grip like iron on my shoulder and said not a word, not a word. With the other he ripped the great blade across my throat and the blood gushed out. Before I died I saw it pour out in a great fountain of crimson, to dye his jerkin and his hands the same colour."

Graeme cried out involuntarily "And now, James Graeme, listen carefully. He carried me to a place I will show you, and there he buried me and there I lie. Come——"

At last she was capable of movement, no longer a rooted sapling, and she took him by the hand, took his trembling, big-man's fist in her own blood-wet, tiny one, and led him a little way up the path.

Then, at a certain great oak, they turned off right and went a few yards through the soaking undergrowth. "Count the steps from the lane," she said, in that voice he recognized as being both the voice of a ghost and the voice, very faint, of Anne Greenwood. "——six, seven, eight, nine, ten, eleven. Here it is."

At first he saw nothing. Then the flaring sky showed quite clearly a neat, well-tidied, grave. With this rain, all trace of loose earth would be washed away by the morning, and a man would find it hard to rediscover the spot.

"Count the steps back again," she ordered, and they did, together. It came, as before, to eleven, and they were standing again at the edge of the lane.

And then she had vanished.

"Where are you, Anne?" he cried out in terror.

An answering voice came faintly, sadly, out of the darkness.

"I have gone. Perhaps forever, to my eternal peace and rest. But, James Graeme, if my killers do not hang for their crime, I will be condemned to stay a ghost forever——"

There came a silence. Then the voice continued,

"But, James, if perchance they should not hang for their crime, I am condemned through eternity to haunt you. Even after you have gone to your own death. I will be condemned to follow you as I have tonight. And you will be condemned until eternity to have me, with the badge of my mortal wound, pursuing you. Until the end of time."

The ghost paused. "But if my killers hang, may God himself bless you, James Graeme."

And now she was really gone. James took to his heels and ran the last half mile to his cottage.

His stupid wife met him in the doorway. "For Heaven's sake, man, have ye been rolling in the mud? Could ye not have sheltered somewhere till the worst of the storm was over?"

He just refrained from hitting her, and contented himself by saying, with dignity: "Get back to your fire. I require nothing from you at all, and in a few moments I will have had a hot toddy and be dry and asleep in my half of the bed. Good night. I have much to do, early tomorrow."

So saying, he went to the kitchen, poured some water from the kettle into a half beaker of strong wine, and drank it in one gulp. As his wife stared in puzzled indignation, James Graeme clumped upstairs, dried himself with flannel and went to bed.

But of course he could not sleep. And an hour later, when his fat wife clambered in beside him, he had to feign slumber until she was snoring and could leave him alone with his thoughts.

Early the next morning he was up and out of the house, without breakfast. The Sheriff lived not far off, and he banged so hard on that great official's door that the man came down in his nightshirt. He was angry.

"I have to report the murder of Anne Greenwood," said James.

"You *what*? Who murdered her? Or are you confessing to the deed?"

"I accuse John Sharp and James Walker, in collaboration, of having killed her. Yesterday. And if we go along to her parents' cottage, they must surely confirm she was not home all afternoon or night."

He spoke with complete conviction, for it did not occur to him even for a moment that he was not stating an absolute fact.

"Come in," said the Sheriff. James followed him and was brusquely pointed to a stool, where he sat thinking while the Sheriff went upstairs and got dressed.

When the official came down again, he was in no better mood. "Stay here, Graeme, and I will go to the Greenwood cottage."

Half an hour later the Sheriff was back and his face had lost its ruby tinge. "Mistress Greenwood is indeed worried. Has been worried about her daughter's behaviour for these past weeks. And as you say, she did not return last night. The first night in all her eighteen years."

"And if I show you the grave, Sheriff, sir. Will you believe, with a great gash across her lovely throat, that she has been murdered?"

"If you showed me all this, there might well have been foul play."

The fool.

The Sheriff continued:

"But this is a most serious charge you lay against two respected citizens of this community. Perhaps you had better make the charge —if you still wish to do so—in the presence of both these citizens. I will summon them."

"And you will not come and inspect the grave?"

"Not yet. If you have as serious a charge as this to lay, then the persons you accuse must be given a chance to deny it."

"But—the body——"

That apparently, could wait. The Sherriff further animadverted that if a body was found, and it proved to be that of Anne Greenwood, who was to say that these gentlemen were in any way concerned? Their rights were the most important in the case, after the foul charge that he, James Graeme, had laid against them. *If* Anne Greenwood was dead, no power on earth could bring her back. But these two gentlemen would lose at least a part of their reputations, and perhaps, ultimately, their lives. *If* they were in any way connected with the deed. And if they were not, the mud thrown, must, a little of it, cling to them forever. The Sheriff concluded by asseverating that that was why the charge had to be laid formally, in his presence, first.

"Without a body? With no evidence of foul play?" persisted Graeme.

"Without a body. This is a most serious accusation you have made, James Graeme, and I will see to it that things are conducted in the right order and with all the dignity of my office."

It was that evening before the two alleged malefactors could be rounded up with their accuser and the Sheriff of Durham. The charge was laid, it was hotly denied, and the counter-charge made that if James Graeme was the only one to know Anne Greenwood had been murdered it stood to reason he must be the murderer.

James went pale on hearing this. Acting up till now under the compulsion of his haunting, he suddenly realized that when he got back to the grave and dug up the pitiful remains of the victim, there was little reason for this strangely hostile Sheriff of Durham, and his court, not to believe he was the culprit.

(James never found out why the Sheriff seemed so unwilling to see his point of view. Perhaps the man simply objected to being dragged from his bed in the early morning.)

But that night, in his own bed, with his wife snoring beside him, James heard, very faintly, that voice which now so terrified him. Very, very soft, and quite unmistakable. "Remember, James Graeme, what I said. Or I will haunt your dreams forever."

And so, nearly two days after being shown the grave in a thunderstorm, James was invited—ordered—to lead the Sheriff back to it.

But, oh God in Heaven, which was the oak tree? The light was different, the circumstances decidedly so, and the only thing that seemed to be firm in James's mind was the "eleven paces". In daylight there were dozens of trees which might be the right one. After an hour of counting paces and getting wet, the Sheriff lost his patience and refused to wander about the muddy undergrowth any longer.

James went back the next day and spent the whole forenoon searching. But now, even if he found the right tree, took the right number of steps in the right direction, the grave might well be completely obliterated.

The Sheriff of Durham gave orders for "The Case Laid by James Graeme against Two Others, Rightly or Wrongly Accused". The wording, to James, seemed as if he himself were being tried for some foul slander, and that whatever the verdict the other two would go Scot-free.

That night (and he was wide awake with a raging toothache when it happened) the voice came back again. "Remember, James. Eternity is a long time. Eternity is for ever."

A week later the case began in the Sheriff Court. And every morning, of course, James Graeme hunted for the grave and never found it. He then spent the rest of the day confronting people who to a man seemed convinced he was a malicious liar at best, and that if Anne Greenwood had been murdered at all it was in all likelihood by his own hand. Did he, James Graeme, realize that the onus was upon him to prove his charge or face the most dire penalties?

Then one night, at his wit's end and almost out of courage and time, the terrifying voice came back, and it was almost as a sleepwalker that he leapt from his bed. Perhaps now, in a similar darkness, he might find the grave. He took a long tallow candle and a spade and set off. It was, fortunately, a dry night. His wife snored loudly and steadily as he left the house, carefully closing the door behind him.

Somehow, tonight, he knew he would find the grave.

And when he had travelled near half a mile, he stumbled and fell over a root sticking out of the ground. As he picked himself up he noticed, with a jump of the heart, that he was right beside the oak tree. It was the right one, of that there was no doubt. After a second's deliberation as to whether the steps should be taken right or left of the lane, he set off in what turned out to be the right direction. After eleven steps, his candle held high, he had found the grave. Weather had all but obliterated the outline, but he could make it out. He stuffed the candle into the soft earth and began digging as if demons were after him.

The first thing he found was the most important, and he almost sang with delight. Only inches beneath the soil was the hideously blood-soaked jerkin of a small man. It was a very recognizable jerkin. A moment later he had seen enough to know the body was there. He left the grave open and retraced his footsteps, this time slashing the bark of trees and in particular of the big, direction-setting oak.

A few hours later, changed and clean, he had reached the Sheriff's house again, told his story and demanded that some witness come immediately. So impressed, almost frightened was he by James Graeme's manner, that the Sheriff forthwith set out with him, bringing two professional grave-diggers.

The body was completely exhumed, with the bloody jerkin, and when the hitherto inimical Sheriff cried, "Oh! The fiend, the fiend!" James knew he had won his case and that he would no longer be haunted by the spectre of Anne Greenwood.

Within three days it was all over. All but the hanging of the two men, which was delayed another week while they went on alternately incriminating each other and wailing for mercy. The theatricals, as some men called them, brought in a large crowd to the Sheriff's Court, and the accounts of what went on (which are written down, and available) during that week of 1681 in Durham would make entertaining reading were the underlying theme not so ghastly.

John Sharp and James Walker were hanged. And that night, as James Graeme was about to go to sleep, the sweetest, softest, voice in the world or out of it, whispered in his ear:

"Thank you James, and may God bless you. I will trouble you no more.'

THE SOUTAR AND THE GRAVE

Rabbie Henspeckle was well known as the best soutar, the best
cobbler or shoe-maker, in the Scottish seaside town of St Andrews.
However cold the winter wind might be, sweeping in from the
North Sea, Rabbie was up and at his last by six each morning.

Not that he had far to go, as his workshop was a wee room on the
ground floor of his cottage, overlooking The Scores, that ancient
street which today prides itself on sweeping past the famous Royal
and Ancient Golf Club, home of that ancient game, with the sea
just beyond.

Rabbie Henspeckle's time pre-dated that of the Royal and Ancient
by quite a few years, and where that pile of masonry now leans
against the easterly wind from Siberia, near the first tee of the
famous St Andrews Old Course (of the five or so the town now
boasts) there was nothing but sand dunes, ever shifting. In winter,
nights are long and days proportionately short in those northern
latitudes. One December morning Rabbie had been hard at work for
more than two hours when a customer came in, just as the clock
struck eight.

There was hardly a sign of daylight in the street, just a pale pink
luminosity out over the eastern sea, somewhere in the direction the
soutar vaguely believed Norway to be. The stranger banged the
door shut behind him, and Rabbie looked up.

He was vaguely annoyed, as he had been finishing the delicate
stitching of a fine black shoe with a silver buckle. He noticed, with

118

continued annoyance, that the stranger was unsmiling, very tall indeed, and wearing a long black coat. He must have towered a head and a half over Rabbie Henspeckle, even when the latter stood bolt upright and said, "Yes?"

The stranger stood absolutely still, leaning over the soutar's last.

"*Well?*" said Rabbie again. It was annoying having customers so early, for this was the time of day one got most of one's real work done. The stranger seemed to wake as if from a trance. "Och, but I'm sorry, and it was rude of me now. Just standing here, gawping at your fine, fine work."

Rabbie was only partly mollified.

"It was just that, well, just that it was so very fine. Hae ye been a soutar long?"

"Since I was ten years old. Twenty-six years," said Rabbie. "Apprenticed to my ain father, right in this wee shop."

"Really?" said the stranger.

"Aye. And *he* was a soutar for ye. Man, there wisna a finer maker of shoes in the whole wide world than aul' Tam Henspeckle."

"Then ye'll be following in his—in his *footsteps*". And the stranger emitted a strange, rather eerie, laugh, presumably at what he considered a witticism.

"Aye," said the soutar, disliking the man more than ever. "I'm proud tae follow in my father's footsteps. Proud o' the fact that there's nae a soutar in Scotland that can touch me. And yet, I'm the first to be telling ye, I'm not the equal of my father."

"Oh, I think you shouldn't be so modest," said the tall man in the black coat. Rabbie saw now that his face was pale, remarkably pale even in the orange glow of the pair of candles by which he was working. And with true Scottish thrift he noticed that those expensive candles were melting fast, while this uncongenial stranger occupied him in time-wasting conversation. He looked at the candles, then at the customer (if such he was). "Would ye be wanting anything yoursel'?" he asked, trying to keep the irritation, frustration, from his voice.

"These shoes you're working on now. Are they bespoke?"

"No. They're nae bespoke. When they're finished, they'll go, the pair of them, into my wee window. And then, somebody'll see them, I fancy. And they'll come in and try them on, and if they fit, they'll buy them. And they'll go out, happy with their bargain. For I dinna charge over much, ye ken."

119

"And what then would ye be charging for this pair, the ones you're working on?"

"It's only the first o' a pair. It would be the afternoon of tomorrow before I finished the second."

"Never mind," said the black-coated stranger. "What will ye be charging for the pair?"

"Eight shillings. Eight shillings the pair.'

"Well, I shall buy them, then."

"But ye haven't tried even *this* one on. How d'ye ken they'd fit?"

"I know they'll fit. I can tell at a glance."

"I see," said Rabbie Henspeckle and went back to his last. In two more minutes the singleton shoe was complete, with its shiny silvery buckle sewed firmly into place. He took it off the bench and, shrugging his shoulders, handed it to the other man. The man in the black coat slipped off one of his own shoes, scuffed and horrible brown ones they were, and slipped the new one in its place.

"There you are," he said, without making an effort to walk across the room in his new shoe. "Fits like a glove. I'll buy the pair."

"There *isn't* a pair. It'll be more than a day before there is, and then mebbe the second one won't fit ye."

"I'll take my chance," said the other. He reached into a deep pocket of the long black overcoat and produced a few pieces of silver. "Here ye are," he said. "Eight shillings."

"And ye'll be back for the other one tomorrow? Late tomorrow afternoon?"

"Yes. And what time would they be ready, then? The second one of the pair, that is——"

Rabbie thought for a moment. "Four o'clock."

"That's fine, I'll just be taking this one now, and I'll be back at four tomorrow. Four o'clock sharp."

"Er—yes," said Rabbie. "Four o'clock sharp."

Then the tall man, to the soutar's amazement, didn't walk out with the new shoe under his arm, but carefully removed the old scuffed brown one and put it in a deep pocket, perhaps the deep pocket from which he'd taken out the coins. Then, clacking away lop-sided, for the new shoe had a much thicker sole than the old, worn, one, he left the shop with one brand new black shoe and one very old brown shoe on his feet.

With a muttered, "Good day, then," the stranger was gone, and Rabbie found himself looking at the shining new coins in his hands. They were so shiny they might have been new minted, and they chimed oddly with the down-at-heel appearance of the man who had handed them over. And yet the fellow had a rather, well—*educated* —way of speaking.

And he'd been so eager to have the shoes Rabbie could probably have asked ten shillings for so fine a pair—with buckles, too—and been paid it. Still, that wasn't the way Rabbie Henspeckle did business, so he dropped the coins into his pocket, and decided to forget everything about the encounter. Everything, that was, but getting busy on the second shoe.

Suddenly he felt himself turn ice cold.

What could it be? The workshop was warm enough, and he'd been well enough on arising. He realized with a sudden dread that he was terrified, absolutely terrified, about how the stranger might behave if he came back at four o'clock the next day and found the shoe unfinished. Despite his grave courtesy there was something very sinister about the man. Hastily, Rabbie began tracing the outline of a new sole on a fine new piece of leather.

But it was no use, and the soutar was suddenly aware that the cold which was still making him shiver had come into the shop with the stranger. He realized too that some spirit had taken possession of him. The occult tendency so widespread in Scotland was even more evident in the mid-eighteenth century of Rabbie Henspeckle. "The sight" was an everyday occurrence, and if a man were wise he listened to the spirits and did their bidding.

He listened; and he put down the shoe, reached up to a nail in the wall for his own grey cloak, and his green and black cap. A moment later his shop door banged shut behind him and he was off in the semi-darkness of the winter morning, following his own customer through the narrow streets of St Andrews. Once out in the windy street, with the roar of the sea behind him, the soutar began to wonder just why this spirit visitant was impelling him, out of the warmth of his shop, into the icy open. But he knew he had to follow the man, and follow him he did.

Heaven knows, it was easy. However dark the street, there was that unmistakable emphatic rhythm of the new shoe and the old, and even if he'd been stone blind Rabbie could have caught up with the man. But Rabbie was far from blind, and as the dawn pressed upward into the sky he could see the stranger and take action to get closer to him.

The tall figure stopped suddenly at the entrance to the cemetery. The soutar, almost on his heels by now, stopped too, just in time.

But what could this strange man want here, with his pair of odd shoes?

Rabbie was given little time for conjecture. The man was now proceeding along the gravel path between the headstones. His pace quickened, the alternate footfalls of the new shoe seeming to emphasize his increasing pace. Rabbie had to break into a run to keep up. And what would the fellow say, with the sun nearly up, if he turned round and saw he was being followed? It was too late now for thinking of this sort. The soutar, obsessed with a morbid curiosity, moved swiftly and stealthily behind the dark figure.

Suddenly the man stopped again. Rabbie, his heart in his mouth, checked his stride, almost overbalancing.

But what happened now was far more terrifying than the chance encounter with an angry stranger. And yet, strangely, it was something that the soutar had been almost expecting. He looked in horror, and then quickly hid himself behind a tombstone. His heart was beating so loud he felt the noise would betray him, and his legs were so weak they would hardly support him. For the man had calmly looked down into a newly dug, empty, grave. And then jumped in. Terrified, Rabbie peeped out from behind his stone and saw the man re-appear, just the head and shoulders. And then he began, like a mad thing, to rake in the loose earth about him. Burying himself, just as fast as he could do it.

Hardly able to believe his eyes, wanting desperately to flee yet riveted to the spot, he stared as the tall man, projecting a foot and a half above the grave, swept the earth into it. Then he disappeared from view—for he had lowered himself down into his self-made grave and presumably was burrowing like a mole deep into it.

The soutar was too frightened to go near the grave. Finding the use of his limbs again, he took to his heels and ran down the little street which led to the cemetery, to the house of a friend. And there, like a madman, he banged and banged again on the knocker.

Eventually Jock Lumsden answered the door. He was not amused. "And what would a soutar like yersel' be doing, disturbing honest folk at this hour, when ye've got a job of your own?"

"Jock—Jock, ye've just got to come. And bring some others. A terrible thing's happened at the cemetery. We'll be needing to dig up a grave, so we'll want spades——"

"*Dig up a grave?* But——"

"But ye'll come now, or the Devil himself will ride in this town tonight. There's terrible, evil, things happening, Jock——"

At this, Jock Lumsden made no further fuss, just came out into the street, walked down a little way and disturbed two of his neighbours. Within a few minutes the four men—three puzzled and one very frightened—all carrying spades, were striding out to the cemetery.

"There it is!" said Rabbie.

"What?"

"Yon new grave. Just over there, hae ye no got eyes in your head, man?"

"Aye, I see it. But there's new graves every day here——"

"Och, but this is different. I've just seen the man himsel' get into this one."

"*Get into it?* By himsel'?"

"*Yes, yes*—I'm tellin' ye. Just walked boldly up to it, hopped in and pulled the earth in round about himsel'."

The four men started to dig. Within minutes their labours were rewarded. At a strange angle, midway between the generally accepted horizontal for a corpse and the vertical for a living man they found the black-coated stranger. He was dead. Undoubtedly dead, and without a coffin.

"What are ye wanting us to do, Rabbie Henspeckle? Is he not better there, in his own grave, than dug up? And in any case, it's a sin to dig up a dead man. *And* it's agin the law."

And then, unaccountably, for he had never in his life stolen from the living leave alone from the dead, Rabbie Henspeckle told his lie.

"I'm wanting him up," he said, "because he stole a shoe from me, and he's wearing it.'

"Stole a shoe?"

"Yes. Came into my shop this morning, och, an hour or so ago it'll be now; picked up a fine shoe I'd just finished, tried it on his own foot—and then rushed out."

"With one old shoe—and a new one he hadna paid for?"

"That's right. He hadna paid for it."

"Och, that's different, then. But it's a funny dead man that goes around stealing shoes."

"I ken that. But that's what he did. You mark my words; dig down to his feet and you'll find on the right foot one of my best black shoes, with a silvery buckle. And just a pitiful, thin, thing, on the other, with its pitiful mate in the pocket of that black coat. You mark my words——"

They went on digging, and the soutar was right. It took time, of course, digging around a very tall man who was securely wedged into his own grave, so that they were unable to pull him, had to take turns at standing in the grave and hacking away with their spades at the earth about the long, long legs.

"*That's it!*" shouted Rabbie in triumph. "That's my shoe. Just let me pull it off him and then we can tuck him in again, all nice and cosy——"

The shoe was soon off and cleaned of the wet earth which had adhered to it. They filled in the grave and walked slowly away, spades over shoulders and Rabbie polishing the buckled shoe against the side of his jerkin as he went. Why, it would soon be as good as new. A little sanding and the few scratches on the sole could be removed. By tomorrow afternoon he would be able to sell the pair. And probably for a bit more than eight shillings. The sudden, strange avarice had made the soutar lose his fear.

As they came to the street where the three others lived, Rabbie thanked them heartily for their help. "But ye know, lads, that I'd do the same for you, any time. Ye ken that, don't ye?"

"Aye, Rabbie, we ken. Glad to have been of service. And it's not often fellows get a chance of digging up a man who's just buried himself——"

"If he'd been alive, we'd hae been able to congratulate ourselves on saving a life," said one of them. "But he wasn't alive."

"No, that's for sure. Goodbye, then, Rabbie."

"Goodbye," said Rabbie Henspeckle. He sauntered away down the street, admiring the shoe and asking himself how much he might get for the pair. Well, even if it were the usual eight shillings, that would make sixteen. And sixteen was a lot more than Rabbie Henspeckle had ever been paid for a pair of shoes.

He had said the second shoe would be ready at four o'clock of the next afternoon, and he might as well stick to that time-table, though in all conscience Rabbie would be well able to do a shoe in half the time. He must have said that because the tall stranger annoyed him.

Well, one thing the Henspeckle family would do—they would celebrate. There was no need to tell Madge that he'd cheated; he'd just tell her he'd sold a fine pair of shoes for a fine sum of money; and she was never one to ask questions.

They went out that night, armed with a few bottles of ale, and called on a neighbour who had a good still; and it was late, very late, when they got back to bed. But after four hours' sleep the soutar was up with the sun and singing away at his last.

Madge cooked them both a midday meal, but she was far from

well. These late nights, and all that whisky drinking, never agreed with her and by one of the afternoon she was back in her bed, feeling exceedingly sorry for herself, even cursing Rabbie's "fine shoes". But Rabbie was in fine fettle, a late night never disturbed him, and he was singing away so lustily downstairs that she closed the bedroom door. She was unable to sleep, though, and she heard the clock below strike two, then three. All the time Rabbie kept up his singing, and his hammering away at the last. Oh, well, if one married a soutar, this was what one had to expect——

Another hour went by.

The clock downstairs started to strike four, and at the last chime Rabbie's happy song was cut off. Cut off as if by a knife. In that instant, and without knowing why, the soutar's wife had a feeling amounting to certainty that something horrible was about to happen.

And then, less suddenly than the song had ended, the music was replaced by the most dreadful scream she had ever heard. It swelled from nothing into a sickening loudness that made her put her head under the bedclothes.

As suddenly as the song, the scream ended.

Madge Henspeckle leapt out of bed, shivering so much with cold and absolute terror that she could scarce get into the old coat she used for such excursions below. She stumbled down the narrow wooden steps. There was no sign of Rabbie. Heart pounding, she looked round the workshop. Gone was her husband, gone his green and black cap. Gone was the buckled shoe he'd been working on. Gone was its mate, which had been in the window.

The next hour of Madge Henspeckle's life was so confused and horrifying that for years she would wake up, night after night, screaming. Somehow she seemed to get to Jock Lumsden's house, up by the cemetery—though it must have been a demon that impelled her there. Somehow she poured out her story, her terrible story. Told of the bright buckled shoes.

Ten minutes later the same good neighbours as had accompanied her husband to the cemetery little more than a day before, were marching back to it. With them came a weeping Madge Henspeckle —weeping she knew not why, but mortally certain that something dreadful had happened. They reached the grave; Madge felt her gorge rising but said nothing.

It had been freezing and the soil was harder to remove than it had been the day before. And now the corpse was completely stiff and the limbs could not be bent aside to make digging easier. It took half an hour of strenuous exertion to throw out all the frozen earth, and the men were sweating despite the cold; at last the body lay exposed in the dying light of evening. It was clutching something in both its hands.

"Madge, woman ye'll have to go home. This is no place for you."

For answer, Madge Henspeckle pushed her way to the open grave, and looked in. Then the air of Fifeshire—for miles and miles, people said—was rent by the most appalling scream any man could remember. The scream started as Madge stared into the open grave and it went on as she took to her heels and ran. The three who had done the digging looked in mute shock at the grave. The sun had vanished altogether now, but there was sufficient light to make out its contents.

They were clear for all to see.

The corpse was clutching with wild white twisted fingers of incredible length the green and black cap of Rabbie Henspeckle.

A cap for which Rabbie Henspeckle would have no further need, for no one was ever to see him again.

And on the dead man's feet, shining with some miraculous lustre in that darkened grave, were both the shiny, buckled, shoes the soutar had made.

SOME NORFOLK GHOSTS

We were coming home under the winter stars across the wild, house-less wet marshes of the Brograve Level which lies between the sand-hills and the cold North Sea and the reedy wilderness of all that undrained, untamed land of reed and water which lies between Hickling Broad and Horsey Mere on the bleak East Norfolk Coast. It is the remotest corner of Broadland. One of the loneliest places in England, And one of the coldest. Southward a few miles along the coast Winterton Ness thrusts, blunt-nosed, into the grinding tides of the North Sea. This whole coast. is a graveyard of ships, and Winterton Ness has been the sombre witness of more than its fair share of maritime misfortune.

I thought as we squelched in long water boots, with snipe springing on wing, wild geese chanting overhead, that we walked in a land which had not changed greatly for centuries. Ahead loomed the tall dark tower of Brograve Mill, lonely, uninhabited. We used to eat our shooting lunches in the little room with a Queen Anne fireplace on days when the east wind cut to the bone, when all the wild sky was a tumult of driven clouds and snow whitened the Level.

"It's a good thing we know the cattle track across this marsh," I said to Dick Jettens, the marshman and millman who plodded along-side. We both carried heavy duck guns, gamebags full of wildfowl, and a couple of hares which seemed to weigh a ton apiece. "I'd hate to be lost out here on a night like this."

"Ah! Rum owd place at the best of times," Dick grunted. "I wouldn't be out here on a dark night fer a bagful of gold. You never know when owd Sir Barney is about, galloping on his high hoss, snortin' flame out of its nostrils. Him and the Davvle ride together they say. That wouldn't be a mite of good a' shootin' yar big gun off at them tew. Many a strong man hev half died of fright when he seen them tew davvles ridin' the Brograve Level. Thass named arter owd Sir Barney Brograve. So is Brograve Farm and Brograve Mill. That was all his land in the owd days, far as you could see— and a damn sight farther than that."

Now this legend of Sir Barney Brograve, the ghostly Baronet of Waxham Hall, which lies just south of Sea Palling, is well founded in Norfolk history. Sir Barney, they say, sold his soul to the Devil. If so, the Devil let himself in for a bad bargain.

First, before we recapture the legends of Sir Barney which were sown in my mind on that dark winter night, let us consider Waxham Hall. No one who loves architecture, ancient history and lonely beauty, should miss seeing that striking manor house with its magnificent church and great barn. They are set like a trinity of jewels close under the sand hills, within a hundred yards of the groaning thunder of the North Sea. More than once it has broken through the rampart of high and hairy sandhills and swept inland drowning men, women, children and farm stock. The last such inundation happened at 6 o'clock on a dark night in the bitter winter of 1937–8 when the Great Flood put back the clock. All day the sea had pounded in shouting gales against the thin sandhills. Then it broke through at Horsey Gap. A hell's pool of sea water poured through— a wide, deep mill-race with all the North Sea behind it in power and volume. Mountains of sand fell into the flood and were swept away. The marshes first became a thin film of glimmering water. Then a racing succession of spreading pools. By 7 o'clock on that February night in 1938 thousands of acres were under water, a great sea lake as far as eye could see. The sea had come back to claim its own again.

In the dark night the sea-flood spread from Somerton to Hickling, from Martham Holmes to Waxham Hall, to Horsey and to the ancient harbour of the Hundred Stream, where the Vikings laid up their longships a thousand years ago. Brograve Mill stood like a dark lighthouse in the wind-whitened flood. All the Brograve Level was a lake. Waxham Hall and church stood up as on an island. Cattle were drowned in scores. Rabbits and hares, moles, voles, rats and field mice and worms were slaughtered in thousands. Between ten and fifteen thousand acres of marshes and farmland were under water.

"And they do say," said Dick slowly, "that the ghost of owd Sir Barney come splashing through the water on Somerton Road across the marshes. He rode his gret hoss right up to the walls of Waxham Hall where he lived and there he rose up in the stirrups, shook his fist at the floods and the tempest and laughed like thunder.

"'You drowned my lands and manors under the sea', he roared into the wind, 'and now you've come back to drown the lands of them that hold the manors that were mine.'"

I thought of this wild fantasy as I stood not long ago on the top of the high sand hills with the sea curdling in peace on the yellow sands behind, and below, sitting within its embattled wall, the old and lovely Hall of Waxham. It is one of those middle-size manor houses which have a lasting dignity.

Built probably about the fifteenth century of faced flints with stone quoins it has, like many Norfolk manor houses, a proliferation of buttresses, angle-shafts, finials and other architectural flourishes. It was here that Sir Barney Brograve lived, fought, drank, roistered and died. He was king of his own little country, an out-of-the-world wild land of marshmen, marsh farmers, smugglers, poachers, eel-catchers, reed-cutters, sea fishermen and bare-fist fighters.

Today the Hall is lived-in and looked after. The church, beyond the duck pond, has a cold nobility, but, alas, too much is in ruins. It stands in austere dignity among the bitter sea-fields with a few cottages and the Hall to owe it spiritual allegiance. There were once many manors which now lie drowned beneath the sea. Blomefield, in his *History of Norfolk* published in 1775 says:

"Oliver de Ingham was Lord of it in 1183, (when the 3d. part of his great tithe belonging to it was confirmed to the monks of St. Benet) as was Sir John de Ingham in the reign of King John.

"From this family it came by marriage, to Sir Miles Stapleton, and from that family, by marriage to Sir William Calthorp, whose grandson, William Calthorpe, Esq., sold it to Sir Thomas Wodehouse, who was lord in the reign of Queen Elizabeth, and of the manor of Ingham, as may be seen there at large.

"This family of the Wodehouses is a distinct family from that of Kimberley, and bore, for their arms, quarterly, azure and ermin, in the first quarter a leopard or; which arms belong to the family of Power, and I find these Wodehouses to be formerly stiled Woodhouse, alias Power."

The hall is said to be haunted by the unshriven spirits of the Brograves who died violently. First, Sir Ralph who died in the Crusades on a Saracen's spear, then Sir Edmund who fell in the Barons' Wars. Sir John was killed by an arrow at Agincourt and Sir Francis in the Wars of the Roses, fighting for the Lancastrians. Sir Thomas was slain at Marston Moor and Sir Charles fell at Ramillies under Marlborough.

Sir Barney—I suspect that the original spelling was Berney as he was almost certainly connected with the ancient Norfolk family of that name—was the epitome of the raffish bachelor Squire. Not precisely "the wicked Squire" because he did little harm to other people and most of it to himself. A bold, fine, upstanding man with immense physical strength, he would fight anyone for a bet, gallop a horse over the stiffest country, jump hedges, ditches and five-bar gates, and drink any of his neighbours under the table. He died a bachelor, but dotted the countryside with his portrait. Few rustic maidens could resist his overpowering charm. To give birth to one of Sir Barney's love-children was regarded as something of an honour —but by no means a unique honour.

Dick Jettens remembered old men who spoke of the fantastic New Year's Eve dinner party which Sir Barney gave at Waxham Hall to the ghosts of Sir Ralph, Sir Edmund, Sir John, Sir Francis, Sir Thomas and Sir Charles, those ancestors who all fell in battle.

The long oak refectory table in the dining room was ceremoniously set out with silver, glass, cutlery, china, decanters and great three-branched silver candle-sticks. Covers were laid—but nothing more— for the six ghostly guests.

At the head of the table sat Sir Barney, with three invisible ancestors seated on either side of him down the table. Their glasses were filled for each course—the sherry, white wine, a noble Burgundy, vintage port and rare old brandy.

The servants solemnly brought in each course and set it before Sir Barney who ate heartily and, at each course, ceremoniously raised his glass to his forebears, saying: "I drink your health Sir Edmund —Sir Ralph—Sir Charles", as the case might be. Not one was forgotten. Nor did Sir Barney forget to drink his guests' wine himself.

He sang hunting songs to them, roared out old Norfolk ballads, praised their valour in battle and, whether they were fox-hunters or not, gave them a roof-raising "View-holloa", followed at the end of the meal by a stentorian "Gone Away" which echoed down the sea wind and scared the owls out of the church tower.

At midnight, with the candles swealing, the shadows flickering, the half-seen, half-guessed wraiths of his ancestors mailed in armour or splendid in Carolean and Georgian silks and ruffles, the feast ended. The ghosts departed. Sir Barney vanquished not by supernatural forces, but laid out by old port and brandy, collapsed at the head of the table and, with his head on his arms snored into the dawn. His was the memory when morning came over the cold sea. His was the hangover which only a five-mile gallop in the sea-wind could dispel.

So, if you meet the ghost of Sir Barney galloping on a windy night of stars along the lone sea levels where also runs that ghastly black hound of Viking days, Black Shuck, you may guess that the man on the galloping horse is merely shaking off a hangover.

The later Walter Rye, a Norwich lawyer of distinction and an outstanding antiquarian and historian of Norfolk families—he torpedoed the Gurneys' claims to Norman descent with paralysing finality—told this enchanting tale of a local marshman's verdict on Sir Barney, in the language of the Brograve Level:

"Owd Sir Barney Brograve he wur a werry bad old man and he sold his soul to the Davil and guv him a parchment bond. When he died he went and called on the Davil and say to him, 'Here I be' and the Davil he say; 'Sir Barney, I allus sed you was a perfect gennle-man' and Sir Barney he say: 'Well, you might ask me to set down' but the Davil he say: 'I've been looking trew your account and it fare to me if I hev you in here twon't be a sennight afore yew'll be top-dog and I shall hev to play second fiddle, so there's your writin' back, and now be off!'

"And Sir Barney, he say: 'Where am I to go tew?' and the owd Davil he forgot hisself and got angry and he say: 'Go to hell!' Sir Barney he had no idea of wanderin' all about nowhere, so he tuk him at his word and he sat down and stayed. And they du say there's tew Davils there now."

Today if you stand on the Waxham sand hills and look down upon the old Hall with its embattled wall and pinnacled gateway, you may look for miles upon the loneliest, bleakest and most austerely beautiful stretch of coast on all the eastern sea-line of Norfolk.

In summer it is a place of infinite peace and sunlit horizons. In winter a bitter land of bitter spaces. A land of ghostly mists and sea fogs stealing like grey armies. A land of shouting gales and thunderous surges. A land, too, of wide, quiet meres and secret waterways, of sighing reed-beds and the whimper of endless wings, of old, small woods of oak and monstrous fern, and of blown, stinging sand and the whipping feet of sleet before the strong sea gales.

That is the kingdom of Sir Barney Brograve.

There is another ghostly rider of Broadland, Colonel the Hon. Thomas Sidney, who on 31 December, 1770, was kidnapped by the

Devil who threw him over the pommel of his saddle on a seventeen-hand ghostly hunter and then galloped madly across Ranworth Broad. Each time the horses hooves struck the water they raised a jet of steam! This ghastly steeple-chase takes place at midnight on the last day of each year—for those who have eyes to see.

Ranworth village is full of ghosts and in its splendid church, the best in Broadland, it preserves an unique treasure. That is the world-famous Ranworth Missal or Sarum Antiphoner, a superbly illumin-ated book of early medieval workmanship. I doubt if it is surpassed by any similar work in England other than the Luttrell Psalter. The church contains a painted screen of incredible beauty, which has been described as "suggestive of a great initial page of some splen-didly illuminated manuscript". The paintings are said to have been the work of German members of the School of Meister Wilhelm of Cologne, who settled in Norwich during the fifteenth century at a time when this church was building.

The gentlest, most lovable of all the Broadland ghosts is that of a monk, the man who painted the Ranworth screen. He, they say, rows up Ranworth Dyke at night, under the moon, in a boat of medieval design with the friendly ghost of his little brown dog sitting beside him. He, I think offsets most charmingly all wicked squires and co-partners of the Devil.

Finally, the Horning Donkey as told in the last century to that charming writer on the Broads, Suffling. An aged marshman told him the tale thus:

"I can't say as I've seen a human ghost, but I have seen the Horn-ing ghost in the Long Lane—that's the ghost of a dickey (donkey) yer know.

"I wuz coming from Walsham one night in the winter time, and I don't know how it wuz, but suthin' fare tu say to me—'Look behind'.

"Well, I must fule like, look roun', cause I fancied I could hear sumthin' go clickerty click, clickerty click, behind me. Sure nuff there came a white dickey lopin' along, all alone. I felt a bit scart and my old hobby pricked up har lugs as much as to say 'Hello, hu's this a follerin' me?' Presently I pulled up short like and the white dickey he pull up tu. Then when I go on, he go on, and we'en I stop, he stop. So thinks I, yew ain't no ghost anyhow. Then a bright idea cum inter me hid. 'I'll go back and see whose donkey 'tis.'

"So I tarned round and back I go, and when I'd got almost up to the white dickey who stud right in the middle o' the road facin' me, my old hobby stopped short and nearly hulled me outer the cart.

Poor ole girl she whinney'd we' fright and roun' she came of her own accord and along the lane she go as hard as she could clap her fower huffs to the ground.

"But it worn't no use; this here white dickey sune began to shorten the distance and every time I looked roun' it wuz nigher. Lord, I felt all of a muck sweat and I know me eyeballs stood out so that any one might ha' chopped 'em out wi' a hook. Closer it cum, and close; an' when I looked roun' again, it wuz just behin' with smoke comin' outer its nostrels like out of a furnace, and I du believe there wuz a little pink flame with it, but thet I ain't sure about, cuz I wuz upset. But this I du know the smell o' sulphur was right powerful.

"I pulled old Cally—short for California—inter the deek (dyke) and past came this here white dickey and sure nuff it wuz a ghost arter all, for I could see every bar of a gate by the rodeside rite trew its maizey body.

"My ha'r must 'av' riz on me hid, for orf went me hat. Away went the dickey up the Long Lane leading past the church to the village, and away went old Cally arter it, full tare, and think's I wot's agoen to happen nixt.

"Why it came to an ind like a flash. When the dickey come to the churchyard wall it plumped trew jest as easy as I could poke my finger trew a pat of butter and wot's more it didn't distarb a single stoon of the thick wall.

"Ye may laff, but nex' morning' when I went ter look for me hat —'cause I dussen't goo back that night—I took a good view o' the churchyard wall, and there worn't a hole in it nowhere, and not a single print of a dickey's huff in the roadway."

THE GHOST OF HIGHBURY HOUSE

When my first wife died, I was living in a small Kentish village on the edge of the Weald.

We had first come to Kent from the Channel Islands some five or six years previously. After a short spell in squalid industrial Erith, we had had a slightly longer stay in a flat in Mystole Park, near Chatham, a gracious country mansion often visited by Miss Jane Austen, when she was staying with her brother at nearby Godmersham.

I have never been able to make up my mind, until very near the end, whether my wife knew she was dying. When doctors had removed the malignant melanoma from her arm, they had told me that she was under sentence of death; but they had also said that she was not the type who could accept the dread news with psychological equanimity, and they had strongly advised me, to weave around us a fantasy world in which this reality at least had no part. I succeeded in doing this so well, that when she died three years later, the shock was far greater, I am convinced, than if I had lived with the inevitability of it from the moment I first knew.

As I say, I cannot be sure that she did not know. I believe, however, that the psychologists were wrong, that she had sensed the truth and had herself created a fantasy, very like mine, to prevent my knowing. One of the reasons for my thinking this is that as soon as she was about again after the operation, she pursued with a dogged singleness of purpose a determination to exchange our tiny Mystole flat for a house commodious enough to accommodate our children and their families whenever they could all visit us at the same time. In her search, she found Highbury House, a Georgian village-house, built in 1764.

As a matter of fact, for the last twenty or thirty years, Highbury House had also comprised the three-roomed, three-storey adjoining cottage. This meant that we had at our disposal, three rooms on the ground floor and seven bedrooms on the first and second floors. The ground-flour room in the cottage was set aside as my study. Over it was a large bedroom which was reached via a bedroom in the Highbury House section. A staircase in the House led up to the four bedrooms on the second floor.

On the ground-floor, my study in the cottage was separated from the dining-room in the House by the passage-hall of the cottage, the front-door of which had been permanently closed and was unusable. The dining-room was separated from the sitting-room by the hall of the House, from which rose the only staircase giving access from the ground-floor to the first-floor. We used the dining-room only when we had guests, but made constant use of the sitting-room, which was separated by two halls and the dining-room from my study.

The reason for my describing the lay-out of Highbury House in such detail will become apparent presently. But I would like to stress now that the distance between the sitting-room and the study must explain why the supernatural activities which are the core of my narration were not brought to our attention earlier.

On 14 December, 1964, we drove to Canterbury for the dual purpose of Jo having her periodic check-up at the Kent and Canterbury hospital, and of doing some Christmas shopping. On leaving the hospital, we went to Slatter's Hotel for lunch. Jo had been given a "clean bill" once again, but on the way from the hospital back into the city, she had seemed worried. Our own surgeon had, apparently, brought down a consultant from London, who had applied some very stringent tests to Jo, and she had said to me at one point, "I'm certain they think I have leukaemia".

This was so wide of the truth, that I was able with honest conviction to tell her that she must not have such wild imaginings. I felt her looking at me, as though trying to discover whether or not I was lying. Then she put her hand on my knee, and smiled. "All right, darling," she said. "I believe you, as always."

Over lunch we discussed plans for shopping, and though she seemed a little weary, she was full of enthusiasm. However, as lunch progressed I became aware that she was growing more and more tired, and over coffee her speech became a little blurred.

"Darling," I suggested, "they've obviously tired you out at the hospital. Let's go home now so that you can rest, and come back tomorrow."

To my surprise, she agreed at once. I paid the bill, and we got up to leave. On the way she said she must go to the ladies' room. As I waited for her, I put on my coat and sat in the hall. When she did not reappear for what seemed an extraordinary long time, I got up and went towards the ladies' room. At the door I was seized with an awful foreboding that something was very wrong. One of the chamber-maids, with dust-pan and brush, was making her way towards the back regions of the hotel. I called to her, and puzzled, she came to me.

I explained that my wife had been in the ladies' room a long time and asked her if she would be kind and go where propriety prevented me from going, to see whether all was well.

"Of course, sir," she said, and went through the door.

Seconds later, she reappeared in great distress. Ignoring propriety, I rushed into the room. In a cubicle, I found Jo, collapsed on the floor. I dragged her out, and laid her on the floor. She looked at me, and tried to move her lips in speech. Except for her left arm, she was completely paralysed.

A man appeared, whom I later knew to be the manager. I explained what had happened and asked him to telephone the hospital. The ambulance seemed hours in arriving, and I followed them back to the hospital in my car.

Hours later, though it seemed like days, the surgeon came to me.

"I'm afraid this is the end," he said. "It seems, though we can't be sure, that the cancer has attacked the brain without showing any intermediate symptoms. It could be a matter of hours, or some days. I'm sorry."

"The end!" What was the man talking about? How could this be "the end"? The shock, as I have said, was greater, I am sure, because of our fantasizing than it would have been had the awful words come out of the blue.

Jo lived ten days, for the most part in a coma, but with a lucid moment or two, during which happily I was at her bedside, to share in them. But she could not speak, only gesture with her left hand. She died at 2.30 a.m. on Christmas Eve.

If only I had not woven round me these past three years my make-pretend world, but each moment faced the truth, I am sure that the sudden solitude would not have affected me as it did. We had been married for thirty-two years, the last twelve of which had drawn us together as only two mature human beings can come together. She was only fifty-one, and could have had a third of a lifetime before her. Kindly people insisted, "Time heals". But time went by and my misery was unalleviated. The vast house, with its eleven rooms, became my mausoleum. I left it only to buy food, and hurriedly returned to it. As an anaesthetic I turned to work.

Since the war, I have only slept four hours a night. From the time that I became a full-time writer, I had got up at 4 a.m., written for three hours, breakfasted, worked, lunched and worked until 5.45 p.m. Then I had put work aside until bed-time. I made it a firm rule never to work evenings or on Saturdays or Sundays.

But now, so successful was work in shutting out the reality that was my half-life, after I had eaten my solitary supper at 7 p.m. I returned to the study and my typewriter.

It was on an evening in early spring that it happened. I was bashing away at my typewriter when I became aware of footsteps on the floor of the bedroom above the study. For a moment or two, I was quite sure that my imagination was taking over. (I am *not* a writer of fiction, by the way.) But as I rested my fingers on the bar of the typewriter, the footsteps in the room above were only too real.

There was, in the village, one of those "irresponsible" families. The irresponsibility is begun by the illiterate, ignorant parents who, believe it or not, do not connect sexual intercourse with the subsequent appearance of children. I am not joking. In a number of rural areas in mid-nineteen-seventies England there are still couples who, intuitively responding to their sex-drives, believe that having intercourse is one thing, and producing babies is quite another. Invariably, the off-spring of such parents are totally—and, I suppose, naturally—without any moral standards. This was certainly true of "our" family.

My first reaction, then, on becoming convinced that I was not "hearing things" was, "Oh, Lord! I've forgotten to put the latch down on the front door, or forgotten to lock the back door, and some of those blasted Baker children have got into the house and upstairs."

My bile rising, I stood up, went through the "cottage" hall and the dining-room, and taking the stairs two at a time, reached the landing in under a minute. From the landing, looking through the door of the first bedroom, I could see that the door of the farther bedroom—"the" bedroom—was open. There was no escape for anyone in the farther bedroom except via the first bedroom, which meant that to get away, whoever was there would have to pass me. On tip-toe I went towards the farther bedroom.

As I reached the door it was slammed to in my face. I tried to turn the handle, but it would not yield. I banged on the door.

"It's no use," I shouted. "You can't get away from there, so you may as well come out."

There was no response.

I banged again on the door, and again shouted to the intruder to come out.

Again, there was no response.

I was now angry. I would not tolerate the Baker kids making free with my house. I would teach them a lesson.

With my hand on the door-handle, I put my shoulder to the door and heaved. At first there was a resistance so strong, that my shoulder felt it had come into contact with a brick wall. This made me more angry still. Frantically, I heaved my shoulder again and again at the door with all my weight behind it. Three, four or five times I heaved, and then suddenly the door gave way and I fell headlong into the room.

As I did so, I felt that I was pushed sideways. I lost my balance and collapsed on to the bed struggling under a sheet that had been thrown over me. After minutes of struggling, I freed myself and switched on the bedroom light. It was then that I noticed the first strange thing—there was no sheet, no cover of any kind that could have been thrown over me, lying either on the bed or the floor. But the implication of the missing sheet did not strike me at the time.

Muttering to myself, I hurried downstairs, but I knew that by the time I got to the door, the intruder would have escaped. The latch on the front door was down, but when I went to the kitchen, I found that I had not locked the back door, which opened on to the walled garden, from which a gate gave access to a lane which led to the yard of the Nag's Head, and to a footpath to the council estate on which the Baker family lived. The unlocked back door convinced me that it was one or more of the Baker children who were up to their pranks.

I went back into the house, locking the door behind me, and searched through all the rooms to see if anything was missing. Everything was in its place.

I poured myself a drink and returned to my study. Fortunately I was copy-typing, otherwise I think I might have had to abandon my work for the day, for my adrenalin was still racing and I knew it would be some time before I calmed down. I found the place in my copy and began to type. I may have been typing a quarter of an hour or twenty minutes when I stopped abruptly, unable to believe my ears.

The footsteps had started up again! Slow measured steps going up and down, up and down, in a deliberate, unvarying rhythm.

I sat listening for a moment or two, then quietly made my way through the dining-room and up the stairs. This time I did not switch on the light in the outer bedroom. There was no need, for the street-light outside had come on and was illuminating the room sufficiently for me to see my way across it. As I tip-toed towards the far bedroom I could see that the door was shut. I could not remember having shut it when I had hurried from the room on the first occasion, though I had a pretty strong feeling that I had not.

With my ear to the door, I paused and listened. Through the solid wood I could hear, faintly, the footsteps going up and down, never faltering, never altering pace, rhythm or length. And as I stood listening something odd struck me.

The Baker boys who, at the present time, had taken over the role of village plagues from older brothers who had been put to work by their needy, thriftless parents, were undersized shrimps of pubescents. It would, I thought, not be possible for any of them to make such long strides without occasionally faltering in their rhythm during the several minutes they paced up and down. They were the strides of a male at least eighteen years old, and between medium height and tall.

I have to admit that for some seconds frissons of cold apprehension ran down my spine. An adult was quite a different proposition from one or two weedy boys when it came to confrontation. But that it was an adult would explain the strength of the resistance to my heavings and the brusqueness with which I had been toppled on to the bed when I had eventually broken into the room.

And who on earth could it be?

To quieten the pounding of my heart a little, I took a number of deep breaths. Then knowing that every minute's hesitation would weaken my courage, I seized the door handle, turned it and flung open the door.

Feet planted firmly apart, leaning slightly forward to off-set the impetus of the attack when it came, I waited.

But no attack came! And whoever had been pacing up and down, had stopped. Thinking that he might be manoeuvring into position to rush me, I quickly put up my hand and switched on the room-light.

It was a narrow oblong of a room containing a double bed, which was close to the door so that an ancient heavy wardrobe could be placed against the windowless end wall. Besides bed and wardrobe it contained a bedside table (on the wardrobe side), two small chairs, and a small book-case full of books.

There were no nooks and crannies where a grown-up man could conceal himself. The bed was too low, and of the wrong construction, to allow even the Thin Man to hide under it. The only hiding-place was the wardrobe itself. But the doors of the wardrobe creaked shrilly at the slightest movement. (Jo had begged me again and again to oil the hinges; again and again I had promised, but I had never got round to it.) Had anyone got into the wardrobe, I would have heard the doors open and close.

There had been no such sound!

By now I was distinctly puzzled, and my bewilderment had the effect of calming me down. To make absolutely certain, I skirted the bed, and pulled open the wardrobe doors together. As I had known, there was no one lurking within it.

My bewilderment increased, and I sat down on the bed, slightly weak at the knees by now, and tried to bring a degree of rationality to my thoughts. As I sat there, presently it struck me that everything that I had so glibly taken for granted up to this point was impossible.

Why?

The room was carpeted from wall to wall, with a deep-piled carpet, under which was a thick rubber underlay! The footsteps of anyone pacing up and down this room would have been completely muffled by the carpet! Certainly I could never have heard them in the study below!

As I sat on the bed pondering this, a cold sweat broke out over my chest and in my armpits. Not daring to give even mental form to the alternatives, I hurried from the bedroom, took the stairs two at a time, lifted the whisky decanter from the sideboard as I went through the dining-room, and in the study, drank half a glass of neat scotch almost in one gulp. Refilling my glass, I flopped into my easy chair and tried to restore some semblance of order to my thoughts.

There were two alternatives, I eventually concluded: either my cloistered, solitary existence in the rambling old house was affecting my mind, or Highbury House was haunted.

It was because I did not wish to reveal my apparent mental instability to my fellow villagers, nor subject myself to their ridicule if I asked if Highbury House was haunted that I kept completely silent, even though, during the next nine months or so, on seven other occasions I heard the footsteps, but never again attempted to investigate.

In the autumn of that year, I found my present wife, and in the following spring we married. Barbara lived in a neighbouring village and I left Highbury House and moved into her house.

Highbury House was bought by a couple who had a young family of three girls and a boy, the youngest, a girl, aged twelve, the oldest, the boy, aged twenty. They practically gutted the old place, putting in central heating, and turning the four second-floor bedrooms into flats for the boy and the oldest girl. The middle girl, aged sixteen, had the room over the study; the youngest girl, the room through which one had to pass to get to it.

There is an extremely good grocer's shop opposite Highbury House—known as the local Fortnum's—whose owners had been very kind to me while Jo was ill, and since she had died, had become good friends. As our own village store did not carry half the lines (in those days) that Bonham and Ward's did, and, also partly out of gratitude, after I had married Barbara and moved out of the village, we continued to give B and W's most of our custom.

I had married Barbara in 1966, and immediately the new owners of Highbury House had moved in. A week or two before Christmas 1967, I went into B and W's at Barbara's request, and while I was making my purchases, Eddy Ward said to me, "Ronald, what do you know about the Highbury House ghost?"

His forthrightness took me unawares, and for a minute I had to collect myself. Remember, I had not told a soul, not even Barbara, about my experiences, and, in fact, I don't think I had thought about them once since moving out of Highbury House. When I had pulled myself together, I said to Eddy, "You tell me what you know, and I'll tell you what I know."

"Well," said Eddy, "last Friday all the Barlows were out. Jane, the youngest, was at Guides and she came home first. She let herself into the house, and thought she heard Margaret moving about in her room upstairs. (Margaret occupied the room over the study.) So she went upstairs to ask Margaret what was for supper. The door to Margaret's room was half open when she got to her room, but as she went towards it, it was slammed to in her face.

"When she tried to open it, she couldn't. She thought Margaret was having a joke, so she banged on the door and kept trying to open it. All of a sudden it did open, and she fell into the room. When she picked herself up she realized that the light wasn't on, and when she switched the light on, there was no one there.

"That frightened her, and she came rushing over here. She was really in a state, trembling all over and she couldn't get out plainly what she was trying to say. Unfortunately, Joy (Eddy's wife) was out, but I calmed Jane down as best I could and in the end I got a good idea of what had happened."

"And what did you do?" I asked him.

"She wanted me to go over to the house with her, and make sure no one was there."

"And did you?"

"Well, no. Er ... you see, I couldn't very well leave Amanda (Eddy's small daughter) here on her own. O.K. I know she was in bed asleep ..."

"So what did you do?"

"I gave Jane something to eat, and when Joy came home, I sent her over with Jane. Margaret was just letting herself in. She hadn't been home since she had gone out about six."

"And that's all?" I said.

"Not quite. Doug Barlow uses your study as an office, and he was in there a couple of evenings ago. He was alone in the house, by the way. Well, he heard these footsteps up in Jane's room. He hadn't heard Jane come in, and he wondered what on earth she was up to making such a commotion. So he went to the foot of the stairs and called up to her, and when she didn't answer, he went up and found the room empty.

"He was sure he'd been imagining things, so he went back to his office, and after a minute or two, the footsteps started again. He was peeved by this time—you know what he's like. He thought Jane must have been hiding in the room, and was stamping up and down just to annoy him. He rushed upstairs. Jane's room was in darkness, and what had happened to Jane happened to him—when he got near the door, it was slammed to in his face. Like Jane, he couldn't get into the room at first, then suddenly the door flew open. But the room was still in darkness and there was no one there. What's your story?"

"How do you know I've got a story?" I said.

"Well, you said, 'You tell me yours, and I'll tell you mine'. So give!"

I gave

While I was reciting what had happened to me, Gordon, Eddy's assistant, had come up. Gordon had been born in the village, and had lived there all his life.

When I finished, he said, "There! What did I tell you? It's old Joe Winter's ghost, I reckon."

"And who was old Joe Winter?" I asked.

"He was the Poor Law Relief Officer when I was a boy," Gordon said. "This end of Highbury House was still a cottage then, and he lived there with his sister. He went potty as he got older, and night after night he used to walk up and down that bedroom, with a candle in his hand, for hours on end. Us boys used to go and shout up at him, and sometimes throw handfuls of pebbles at the window. That was more than fifty years ago.

"They had to shut him away at the end. When they came to fetch him, he put up a heck of a struggle. There was quite a crowd gathered round in the street. I was there when they brought him down in a strait-jacket and loaded him into the van and took him off to the asylum.

"There's one thing I don't understand, though," Gordon went on. "The cottage didn't become part of Highbury House until thirty years ago. Joe's sister died in 1930, and after her the cottage was lived in by two or three families. I don't recall any of them saying anything about footsteps or ghosts. Nor did the Ferrises say anything, and they lived there for nearly twenty years, nor did the Shipmans, that you took over from. Funny that. Has old Joe only just begun to 'walk', do you reckon? Or is it some people can't hear or see ghosts and others can? It's a rum old do, in any case."

Gordon shook his head gravely, and repeated, "A rum old do!"

"Why didn't you say anything?" Eddy asked me.

"Well, you know I wasn't very happy at the time," I told him, "and I was quite sure that if I told anyone, they'd think I'd gone round the bend."

"Maybe they would," Eddy agreed. "That will be thirty-seven and eightpence ha'penny, Ronald."

At the shop door, I turned and called to Eddy who was still at the counter: "What about young Margaret? Hasn't it put her off the room?"

"No. She's never heard the footsteps, and she says she's not impressed. Doug Barlow says he's heard them once or twice, though, when he's been working late in his office. Cheers, Ronald."

"Cheers," I said.

Strange Hauntings

THE INTRUDER

"Buster" Lloyd-Jones—Llewellyn to give him his Christian name
—was a busy veterinary practitioner near war-time Feltham when
the poltergeist made its appearance. For close on two years he
showed extraordinary patience with this tedious and sometimes
alarming joker before being obliged to take drastic steps.

For Buster, be it understood, was no ghost-hunter and in no way
interested in the occult. Animals were his life and he had no time or
interest for "entities", whoever they were, quadruped, biped or
with no feet at all, and frankly disbelieved in them—till the poltergeist came in the midst of a bustling life and started to be very,
very tiresome. Even then he was not easily upset, and reacted to
this further addition to his household, which already included one
hundred and sixty dogs, with something like humorous tolerance.
If only the poltergeist had shown the same ...

But it was not only because of the poltergeist that Buster needed
a broad sense of humour. Throughout his life it had been a useful
ally. In the first of his two delightful books of autobiography* we
read of the small boy Llewellyn living after the First World War
with his well-to-do parents and sisters in a large house at Feltham.
Years before, his father had come penniless to London from Wales
and made a fortune in the dress business, fully intending that in

* *The Animals Came In One By One* and *Come Into My World*, published
by Secker & Warburg.

due course his son should follow in his footsteps. But from an early age Llewellyn had only one passion in life, animals.

As a four-year-old he would lie restlessly awake at night agonizing about the safety of the bats that in darkness often got entangled in the netting surrounding the tennis court. And if it wasn't bats, it was cats that drew his passionate concern, poor little things catching their deaths in the rain he could hear beating against the bedroom windows. Sometimes he got so anxious about them that he had to get up, slip out of the house in his pyjamas and shielding himself against the rain under his father's big umbrella do a kind of sweep of the area, scooping up protesting cats wherever he could find them, then locking them till daylight in an empty gardener's cottage.

Animals were more real to him than human beings, so when Florence the housemaid offered him a sugar mouse to eat it was natural to refuse indignantly and when pressed to retort with devastating logic: "How would you like a sugar mouse to eat *you*?" A fist-clenching refusal to eat meat of any kind soon followed, not chicken, not lamb, not anything that had hopped or capered or been fed by him. He was scolded and sent to his room, but a self-willed father had produced a determined son and Llewellyn never ate meat again.

There was plenty of wild life around the little town in those days, rabbits, weasels, hedgehogs, stoats, hares, foxes, and Buster got to know all the species, including the smelly goats kept by the vicar's wife (to the vicar's disenchantment) and the cows that the dairyman taught him to milk. Then one day his Irish terrier Paddy impaled himself on some railings and had to be rushed to the vet's where an operation was performed, watched uninvited and unobserved by Buster. Thereupon the five-year-old informed the family of his future plans: when he grew up he was going to be a veterinary surgeon. This from a child could be treated lightly, or so his father thought. But he was wrong.

Two years later, Buster caught polio and nearly died. His bed was moved to the drawing-room where his mother could nurse him more easily and she agreed to the big french windows being left open at all times so that he could be in touch with his wild friends. The room was always full of animals. His dog slept on the bed. Cats prowled and dozed; two had kittens in a corner. Tortoises steered tank-like across the carpet. Ducks, bantams, starlings, thrushes fluttered, strutted and gazed beady-eyed while Maggot, his tame magpie, lectured him industriously from the bed-post.

"God's zoo", his mother called it and surrounded by this wild life, devotedly nursed by her, Buster slowly got better while his father, the stern man of action who had never known illness, watched impatiently from a distance.

At eleven he was ready to go to school where he was able to swim and play tennis, though not other games. In his teens he went protestingly under paternal orders into the family dress business and worked there for some time, uneasily conscious that his real life had not yet begun and sooner or later he would have to face his formidable parent to claim his independence. Then he saw an advertisement by a well-known animal society for trainees in animal husbandry and applied, was accepted and told to start training in a month's time. The fatal moment had come.

His father took the news with a total refusal to consider anything but his own wishes, said he would not allow such a step and when Buster persisted gave his ultimatum: "If you leave your job you will get out of this house and never come back." For the rest of that week, till the training began, he said not one word to his son.

So Buster got out bag and baggage, did his training at Woodford and for five years worked in animal dispensaries all over London, returning home sometimes when his father was out to see his mother and sisters. Socially he enjoyed the gay life, but his deeper self was always involved with animals and he found he had a healing touch with them and sometimes the power of intuitive diagnosis which he took as a great responsibility.

So far he had not had his own practice, but when war came and he was medically rejected for the Royal Veterinary Corps he set up his own surgery at Feltham. On the first day of war his unpredictable father had appeared at his flat unannounced and invited him to return home. There was a reconciliation of a kind, but before long, despite his son's obvious success, the old man, now retired, relapsed into gloomy silence and though they were living in the same house did not speak to him for a year and died, still unforgiving.

But Buster had no time for brooding. In the whole history of Britain's animal pets the year 1940 was probably the most disastrous. Amid food shortages, bombing and the disruption of families they suddenly became unwanted, impossible to keep and were brought to Buster by the dozen to be put down, often by owners distracted at the cruel necessity. But what alternative was there? Buster found an alternative. He took the animals himself till the garden and outbuildings at home became overcrowded and he and his mother had to find another, larger place.

They moved to a house near Feltham called Clymping Dene which had the advantage of a ten-acre garden and there Buster built kennels and a cattery big enough to house yet more unwanted animals. Apart from 160 dogs the inhabitants soon included innumerable cats, ducks, chickens, goats, donkies, ponies, monkeys and a parrot renamed Pollyo, of evil reputation, which decided that Buster was a good thing and went everywhere with him on his shoulder, the shoulder, that is, that wasn't occupied by another reformed character, a Javanese monkey called Wanda.

Feeding the animals was the greatest problem, but none ever went hungry, though the diet was inevitably short on meat. The goats provided a private dairy. There was a large well-stocked kitchen garden. The chickens laid for victory. A lake in the grounds yielded fish and people for miles around brought their parcelled-up kitchen scraps. All the same, running a war-time menagerie amid air-raids was an exacting business and in addition Buster still held his surgeries like any other vet and was often up all night working with the rescue services to extract terrified, wounded animals from bombed buildings. It was an intensely busy but satisfying life with problems which Buster well understood—until the poltergeist arrived.

Soon after the move to Clymping Dene he was crossing the garden one day when a stone flew past his head and landed with a thump in the grass, then another, then another. As he was alone and too far to be reached from the house or the garden boundaries he supposed some youngster was bombarding him from the bushes, and thought no more about it. But when the performance repeated itself, day after day, often when he was far from any shrubbery, he became really perplexed, and not because any stone ever hit him. The joker, whoever he was, was the worst of bad shots. But no human explanation seemed to fit. He knew his staff too well to suspect them of lunatic games and Wanda the monkey who might otherwise have been the culprit was often with him when the stones flew past. So who was responsible? To Buster this was not an intriguing mystery but a very practical problem. Sometimes the stones followed him as he returned to the house, smashing ground floor windows, and glass was very difficult to come by in war-time England.

The stone-throwing went on spasmodically for over a year, but there were other, more unpleasant phenomena. The house was very

large and for convenience Buster and his staff lived in the former
servants' quarters which were reached by some dingy, ill-lit back
stairs. These were frequently used, particularly by Buster, and
before long he was made forcibly aware of something sinister lurking there. One day as he was coming down he felt a pair of hands
squeezing his neck, not choking him but exerting a definite warning
pressure. His reaction was one of horror, but he preserved enough
grim humour to invite friends to walk down the stairs and watch
their reactions. Almost every one felt the invisible hands and the
pressure. When he was on his own, though, Buster avoided that
staircase, particularly at night.

At this stage anyone less level-headed and busy might have
panicked. But stone-throwing and clammy hands could not stop
Buster doing his job. If they had, he would have acted soon enough.
All the same, he was happy to have company when five army
officers were billetted in the house and really delighted to hear one
of them was a padre. For something else had now occurred. After
going to bed dead-tired at night he would be woken in the early
hours by the sound of weird and dismal organ music. His mother in
her room would hear it, too, and his sister. His dogs, of which
several always slept in the room with him, would crouch and quiver
in a corner with hackles raised as though someone were actually
present. But there was nothing visible, either in the room or outside in the corridor. The music seemed to come out of thin air.

The officers scoffed at this story, the padre loudest of all, and in
turn they readily agreed to test it by spending a night in Buster's
room, with the result however that each morning a different face
came pale and pensive to the breakfast table. The padre even insisted on changing back rooms in the middle of the night.

The priestly presence had no effect on the phenomena and in fact
they extended to include other weird, untraceable noises, pictures
dropping from walls, ornaments sweeping off tables and, on one
occasion, peals of girlish laughter—with no girl present—when
Buster tripped in the garden and sprained his ankle. By now his
mother was seriously upset and it was time to do something.

As a Protestant, to his way of thinking, had proved ineffective
Buster now consulted a Catholic priest and this man performed a
service of exorcism, reciting prayers, sprinkling holy water, making
the sign of the cross. This worked for a short while, then the turbulent spirit shook off its inhibitions and started all over again.

Worried more by the window breakages than anything else Buster
then called in the police who arrived with earnest professionalism,

camouflaged their tin helmets with greenery and concealed themselves about the grounds. Buster was then invited to perform a walk
across the lawn and, closely observing, the men noted stones showering around him, coming not from one direction but from several
at once. Such an event lay outside their experience and next day
they asked for a repeat performance, in which the poltergeist obligingly co-operated. Once more they asked Buster to take his walk
and for the third time stones whistled through the air. Then the
policemen conferred and came up with a considered judgement:
"Something very strange is happening here, sir, for sure."

But they were sorry, they could not help and advised Buster to
try the CID. With the CID the same rigmarole was repeated and
they, too, were nonplussed. But why not, said these more sophisticated gentlemen, try the Marylebone Spiritualist Association?

So in due course two women mediums arrived, one being the
well-known Estelle Roberts, in Buster's eyes, surprisingly ordinary
and sensible people. What were the phenomena, they wanted to
know? He told them—and there was a new one now: someone
invisible kept ringing the door-bells, for a professional man the most
aggravating trick of all. The ladies then said they would hold a
séance immediately in the room where the organ played and Buster
was persuaded to sit with them.

The women prayed in the darkened room, then sat in silence
till Estelle Roberts suddenly quoted the first line of a hymn and said
it would mean something to Buster. It was his father's favourite:
"The day Thou gavest, Lord, is ended." The medium then went
into a trance and said his father was trying to get in touch. He was
very unhappy and wanted to apologize to his son for being so difficult in his lifetime.

At first Buster was reluctant to believe in his father's presence,
but the evidence quickly became overwhelming. The medium gave
the dates of his father's birth and death. She described his appearance, down to a small mole on his cheek. A clue was given about
a family Bible which Buster had never looked into, containing between certain pages a record of family births and photographs of
his grandmother. The page numbers were given and Buster was
told where to find the key to the drawer containing the Bible. All
this was subsequently confirmed. Finally, a shattering experience,
his father spoke to him directly through the medium in his own
well-remembered voice. He said he was a lost soul repentant of the
past and asked forgiveness. As for the poltergeist, his words were
mysterious but comforting. He said that when Buster had converted

an old outbuilding into kennels some floor-boards had been re-placed (which was true) and this had "disturbed something" and given rise to the manifestations. But these would now stop.

And stop they did. For the remaining years at Clymping Dene all was quiet. The poltergeist was at peace, Estelle Roberts assured him, and to confirm this said he would receive two signs: the first would be a lily growing out of water, the second, a sign of the cross.

Despite all that transpired that day Buster was doubtful about the signs. But that winter he saw a lily growing out of the centre of the lake, something never seen before, and two weeks later he received the second sign. One night he heard an imperious ring at the front door. With a sinking feeling it might be the poltergeist, he opened it and there was no one there. It had been snowing and, a thing un-heard-of in the war-time blackout, there was a light shining across the porch. Reflecting the light on the smooth, untrodden, snow-covered ground lay a rough little cross made of brass. As soon as he picked it up the light faded.

In his account Buster almost apologizes for what may seem a far-fetched tale, but says that every word is true and nothing would make him part with the cross which meant that his poor strange father was at peace at last.

But this was not quite the end of the story. Some time later, with evening guests, Buster was persuaded to play the game of laying cut-out letters round a table and inviting an upturned wine-glass on which each person lightly placed a finger to spell out answers to questions. The result was dramatic, and uncanny. A person came through, gave a French name and said he had been killed on a con-voy to North Russia in 1942. Many details were given, of the ship, the battle, the tactics and every one of them was subsequently con-firmed from Admiralty records.

Years after this, Buster once more turned to the wine-glass with his friends, and had a conversation with a cheerful and vigorous woman named Hilary who said she had been drowned while swim-ming in Norfolk in 1954. To the company in general and Buster in particular she kept saying that "everything is going to be all right", which was pleasant to hear, though rather vague.

But a shattering blow was in store for Buster. As the result of the childhood polio he had been plagued all his life by illness and been in and out of hospitals, though always returning to his work with animals. Now, in 1958, he began to lose the use of his right leg, then progressively his arms and his lungs became affected. He struggled on, treating animals from a wheel-chair till, in 1965, he had to give up his veterinary practice.

Five years later, out of pure curiosity he tried the wine-glass for the third and last time at an evening party, wondering idly what would turn up this time. As it happened, it was his father.

He foretold correctly that Buster would be returning to hospital, a day before the doctors in fact made that decision, and also, a more hazardous prediction in view of his state of health, that he would survive to return home. And when he got back his father asked him to get in contact again, using the same method.

Buster did get home, but preferred not to take up the invitation and, reading his books, one may guess why. In early life he had had a tough fight to free himself from his domineering parent and had no wish now to risk further communication. Why should he? He had no need of spiritual advice however sound to boost his morale for in a strangely uplifting way we feel that, despite the ravages of his illness, he has preserved and perhaps even deepened his freedom. He has made a new life for himself. He writes books. He travels. He enjoys the company of his many friends. And he has a lot of interesting things to say about faith, which has been the basis of his work with animals.

This it is, no doubt, coupled with a fundamental acceptance of his lot, which has turned the coin of suffering to reveal its positive side, shown beneath the pain and weakness an indestructible core of personality and given solid meaning to the message spelt out years ago by the cheerful Hilary. This at any rate is the effect of his books on one of his readers.

GREEN DEVILS AND WHITE BONES

A doctor's surgery is almost as secret as the confessional, so doctors hear many strange stories from their patients. Here are two such stories taken from doctors' casebooks in the nineteenth century. They were told to Sir Walter Scott by doctor friends. He does not give their names and they do not give the names of their patients, as the matter was private and confidential.

*　　*　　*

"It's the green devils," said the patient. "I can't get away from them."

"What green devils?" asked the doctor.

"I don't know what or who they are. They're a band of men dressed in green. They dance in my drawing-room, a special dance, peculiar steps that I've never seen before. Whenever I go into the room, there they are, dancing their weird ballet among the furniture."

"You're drinking too much," said the doctor bluntly. In those days the blue devils was the nickname given to d.t's, or delirium tremens, that disease which besets alcoholics and gives them hallucinations. In this case the colouring differed, but the doctor presumed the cause was the same. He had good reason to think so, for his patient was a rich young man leading a wild and dissolute life with plenty of wine, women and song. Particularly wine.

He owned two houses, an elegantly furnished place in town, where he was living at the moment, and an old manor-house in the country, which he neglected because life there was a bore.

"Cut out the drink and you'll cut out your green devils," the doctor advised him. "Go and live in your country house. Take things quietly. Rest yourself. Early to bed and early to rise. Moderate diet. And no alcohol."

It sounded a gloomy prospect, but the young man was sufficiently frightened by his visions to take the advice. He went to the country and a month later the doctor received a letter from him. It was a sober, grateful letter, saying that the cure had worked. He was feeling fit again—and not a green devil in sight. He was so pleased, in fact, with his new-found well-being that he decided to give up town life for ever. He would settle down in the country. He sold his town house, since he badly needed the money, having wasted so much previously on drink and other extravagances. But he decided to keep the town furniture and have it transferred to his country place.

The furniture arrived. Happily he watched the men arrange it in the gallery of the manor-house. It looked perfect in the new setting and he was delighted. He paid the men, sent them away, then stood alone, admiring his furnished gallery.

And suddenly they were back.

Among the familiar articles of furniture, the green figures formed, mistily at first, then taking on definite form and shape. They began to move in that pattern he had seen before, making those strange, intricate steps of some unknown dance. He blinked and stared and willed them away. He'd had nothing to drink for weeks so it couldn't be that. Far from vanishing, they became even clearer.

The green devils capered and frisked about, delighted to see the young man again, and expecting him to be equally pleased.

"Here we all are!" they cried in chorus. "Here we all are!"

His peaceful life shattered by the green haunting, the young man left everything behind him and fled abroad. He never came back, and his doctor never learnt whether the green devils followed him or whether they stayed with the furniture, which was apparently their material anchorage. Maybe they still dance greenly somewhere in some old junk-room of Victoriana, or haunt the gallery of a "stately home" whose owners have long since been frightened away.

*   *   *

The second patient to be haunted by apparitions was a distinguished lawyer. It would have ruined his career if anyone had known the terror in which he was living, and even his doctor couldn't win his confidence until almost the end.

He was sent for when the lawyer had collapsed and was staying in bed. His pulse was slow, his appetite poor, and he suffered from fits of depression, but none of this could account for his shattered state. His family was mystified. The doctor questioned his wife and son, but they could think of nothing to account for the patient's condition. There had been no family disasters recently. Everything had been going smoothly.

There had to be a secret, and it must be revealed. The doctor determined to get the patient to talk. He sent everyone out of the bedroom and then locked the door, so that he and the lawyer would be completely private. His guess was that the man might have committed a crime and was suffering from torments of guilt.

"Confession will help you," he told the man. "Come on now—any skeletons in the cupboard?"

"How ironical that you should say that. How ironical," murmured the sick man. "All right, I will tell you. Although you'll find it hard to believe."

He said that twenty-seven months ago (he could, in fact, remember the exact date), he had begun to see things which others did not see. He had been in perfectly good health and quite content; his practice was prospering and he was happily married. His first "vision" was only of a cat, and he thought it was real for a long time; then it dawned on him that the animal was for his eyes alone. He wondered whether there was something wrong with his eyesight, or his mind, and then he felt afraid. Yet it didn't affect his everyday life in any way; he quite liked cats, so he grew accustomed to its mysterious presence. He didn't mention it to anyone for fear of being thought mad.

A few months later the cat disappeared and a human figure took its place. This was an apparition of a gentleman usher, the type whose job it was to announce guests' names at grand parties. He was elaborately arrayed in court dress, complete with sword, and accompanied the lawyer wherever he went. In his own house or anyone else's, the usher would always walk up the stairs in front of him as if to announce him to waiting company at the top. The lawyer attended many receptions, and the usher always came with him and mingled with the crowd—but they never saw him.

As in the case of the cat, he grew accustomed to the situation, his only anxiety being the necessity of keeping it secret. Clients would hardly trust their cases to a lawyer who claimed a ghost for company.

More months passed and the ghostly usher vanished. The lawyer was vastly relieved. He thought he could now look back on the whole experience as some minor brain disorder from which he had spontaneously recovered.

But worse was to come. One day, when he was walking by himself in Regent's Park, he had a sensation that he was no longer alone. He looked round warily, half-expecting to see that either the cat or the usher had returned. Instead he saw the image of death itself—a skeleton. He started to run, but it came with him, silent, insubstantial, its white bones gleaming, its skull horribly grinning. It accompanied him down Baker Street, back to his home in Mayfair. And from that moment it never left him.

When he walked alone, it walked with him. When he sat down to a meal, it joined him at table. When he was with his family, the skeleton hovered among them. When he went about his business at the law-courts, the skeleton appeared in the corridors and courtrooms. He had tried to carry on as if nothing were the matter; but of course he couldn't. The apparition made him ill. He couldn't eat or sleep and his nerves were being torn to shreds. The thing had gradually worn him down.

"Promise you won't tell my family," he begged the doctor. "I couldn't bear it if they knew. A story like that would spread like wildfire, and their lives wouldn't be worth living. You see, I tell myself over and over again that it can't really be there—and yet it *is*! It's driving me to my death. It's an emanation from some other world and will be with me to the last."

"Can you see it now?" the doctor asked.

"Of course I can. I've told you. It's before my eyes all the time. But it's no use your looking round like that. You won't see anything. No one does, except myself."

"Tell me whereabouts in the room it is."

"At the foot of my bed."

There were curtains round his bed. The two curtains at the foot were not quite closed. The patient said:

"It's standing in the space where the curtains are left open."

The doctor looked at the empty space. "There's nothing there. It's a delusion. Let's prove it. I want you to get up and stand in the place where you now see the skeleton."

"Oh, no—no—I can't—for God's sake . . ." The man was so distraught at the very idea that the doctor didn't insist.

"All right, old man. Calm down. *I'll* go and stand there."

He got up from his chair and stood in the space between the half-open curtains.

"Right. Have a good look," he said. "No skeleton there now, is there? Just your solid old down-to-earth doctor."

Yet despite his hearty manner, the doctor felt uneasy standing there. A chill passed through him. He felt the lightest of touches on his shoulder. But he stood his ground and kept a consoling smile on his face. "Well? Tell me if you can see it now."

"Not entirely," whispered the patient.

"How do you mean 'Not entirely'?"

"Never mind. I don't want to alarm you."

"My dear fellow, you're the one who's alarmed, not me. Just tell me if you can still see it with me standing here."

"Not entirely," said the sick man again, "but the skull is peering over your shoulder."

Forgetting his "bedside manner" for a moment, the doctor jumped and looked sharply behind him. He saw nothing, but he still felt oddly cold and moved quickly away. The patient said hopelessly: "You're very kind, but these powers, whatever they are, are too strong for you. You can't help me. No one can."

The doctor tried other methods of getting rid of the ghostly skeleton, but they all failed. The patient still saw the vision in all its macabre clarity. He gradually grew weaker and more ill during the next two months and never rose from his bed again. He faded, and died. As he drew his last breath, the skeleton, with its static, ruthless grin, hovered near him. It was with him to the last.

The doctor kept the dead man's secret. His family never knew about it. And it makes one wonder which of the distinguished lawyers of that period had a skeleton by his side as he conducted his cases—and whether anyone in an ultra-sensitive state of mind ever did see it, in some crowded courtroom, and wonder if he himself were going mad.

Perhaps many people see more than they ever admit to seeing—unlike the poet, a contemporary of the lawyer, who, when a woman asked him if he believed in ghosts, answered:

"No, Madam. I have seen too many myself."

A FACE IN THE MIRROR

To enter the august portals of *Who's Who* and be enshrined there among the aristocracy of talent may be the ambition of many people, but only one man, so far as I know, has achieved it exclusively as a writer of ghost stories. If we search those pages for the name Elliot O'Donnell we find a three-inch column listing over fifty publications, all of them on ghostly themes, but no other claims to fame.

But the writer's biographical details show that he came from a solid middle-class background more likely, one would have thought, to lead him to a conventional occupation. His father was a clergyman with a living near Worcester. He himself was educated at the reputable Clifton College, Dublin, and later married an English doctor's daughter. From his books we learn that as a young man at the turn of the century he tried to enter the Royal Irish Constabulary, but was failed on medical grounds. At this point it seems that something in his personality took over, impelling him to write about ghosts, so that by 1916 he had already written twelve books with such titles as *The Unknown Depths*, *Ghostly Phenomena* and *Twenty Years' Experience as a Ghost Hunter*. At the same time he was struggling to earn a living by other means, as a fruit farmer in Oregon, then as a prep-school master in England, then as an actor in an English touring company. But all this finally petered out before his one lasting enthusiasm which he followed for close on sixty years, dying in 1965.

Elliot O'Donnell seemed to feel that some explanation was required for his preoccupation with the occult and in one of his early books he claimed that he did not hunt ghosts as much as ghosts hunted him. He did recount the experiences of other people, but many of the strange events had happened to himself; he had not sought them. He seemed to attract phenomena, and it was not a happy fate. "I am often sorry," he wrote, "extremely sorry I was ever brought into contact with the Unknown. It has never given me any peace. I feel its presence beside me at all times ... I hope that some day, when I am brought face to face with it, I may be able to hit upon some mode of communication and discover something that may be of real service both to myself and to the rest of humanity ... If only I could overcome fear!"

Seen in this light, those fifty books may have been a means of preserving his own sanity, of providing explanations, however tenuous, of the strange phenomena which bombarded him whether he welcomed them or not. Several of his own experiences concerned entities assuming sinister, half-human shapes which came at him in the night with bony fingers outstretched to throttle him, and perhaps it was the relationship between murderer and victim which intrigued him in the outline of this story, told to him as a young man in America.

In the early 1900s the town of Denver, Colorado, like many other settlements in the United States, was at last looking forward to the prospect of steady, uninterrupted progress. It had clean stone-built and brick houses, well-paved streets, a municipality and a well-organized medical service. It even had a zoological garden, the pride of older citizens who remembered the treeless, arid waste they had come to as children. But law and order was still a plant of tender growth and not surprisingly, for Denver was only forty years old and in that period self-help had been the watchword of all its citizens.

It was the rumour of gold that had attracted the first settlers and within a year, by mid-1859, no less than fifteen thousand prospectors, among them some of the most ruffianly characters to be found on two legs, were swarming into Colorado to scrape, squabble, steal and murder one another in an area bearing alluvial gold only two-thirds of a mile long and two hundred yards wide. For three years the hunt went on, while in Denver the squalid cabins hastily set up reverberated nightly to the roars of drunken men and the cries of half-starved women and children.

But then the gold ran out; Denver obstinately survived and some people thought: why not settle here for good? The men decided they needed a bank and a coinage, so a private mint was set up to issue gold pieces. Thirsty for culture, the ladies started a literary and historical society. From the north an enterprising person arrived with a mule-train carrying printing equipment and soon Denver's first-ever newspaper, *The Rocky Mountain News* appeared, the proprietor and his staff working with pistols and shotguns at the ready to ward off desperadoes who tended to react violently to printed criticism.

Denver survived the Civil War unscathed, but then came serious assaults by Red Indian tribes when every road to the town was cut and for a whole year it was under seige. The Indians were defeated, but later the town was destroyed by fire and had to be rebuilt, house by house—all this with practically no help from outside, through the initiative and daring of its own citizens. It is no wonder that a tradition of rugged individualism survived for many years.

One of the younger generation who, around 1900, absorbed the full force of this tradition was a girl named Stella Dean, tall, handsome, but over-masculinized. She was fond of thinking over the story, so often told her, that she would not have been born at all if, one night during the Indian seige, her mother had not seized a hatchet and sliced clean through the skull of an Apache prowling round the house. Her mother, not her father; father had made himself scarce under a bed. So Stella drew the lesson: women are strong, but men are weak. Then she thought what she would do with her own strength, which was considerable, and here, too, her mother was a help. "Decide what you want," she said, pointing the breadknife at Stella till she almost winced, "and then go straight for your target. That's the way to get on in life. Stake your claim and then work it, and to hell with everyone else!"

So Stella thought hard and decided she wanted two things: some money to gain a degree of independence and, concurrently, a young man named Peter Simpkins, whom she summed up as pliant, good-natured and not impossibly stupid. Peter, she felt sure, would be happy to see her wear the trousers.

Stella went to work at a typing agency in Denver main street run by a Mrs Bell (widowed daughter of the embattled newspaper proprietor) where she found that the only other employee was a frail but beautiful young girl named Hester Holt, for whom Mrs Bell showed a motherly concern. There seemed to be tragedy lurking in Hester's background—Stella discovered she was an orphan living in lodgings—and it was this perhaps which impelled her as compensation to a romanticism which Stella found very tiresome.

"Somewhere there's a rainbow", Hester would say, her eyes misting with tears, and then would make typing mistakes. Her ignorance of harsh facts, of the practical side of life at first amazed, then flattered Stella who lost no chance of bringing them home to the shuddering Hester, eliciting such responses as "Oh, my, you don't say!" and "Stella, what a lot you know". On this basis they got on well enough, yet Hester had a warmth, a capacity for something which Stella could not define but knew she lacked, and it made her jealous.

Three months passed and then one morning Hester failed to turn up. "She's indisposed, I dare say," said Mrs Bell. "Back tomorrow for sure." But next morning there was still no Hester and at the dinner-break Stella was sent round to inquire at her lodgings, to find the landlady in great agitation. "I know what you've come about," she said before Stella could open her mouth. "She's not been here for two nights, not last night, not the one before. The poor thing, wherever can she be?" She thought it just possible Hester might have gone to her sister's in Baltimore, but that was a long way, a difficult journey. "However will she manage, all on her own? Anyway, I have the address; I've written, we should hear soon." "Then let us know, please," said Stella, and left.

A few days later, the landlady came to see Mrs Bell. She had received a reply. Hester had not been to her sister's, but the sister made a suggestion. Hester had often written to her about a young man she was very fond of and he might know something. His name was Peter Simpkins.

"Simpkins?" said Mrs Bell. "Not the son of the building contractor?"

"Yes," said the landlady. "Don't tell me you didn't know. Surely everyone knows about Peter and Hester. They've been going together for a couple of months now."

"Really? Well I am glad. I'm sure they are made for each other." And in Mrs Bell's mind rose a picture of the couple, like the Suchard chocolate advertisement, surrounded by fluttering love-birds, beamed on by a conspiratorial sun, naïve, tender, thoughtful for one another, rather old-fashioned, very touching. "That really is good news. I will go and see him."

"Hullo, Mrs Bell," said Peter, opening the door for her at his parents' home, and she thought again what a nice voice he had, what a friendly smile. "I'm so pleased you have come because I wanted to ask you: have you seen Hester lately?"

"But that's what I wanted to ask you."

Peter had not seen Hester for three days, which was very worrying, because usually they met every evening when Hester left the office—round a street corner, in fact, out of sight of the building in case Stella Dean should see them.

"But why?" said Mrs Bell. "What have you to fear from her?"

"I've got nothing to fear, Mrs Bell. But I know Stella is very jealous of Hester and if she saw us meeting, well—she could give Hester a very bad time, and she would, too."

"But why should she be jealous?"

"Because a few months ago Stella and I were engaged."

Peter had "succumbed", as he put it, rather as a general in the field might succumb to superior forces. Stella had cornered him, and one day he had hoisted the white flag and proposed. But then . . .

"Oh, then, what a change, Mrs Bell. From that moment on she thought I was her property and even the good qualities I had seen in her vanished in a wave of possessiveness. She was horrible to my mother. She was even jealous of my men friends. She was trying to wrap me up like a parcel, isolating me more and more. In a very short time I got so depressed I just had to break off the engagement."

"And where was Hester when you last saw her?"

"Now that's the extraordinary thing, Mrs Bell. On the evening of that day when Hester was last in your office I saw her and Stella taking a buggy ride together. I was cycling back from the building site where I work for my father, east of the town. It's a lonely track, overgrown, dark, not much place for a buggy ride. Stella was driving. But what really astonished me was that they should be together at all, Stella taking Hester for a joy-ride: it just didn't fit . . ."

At this moment a sinister thought rose in Mrs Bell's mind. But she said nothing to Peter.

Back at the office she questioned Stella, and got no change. No, she had not been out with Hester that evening. Yes, she had been engaged to Peter Simpkins, but it was she who had broken it off: "Not man enough for me, I'm afraid, my dear Mrs Bell." As for Hester, they were on the best of terms—"and I feel protective towards her, don't you?"

So, with still no sign of Hester, Mrs Bell told the Denver police, who culled a crop of conflicting evidence. An old gentleman thought he had seen Hester enter her lodgings on the night in question. Someone else confirmed Peter's story about the buggy but could not be sure the passenger was Hester. The buggy owner said he had definitely hired out the vehicle to Stella, whom he knew well by sight, and Stella, questioned again, calmly said yes, she had never denied driving the buggy, but it was not Hester Holt, it was her own mother who was with her. This, when interviewed a day later, Mrs Dean obligingly confirmed and the police, too thin on the ground to search for Hester, then put the case on file.

A week after this, Mrs Bell engaged a new typist, Alice Cummings, a farmer's daughter, and with her arrival strange things began to happen. First, she complained of feeling icily cold when she sat typing next to Stella at the same table, and moved to the opposite side. Then she accused Stella of kicking her under the table as they worked.

"Don't be ridiculous," flared Stella. "How can I when I'm sitting four feet away?"

"I don't know. But somebody is."

Mrs Bell noticed that Stella looked frightened.

Nothing more happened for a few days until one afternoon, when the three women were having a tea break, Alice said to Stella: "By the way, who's that beautiful girl I saw following you into the building yesterday morning?"

"What beautiful girl?" said Stella sharply. "I don't know what you're talking about. I saw no one."

"But you must have seen her. She was close behind you, practically touching you. I was crossing the hall making for the stairs when I saw you both come in. She caught up with you halfway to the elevator, then seemed to turn off to one side. Anyway, I didn't see her again. I suppose she works on the ground floor."

"What did this girl look like?" said Mrs Bell. "Did you see her face?"

"Oh, yes," said Alice and gave a description.

"Why Stella," said Mrs Bell excitedly. "That's Hester. It must be. Wherever can the dear child have got to? Why doesn't she come up here?"

But Stella apparently could not speak. She gave a gasp and then, suddenly pale, stared in terror at the door.

This revived Mrs Bell's suspicions and talking alone together later she and Alice decided to watch Stella carefully, with the possibility of discussing the matter with the police again. But events were taken out of their hands.

Next morning the three women happened to arrive at the office together. Mrs Bell had a key in her hand and was about to unlock the door when they heard the sound of a typewriter clicking furiously inside. "And who's got into my office, I should like to know?" Quickly she unlocked the door, flung it wide open, the sound stopped

165

abruptly and she stared into an empty room. The sun was shining on the typist's table and the machines were standing there with provocative stillness. Stella gazed at this scene transfixed, swayed slightly and the next moment ran to a chair and collapsed with her head in her hands. That afternoon she pleaded influenza and went home early.

Stella was away for several days and during that time the phenomena ceased entirely. Then one morning she came back, thinner, ill looking, with a glazed look as though she were ruminating some terrible problem. The day passed without incident until evening when on leaving the building Mrs Bell was intercepted by an agitated Peter Simpkins.

"Mrs Bell, she's come back! Hester's come back! I saw her this morning about ten o'clock, going in through the main door there. I didn't like to follow her and disturb your work, and also, to be honest"—Peter gave her an imploring look—"to be honest, I was afraid."

"Afraid? Tell me why."

"I can't quite explain. It was a very curious experience. It was Hester, and yet it wasn't. I know it sounds silly, but I have an awful feeling something terrible has happened."

Mrs Bell saw that Peter was very upset. She put an arm round his shoulder, steered him to a café, sat him down, ordered two cups of coffee and said: "Peter, it is time I told you something. I'm very afraid that what you saw this morning was not the living Hester, but—something else."

Then Peter said quietly: "I know what you mean. I think so, too. It was Hester's ghost . . . Oh, Mrs Bell . . ." And he was in tears.

Mrs Bell herself was now taken ill and for a few days had to leave the girls to work together. Later, Alice told the police what happened. On the very first day they were alone, at about eleven in the morning, Alice glanced up from her typewriter to see Stella staring hypnotized at something on the floor. It was a black dispatch-case with the initials "H.H." clearly embossed in gold on the side facing Alice and it was jumping to and fro, "like a child playing hopscotch," she said, a few inches in one direction, then back again a few inches in the other. She had not noticed the noise because she was typing, but now she heard a distinct thump each time it landed. She thought at first there must be some rhythmic vibration in the building, but everything was as steady and solid as usual. Stella was petrified.

The movement stopped after a while and Alice saw Stella dabbing her face bathed in sweat. Then lunch-time came and they both got ready to go out, Alice intending to eat separately. She had put on her hat and was moving to the door when she heard a cry of sheer terror behind her. There was a mirror the size of a large picture frame on the wall opposite the door. Alice at that moment was at a slight angle to it, so that she could see the reflection of Stella's face as she stood there with her own hat in her hand. But there was something else in that reflection, another face, and Alice's blood froze as she saw it: the face of a beautiful girl staring into the mirror over Stella's right shoulder, the same face that she herself had described some days earlier and Mrs Bell had identified as Hester Holt's.

Alice fled the room and without her touching it the door slammed shut behind her. She stood for a moment in awful fear then, ashamed of her cowardice, tried the door handle. It turned, but push as she might the door would not open. Alarmed now for Stella, she ran to the elevator and fetched the man in charge. They tried the door again; again it would not budge. Then, as they were considering what to do they saw the handle turn and the door swung silently back on its hinges. In front of the mirror was Stella's body motionless on the floor.

Stella had fainted and was taken home. But she died that same night, from natural causes, her mother said—"she always had a weak heart". After the funeral Mrs Bell came back and rented another office in the same building for her typing agency, where Alice joined her. One day Peter Simpkins came to see them in a strangely quiet and solemn mood. "Have you seen what I've seen?" he said. "They've come back, both of them this time. I saw them just now, only five minutes ago, walking in through the main entrance, just as before, Stella in front, Hester behind. And they both looked ghastly. They were the ones that looked haunted."

"Come back?" said Mrs Bell horrified. "But why?"

"I think because there's a problem between them—it's the problem of giving and accepting forgiveness."

Then Peter said a strange thing. "I'll talk to Hester about it. I'm sure I can get her to understand."

THE BLUE LADY OF VERDALA

Very roughly in the middle of Malta is a 725-feet-high "table-land". At the northern end of it lies Mdina, the medieval walled capital of the island, which surrendered its supremacy as the seat of government in the middle of the sixteenth century to Valletta, newly founded by Jean de la Valette as the headquarters of the Order of St John, of which he was then Grand Master.

At the foot of the table-land, perhaps two miles from Mdina, is a small wooded valley, called Boschetto or Busket. Here migrant birds moving backwards and forwards between Africa and Europe made a staying post. They represent practically the only prey for hunters, and it was on this account that the knights and their falcons were attracted to Boschetto, where ornamental gardens and games enclosures were eventually laid out. It was for this reason, too, that Valette built himself a small hunting-lodge and stables just above the valley—and where he developed the pneumonia that killed him.

Compared with Mdina, Valletta was low-lying. In some parts it was at sea-level, and it was, therefore—as it is today—an oven in the high summer temperatures. To escape this worldly purgatory, a successor of Valette, Grand Master Hughes Loubenx de Verdalle, in 1586, commissioned the Maltese architect, Girolamo Cassar, who had built most of Valletta for the Order, to design a palace not far from Valette's hunting lodge. He intended to move there permanently during the high summer months, instead of spending occasional days at the hunting lodge, as Valette had done.

168

Cassar's Verdala Palace is almost a perfect square—176 feet by 188 feet—and in appearance is not unlike a Norman keep. Solidly built, with a turret at each corner, it is surrounded by a dry moat, and is complete with torture chamber—not in the dungeons, because there are none—and a secret stairway leading from the Grand Master's bedroom down to the moat, by which he might retreat in case of need. It was, in fact, a fortress-like dwelling, so designed to protect its inhabitants against any attack that might be made on it by a Barbary corsair in search of slaves.

When the British ousted the French from the islands in 1799, and began an association with the Maltese that was to last for a hundred and fifty years, various Governors used Verdala Palace as their summer residence. One of them was Lord Methuen, who was Governor during, and in the years immediately following, the First World War.

Lord Methuen was attracted to Verdala as probably no other Governor has been, and like Verdalle, he spent the greater part of the summer there each year. There he entertained an almost continuous flow of guests, among whom in the summer of 1918 was a famous pianist, who was giving a number of recitals in the island.

The pianist was given a bedroom on the upper floor, adjacent to one of the turret-rooms. (This, like the other three, was approached from the bedroom up a short flight of steps.) The room was spacious, and though sparingly furnished, was comfortable, and there was nothing about its atmosphere that had so far caused its occupant any apprehension.

It was with considerable surprise, therefore, when one morning while he was tying his tie before the mirror, that he saw himself looking into the face of a beautiful woman. Her black eyes, accentuated by her olive skin, held a pleading expression. Any moment he expected to hear her voice, but when she did not speak, he turned, only to discover that he was alone in the room.

The image in the mirror had been so clear, so well defined, that he was certain he had not imagined it.

"After dinner it might be a different matter," he told himself, "but in the cold light of morning, the mind does not play such tricks."

When he returned to tying his tie, he found that his hands were shaking a little.

"Idiot!" he muttered. "You must have imagined it! A man of your intelligence does not believe in ghosts!"

With an exclamation of irritation he pulled off his tie, and began to tie it again, but his fingers would not do as he bid them. When he failed yet again, he went over to the bed and sat down, trying to calm himself.

"It isn't that I'm afraid," he tried to convince himself. "It was the unexpectedness of it. But she looked so real, too. Of course, one shouldn't be surprised by ghosts in an ancient building that has so much history. There I go again!" He stood up, and said firmly aloud. "I do *not* believe in ghosts."

Selecting another tie, he willed himself to tie it, but it was still a botched job when he had finished. He decided, with a shrug, that it would have to do, put on his coat and went down to the hall, where he found most of the other house-guests assembled, waiting for the appearance of His Excellency to lead them in to breakfast.

The Governor's A.D.C. was standing near the foot of the stair-case, and came over to him as soon as he entered.

"Is everything all right, sir?" the young man asked.

"Thank you, yes. Why?"

"You look as if you'd seen a ghost, sir."

It was too amusing. The pianist burst out laughing.

"Well, as a matter of fact," he confided, "I've just thought I had."

The other guests, curious at the pianist's noisy outburst, had fallen silent. One of Lord Methuen's daughters asked, "Where did you see her?"

"In my bedroom," he told her without thinking. "But, I say, how did you know it was a woman?"

"There is only one ghost at Verdala," the young lady replied. "We call her the Blue Lady. I haven't seen her myself yet, but the children have seen her quite often in various parts of the palace. As a matter of fact, I'm surprised that having appeared to you now, she has not done so before. You see, she spent quite a long time in that room."

"Surely you don't believe in ghosts, ma'am!" the pianist exclaimed.

"Certainly I do. It's a matter of vibrations, you know; extra-sensory perception. We all have them, but in some they become more highly developed than in others. Those in whom they are developed can see ghosts. They are usually sensitive people, likely to be artistic, or in other ways receptive to the forces that surround us all, but which most are too world-bound to appreciate."

Lord Methuen had come into the hall and overheard his daughter's last remarks.

"My dear, not vibrations and ghosts before breakfast, surely," he smiled. "She needs only the slightest encouragement," he said to the company.

"And that I have given her, Your Excellency," said the pianist. "I've just seen the Blue Lady."

"By jove, have you? I told my wife, or at least, my daughter did, that perhaps it would not be wise to put you in *that* room. When you say you've just seen her, do you mean this morning or last night?"

"Are you a sceptic, then, sir?" one of the guests asked.

"Oh, by no means! You must not misconstrue my innocent words."

"I saw her only minutes ago," the pianist explained. "I was at the mirror tying my tie, and saw her reflection in the glass peering over my shoulder. It gave me quite a shock, because I had not heard anyone come into the room. She looked as though she was going to ask me something, make a plea of some kind, but when she did not speak, I turned round—and there was no one in the room. Who is she, do you know?"

"Yes, I've gone into the history, and I will tell you about it over breakfast," said the Governor. "But tradition insists that I shall mention no names. It is not a very edifying story, and it is best for the reputation of the Order of St John, and perhaps for the peace of mind of the descendants of the other parties concerned."

★   ★   ★

The Grand Master did not set a good example to his celibate knights. Within a short time of entering the Order, he had broken his vow of Chastity, but as he was following a long tradition of the Order in this respect, his behaviour was not checked. Even so, it had been expected that when he was elected Grand Master, he would curb his profligacy as others had done before him. But he did not see things in that light. His natural instincts were still as demanding for a man of his age, as they had been overly active when he was a young man, and he could think of no reason why he should devote his latter years to physical frustration, when there were plenty of women only too willing to have the honour of fulfilling his needs, and benefit from the largesse which he was always prepared to distribute for services well rendered. On the contrary, he considered that he would have been a fool not to have put to good advantage the influence he could wield in making his choices which accrued to him as ruler of the Island as well as of the Order.

Perhaps history would not have had to be so circumspect had

171

he exercised discretion and managed his affaires *sub rosa* ... But again, either he considered himself above man's laws and was prepared to flaunt the law of God as laid down by Holy Church, or he was so completely in the grip of his urges that they utterly overwhelmed his will. Nor was he right in thinking that every woman would go weak at the knees with desire for him. There were many, indeed, who surrendered out of sheer fear, and considered themselves defiled for the rest of their lives; the thirty pieces of silver he paid them they threw secretly into the sea.

Until he saw the Blue Lady, there had been little, if any, emotional involvement with any of his partners. Rarely did any of the women serve him more than two or three times. But the moment he cast eyes on her, he became madly infatuated with her beauty, and knew that he would never have peace of mind, or of body, again until he had possessed her.

It had happened on the way from the palace of San Anton at Attard to Valletta. The pin in the wheel of a carriage had been worked loose by the unevenness of the road, and the coachman and footman were struggling to replace the wheel when the Grand Master and his bodyguard rode up.

Ordinarily, the Grand Master would have ridden by un-noticing, but now his attention was at once attracted to the occupants of the carriage—a lady and her maid. The accident had clearly shaken the lady badly, and she was still trembling as the maid tried to comfort her.

Immediately the Grand Master halted his troop and ordered two of them to give the coachman and footman assistance with the wheel. While the repair was being completed the Grand Master rode over to the two women, to ask if they had been harmed.

Both dropped a curtsey when they recognized who he was, and the lady told him that she had been shaken by the suddenness of the accident, but was otherwise unhurt.

"I am most grateful, Your Eminent Highness," she said, "for your consideration, and for your assistance."

It was as she spoke that the Grand Master first realized her beauty. It would be a gross misrepresentation to say that the Grand Master's heart leapt; nevertheless, it was at that moment that he knew his body would know no peace until it had had its will of her body. Up to now if he had ever given a moment's thought to the attractiveness of his partners, it had been merely to subscribe to the rake's maxim that all cats are grey in the dark. Probably for the first time in his life, he was stirred by a woman's beauty.

By this time the wheel was fixed.

Before remounting, he held out his hand, and when she responded bowed over her hand, lightly brushing it with his lips.

"Madame," he said, "I should have been breaking one of the great rules of the Order had I not had the chivalry to stop when I saw your distress."

As he had kissed her hand, she had shivered, and the *frisson* had communicated itself to him. Wrongly, he had interpreted her reaction of disgust as a thrill of erotic pleasure.

"I hope," he said, "that I shall have the honour of meeting you again in less distressing circumstances."

She did not reply, but curtsied again, remaining with her head bowed until she heard his horse move away.

"And I hope," she told herself, "that I never encounter such wickedness again."

As he rode towards Valletta, the Grand Master's mind was in a torment. What had happened to him? Never before had his loins been so stirred by any woman. Was this love? he wondered, and could not decide.

On the way, he beckoned the captain of guard to him.

"Who was the lady?" he asked.

"I do not know, Highness," the captain of the guard replied.

Arrived at the Auberge in Valletta, he immediately summoned his secretary, and gave instructions that the lady's identity should be discovered without delay. Some hours later the information was brought to him.

"She is . . . twenty-eight years old, the mother of three children, the wife of a prominent merchant," he was told.

"It is a pity she is married," he commented. "No matter. No one is to disturb me until I summon you."

Alone, he paced up and down the room, his mind concentrated on finding a plan which would allow his passion for the lady to be assuaged. Presently he called for his secretary.

"Bring the merchant to me with all haste," he ordered.

When the merchant came before him, the Grand Master treated him with all courtesy, making him sit down and offering him wine.

"I have asked you to come," he said, "because I have heard of your reputation as the striker of a good bargain, and am so impressed by it that I would be grateful if you would undertake some urgent private business for me in Naples."

"I am flattered by Your Eminent Highness's attentions," the

merchant told him. "If I can be of use, command me. What is the nature of the business, Highness?"

The Grand Master explained, concluding, "If you will undertake the mission and carry it out successfully, you may ask for twice the usual commission. What do you say? I will place one of my ships at your disposal."

"Agreed," replied the merchant. "When do you want me to leave?"

"Tomorrow."

The following morning the Grand Master watched from the Barraccas as the ship slipped her moorings and sailed out of the Grand Harbour. He then returned to the Auberge, where he ordered his secretary to go in person and command the lady to dine with him that evening at the Verdala palace. He would send a carriage to fetch her.

Impatiently he awaited the secretary's return. The message the man brought momentarily stunned him.

"The lady regrets she is unable to obey Your Highness's command to dine," he was told.

"For what reason?" he asked.

"No reason was given, Highness. That was the message as I have repeated it."

The Grand Master took a turn or two about the room, and presently called the captain of his guard to him, and gave him instructions.

At dusk the captain took his troop to the lady's house, where he repeated the Grand Master's command. On receiving a second refusal, he ordered the maid to bring the lady a cloak, on pain of a beating. When the maid returned with a blue velvet cloak and hood, he said, "I hope you will not require me to use force."

The lady said nothing, but stood with her head erect, her hands clasped, and let him put the cloak about her shoulders, and lead her out to the waiting carriage. At Verdala she maintained her cold composure as she told the Grand Master, "You are a wicked man. My husband will kill you when he returns."

"If he returns," said the Grand Master. "That depends on you."

"How do you mean?" she asked, suddenly afraid.

"Unless you come to me freely, and swear a sacred oath to remain silent for ever, he will never return. Or if you break your oath at any time . . . Do I need to say more? The servants will take you to your room. I will come to you presently for your decision."

Immediately the door was locked on her, she fell on her knees beside the bed and prayed God to forgive her for what she was about to do. She remained on her knees until she heard the Grand Master's footsteps crossing the ante-room.

With a little cry, she rose and ran to the window and threw it open. As the Grand Master entered the room, he caught a glimpse of the hem of her cloak as she threw herself out.

They found her crushed body, lifeless in the dry moat.

THE WATERFALL

There are two things I'll say for Dudley Barrington; he is neither a bore nor an intellectual snob, which is admirable, for a man of his eminence and attainments might understandably be either or both. But not Barrington; his presence in the Smoking Room is always welcome, which in itself is testimony to the ease and grace with which he can shrug off the mantle of a master of music, for it must be admitted that the Club tends to attract men whose honours have been won on the turf of Twickenham or the sands of North Africa rather than on the podium of the Festival Hall or the Berlin Opera House.

We remember Obolensky's try against the All Blacks more readily and with greater relish than Sir Dudley's more recent *tour de force* with the Philharmonic, and one of the reasons we are so fond of Barrington—though not the only reason by any means—is that he is not only content but delighted that this should be so. He summed the matter up neatly enough for us many years ago. "Of course I love music; it's an unhappy fellow, surely, who doesn't love the profession he follows. But when I sit in the sunshine at Lord's the scores I am interested in are those of Compton and Edrich, not Beethoven or Bartok. And I come to the Club for conversation and companionship, not for a fault-by-fault remembrance of the horrors of four hours' rehearsal of an orchestra apparently smitten by arthritis of the elbows and a pianist labouring under the impression that the Emperor was there to be overthrown rather than interpreted.

176

Do join me in a glass of this most excellent Cockburn, and tell me about Harold's performance in the House today—one hears it was quite remarkable even by his own incomparable standards of sophistry." Yes, a Clubman through and through, Sir Dudley Barrington.

And we in our turn are not entirely Philistine. It was wholly natural, for instance, that the conversation last evening should have turned to the subject of music, and several of the men gathered around the great fire in the Smoking Room had quite intelligent things to say. But eventually, of course, we looked to Barrington for some contribution to the general talk.

He had been sitting quite silent, but he was not being supercilious; his occasional smile had registered appreciation of a good remark rather than scorn over a *gaffe*. It was Penfold, I believe, who finally made the approach direct. "Well, Dudley," said Penfold, "you have a pretty fair idea now of our tastes, from Sibelius to Gilbert and Sullivan. I appreciate that this is rather like asking a man-of-letters to name his favourite book, but can you tell us—is there any single piece of music, any work or melody that stands in your memory or affections above all the others?"

Barrington leaned back into the depths of his leather armchair, stretched his long faultlessly-tailored legs luxuriantly towards the blazing logs, and spent a reflective moment over the selection and ignition of a cigar. We were content to wait; it is not in Barrington's nature to create silences merely for dramatic effect. When he spoke, his manner was almost apologetic. "As a matter of fact there is such a piece of music, but I fear I can only reply to your question properly with an anecdote. A simple answer would not suffice, for strangely enough—there is no simple answer."

The stewards replenished our glasses, we settled in our chairs, saw to our smokes, and listened expectantly. Barrington, as I have said, is not a bore.

"To tell you about this music," he began, "I must ask you to accompany me on a walking-tour I made some years ago—five, I believe it was, yes five—in Scandinavia. Such expeditions have for a long time been my answer to the call for relaxation, sometimes alone, sometimes with a well-chosen companion. On this occasion there were two of us, for I was being introduced to Norway by young Gerald Brandon, who served there during the war and who knows the country well. A good fellow, Brandon, and a good conversationalist; he had talked to me many times of the incomparable beauty of the Norwegian scenery, and I was happy to accept his suggestion that we visit there together. And so that Easter we set off, boots and rucksacks at the ready, on a journey that, to me, was an exploration of unknown delights.

"We walked the south-western coastline, marching many miles inland along the banks of the great fjords, Hardanger, Lyse, Geiranger and the rest, and it was soon obvious that Brandon had in no way exaggerated the splendour of the country. Every bend in the road brought one upon some new scenic delight, glories of nature ranging from gentle charm to wild magnificence, orchards of cherry and apple waving gently in the breeze, vast and craggy glaciers reflected in the deep blue waters of the fjords. After more than a month of such wanderings, as we settled at last into the comfort of the Ernst Hotel in Kristiansand, on the south coast, to ease our muscles in deep baths and to await our passage to Harwich, I felt I had enjoyed not only a holiday but an experience complete in itself, a segment of life that could be neither added to nor improved. And that is how that Easter vacation would have remained in my mind, had it not been for a chance encounter on the evening before our planned departure for home.

"The old gentleman who addressed us as we sipped our post-prandial brandy was remarkable only for his charm and courtesy and the fact that he knew my name—two circumstances that may perhaps be not wholly unrelated in my recollection of them. Well into his eighties, I should say, yet clear in the eye and complexion as a youngster—a man of the outdoors, unquestionably and yet, with equal certainty, a man of culture and breeding. We talked agreeably for half an hour or so, by which time he had become well aware of the nature and purpose of our visit to Norway, and at length he leaned forward and said with a strange eagerness: 'Now tell me, gentlemen, what did you think of Setesdal?' The name, I confessed, meant nothing to me, and for once Brandon too was at a loss; understandably enough in what is after all a foreign country to us, and yet we both felt unreasonably apologetic, almost guilty, as we saw the old gentleman's palpable disappointment, and we urged him with genuine insistence to tell us what it was that he had missed.

"The picture he painted for us was of a long and beautiful valley stretching many miles north-west of Kristiansand—a valley green and fertile in its lower reaches but narrowing to steep and rugged grandeur as it climbed inland past Evje and the blue waters of Byglandsfjord. This in itself was of small significance; Norway, as I have indicated, abounds in beautiful valleys. What made Setesdal something out of the ordinary, said our companion, was the fact that for countless centuries the mountains and the lakes had combined to seal off the people of the valley almost completely from contact with the world beyond. 'Should you decide to visit there,' said the old gentleman, and it is a measure of his persuasive charm that already such an unplanned and inconvenient intention was forming silently in our minds, 'you will see if you look closely that there are three entrances to Setesdal from the south. The first and earliest, the merest trace of a track, climbs over the top of the mountain; the second, also rudimentary, winds its way circuitously around the same mountain; the third, a twentieth-century tribute to the power of dynamite, blasts its way clear *through* the mountain and so provides the only route any normal man would follow for any reason short of sheer necessity. It is, in short, only within the last hundred years that any but the hardiest of travellers have journeyed between Setesdal and the rest of Norway.

" 'The people of the valley', continued our companion, 'have as a result retained their own language, costume, customs and culture, to all of which they cling tenaciously, simply because it seems natural to them to do so, and not in response to any vulgar inclination to exploit their *quaintness* for commercial reasons. The language, I fear, may defeat you, for it is not easily intelligible even to the Norwegian ear, but certain of the more elaborate costumes are very pleasing, heavily embroidered with the silver ornamentations for which the craftsmen of the valley are now justly renowned. And for you at least, Sir Dudley, there is a treat in store, for with your permission I shall furnish you with a letter of introduction to one Torleiv Bjorum, a silversmith in the village of Rystadd who has the reputation of being the finest musician in all Setesdal. He will, I am sure, be honoured to play for such a distinguished musician as yourself a few traditional airs on the multi-stringed Hardinger fiddle that is favoured by the people of the region. I venture, without disrespect, to doubt whether even in your wide experience you have ever heard anything quite like it.'

"Undaunted by the ambiguity of this last remark," went on Barrington with a grin, "both Brandon and myself found ourselves without argument beginning to formulate a plan for cancelling our passage to England, accepting the letter of introduction to the musical silversmith, and making the journey to the hidden valley of Setesdal. It was a decision for which I shall never cease to be thankful. The countryside was as spectacular as any we had seen on our travels, and the silversmith as hospitable—and as talented—as our new friend had promised. The music of the Hardinger fiddle, though

179

strange to my ear, was both interesting and melodious, and with the musician's permission I recorded several of his songs on the tape-recorder that is as basic to my travelling equipment as my boots. Even now I occasionally play it to remind myself of that extra-ordinary journey."

Sensing our unspoken feeling that the journey in question, although certainly interesting, seemed scarcely to merit the term "extraordinary", Barrington stirred in his chair and added with quiet emphasis; "But it was not the music of Torleiv Bjorum of Rystadd that I referred to in answer to Penfold's question. Nor was it the strange sound of the Hardinger fiddle. What has haunted my memory ever since that expedition to Setesdal is the music of a vocal trio that I heard the following evening as Brandon and I made our way south towards Kristiansand and, thence, towards England. I heard it as I lay at twilight in a meadow just a mile or so south of the charming little hamlet of Ose.

"Brandon and I had halted there not because we were tired, but for the best of all reasons—we had found what we considered the ideal place in which to camp for the night. Striding along the high-way we had heard, faintly at first but gradually growing louder, that lovely and most subtle of sounds, the plash and murmur of great volumes of water falling from a height, and suddenly we saw its source, a most beautiful waterfall gushing like a silver fountain from the mountainside many hundreds of feet above us, a misty cataract that bounced and bounded down the precipice to the rocky stream beneath. Without a word we unslung our rucksacks, laid down our bedding-rolls, and made our way to a cottage nestling almost at the base of the falls.

"Our business was swiftly transacted; the sturdy farmer, brushing aside our suggestion of payment, assured us we were most welcome to pitch our tent in his pasture. No sooner had we done so than his small son, dispatched from the kitchen by a smiling mother, brought to us a pitcher of ice-cold milk and a steaming cauldron of Far-i-Kal, a mouth-watering mixture of mutton and cabbage such as used, he assured us, to speed the Vikings on their voyages of conquest. Well fed and hugely content, Brandon and I debated how best to con-tinue the evening, and came to different conclusions. He, perhaps having helped himself more liberally than I to the simmering stew, decided upon a walk before bedtime and set off accordingly; I, perhaps having helped myself more liberally than he, wanted nothing more than to lie in the meadow and watch the sinking sun strike fire and diamonds from the tumbling water of the falls.

"It was as I lay there in the gathering dusk that the music began, and for a moment I wondered if I was dreaming, for the voice, a rich and lusty baritone, seemed to be pouring out from the cliff that towered above me. But no, I was wide awake, and as a second voice, pure and lovely as only a soprano can be, began to respond to the first, I rushed into the tent, fetched my tape-recorder, and switched it on. The ribbon on which I had captured the music of the silversmith still had half its length to run, enough to give me at least thirty minutes of this concert if happily it should last so long. I listened enthralled as yet another voice rang out above me, but this time from far away, its *basso profundo* booming and echoing from the surrounding hills. The music was the most moving, the most dramatic that I had ever heard, and I could scarcely believe in my good fortune in having the means to preserve it for all time. My elderly acquaintance in Kristiansand had spoken with enthusiasm, certainly, of the distinctive culture of the Setesdal valley, but nothing in his panegyric had led me to expect anything like this. I gave myself over to sheer delight in the singing, content to wait until later to discover the identity of the singers—for already I had decided that I must meet them; such talent was too rich to be allowed to languish in the obscurity of this remote Norwegian valley.

"Nor was it the singers alone who aroused my unqualified admiration. The composer too, whoever he might be or have been, was fit to rank with the greatest. Not Verdi, not Mozart, no, not Beethoven himself in his immortal *Fidelio* had, to my enchanted mind, created finer, more exquisite operatic melody than this. Though the words were foreign to me I was in no doubt as to the nature of the tale that was being unfolded; this was tragedy, stark and wild. The strong young voice of the baritone rang with pride, that of the soprano with love, and the bass had a power to it that was at once taunting, challenging, and a source of fear. Once, after the baritone had given out with an aria that swooped and soared like a call to war, the soprano answered with a song of piteous, unbearable grief as heart-rending as Sutherland's mad scene in Lucia, and always, always there was the sinister, threatening voice of the bass to tell us that this tragedy was of man's making and no mere accident of Fate. But at last the mood changed to a strange and eerie blending of a love song with a lament of profound and hopeless sorrow; when the last notes died away I sat silent, enraptured as I had never been before and have never been since.

"I was still sitting there unmoving when Brandon returned from his walk, and my fingers trembled as I rewound the tape-recorder.

'Listen, Brandon,' I whispered, 'just listen to this.' He did not press me with questions; my tone and my intense excitement must have told him there was reason in my failure to offer any explanation. As the reel reached the point where the singing had started—or as near that point as I could judge—I stopped the machine, set the switch to 'Play', and watched eagerly for the look of astonishment that must surely cross the face of my friend. Nor was it only surprise that I looked for, but happiness and pure delight as well, for Brandon's love of music is as great as my own. I smiled secretly in anticipation.

"The drum revolved, and we listened to the dying notes of the last tune played to us by Torleiv Bjorum on his Hardinger fiddle. Then silence; I waited breathlessly. Still silence; I stirred uneasily, uncomfortably aware of Brandon's gaze, polite but unmistakably—and understandably—quizzical. But what was this? The silence, I realized, was not absolute; there was the soft whirring of the motor, and behind that, faint but undeniable, one could hear in the distant background the plangent notes of the waterfall. Brandon tactfully held his peace as I stopped the machine, once again re-wound it, switched the dial to 'Record', and spoke into it a verse or two of doggerel. 'Now listen', I said, re-winding and altering the switch to 'Play'. At once came the sound of my own voice reciting the meaningless rhymes—*on the very strip of tape on which I had attempted to record the voices of the singers.*

"I must have looked distraught—heaven knows I *felt* distraught —but Brandon did me the courtesy of not assuming I had taken leave of my senses as I poured out to him the tale of the music I had just listened to with such enjoyment. I concluded by saying with some heat, 'Now here is proof that I have not been dreaming, for if I could create such music I should not be well known as a conductor, but immortal as a composer', and I sang to him some snatches of the melodies that had been indelibly imprinted in my mind, noting down the music as I did so on a writing-pad. Brandon's response was both gratifying and astute. 'Whatever the explanation, there can be no doubt that you heard this music, nor that it is Scandinavian in origin, for although you hit your notes truly you failed, if you will forgive my saying so, to capture the strange cadences of the original. No, I am not psychic,' he smiled, noting my look of incredulity, 'it so happens I am familiar with this style of singing, though not with the songs themselves. It is an ancient folk-art deriving from the necessity for vocal communication between men separated by great distances and perhaps by insuperable physical barriers; in the wilder regions of Norway you will find many men and women who can so pitch their voices that they will carry clear across a wide valley, ringing from one mountainside to another in a way that would be utterly impossible to even the finest conventionally-trained singer. It must be some such voices you heard—perhaps peasants rehearsing for a festival, or merely singing for their own enjoyment.'

" 'But the *quality* of the voices, Brandon, and above all, the quality of the music. You will allow me, I think, some expertise in this matter, and what I heard, I assure you, was no rustic *chorale* performed by amateurs. No, Brandon, this was great music magnificently sung; it had an air one might almost say of ...' I hesitated over the word, 'of the supernatural'. There was a moment of uncomfortable silence as each of us found his mind ranging doubtfully over the mystery that remained unsolved, the unaccountable failure of a sophisticated and perfectly serviceable piece of electronic equipment to reproduce the sounds that had unquestionably been fed into its receiving apparatus. It was I who finally spoke. 'Brandon,' said I, 'I am a man of music, not of mystery; there must be some logical answer to this affair, and I mean to have it. Our farmer friend seems kindly disposed, and the lights are still burning in his cottage; let us see if he can satisfy our curiosity.' And without further ado we made our way to the farmhouse door.

"The farmer welcomed us most courteously and made to usher us indoors, but Brandon in his impatience blurted out at once the burden of our visit. The change, the reaction, my friends, was unbelievable. A look of sheer terror transformed the face of this sturdy countryman to a pallid, quivering mask, and the cottage door was immediately, almost violently closed fast against us.

"In response to our astounded knocking there came only an incoherent babbling pitched dangerously close to hysteria. Such snatches as were intelligible to Brandon told us merely that we must leave at once, that same night, and that no power on earth would persuade this man once more to open his door to us. The very least we could do was to accede to the man's request; he had been, hitherto, the very soul of hospitality, and his state of terror was so great there could be no doubt that our continued presence would cause him, and presumably his family, acute distress.

"We scribbled a brief note of thanks, enclosed some money with the request that it be put to the purchase of some trifle for the youngster who had so cheerfully brought us our supper, and within twenty minutes we had struck camp and were once again on the road. By common consent no mention was made between us of the events of the past few hours, and at the nearest village we took rooms in a wayside hostel and engaged a car for the following morning; our simple intention was to seek out the old gentleman we had to thank for the strange adventure that had befallen us.

"By noon next day we were once again in the Ernst Hotel, and in response to our inquiries an obliging page-boy volunteered to seek out the old gentleman and invite him to join us over a glass of sherry. He seemed genuinely pleased to see us and quite touchingly grateful that we had disrupted our itinerary to fall in with his suggestion, and when at last I led the conversation gently and without melodrama to the subject uppermost in our minds there came to his face such an expression of wonder and delight as I had seen only in the eyes of little children attending their first performance of *Peter Pan.*

" 'Sir Dudley,' he breathed, almost overcome by emotion, 'my dear Sir Dudley, but how fitting that you of all men, you who have yourself brought magic to audiences all over the world, should have been privileged to hear the music of the Silent Singers of Setesdal. And to think that I myself should have been instrumental—no pun intended, my dear sir, I do assure you—in bringing this about. You have made me the happiest and proudest of men. Come, let us have another glass of sherry, and I shall tell you all that lies behind your extraordinary experience.'

" 'The waterfall beside which you made your camp is known as Reiardsfossen, that is, the Falls of Reiard, and centuries ago that cataract was the scene of a tragedy terrible in its wastefulness and shameful in the wilful malice that inspired it. There lived then in the vicinity of Ose a farmer and merchant of substance, a man possessed not only of land and riches but of an overweening pride and an ungovernable temper. He was also possessed, and more's the pity, of a sweet-natured and singularly beautiful daughter, who as she approached the flowering of her womanhood fell deeply in love with a young man of the district, Reiard by name. The sentiment was reciprocated in full, and since Reiard was a lad of good birth and infinite promise there should have been no hindrance to what all the neighbourhood regarded as an eminently suitable match. But that was to reckon without the ill-natured caprice of the girl's father. This evil creature, while pretending to be all in favour of the courtship, waited until the very morning of the wedding before proclaiming that before the ceremony could take place Reiard must prove himself a man of courage, and must do so by accepting a challenge devised by his prospective father-in-law. He must climb the mountainside, leading his horse, and he must then ride the animal across the very brink of the great waterfall; only then might he claim his bride.

" 'Now Reiard was both brave and proud, and despite the pleading of his betrothed, despite the outraged protests of the elders of the community, he accepted this insane condition; no man, least of all the hated father of the girl he loved, should question his willingness to stake his life for the greatest prize that life itself had to offer. In a strange and unhappy variety of moods the lovers, the father, and a group of villagers made their way up to the very edge of the falls, and there they stood silent, apart from the girl's sobbing, as Reiard gazed at the broad expanse of rushing, roaring water and wondered if his steed's nerve would prove as steady as his own. At last he turned, quietly embraced his bride-to-be, mounted the trembling thoroughbred, and guided it gently, soothingly into the torrent.

" 'To the watchers, no less than to Reiard himself, that hideous journey seemed interminable. Picking each step with infinite care, leaning its flank steeply against the swift-flowing wall of water, the horse edged its nervous way forward, its rider stroking its neck and whispering ceaselessly in its ear flattened backwards in fear. Once, twice, three times and yet again the terrified creature stumbled, and only by crushing her anguished fingers into her mouth did the weeping girl hold back the wild cry that might startle the beast still further and send it and its rider plunging to the rocks so far beneath. And then, at last, a vast sigh arose from the onlookers as the horse seemed to gather its muscles like a coiled spring and, with one mighty effort, thrust itself out of the foaming water to the safety of the farther bank. Reiard, his wedding finery drenched and clinging to him like a beggar's rags, made nevertheless a figure of surpassing dignity as he sat, proud and erect as a captain of cavalry, and raised his feathered bonnet in a gesture that was at once a symbol of defiance and a salute. The girl extended her open arms towards him, the villagers roared their approbation and relief; even the madman who had decreed the whole grisly *charade* was moved to sudden admiration. 'Reiard,' he cried, 'you are a man indeed. Make your way down the mountain; there your bride shall await you, and may she always think with pride of the way you won her this day.'

" 'For a long moment Reiard gazed at him in silence. Then he spoke. 'My bride,' said he, 'is no longer a gift from you. I claim her as of right—and I claim her *now*.' And slowly, deliberately, he urged his mount once more into the turbulent water and set out on his return journey across the treacherous parapet of the falls. Step by fearful step the quivering beast carried Reiard towards the now-silent gathering until at last he was within three paces of safety and the girl was moving joyfully to embrace him. And then the horse stumbled, whinnied in a piercing shriek of mortal terror, and was swept with its rider to destruction on the jagged rocks below. For an eternity of horror there was silence broken only by the rumbling thunder of the falls, and then with a wild cry of grief the demented girl snatched herself free from her father's restraining hand, ran forward swiftly as the wind, and cast herself into the boiling torrent to disappear, a tumbling, tragic scrap of humanity as she plunged to rejoin her lover.'

"A chill," said Barrington, "seemed to have entered the warm drawing-room of the Ernst Hotel. Then the old gentleman leaned back in his chair and said softly, 'So now you will understand, Sir Dudley, why only you and not your electronic gadget were able to receive the music of the Silent Singers, those voices from the distant past that come to life only very occasionally to tell their story of love and hatred, of tragedy and remorse to those who have the ear to hear them. Only to those; oh yes, only to those. That is why your poor farmer was so terrified—for simple people fear what they cannot comprehend, and to him you were a madman, of the type no doubt described to him time and again by his father and grandfather; wandering lunatics who appear only once in several decades and who claim to hear music where all right-minded people know full well no music exists. But you, Sir Dudley, and I, who have no such claim to fame but who many years ago, as a mere boy, used to stroll by the fjords with Grieg—*we* know, do we not, that it does exist.'

"And rising from his chair the old gentleman thanked us for our company and walked smiling from the room, whistling softly and tunefully a snatch of melody whose notes were roughly scribbled on the writing-pad in my rucksack."

Spectres of the Sea

THE HAUNTING OF U-BOAT 65

Ghosts are one thing. Accidents are another. When a ship has a reputation for both she is liable to be shunned by men who might otherwise have signed on with her. But in time of war a seaman has no choice. Whether he likes it or not he must leave his superstitions behind, even though he fears he may be sailing in a doomed vessel. Such was the case with the crew of the U-boat U.65.

She was one of the light submarines launched by the Germans in 1916 to patrol the heavily protected Belgian coastline, thick with mines and nets. The earliest versions of these frail little craft had a surface speed of only 6·5 knots, and carried only two torpedoes. They plodded up and down Belgian waters, dodging British patrols, weaving in and out of sandbanks, edging up to terrorize fishing fleets or sink the occasional Allied ship. They pierced the Dover barrage and defied the famous Dover patrol. Little, but game, were the U-boats.

U.65 was new in 1916. Her surface speed was an improvement on that of her elder sisters—13 knots. She carried a crew of thirty-four, including three officers. The trouble that was to make her the jinx of the German Navy began while she was still building. A steel girder was being slowly, steadily lowered into place. There was a jerk, a shout of warning, and the massive thing slid sideways and fell with a mighty crash. The noise of its fall and the splintering of wood were mingled with fearful screams. It had fallen on two workmen.

Slowly, with difficulty, their horrified mates raised the heavy mass as far as they could. But it was jammed, and the tackle had broken —they could not lift it clear of the two victims. One, it was obvious, was beyond help, a broken, bloody pulp. The other, trapped by the legs, screamed for an hour as they fought to free him. Soon after they got him out he died.

In the Dark Ages a blood sacrifice was made to bring good fortune to a new building. It seemed that U.65 had taken her toll of blood, and would now be satisfied. But she had only begun.

Work was resumed, and for some weeks went on without mishap. Then came a second fatal mishap. The U.65 was almost ready for launching when three workmen, putting the finishing touches to equipment in the engine-room, were heard coughing and calling for help. When help came, the engine-room door was found to be jammed. Inside was a haze of noxious fumes, and on the floor were three corpses. An inquiry produced no satisfactory reason for the escape of the fumes and the submarine was declared seaworthy.

"Deutschland, Deutschland über alles!" The Fatherland had a new weapon to hurl against the enemy. The U.65 slid out for her trials. The day was calm, the omens propitious. She had scarcely got into the open sea before a sharp squall blew up. The sea rose, swamped her deck, and swept one of her ratings overboard. A boat was hastily lowered, but no trace of him was to be seen. Victim Number Six had died by drowning.

Then U.65 was put through the diving trials in which a submarine must prove itself. A certain gloom prevailed amongst the crew. It was justified. Sure enough, when the U-boat was submerged a leak developed in one of her tanks with the result that submarine and crew were trapped underwater for twelve hours. Once again death-bringing fumes filled her, perhaps due to seawater in the batteries—it was never proved. When she finally surfaced and the officers and crew were released they were half-stupefied, sick, choking—but alive, *Gott sei dank*. For once the jinx had only been joking.

The next time was no joke. The submarine's private fiend had dealt out death by crushing, by asphyxiation and drowning. Now it experimented with explosives—and most successfully. The U.65 made an uneventful maiden patrol, returned to base and started taking in torpedoes. Without warning, or reason, a warhead exploded. A fearful detonation, screams, chaos, followed, and five dead men lay huddled and twisted on the submarine's deck. Others were badly hurt. The fateful submarine, itself considerably damaged,

went out of action for repairs during which any workmen in possession of good-luck charms undoubtedly wore them. A cemetery at
Wilhelmshaven, the chief German naval station, received the bodies
of the dead, including that of the second officer, a man of striking
appearance.

Once more fighting fit, U.65 was manned and prepared to sail.
It was evening, and her captain and his officers were discussing plans
in the wardroom while the crew settled in. Suddenly, the door burst
open and a white-faced rating stood before them, panting and
trembling. The captain's head jerked up, his beard bristling with
affront.

"What's the meaning of this, Schmidt? Don't you know better
than to enter the wardroom without knocking?"

"I beg pardon, Herr Oberleutnant, but the second officer ... I
—I've just seen him!" gasped out Schmidt.

The captain's lip curled sarcastically. "Not unlikely, Schmidt, as
you're looking at him now!" The new second officer who was indeed sitting at the captain's side, looked in surprise at the seaman.

"No, sir," stammered the man. "I mean the late second officer—
the one who died in the explosion!"

The captain banged the table. "You're drunk, man—get out!
You'll be in trouble for this!"

But the bluejacket stood his ground. He had seen the dead man,
he repeated—strolling up the gang-plank. And somebody else had
seen him, a man called Petersen. They would both swear to it, and
they were stone-cold sober.

The captain sighed.

"All right. Bring Petersen here, and let him tell his own fairy-
tale."

"He won't come, Herr Oberleutnant. He's up on deck, behind the
conning-tower. Shaking like a leaf, he is."

"Come along, gentlemen—we'd better investigate for ourselves,"
said the captain, and led the way on deck. There, indeed, was
Petersen, huddled in a corner, in a worse state of fear than his
shipmate. Patient questioning produced the information that he had
seen the ghost of the dead officer come up the gang-plank, stroll
along to the bows, and stand there, arms folded, looking calmly out
to sea. Petersen had rushed in panic to the corner where he was now
crouching. When he dared to peer out again the phantom had gone.

The captain was a reasonable man. He knew the symptoms of
drunkenness, and neither of these men had them. They had obviously seen something—but what? The captain had never believed

in ghosts; he did not intend to start now. In his opinion, someone was either playing a grisly joke or deliberately trying to undermine the crew's morale. He investigated every possibility, questioned everyone who might have had access to U.65, checked on the activities of other members of the crew. But no evidence of trickery came to light and he was obliged to let the matter rest. If a fake ghost had been produced with malicious intent, the faker must have been thoroughly satisfied, for the experience of the two sailors had infected the crew with panic. Petersen could not face the prospect of sailing on a death-boat. Two days before she was due to sail he vanished, risking the chance of a deserter's punishment.

Two years had passed since U.65's keel had been laid. In the latter part of 1917 the U-boat menace had slowly been overcome by the Allies. Until the summer of that year the terror under the sea had been destroying British shipping at an alarming rate. In May, 1917, out of every four vessels that left British shores one had not returned. In April, U-boats had sunk 840,000 tons of British and Allied merchant shipping. But by the autumn the picture was changing. The Ministry of Shipping had boosted production; the convoy system was working. Germany would have to think hard and quickly if she were to win the war at sea, and would need to throw every vessel she had into the fight. So U.65, which in less needful times might have been written off, was kept in service.

On New Year's Day, 1918, she cruised from Heligoland to Zeebrugge where she spent ten days. To the immense relief of the crew, nothing untoward happened. They felt that their luck might have changed with the calendar. Then orders came to sail into the Channel, in search of merchant and fishing fleets.

The evening of 21 January was wild as U.65 ran on the surface. A gale was rising, the sea threatened to wash over the conning-tower. It was a night to be down in the stuffy warmth of your cramped quarters if you were not absolutely obliged to be outside, like the starboard look-out, keeping his lonely watch. But suddenly, to his amazement, he saw that he was not alone. Below him, on the narrow, plunging deck, bathed in recurrent showers of spray, was the figure of an officer.

Cupping his hands, the look-out shouted a warning. "Don't stay there, sir—you'll be washed overboard!"

The officer looked up—with the face of the dead man who had appeared to Petersen and his mate. It was a frightened look-out who stammered out his tale to the captain as he came up through the hatch. Looking from the conning-tower, the captain was just in time to see a figure. By the time he had blinked and looked again it had gone.

We are not told what eventually happened to the deserter Petersen, or to the other sailor who had first seen the apparition. But to the captain the sight he saw on 21 January was a death-warning. A few weeks later, while U.65 was moored in a bomb-proof pen in a canal dock at Bruges, he went ashore to pass the evening at the local casino.

The air-raid sirens sounded as he walked through the streets: British planes were approaching. The captain's place was with his ship. He turned to go back—and a shell fragment severed his head from his body.

After this dreadful happening an official inquiry into the submarine's troubles was held. The investigating officer in charge of it did not transfer the crew wholesale to another vessel as they asked, but some neat paper-work resulted in most of them being drafted, one after another, to less alarming environments. The German Navy could not afford to have even one boat manned by demoralized men.

While the jinxed U-boat lay at Bruges it was someone's bright idea to have a pastor come aboard and hold a service of exorcism, bidding any devils who might be aboard to leave the ship, in the name of God. Nothing more tactless could have been planned. The new crew had heard unpleasant rumours from their predecessors and at this confirmation that there were devils sailing with them they became infected with fear. Ghost stories flew about until the captain issued an order that anyone who claimed to see even a vestige of a phantom would be heavily punished.

A first-hand account exists of the events of the next few months. A petty officer who served on U.65 from beginning to end of her career wrote frankly of his experiences and beliefs.

"U.65 was never a happy ship," he wrote, "though we were always fortunate in our officers. There was something in the atmosphere on board which made one uneasy. Perhaps, knowing her evil history, we imagined things, but I am convinced myself that she was haunted. One night at sea I saw an officer standing on deck. He was not one of us. I caught only a glimpse of him, but a shipmate who was nearer swore that he recognized our former second officer walk through the ship. He always went into the forward torpedo-room, but never came out again. Several of the bluejackets saw the ghost quite often, but others were unable to see it, even when it was pointed out to them standing only a few feet away.

"Our last captain but one would never admit the existence of anything supernatural, but once or twice, when coming on deck, I observed him to be very agitated, and was told by the men that the ghost had been walking on the foredeck. When the captain's attention was drawn to it he pretended to see nothing and scolded the watch for being a pack of nervous fools. But afterwards I heard from a mess steward at the officers' casino that our captain openly declared his ship to be haunted by devils."

During May, went on the story-teller, the U-boat was cruising up and down the Channel and off Spain. It was a terrible trip. After two days at sea a torpedo-gunner named Eberhard went screaming mad and had to be tied hand and foot and given morphia to quieten him. The treatment seemed to take effect and he was released and sent on deck for air in the company of another of the crew. No sooner did he reach the deck than he again went beserk. Pushing away the man at his side he leapt over the rail and went down like a stone. His body was never recovered.

Off Ushant, when high seas were raging, the chief engineer slipped and broke a leg. The submarine was hopefully chasing a British tramp steamer, firing with her deck-gun, when waves towered over the gun-crew and washed one of them, Richard Meyer, overboard. He, too, was never seen again.

Now the submarine began to avoid encounters with British or Allied boats that would otherwise have seemed her natural prey—for each one might be the instrument of the final fate that her entire crew were sure was in store for her. "The men were so depressed that they went about like sleep-walkers, performing their duties automatically and starting at every unusual sound." They were not reassured to find themselves approaching the dreaded Straits of Dover, where three U-boats—U.55, U.33 and U.79—had just been blown up.

Their fears were justified. They were shot at on the surface, depth-charged when submerged and Coxswain Lohmann received injuries from which he died. A battered U.65 limped away to Zeebrugge, almost sorry to have escaped. "Most of us felt that it was merely prolonging the agony."

At this point the story-teller, to his own immense relief, was attacked by such severe rheumatism that he was sent to hospital. He was visited there by another officer, Wernicke. The U.65 was due to sail next day, and Wernicke felt that it would be her last voyage—and his. He brought his messmate most of his personal belongings, to be sent on to his wife when the news everybody expected came.

It broke on 31 July. U.65 was posted as missing. Her end was as mysterious as everything else that had happened to her.

On 10 July an American submarine off Cape Clear, on the west coast of Ireland, sighted a U-boat. Through the periscope her number could be made out—it was U.65. Hasty orders were given for attack.

But just before the American torpedoes were fired, something happened that made it unnecessary. With a fearful detonation, U.65 blew up.

The reason was never known. Possibly one of her own torpedoes exploded in its tube, or another U-boat attacked her by mistake and made off without being sighted by the American. But there were no remains on which to hold an inquest.

The mystery of U.65, surely one of the strangest in naval history, was investigated thoroughly after the war by a psychologist, Professor Hecht, who published a pamphlet on the subject. In 1932 Hector C. Bywater, the English naval historian, followed this up with an investigation of his own, carefully checking all the evidence and testimonies. Neither Professor Hecht nor he was able to draw any firm conclusions. As a scientist, Dr Hecht did not care for the supernatural explanation, but he could not suggest a watertight rational one. Today, so far away in time from the events, it would be even more difficult to do so. The ghost stories are convincing and well attested, and there are many who have continued to believe that she was haunted.

On the other hand several who had sailed in U.65 felt that there was malicious human agency behind the "accidents". Were they the work of a British secret agent? It is hard to see how some of them were contrived, and others, like the washing overboard of the gunner, and the beheading of the captain, were obvious coincidences. But the whole thing has a very strong smell of sabotage. Another possibility is that the "ghost" and various disasters were the work of some Till Eulenspiegel with a grudge, or a taste for killing. If the last accident of all was a planned one, the saboteur must have blown himself up with his victims. He might have saved himself the trouble, for within four months the war was over, and 138 U-boats were meekly brought as captives into Harwich.

PHANTOM SAILORS AND SHIPS

The sailor has always been the most superstitious of men. Isolated by great stretches of ocean for months at a time from his fellow-men ashore, he remains more unsophisticated than the soldier, even in these days of vastly improved communications. And, far more than the soldier or the landsman, he is a prey to the "skyey influences" of legend and hearsay.

In the days before the blessing of electric light he lived through his night-watches in a world of illusory shadows and flickering lanterns, his eyes misled by sea-mist and moon-ray. Anything could happen at sea, however fearful or miraculous. Jack might be terrified, but he was never wholly surprised by phantom hulk, long-dead pirate, monster, mermaid, or (possibly most horrible of all) the apparition of a drowned messmate in his hammock. Whatever fears he suffered would all be repaid by the breathless interest of shore audiences when he spun his yarns in a Portsmouth tavern—perhaps adding a few colourful details which might earn him an extra pot of porter or pipeful of baccy from some sensation-hungry landlubber.

But even allowing for superstition and imagination, there are countless stories of strange appearances at sea which have been seen by whole crews at a time and by different ships on different occasions. Phantom sailors and the ghosts of their vessels seem to outlive land-wraiths, remaining as active in the days of steam as in those of sail. The theory has been advanced that the gradual fading of familiar spectres ashore is due to the glare of electricity, in which the

196

frail shadows cannot survive. On the dark surface of the sea conditions are most favourable.

This may explain the apparently endless voyage of the most famous of all sea-spectres, the *Flying Dutchman*. For some three hundred years Cornelius Vanderdecken has been afloat, ever since that day in the seventeenth century when he set sail for Holland from Batavia. Captain Vanderdecken had the reputation of being as merciless to his ship as he was to his men, pushing her on through storms and turbulent seas that would have deterred a more reasonable skipper. He had also a name for godlessness and blasphemy. On this particular fateful voyage his ship ran into violent headwinds when she reached the Cape of Good Hope. For nine weeks Vanderdecken and his weary crew urged her on, but in vain.

Understandably enough, it is said, Vanderdecken's patience gave way. He fell to his knees on the deck and cursed God, swearing a terrible oath that he would round the Cape if it took him till Judgement Day. And then followed a sequence of events which have since become legend.

As if unseen powers had heard him the winds rose higher. Vanderdecken's shrieked curses rose above their howl as he tramped the deck, shouting snatches of a blasphemous song. Suddenly, from the blackness of the night, a brilliant light shone out and formed itself into a dazzling figure which floated down until it rested on the poop of the ship. The sailors knelt and prayed, some taking it for an angel, others for the Holy Ghost. But Vanderdecken stood his ground, not even bothering to remove his hat, and to the gentle salutation of the visitant replied with a volley of curses. The figure stood unmoved, and Vanderdecken then did something which paralysed his crew with horror. He drew his pistol and fired at the spirit, ordering it to leave his ship at once.

The bullet made no impression on it. Then it spoke.

"Captain Vanderdecken, you have taken an oath to sail until Judgement Day, if need be. For your blasphemies you shall do so. You shall neither eat, dring, nor sleep, nor ever see your home port again, but sail the Seven Seas, a portent of disaster to all who see you. God is not mocked, Captain Vanderdecken!"

And so it is that ever since that night seamen have shuddered and crossed themselves at the sight of a phantom vessel rising from the waves, topmasts first, in the waters round Cape Horn and the Cape of Good Hope, or even farther south. Accounts of her appearance differ. Sometimes she seems like a sloop or a schooner. The *Bacchante*, sailing in 1881 between Melbourne and Sydney, saw her as a brig. Aboard the *Bacchante* was a young man who was to be King George V, and he among others saw the sight as recorded in the ship's log:

> "The *Flying Dutchman* crossed our bows. A strange red light, as of a phantom ship all aglow, in the midst of which light the masts, spars and sails of a brig two hundred yards distant stood up in strong relief ... on arriving there, no vestige nor any sign whatever of any material ship was to be seen either near or right away to the horizon, the night being clear and the sea calm. Thirteen persons altogether saw her."

One of those persons, the sailor who had first sighted her, fell from the fore top-mast crosstrees to his death on the deck, and at the next port the Admiral who had been aboard the *Bacchante* became fatally ill. The curse of the Dutchman still had power.

The phantom was said to have appeared in 1911 to a whaler, the *Orkney Belle*, off Reykjavik, her sails swelling in a non-existent breeze, her bows almost ramming the side of the real vessel. Then, from her depths, three bells sounded and, heeling to starboard, she drifted away. There is no record that disaster followed this appearance.

Another Dutchman who still wanders the seas is Captain Bernard Fokke, also of Vanderdecken's time. He was a brilliant navigator with a bad reputation, reputedly in league with the Devil. When his ship vanished it was said that he had been condemned by his Master to sail for ever. But a sight of him does not automatically bring misfortune. His legend and that of the two Waleran brothers of Falkenberg Castle in Lower Lorraine have become inextricably mixed with that of Vanderdecken.

The waters of the Solway sometimes carry ghostly longships, the dragon-prowed galleys of the days when Danish raiders were the terror of the seas. Two of these, which sank at their moorings taking all hands down with them, have been seen on light nights, and a venturesome little boat which went out to investigate them about the turn of the eighteenth century was caught up in the whirl of waters as the galleys sank from sight and vanished with them. Today nobody cares to take too close a look at those warrior-laden shapes, when they still appear.

Another ghost of the Solway is a shallop, sunk out of spite by a rival ferryman as it bore a young bride and bridegroom and their attendants across the bay. The man who wrecked it is still aboard, in skeleton form, and like Vanderdecken he brings ill-luck. A similar story is told of a ghostly bridal party seen off the Goodwin Sands.

The Gulf of St Lawrence, between Quebec and Newfoundland, is said to be haunted by a British flagship, one of a fleet sent by Queen Anne against the French. She sank under the cliffs of Cap d'Espoir in Gaspe Bay, but every year, on the anniversary of the tragedy, can be seen as a gay vision—her decks crowded with red-coated soldiers in mitre hats, her ports ablaze with light. In the bows stands an officer pointing landwards, one arm round the waist of a pretty girl. Then the lights fade, the vessel tosses, heels over and vanishes beneath the waves.

The coasts of New England are famous—or notorious—for ghost ships. The most terrifying is the phantom *Palatine*. When she is seen scudding down Long Island Sound it is a sign to prepare for storms—hardly surprising, in view of her story.

The *Palatine*, a Dutch trader, left Holland in 1752, with a load of emigrants bound for New England. She was not a happy ship. The captain and crew were a drunken, brutal lot who terrorized and robbed their passengers and their heavy drinking was probably responsible for the ship grounding on Block Island, though the island was the headquarters of wreckers, who may well have lured the *Palatine* with false lights. As she lurched ashore, bands of these human vultures fell on her, seized all they could get in the way of valuables, flung overboard or knifed any passenger who tried to resist and raped or dragged away any women who happened to take their fancy.

One woman remained, cowering below decks. Some stories call her a young mother whose baby had vanished in the pandemonium. She was driven from her hiding-place by a dreadful sound, the crackling of flames. The wreckers had fired the *Palatine*, having taken from her all they wanted. Now she was drifting out to sea with the wretched survivor aboard. The girl scrambled up to the deck and stood there shrieking for help, the flames mounting behind her. Then the masts crumpled, the decking fell in and the frantic figure vanished into the blazing inferno. Still, in those waters, the ship is seen, still the woman signals desperately for help and the "Palatine fire" lights up Block Island. But sceptics say that there may be a natural explanation of this light—perhaps phosphorescence.

Another burning ship is the *Packet Light*, wrecked, like Queen Anne's flagship, in the Gulf of St Lawrence. She appears first in the form of a ball of fire.

Not all sea apparitions are bringers of bad luck. Some, like phantoms on land, seem sent to give help or well-meant warnings. Captain Rogers, of the *Society*, was lucky enough to receive such a warn-

199

ing in the year 1664. The *Society* was cruising along the east coast of America, bound for Virginia, apparently in no trouble. The captain, thinking all was well, retired. He was deeply asleep when he was roused by a cold touch on his shoulder. "Turn out, captain, and look about," said a voice. The captain shook himself awake. There was nothing to be seen, but—a true sailor, ready to believe the unbelievable—he returned to his cot. A second time the touch and the warning came, and a second time he investigated, without result. The *Society* was about three hundred miles from land, he calculated, and could be in no danger of rocks or grounding. But a third warning came. This time the voice said clearly: "Go on deck and cast the lead." The captain obeyed—and found to his horror only seven fathoms. Hurriedly he gave orders to anchor. When dawn came, it was seen that the *Society* lay close inshore, under the Capes of Virginia, instead of far out at sea. The ghostly visitant had saved her from certain destruction.

Another lucky skipper was Joshua Slocum. He was an old professional master mariner who had worked his way up from a deckhand to being master of his own small barque.

But she had been wrecked and Slocum was reduced to working for two years in a Boston shipyard. Then, in 1892, the captain of a whaler made him a present of a little old sloop called the *Spray*. She was in poor shape after seven years lying beached, but Slocum vowed he was going to make her a new keel and ribs and worked for tl :teen months until the *Spray* was as good as new, if not better. Slocum then methodically turned an old dory into a lifeboat, took aboard supplies and equipment and on 1 July, 1895, put out from Yarmouth, Massachusetts, to sail round the world.

It was a lonely venture, even for a man of Slocum's sturdy character. He comforted himself by shouting questions to an imaginary hand as to how the voyage was going, answering himself. "All right, sir; all right, sir!" There were human contacts, of course—notably on the island of Fayal, in the Azores, where Slocum was given a warm welcome, plenty of fruit and an enormous white cheese. A young woman proposed that for a small wage she should accompany him as domestic staff. Slocum politely declined the offer and sailed for Gibraltar.

So tempting was the food given to him by the people of Fayal that Slocum spent a whole day doing little else but eating it. Not surprisingly, the prolonged banquet of cheese and plums resulted in agonizing stomach cramps. As Slocum battled with his digestion, the wind began to freshen. Painfully he crawled up on deck and struggled to get reefs into his sails, doubling up in agony every few moments. Then, having lashed the helm, he somehow got back to his cabin, where he lay writhing on the floor, delirious with pain. At last he fainted.

When he recovered his senses, the *Spray* was tossing about like a cork. He knew that he would have to take the helm, though in his state it seemed impossible. Once again he struggled on deck. There, to his incredulous amazement, he saw at the helm a tall man, in clothing which seemed unfamiliar. Reassuringly, the stranger swept off his cap with a smile and, as though it were the most natural thing in the world, introduced himself as the pilot of the *Pinta* which had set sail from Spain to the New World as part of the fleet of Columbus—in August, 1492, almost four hundred years before Slocum had put to sea. Slocum was to return to his cabin and rest, he said, while he guided the *Spray*.

Too ill and bemused to think clearly or even consider all this particularly extraordinary, Slocum accepted the offer and asked his helper to stay aboard until next day. As the ghostly pilot returned to his duty he turned smilingly to Slocum, remarking that it was never wise to mix cheese and plums—or to eat white cheese at all without knowing its origin.

And the *Spray* sailed safely on to Gibraltar.

A similar experience befell Captain Johansen of Liverpool in 1900, but this time the vessel was sailing from Gibraltar to America. She was the *Lotta*, a small open sailing-boat, manned only by Johansen and his fourteen-year-old son. Their daring venture was rewarded by eight days of calm weather. On the morning of the eighth day both Johansens were basking in the sunshine, the boy asleep. Suddenly Captain Johansen heard a voice speaking—"making a remark" was his impression. He looked round, but saw nobody except the sleeping boy. It had been imagination, he decided. Then another voice spoke—and more voices, chattering away in a language he did not recognize. The boy woke, and listened with his father. Both were amazed, and neither could think of an explanation.

Two days after this strange event, a gale blew up while young Johansen was at the helm. "Let go the jib-sheet!" called his father. But the inexperienced boy let go of the tiller in order to obey. The boat at once began to turn beam-on to the sea. It was a moment of peril, until, as if waiting for their cue, a band of four shadowy men materialized. One grasped the tiller and wrenched the little boat back on course.

All night he steered her, a strange figure in rough, primitive clothing, with an iron prop where his left leg should have been. He and his companions talked continuously to the Johansens, who could not understand a word they said, and showed them great kindness and goodwill. Seeing the *Lotta* in safe hands, father and son slept. When the sun rose, the spectral crew had vanished. Next night they returned and seemed to signal other craft which the Johansens could not see. Concerned at the possible effect of their weight (if weight they had) in the bow of the tiny *Lotta*, Johansen sent the boy to tell them to move aft. As he moved towards them they vanished once more, and never returned.

Johansen was hard-headed, sober and sceptical. He recorded the occurrences of 30 and 31 August, 1900, as a matter of solid fact.

Nearer to our own time was the curious incident that befell a British submarine during the First World War. One of the most popular submarine commanders at a south-east coast depot was Ryan—not his real name, but that given by the recorder of the story in 1919. He was a cheerful, handsome man, distinctive in appearance, popular with everyone, and there was general mourning when his submarine failed to return from one of its routine patrols off the Dutch shoals. Either the Germans had sunk Ryan or an accident had happened, for he should have returned to base in three weeks and eight passed without news of him.

Another submarine set out on the same trail, moving on the surface of the sea by night, submerged by day because of the danger from German aircraft patrols. Proceeding slowly one sunny morning, she broke surface with her periscope. As the second officer scanned the sea around them he suddenly turned and cried: "By Jove! There's jolly old Ryan waving to us like mad from the water!"

The commander instantly gave orders for the submarine to be surfaced, life-lines to be thrown out, and all preparations made for the rescue of their friend who had been so miraculously preserved. Excitement reigned on deck as they drew near the place where he had been seen. But not a trace of him was visible, though only a few minutes had passed. Had he sunk? He had not looked like a drowning man—indeed, his face had been cheerful and smiling. Had the officer made a mistake? No, he could swear it was Ryan. Had he been thinking of Ryan at that moment, and translated his thought into a vision? Not in the least, he said.

The commander gave orders to press on; it was no use searching farther and exposing themselves to danger. Then, just ahead, an object was sighted. As they skirted it carefully they saw what it was —a pair of mines, right in the path the submarine would have taken, if Ryan—or his spirit—had not appeared and made her change course.

A less welcome return by a departed mess-mate was that of the paymaster of the *Monongahela*, a corvette of the United States Navy in the First World War. The red-bearded, one-eyed "Pay" was much liked and convivial; too much so, for it was his fondness for whisky which eventually caused his death. As he lay dying on board, he said to his brother officers: "Dear boys, you've been good to me, and I love you for it. I've loved the ship, too, and I can't bear to think of leaving it. I'll come back if I can, and you'll find me in my old cabin, No. 2 on the port side."

It is a measure of sailors' superstition that cabin No. 2 was allowed to remain vacant for three cruises. Then a young Assistant-Paymaster joined the ship, and being a man not given to fancies took possession of No. 2 and settled comfortably in it. The *Monongahela* was homeward bound from South American waters, after a peaceful cruise, when, one April night, awful screams brought everyone running to Cabin No. 2. Outside, on the floor, lay the Assistant-Paymaster, unconscious. They brought him round and asked what had caused his collapse. "A corpse in my berth," he managed to say. "One eye and a red beard. Horrible!" He had wakened feeling strangely cold. In the bed with him seemed to be something chilly and wet. With indescribable horror, he had pulled the bedclothes aside to reveal the awful dead thing, seaweed entangled in its straggling beard.

The ship's company crowded round and peered nervously into the cabin. The berth was empty—but the blankets were wet, and on them a few trails of barnacled seaweed.

One of the oddest things about such stories of sea apparitions is that it is always ordinary seamen or officers who come back, never the great naval commanders of the past. What has happened to the spirits of Nelson, Howe, Collingwood, Rodney, Benbow, Blake? Nelson's shade, we are told, used to be seen walking briskly across the quadrangle of Somerset House, to disappear into the Admiralty offices.

Yet it is strange that they have never been seen transfigured aboard Britain's fighting ships at times of peril, urging the sailors on to victory and glory. Only one among them is reputed to return— Sir Francis Drake—perhaps because his body never came home, but lies "slung atween the roundshot in Nombre Dios Bay", the blue Caribbean rolling eternally about his bones. His ghost is not seen, but the legend goes that when England is in danger his famous

Drum of State will sound in warning. As he lay dying, he told those about him to bring it home to England and strike it when danger threatened. But it is said to have sounded sometimes of its own accord, summoning Drake to rise again and lead his Devon men against the Dons, or whoever the enemy happened to be at that time. The last occasion when it was heard, perhaps beating in triumph, was at the surrender of the German High Seas Fleet at Scapa Flow on 21 June, 1919.

There are tales, too, of Drake's haunting a fortress-like house on Dartmoor, and of the discovery under its lawn of the skeleton of a gigantic man with an Elizabethan watch by its side. Perhaps these were the remains of one of Drake's daring crews who sailed aboard the *Golden Hind*.

From the farthest shore of the Seven Seas to the galleon-haunted Goodwin Sands, phantom ships and their sailors float eternally, terrorizing or protecting the living. Are they really fog wreaths, shapes of illusion caused by changing light and poor visibility? Or the result of over-generous grog rations? Or, simply, what so many witnesses have believed them to be throughout the centuries?

They Came Back

THE RETURN OF ADMIRAL TRYON

It had been a glorious day—a Midsummer's Day, said some, which deserved to go down in history, simply as that. For whether the pundits agreed on the 21st or 22nd of June as the astronomical "middle of summer" in England, it was palpably obvious that the real heat of summer invariably came after this oddly chosen date.

But, in 1893, the 22nd of June was a glorious, sun-drenched scorcher. As many of Queen Victoria's subjects as had been able to get there had spent at least a part of that day paddling, or even recklessly bathing, along the circumference of Her Majesty's coastline. One refers, of course, to the "United Kingdom", as it is now styled. But the good Queen's empire spread across the world, even as far down and under the globe as Australia and New Zealand, where today, incredibly, it was mid-winter. Her Majesty, in 1893, had more coastline than she could add up.

In London, where the only coastline belonged to the not too salubrious Thames, the day had been almost alarmingly hot. And when the early evening brought a pleasant breeze to lower the temperature, it lowered at the same time the very real anxiety of Lady Tryon.

For scorching summer days are all very well at one's country seat, or even at the seaside, but to a London hostess giving a large and expensive ball indoors, in the most exclusive (and expensive) part of that metropolis, they are a nightmare. In those well-starched, well-stayed, days, many a guest would rue the fact that he or she had accepted, weeks in advance, an engagement which turned out to be formal, constricting—and hot. How much better to laze in one's own garden, eat a pleasant, simple meal, washed down with a few glasses of a lightly chilled white wine, rather than get oneself up in this boiled shirt, or those hideously uncomfortable stays.

And dance!

But to Lady Tryon, a Clementina still beautiful after thirty-four years of marriage to her gallant, handsome and distinguished naval officer, the elements decided—in the nick of time—to be kind.

Before the day was out, fate would have dealt her a crushing blow. But busy with preparation for the ball that evening at her Eaton Square home she was of course unaware of this and delighted by the change in the weather. There was now a pleasant chill in the air, and her hundreds of candles vied for attention with an unclouded summer twilight on the other side of the windows. Many of these she had even felt obliged to get the servants to close.

Have we perhaps suggested in an earlier paragraph that a hot and humid evening might have made some of Lady Tryon's guests rueful at having accepted her invitation? If so, then we hasten to correct the impression. She was one of the few exceptions for whom every single one would willingly have braved terrors far more alarming than dissolving stiff shirts or agonizing stays. For Lady Tryon's orchestra would be superb, her refreshments, delectable: but had Her Ladyship provided only a lone fiddler and a few dozen bottles of stone ginger beer, this would not have deterred anyone. For to be invited to one of Lady Tryon's parties was to have arrived in the really important sense of the word; one was somebody.

For this, Clementina deserved a good share of the credit. She was, as we have noted, still a beautiful woman, but, far more than that, she was intelligent, understanding and witty. With the whole of London society to choose from, a society excitingly bolstered by visiting dignitaries from abroad, Clementina could ensure that her parties were a success. But her real sympathy, her understanding of lesser mortals, were such that no wallflower stayed glued to the wainscotting, no embarrassed young man remained blushing in his corner, before the kindly Clementina swept into action. She had, they said, eyes in the back of her head. These took in everything, and then her lightning, hostess, brain decided whether the pair should be united, joined to each other—or linked with other partners.

Whichever decision she took, it rarely turned out badly, and it was common knowledge that more than one romance had flowered into marriage from a chance meeting in Eaton Square.

But Clementina would have been first to admit that much of her success stemmed from that of her extraordinary husband. Sir George Tryon was a truly remarkable man whose naval career to this moment spanned forty-five years of unblemished success. To mention his name in the Admiralty itself was to cause a hush to swell up and fill those high-ceilinged rooms, perhaps followed by the respectful query, "Wonder what the extraordinary fella's up to now?"

This very question, phrased perhaps more delicately, was being asked by half the guests at Lady Tryon's party.

Only a dolt would be unfamiliar with the fact that Tryon had been commanding the Mediterranean station for four years, since his elevation to Vice-Admiral in 1889. But news in those days took long to travel, and Vice-Admiral Sir George Tryon might be at one end of that inland sea or the other, and it would be weeks before anyone found out. He might even be ashore, perhaps in Naples, finishing another of his books on naval tactics.

"Yes," said Lady Tryon for the twentieth time that night, "it *is* the most awful shame he can't be with us tonight. He'll be back soon, his tour of duty's almost up, but at the moment his work takes up all his time. Yes, he's still with *Victoria*, his flagship. He'll be very upset he missed you: I'll write him——"

Within an hour there would be plenty of people, stunned people, to recall that phrase, "He'll be back soon". And there would be many others who would wonder why the woman who said those words should be the only person not to see him.

But George Tryon is not going to make his appearance just yet, and as he is a very real historical figure whose exploits occupy many chapters of naval history, we can await his arrival by having a quick look at a brilliant, eccentric, career.

He was the third son of Thomas Tryon, a country squire who ran a large estate, Bulwick Park, in Northamptonshire. There were gossips (even then) who could always dig up something slightly discreditable about the famous, and these maintained about the family: "Why, they were a lot o' immigrant Dutchmen, come over here and made their pile, they did——" Quite possibly this was true, but the "immigrant Dutchmen" were proud of having lived at Bulwick since early in the seventeenth century. They had been there at least when James I-and-VI (an immigrant if ever there was one) came to England.

George Tryon was a clever child, and it seems likely that his decision to join the Royal Navy, rather than do any of the hundred and one things open to a man of his standing and his gifts, came a little later than it usually does. He left Eton halfway through his studies and became a Royal Navy Cadet. As a result, he was not only older—at sixteen—than the others, but also a lot bigger, standing over six feet in his naval socks.

His first foreign posting was to that Mediterranean Station which half a century later would become his final, tragic, resting place. He travelled out as a sea-going midshipman and was then a little nonplussed by being landed as a soldier, to fight in that gallant and desperately needed "Naval Brigade" in the Crimean War. Midshipman Tryon distinguished himself as a soldier, and his promotion to lieutenant was accordingly sooner than it might have been. He owed it, his Admiral told him, "to the conduct and character you have displayed".

Not the sort of citation to set Fleet Street afire. But from a mid-nineteenth-century British Admiral, this was praise indeed. And George Tryon's promotion continued, ahead of his contemporaries, and always for some very good reason.

It was in 1867 when he had reached the rank of Captain that he took leave in Norway. Not for George Tryon the waters, placid or shallow, or both, of a British river: he would fish dangerously on a Norwegian fiord. And, incongruously, he was recalled from mid-fiord, in effect, to rush back to England and take charge of naval preparations for the Abyssinian War. He took this, like everything else, in his long stride, and although Britain's Abyssinian War may not have entered world history as a Great Campaign, no one could fault its naval handling. This involved not only the delivery of all British troops, against some opposition, but their continued supply. George Tryon's powers of improvisation were taxed to the utmost.

The Abyssinian War was only an episode. Already Tryon was working hard on two apparently unrelated aspects of seamanship. One of these, and far the more important, was Naval Intelligence, the ascertaining of what one's enemy plans to do and what he has to do it with. Naval Intelligence can accurately be called the brainchild of George Tryon, R.N. And it was during a brief spell of shore duty, with the Admiralty, that Tryon actually started the Department of Naval Intelligence.

His other naval interest seems odd indeed to us today: almost a circus trick. But we must remember that this was long before the day of wireless telegraphy, and secret cyphers. In the nineteenth century, if you wanted your fleet to perform a manoeuvre in action, you ran up flags. And you knew that the enemy could read them just as well as your own captains. So Tryon tried "Naval Manoeuvring Without Signals". His contemporaries were loud in their contempt. It was a circus trick, highly dangerous, suicidal. And more in the same vein.

Nowadays, with radar, cyphered W/T, scrambled R/T, and At-Sea-Conferences on closed-circuit television, it may seem strange that a fleet could only take action on the basis of a few brightly coloured bits of cloth hoisted up by the appropriately-named "flagship". But it is even stranger that a fleet could be made to perform the most intricate manoeuvres simply by the sudden movement of a *flagless* flagship.

"George Tryon gets away with this damn silly nonsense, doesn't get cashiered, as he damn well ought to be, simply because the damn fella's so far away." So said a contemporary, and there was an element of truth in his remark: Tryon was now a Vice-Admiral, knighted in Her Majesty's Jubilee Honours—and commanding the Australian Station.

But at the time of our party—22 June, 1893—Sir George Tryon was back in the Mediterranean where his career had begun. And although there were people who continued to object to the Naval Manoeuvring Without Signals he still from time to time tried out (and those who assured all who would listen that Tryon would try it on just once too often and send the entire British fleet to the bottom), it is sadly ironic that what now took place had no connection with the "flagless madness" which had earned him both fame and notoriety.

Back to Eaton Square. The party soon filled with happy, confident, guests. The string orchestra was playing, in those pre-ragtime days, soothing yet rhythmic music, and a few couples had taken the floor. Others were busying themselves with the champagne, the astonishing variety of hot and cold foods, all of which was being dispensed in the next room. Some of the guests had been invited for their first time to this social Mecca, and their delight at the honour was impossible to conceal. Others had been to Eaton Square before (Lady Tryon's Eaton Square, that is) and were confident that they had scaled the social ladder to its topmost rung. These too were happy.

By eleven the ballroom was crammed to overflowing with handsome men and women, and others who made up with the distinction of their manner and their attire for the shortcomings of nature. It had become almost uncomfortably warm, what with the exertion and the refreshment, and when the sweating orchestra played a final bar and put down their instruments for a short interval, most guests were relieved. Here was a chance, without feigning gout or the vapours, to cut back on the violent physical exercise and go back for another glass or two of bubbly.

No one ever knew how the big door at the east end of the ballroom opened. It had been closed all evening, on purpose, for it spoilt the look of the room when open. Perhaps, at eleven twenty-five, a servant or a presumptuous guest had swung the vast thing back on its hinges to let in a little cool air.

Discussing this for months later (and still in hushed whispers) the guests seemed to remember that there had been no one near the inside of the door, no one in the ballroom in a position to open it.

And no servant would admit to opening it from the outside.

Vice-Admiral Sir George Tryon, KCB, Commanding the Mediterranean Station, had simply opened it himself.

The music had halted, the centre of the floor was empty, but there were about fifty people, including Her Ladyship, standing around the edges of the room, talking. Lady Tryon had her back to the door and was talking to a voluble little man who had been invited for the first time, with his over-dressed, overweight, little wife, and was determined to make an impression. Some of the other guests had made no effort to conceal their contempt for the couple, and for this reason alone the wise and kindly Lady Tryon was listening to the man with every show of interest.

She noticed suddenly that her conversant's eyes were wide, were on stalks. He had stopped his flood of banality in mid-sentence. Lady Tryon noticed too that every other soul in the room had stopped talking. It was uncanny, as if every single person at her party had been struck dumb.

She turned round, took in that the east door of the ballroom was unexpectedly open, and felt the draught from it on her flushed cheeks. But what struck her most was the look of shocked surprise on the faces of each and every one of her guests.

She watched them as their eyes, their heads, swivelled, very slowly from east to west (or from left to right as she faced those on the far side of the empty ballroom floor). And what was most startling, in Lady Tryon's view, was the variety of expression displayed. For while everyone present seemed to evince surprise, there were superimposed on this basic human expression tiny variations as in music.

For some of her guests seemed surprised and delighted; others seemed surprised and uncomprehending; many of her own sex seemed surprised and about to faint.

One man, with an especially annoying surprised look on his face (brought on doubtless by an excess of the Bollinger) lurched forward and stuck out an arm, as if he were shaking hands with someone who existed only in the fuddled recesses of his own imagination. Lady Tryon made a mental note that although she would invite the humble Cartwrights again, Lord North would not be on her list for some time.

The eyes, the faces, continued their swivelling. To the hostess it was baffling, upsetting. The floor was absolutely empty and yet here were her guests, mouths open, gawping at it.

Whatever it was they were imagining, whatever "ghost" (and Her Ladyship had no time for "ghosts") had swept through her ballroom, it seemed to make its exit through the open western door. She watched in wonder and some discomfiture as her guests stood looking, inexplicably, at the open, empty, west door of the ballroom.

The string orchestra, glasses in hand, were in position. "Gentlemen," she said, and her voice had a strange, far-away, sound to it. "Gentlemen, play us something gay." The orchestra, as if this was the one thing they too most wanted from life, put down their glasses and broke into a lively air. Under its influence people began to move again. A servant closed the east door.

Two couples, ashen of complexion despite the perspiration pouring down their faces, got bravely up to dance.

Months later Sir Jasper Hoad was to explain what had happened. And his account, verified by every other guests present in the ballroom at eleven twenty-five that evening, would go down in history. "I had to summon up a bit of courage to ask Clementina if she'd seen what I'd seen. But I did. And she let me have it.

"'I don't know what *you* saw, Jasper. I only had the sensation of watching as all my guests ridiculously moved heads, like mechanical toys, from one side to the other. I saw nothing else, not a thing. Yet it seems that they imagined they were seeing something ...

"'But Clementina,' I said to her, 'it was George.' That's what I said to her, and she said, 'Don't be ridiculous, Jasper, George is at the far end of the Mediterranean. If he'd got back, on some sudden leave, well then obviously I'd have seen him too.'

"'Clementina, my dear. I only hope and pray that this means nothing sad and—supernatural. But I assure you that every man and woman in that ballroom saw your husband walk in the east door and out the west. He turned and smiled at everyone—including you, my dear—but he didn't stop. And when he got to the west door, well, he just vanished.'"

There were at least fifty people to back up Sir Jasper's story.

And the only person in the room who had not seen the ghost—for surely that was what it was—was Lady Tryon herself.

Few ghost stories, tales of the supernatural, lend themselves to exact chronology. But the visit of Admiral Tryon to his wife's ball does just this. He had died, tragically, as the first of his wife's guests was entering the Eaton Square house on the evening of 22 June, 1893. And each and every one of his wife's guests had seen him stride through the room.

What had happened?

After all, the Mediterranean Station was a fairly peaceful one in June, 1893. How had its Admiral died?

Through a tragic error in signalling.

No, it was not a "Manoeuvre without Signals"—very much the reverse. Tryon's fleet had moved that day to the coast of Syria. And off that coast, as his command approached in two columns twelve hundred yards apart, Tryon in his flagship *Victoria* gave the clear, well-understood, flag signal, "Invert Course in Succession".

For some presumably quite orthodox reason Tryon wanted his fleet the other way about before it dropped anchor for the night. But, incredibly, he had not made allowance for the fact that his *Victoria* and his Second-in-Command's *Camperdown* were very large ships, too big and unwieldy to turn inwards and reverse direction, like marching soldiers, and miss each other—in twelve hundred yards.

Horrified, the crews of every other ship watched, praying that Tryon was planning a wide unorthodox sweep which would take him and his column outside *Camperdown* and hers. *Camperdown* would thus remain on his port beam and not change, as the manoeuvre usually implied, to being on his starboard, and a great deal closer.

But no. Admiral Tryon's last words have been recorded as "It is entirely my fault". At that moment his *Victoria* had her starboard side cut open by the sharp steel bow of *Camperdown*.

Within seconds *Victoria*'s bow had dipped below the sea, her stern had cocked up. She capsized, sinking straight to the bottom.

Admiral Tryon was never seen again.

Except once. In Eaton Square that evening.

THE FIGURE ON THE WHITE ROAD

The funeral procession made its way slowly down the winding roads shadowed by the hills. The burial was over. Everyone was very tired. They were on their way home again. During the journey they had watched the sun set, and now in the valleys it was already dark as night.

At last they left the hills behind them and came out on to the white limestone highway where an illusion of daylight returned, as the white road reflected the light of the night.

It was then that the two men in the leading car saw a figure coming down the slope towards them.

"Who's that wandering about at this hour?" asked one.

"God knows," said the other. "So shall we in a minute. He's coming straight towards us."

The figure drew closer. First they identified the clothes, the black frock-coat which had been a familiar sight in the parish for many years, and then the face. A face they knew well. Yet horribly changed. The familiar turned unfamiliar. The nightmare come true.

"It's *himself*!" gasped one of the men. "Lord have mercy on us. It's *himself*!"

And who was "himself", the stranger who was yet no stranger, and who now terrified the mourners?

His name was Bernard McSweeney, and he belonged to a farming family which had lived for generations in this county of north-western Ireland. He had been born in the 1870s, and at first he worked on the land and lived with his mother in a little white-washed farmhouse. He was thoughtful, dreamy, always a little strange. His mother loved and admired him, but felt she never really knew him. When he told her that his humdrum life was not enough, that he wished to train as a priest in the Roman Catholic Church, she was proud of him, revered him for his decision. She talked about him to the neighbours: "My boy in the Church, he's so good, so clever. He's a wonderful son. My son—a priest!" To her it was better for a man to be a priest than anything else in the world.

Time passed, he did well, and at last was appointed priest in charge of the hill parish not far from the farmhouse of his birth.

In his work Father McSweeney proved efficient and conscientious. He carried out parish business without sparing himself. He kept his records straight. He gave excellent sermons, although sometimes they were rather above his parishioners' heads. He studied alone at night, and the light would shine out from his little house long after everyone else was in bed.

Strangers visited him, casual travellers and tramps. He would put up temporary beds for them in his own rooms. He never turned anyone away, however unpleasant they might seem to the more respectable people round about.

Apparently he did nothing wrong at all, and no one could pin down exactly what *was* wrong. Yet he wasn't liked. His parishioners never quite regarded him as a friend. They didn't come to him with their personal troubles. They were ill at ease with him. Some of them were even afraid of him, without knowing why.

Members of his own family, of which there were many in the area, felt separate from him. They put it down to the fact that he was the priest and they were ordinary farming folk. Yet somehow there had always been this chilling barrier between him and ordinary people.

When Father McSweeney was just over fifty he became ill, mysteriously. Within a few months he wasted away and died. People were shaken by the sudden death, but not particularly sorrowful. They hoped that someone less meticulous and more warm-hearted might take his place.

However, with family loyalty the surviving relatives planned to give him a grand funeral. The body was taken to his mother's house. She was old now, frail and distraught with sorrow. Her "boy in the Church" was gone for ever. She wasn't well enough to go with the funeral procession herself, but it would start out from her house and the mourners would all return to her afterwards.

So on the funeral day she stood alone at her door and watched the procession of traps, carts and cars—the year was 1925—start on its journey to the hills. Among those mountains was the rocky grave-yard where members of the family had been buried for centuries. Before the day ended, she was to receive the strangest visit of her life, but of course she had no notion of that at the time.

The long, sad procession reached the graveyard. Other parish-ioners and priests were there aside from the relatives. The burial ceremony was quiet and formal, and when it was over they all felt that sense of relief which follows a funeral. The dead man is under the ground. Life goes on for the living. So they were in a weary but placid state on the way back. Many of the women were asleep or half-asleep in the vehicles. All they wanted now was to reach the cosy farmhouse where the priest's mother waited, with her warm fire and hot drinks for them all.

But before they reached that bright fireside, they were to meet *himself* on the white limestone road. For the figure which steadily approached the leading car was the priest whom they had just buried ... the priest, not in graveclothes, but in the frock-coat in which they'd last seen him alive.

After the first gasps of horrified astonishment, those who saw him were too petrified to speak. They could only stare.

The priest turned his head away slightly as he passed the leading car and walked the full length of the following vehicles. But they noticed how horrible he looked. His skin seemed lividly white, far whiter than living pallor. His eyes were wide open and stared with-out blinking. They glittered diamond-bright. His teeth, strong and white, seemed to be thrust forward, the lips drawn back and the gums exposed.

Everyone saw him, except a few who were sleeping, or who were on the far side of the vehicles so that their view was blocked by others craning forward.

When he had passed the last car, he disappeared round the bend of the road—as if he had never been.

A wave of terror passed through the whole procession. Some of the women wept with fear. There were whispered exclamations and questions: "Did you see him?" ... "Yes, but I couldn't believe my eyes. Did *you*?" ... "I saw him. I thought I must be dreaming" ... "You weren't dreaming. I saw him too" ... "So did I" ... "And I" ... "He looked like some devil" ... "Or a wolf" ... "It couldn't have been him!" ... "But it was! It was himself!" ... "I always knew there was something terrible about him" ... "This is why we never liked him" ... "Sh, don't speak ill of the dead" ... "The dead should stay buried!"

Panic, passion, anguish, terror. They had seen a dead man walking and were frightened out of their wits.

"Shall some of us go after him?"

"No! No! Let's get home!"

No one was placid or sleepy now. The cars and traps and carts were full of people who had never felt more awake in their lives. They put on speed. They wanted to get away from the white limestone highway. They wanted the security of walls about them, a fire to warm them and curtains to shut out the dark and whatever creatures might be wandering there.

But as they drew nearer to the farmhouse where Mrs McSweeney waited, they stopped and held a conference. What should they tell her? Anything or nothing?

"Nothing," said one of the mourners. "Not a word of this to his mother. We must all swear to keep our mouths shut. The poor woman's grief-stricken enough without hearing a story like that about her son."

"Are you sure it was him?" asked a woman who had been asleep through it all.

Those who had seen him were sure, and they were numerous. This was no case of one man's flight of fancy or one woman's succumbing to hysteria.

Now they gathered in the porch outside the mother's house. They were still whispering together, whispering voices among the whispering trees, but on one thing they all agreed—Mrs McSweeney was to be told nothing of the vision they had seen.

Calming themselves, exercising all their self-control, they knocked on her door, ready to smile and greet her comfortingly when she opened it. But she didn't come. The house was silent. Surely she should have been waiting eargerly for their return, listening for their knock.

"Hello! We're back!"

"Open up, darling. We're here!"

They knocked again and again. Nothing.

On either side of the porch were two small windows through which one could see into the hall. They had hesitated to peer inside, like people looking through keyholes, but now one of them did.

"Well, can you see anything?" he was asked.

"Yes. She's there. She's lying face down on floor. We'll have to break in."

They broke open the door and gathered round the prostrate figure of the old woman.

"Is she dead?"

"I don't know. She's as cold as ice."

"No, she's not dead. She's breathing. Oh, thank God!"

They called to her and chafed her hands. They lifted her on to her bed. At last she opened her eyes. They gave her something to drink: "Drink this, darling. You're all right now. You fainted, that's all. And no wonder, after what you've been through."

All around her they hovered, trying to give her solace, but all she could do was stare ahead of her in horror.

"What happened?" they asked her. "Did something happen to frighten you?"

"Yes. I had—a visitor."

"A visitor? What sort of visitor?"

"Where is he?" she said.

"There's no one here but yourself and us. You're quite safe. Who was this visitor?"

"I must have fainted from the shock of seeing him. You won't believe me. I don't know how to tell you."

They exchanged glances, half-knowing what was coming.

"Tell us what happened," they said.

"What time is it?" she asked.

They told her the time.

"Then it happened about half an hour ago. I heard footsteps outside, then a knock on the door. At first I thought it might be you, back earlier than I expected. Then I realized it couldn't be all of you or I'd have heard the carts and cars. Those new-fangled cars make quite a noise, don't they?"

"Yes, go on. You heard a knock on the door ..."

"I couldn't think who it would be. Everyone was at the funeral. Who would be calling on me? So I looked out through the side-window to see who was there."

She began to gasp and wail: "It was him! It was my Bernard! He was standing there by the hedge just as if he were still alive. Yet I saw his dead body in the house only this morning—so I knew it couldn't be him—but it *was*!"

"You saw his face?" they asked her.

"His face—his poor face—such a terrible expression. The light

219

from the window shone directly on to him. He was turned away from me a little, but I saw his features all twisted—his teeth jutting out—his lips pulled back—his eyes glaring as if he were staring at horrors—and his skin was as white as—as white as——"

"As a ghost?" someone murmured.

"Yes. I believe I saw the ghost of my son," she said.

"What did you do? Did you let him in?" And they looked round warily, half-expecting the dead priest to walk into the room, baring his teeth at them and fixing them with that inhuman glare.

"Of course I was going to let him in, ghost or no ghost," said the mother proudly. "He was still my boy, whatever terrible thing had happened to him. I moved to open the door, but then I was so terrified that my legs went weak under me, and everything went black. I don't know what happened after that—until you came. Please believe me! I really did see him!"

Her relatives exchanged glances and nods. They changed their decision to say nothing.

"We believe you," said one of them. "We saw him too."

And they told her of the figure on the white road.

None of the members of that family, especially the mother, ever forgot that day of the funeral when the man who had just been buried appeared to them afterwards with an aspect of fleshly life—and a look of cruelty which they had often sensed beneath the surface of his quiet manners, and which had made them withdraw from him and fear him.

He had always been a secret man, and he left this fearful mystery behind him. He was not seen again.

THE LOVERS OF PORTHGWARRA

Down in south-west England, they will still—almost eagerly—tell you the story of the Lovers of Porthgwarra. And if you ask them, at that little fishing village, they will even show you Sweethearts' Cove.

The story has been current so long, its details virtually unchanged, that it would be a brave man who questioned its veracity. The actual Sweetheart Rock is still there to be seen, washed smooth by the surging tides of that south-western coast, and no doubt it is even smoother now than when Nancy and her William sat there a hundred and fifty years ago.

But, to start at the beginning.

Nancy Hocking was a strikingly beautiful black-haired girl, with the hair and features that belong to that ancient corner of Britain. She was a small-boned, delicate-looking creature, whose long black tresses were strikingly set off by a pair of wide-open, light-blue eyes. By the age of nineteen she had had many suitors and rejected them all.

And then, to the great distress of her parents, she fell hopelessly in love with a sailor, William Pullen.

There was nothing wrong with William; he was a fine-looking man excelling at games and much admired by the young boys of the area. Nor did he lack for adoring females who wished to make him their own for ever. But to Nancy's parents, no husband could be less suitable. Sailors, in their estimation, were rough, drunken creatures. And although this was the most arrant nonsense in William's case (as it is in the case of most sailors), there was no denying their second objection: sailors went away for long, long periods.

The very fact that William was the reverse of a rough, drunken creature provided an adequate reason for his own mother to raise objection to the union. He was a wonderful son who supported her in her widowhood from his earnings at sea. And he was greatly admired and respected by all from old Mother Treglown of Porthgwarra, whom in his warm-hearted way he often helped behind the counter of her general shop, to the children whose toys he repaired when they broke.

William's mother was none too keen to be exchanged, as she saw it, for another, much younger woman. But when at last she met Nancy (for the Pullens, mother and son, lived in the neighbouring village of Porthcurno), she fell almost as much under the girl's spell as her son. She took to Nancy immediately.

But unremitting opposition continued from Nancy's parents. If William got himself a job on dry land—after all, he did seem to be good at everything he put his hand to—they might change their minds. As a sailor—they would ever remain bitterly opposed to such a union.

The young couple gave this a lot of thought. But seafaring was so obviously in William's blood that Nancy knew a marriage on her parents' terms would make him unhappy. William hopefully pointed out that he would soon have command of his own small vessel, and as captain he could and would take his wife wheresoever he went.

Soon? Well, that did depend on a number of factors. But there was no reason to believe that within five years, with the money he was saving and the blessing of the line which employed him, he could not be his own skipper. And then Nancy would see sights of which she had never dreamed, places where beautifully coloured birds sang and fluttered among tropical trees, and where strange and exciting wild animals roamed. And she could bring back rare and precious presents for her mother and father.

Still this wasn't good enough for that stubborn pair. Five years was a long time, and in any case they didn't want their daughter gallivanting at great risk over the seven seas. They wanted her in Porthgwarra, married to a man who worked in a shop, or at a steady trade. Or even to a farmer. Young people heeded their elders much more then than they do now; and so when the time came for William's ship to sail, taking him away for three months, there was no question of their getting married first, as they both so dearly wanted.

But on the night before William sailed for the Spice Islands, they arranged to meet in a little cove beyond the village. There they could sit, as they had in the past, with their arms about each other. They could say again, to the murmuring of the sea, the thing lovers say. And next time, for sure, if William were not yet in a position to take Nancy with him, they would get married none the less—and the devil take all their parents. He would set her up in a little cottage he had already found, many miles from Porthgwarra.

He might even get a long shore leave, these things could be arranged, so that he could get a shore job for a few months. And then they could live happily together as man and wife.

So, on this March night, at different moments and from different directions that there might be no gossip, they arrived at their cove. The milky whiteness of a full moon was streaming down—not an entirely unmixed blessing, as it meant they could be seen by some chance passer-by. Soon they were sitting, arm in arm, with their bare feet on chilly sand. "I love you, William," she said. "You'll never forget that, will you?"

"How could I, my darling? And I love you, too. I'm keeping myself for you, Nancy, you must believe that——"

"And I'll be faithful—if I have to wait forever——"

"You won't have to wait long. I promise."

And so they sat, till the tide turned, and the water started to rush in again. At Porthgwarra the tide is rapid, channelled in the throat of the bay, and once it starts to come in it is a foolish man indeed who stays there, admiring it. Within a few minutes he can be surrounded by seething water, and will need to be a strong swimmer to regain the shore. They left their rock with the water beginning to lap their ankles. A few hundred yards' walk together arm in arm, a brief embrace, and they parted to go to their separate homes.

William's ship sailed with the next day's ebb tide for the Spice Islands. They had said their farewells and Nancy watched from a distance as the three-masted vessel made its way out to the open sea. It headed down the bay, its square-rigged sails filled with the easterly wind, and in a few minutes it had shrunk to a tiny speck. A moment later it slithered gently over the horizon.

Later that day Nancy went to the village shop, old Mother Treglown's general emporium. Mother Treglown was a kindly soul and had good reason to feel affection for the sailor who so often lent a hand when her rheumatism made a shopkeeper's job almost impossibly painful. She knew all about William's love for Nancy, and approved. When Nancy came in, the old lady served her and then, as the shop was otherwise empty, asked her back to the little store-room and gave her a glass of mead. She took one herself and they clinked them together.

"To William's speedy return," she said. "And then to your marriage and a long, happy life together."

"Thank you," said Nancy, a tear trickling down her cheek. "But you know, Mrs Treglown, I sometimes think it can never happen. My parents, it doesn't seem as if they'll ever change. Not for years——"

"Nonsense, my child," said Mother Treglown. "It will happen, and soon. And you will be happy, forever."

Forever. Nancy took that word and cherished it.

But the months went by, and never a word came from William, nor news of his ship. At first, this was not too alarming, as ships were often diverted at various ports of call, and sent on different, often very long, detours. And communication with home was difficult at the best of times, for these were days before wireless or telegraph. But after five months without a word Nancy was not only upset, she was terrified. Surely, even if the ship were being re-directed right round the globe, it must pass other vessels and be able to send messages home via them?

Nancy's heartless parents were openly pleased. They began to extol the virtues of other young men in and around Porthgwarra.

Then Nancy vanished.

Her parents now became filled with remorse. Obviously the girl, goaded to breaking point and tense with strain, had left them to go to London. There was a coach once a week, and her disappearance was noticed a few hours after it had left.

But even now her parents' feelings were more of shame than of compassion. If marriage to a sailor were bad, the prospects for a young, attractive and penniless girl in the sinful capital were appalling. They suddenly took to attending both matins and evensong each Sunday, and whatever other service might be conducted by the rector during the week.

But not a word from Nancy.

Nor—and the months continued to go by—from William, or his ship. Spring had ripened into summer, autumn was slipping towards winter. And then—to the whole village's delight—a letter for Nancy, in William's hand, from New Zealand, and in the same post-coach delivery, one from William for his mother. At last—everyone would know the news!

Nancy's parents controlled their eagerness to rip her letter open and see what had caused the long delay which had indirectly made their daughter leave them. The information was supplied by William's omther, who came in from Porthcurno to show her letter to Mother Treglown. William explained that in his much-altered trip he had written at least weekly and posted a large batch of letters in South Africa. Five months later when he himself was worried that he had got no reply to the Australian address he had given, he learnt that the vessel carrying all his letters had sunk off Lagos.

It was exactly a week after this letter had been read, and the one for Nancy placed carefully, unopened, on the mantelpiece, that the girl appeared again in Porthgwarra. It was old Mother Treglown, hobbling up the High Street, who saw her. At first she couldn't believe her eyes. The girl was changed in some odd, indefinable, way. "Nancy, oh Nancy——" she croaked, and the girl turned round. She didn't smile, though.

"It *is* you, Nancy?"

"Yes, Mrs Treglown, it is."

"And—you've been away?"

"Yes, that's right. I've been away——"

"You've been sadly missed, Nancy."

The girl said nothing.

"And would it be prying if I asked you where you'd been? You don't have to tell me, you know." Mrs Treglown, Old Mother Treglown, with the middle-aged daughter in Bristol, knew about these things. There were some with long memories and unkind tongues who called her Miss Treglown. Whatever her title, the old lady knew all about girls who left the village, went somewhere distant with a story of widowhood or separation and there gave birth to a child. Sometimes it was fostered out, sometimes it was properly adopted into some kind family.

"You wouldn't be prying, Mrs Treglown. But—oh, I've been a long, long way——"

And that seemed to be the end of it.

"You've seen your parents yet? You know there's a great thick letter on their mantelshelf for you, from William? But you haven't been home?"

"I haven't been home."

"Oh. I see." Mrs Treglown felt she ought to leave well alone, but she couldn't help rambling on. "You see, Nancy darling, he wrote to his old mother too, and he told her he'd been writing ever so often. (So he'd have been writing ever so often, maybe much more often, to *you*.) And of course their ship was ordered all over the place, but they managed to post their letters somewhere, can't remember where he wrote that it was. But the awful thing was, Nancy, that the ship bringing all those letters home, it just sank somewhere. Now, I think you ought to go along home, even if you don't want to see your old folks, and I know they weren't very kind, but they didn't understand, you see, and just open that letter——"

Now while this conversation, or perhaps monologue, was going on, one of Porthgwarra's fishermen, Gerald Matthews, walked by with his wife, Lily. They gave a start of recognition, and Lily—who loved to be the purveyor of news—dragged her husband quickly away. This was a tasty tit-bit of a happening, and she must away and tell Rosie Tregunna.

"Thank you, Mrs Treglown." And the girl walked away very slowly, without any sign of haste or enthusiasm, almost as if she had no idea of where she wanted to go. Almost as if she were a stranger in her own village.

The old lady shook her head in dismay and wonder and limped back towards her shop.

Later that afternoon Nancy's mother was in the shop, looking pale and drawn. "Something very strange has happened," she said.

"Oh?"

"Yes, it's very worrying, uncanny. Someone's come and taken that letter for Nancy. And you know—the worst thing of all? We were out, and the door was locked. And still somebody managed to get in—and steal that letter." The woman bit her lip as the tears started to her eyes.

"But—but didn't you see Nancy?" asked Mother Treglown.

"No. And that's another strange thing. For it's all round the village she was seen talking to you. But there's no sign of her anywhere."

Old Mother Treglown was strangely disturbed. She began to busy herself among the big, dusty jars of sweets. She filled up a large paper bag of the bulls-eyes she knew Nancy was always fond of, and which she would give the girl when she came in, as assuredly she would.

But would she?

Mother Treglown found herself trembling. She recalled now the strange, almost other-worldly look about the girl. The hopelessness of manner, the unfocussed eyes, the sense of utter forlornness she had conveyed now struck a chill into the old woman. It was almost as if—oh, my God, no. But yes, it was almost as if she were already dead.

She shuddered, then with a quick shake of the head put such thoughts behind her. She looked at the tense, tear-stained face of Mrs Hocking, and although she had never liked the woman, her kind old heart melted.

"She'll be back, directly," she said comfortingly. "You'll see."

But Nancy did not come back. There was no doubt about it; she had vanished again as suddenly as she had reappeared, and the whole village was in an uproar of speculation about it.

About a week after her strange meeting with Nancy, as November was moving into a surprisingly warm first week of December, and on a Sunday, when her shop of course was closed, Old Mother Treglown took a "constitutional" during the afternoon. She often went great distances, for one so lame, and today she planned to hobble with her stick perhaps a mile along the sea front before it grew dark.

To her delight, she saw Nancy walking ahead of her. Her unexpressed doubts were suddenly relieved. Nancy was here after all.

She didn't call out, just went steadily along leaning on her stick, and watched the pretty young girl go down on to the moist sand and walk out seawards for a few yards. Placidly she sat on a large, smooth, rock, hands on her lap. The old lady watched for a moment, then decided it was none of her business and went on the little bit extra she'd planned. She was delighted though that the "mystery" of Nancy had been resolved. For reasons best known to herself and not unconnected perhaps with her parents' previous hostility, she must have been living somewhere close by for these last few days.

Mrs Treglown didn't go much farther, for a wintry wind got up very suddenly and dark clouds filled the sky. She turned back and was soon at the cove. Nancy was still there. But now, incredibly, seated beside her on that smooth rock was William Pullen. There was no possible doubt about it. Their arms were about each other, their heads were close together. Anyone could see they were very much in love.

But had they seen how fast the tide was coming in? With this sudden icy wind it was fairly racing up the cove and already it was on three sides of the rock they were sharing. The old lady could see the danger in a situation of which the lovers, totally rapt in each other, seemed quite unaware.

"Nancy! William!" she croaked at the top of her lungs. "Come back, come back!"

They paid no attention.

Horrified at the prospect of imminent tragedy, she started to hobble down towards the sand. And there was very little sand left, for the tide was at the flood. "Come back, oh please come back——" and she found herself weeping with distress. And then she missed her footing and fell on what was, fortunately, the last few square feet of uncovered beach.

It took her quite a time, with the stick flung from her hand and floating in the angry water, to get to her feet. And when she looked out seawards again, there was only the flat top of the rock still visible over the waves. And no sign of the young people. She stared in horror for a few moments, then began to move back to Porthgwarra as fast as her legs would take her. To the first man she saw she shouted, "Two folks caught by the tide, down by the cove, swep' away!"

Men rushed to the scene, launched a boat, made every effort to find a trace of the "two folks". Eventually with tide full in and almost complete darkness, they abandoned the search.

Back in Porthgwarra Mother Treglown told her story. People believed half of it, but not the other half. She was so certain of what she had seen that they were inclined to believe she had seen two people at the cove; but Nancy Hocking and William Pullen? True, the village was still buzzing with the strange, brief reappearance of Nancy; but William was still at sea—everyone knew that.

The next morning brought another shock. Mrs Pullen arrived breathless and grief-stricken from Porthcurno. She went straight to the general store, for Mother Treglown was one of her few friends in Porthgwarra. Almost too overcome to speak, she managed to say slowly that due to an extraordinary oversight she had received a very delayed letter from the shipping company which employed her son, telling her that William had been drowned. His ship had been lost with all hands two months ago.

Slowly, she continued: "The crew came from all over England. It must have been common gossip in all the big towns; but no news ever comes to remote villages in Cornwall. I've been thinking that Nancy in London—and I've never felt closer to the girl than now— must have known about it weeks since."

She paused for a moment, sobbing quietly.

"Oh, dear Mrs Treglown. I no longer wish to live. And I know that girl loved my son yet more than me. I think she will have died ..."

Mother Treglown had gone deathly white.

* * *

As time wore on Nancy Hocking never reappeared; nor was any word heard of her. Her death or disappearance came to be accepted by all.

RAYMOND

The broad categories of human personality known as the extrovert and the introvert have always existed and been expressed through the ages in the artist, the contemplative and the mystic on the one hand, and the man of action on the other. But if ever there was an extroverted age it occurred in nineteenth-century Britain, when the rapid development of industrial technology combined with a scientific outlook of unqualified materialism to give man the feeling that he himself was a finished product, a triumph of nature requiring no further improvement, and progress in future would depend on the exploitation and manipulation of the outside world. Though not exactly in sight, Utopia was felt to be just around the corner.

This blind, astonishing optimism, a bubble of romantic fantasy, should long since have collapsed in the debris of two world wars and their aftermath; yet peoples and governments are still reluctant to abandon the dream that man is no more than the active factor in an economic, financial and industrial equation and once that has been solved he will be free. Though we all know that this is not true, we cling to the belief because reality is more complicated, offering no Utopias, and is therefore unpalatable.

Fortunately in this situation nature herself supplies a corrective by making us uneasy, even neurotic, so forcing us to ask spiritual questions too long neglected: who are we? Why are we here? What must we do? What is the path of evolution for the human race and how can we follow it instead of taking some side-turning? To

230

answer these questions, particularly the last one, we require not only intuition, which does not work reliably for everyone, but a much firmer basis than we yet possess of incontrovertible knowledge about life, the universe and human nature, and in this search all lines of inquiry must be pursued, including that of parapsychology or psychical research.

The Society for Psychical Research was founded by a group of Cambridge scholars in 1882 in the same decade as Freud began his study of psychology, not, as is often thought, with the prime object of exploring the question of survival after death, but to observe and study with the most rigorous objectivity all phenomena called paranormal, for instance telepathy, clairvoyance, telekinesis (movement of objects at a distance), poltergeists, apparitions, hauntings and mediumistic powers; though the interesting fact is that, without anyone's volition, the survival question was forced on its attention at a comparatively early stage. In this development a leading part was to be played by Sir Oliver Lodge.

Oliver Lodge (1851–1940)—he was knighted for his services to physics in 1902—was descended from solid middle-class clergymen and school-teachers on both sides of the family. As a young man he had interested himself in physics and mechanics, obtaining his doctorate at University College, London, and in due course became a pioneer in research into electricity, the phenomena of electrolysis, electro-magnetic waves and wireless telegraphy. In 1879 he was appointed Professor of Physics at Liverpool University, became a Fellow of the Royal Society in 1887 and from 1900 to 1919 served as first Principal of the new Birmingham University. In his objective desire to add to human knowledge and his rigorous scientific approach he was typical of the scrupulous and serious-minded intellectuals who became associated with the Society and its endeavours. But it was only slowly that he became directly involved.

As a young man in the 1870s Lodge had met a student named Edward Gurney who was collecting data on hauntings and apparitions, and somewhat despite himself had been impressed by Gurney's seriousness and his hypothesis that such phenomena might be due to some unexplored extra-sensory faculty operating between agent and percipient.

Over the years Lodge became acquainted with other intelligent men who were exploring the same territory and one of them, who was to be of lasting importance in his life, was a classics scholar, F. W. H. Myers. At the same time impressive facts about telepathy were accumulating until, as interested students, Lodge and his friend heard in the early eighties from William James, brother of the novelist Henry James, who was professor of Psychology at Harvard University. James reported that he had come across a remarkable medium named Mrs Piper who in a trance state seemed to get in touch with the spirits of the dead.

In 1889 Mrs Piper was invited to England and Lodge had a sitting with her, his first ever with a trance medium, in which he was astonished to hear the well-remembered voice of an aunt who had died speak to him through the medium, reminding him in a very characteristic and energetic manner that she had promised to "come back" if she could. From this sitting Lodge got the strong impression that personality survives, but to exclude the possibility that Mrs Piper had recovered some of his own memories by telepathy he arranged a second sitting. At this, information was given about the early life of deceased relatives of a yet older generation, information which was subsequently confirmed by their surviving contemporaries.

Lodge now felt that a *prima facie* case for survival had been established, but he continued to look at further evidence objectively, bearing in mind other possible explanations of the extraordinary phenomena which he witnessed or were reported by his friends. But other explanations were increasingly unsatisfactory, and over the years he personally became convinced that at least something of the human personality survives death and that "communication is not easy, but it occurs". Then came August, 1914.

Lodge had twelve children, six boys and six girls, and his youngest son Raymond was at that time twenty-five. With a marked gift for organization and engineering, he had been hoping to work with two brothers in a firm they had started for making sparking-plugs, but within a month he had joined the South Lancashire Regiment for training as an officer and by March, 1915, was in the trenches in Flanders.

Meanwhile, mediums had been receiving a mass of material purporting to come from Lodge's close friend Myers, who had died in 1901, which further substantiated survival. Now, in August, 1914, Mrs Piper, herself ignorant of classical literature, received a message allegedly from Myers containing a quotation from Horace which when correctly interpreted spelt out a warning to Lodge that he would suffer a severe blow but would receive comfort. Five weeks later, on 14 September, 1915, his son Raymond was killed in action.

On 25 September, Lady Lodge, whose identity was unknown to

the medium, was having a sitting with another person when the message was spoken by the medium in trance: "Tell father I have met some friends of his." Lady Lodge: 'Can you give any name?" Answer: "Yes, Myers". Two days after this, Lodge himself had an anonymous sitting with the same medium, Mrs Leonard, who operated through a "control" believed to be the departed spirit of a young girl acting as intermediary for the conveyance of messages. This girl, who called herself "Feda", said that a young man was with her and accurately described Raymond, though she only gave his name as "R". R, she said, would be as a cross to his father, dark on one side (the suffering caused by his death) and light on the other, "because he is going to be a light that will help you ... to prove to the world the truth", in other words the truth of survival.

From this time on for many years Sir Oliver and Lady Lodge and some of their children were in regular communication with "Raymond" through several trance mediums operating with their controls, and also at their home near Birmingham when they were usually in touch "through the table", a table round which they sat tilting so many times for each letter of the alphabet and for "yes" and "no". This sounds a tedious method, but in time a very happy and intimate atmosphere is said to have developed in which the table almost acquired an identity, beating time on its own, for instance, when the family sang songs, shaking apparently with laughter at jokes, tipping over, righting itself and floating about the room, as well as answering through the alphabet.

Through these and the trance experiences in which the mediums' controls seemed directly to convey Raymond's words, gestures and manner of speech the surviving members of the family became convinced that he was alive, the evidence being of two kinds: (1) intimate knowledge of past and also current family affairs, and in some cases of facts unknown but subsequently corroborated; (2) an overwhelming impression of Raymond's surviving personality, not as a mere synthesis of family memories, let alone as a product of wishful thinking, but as something dynamic, independent and unpredictable in its action. To the family at any rate any suggestion that all this might have some other explanation or that all the evidence produced at sittings with mediums was the result of telepathy between the people involved was past belief.

So it was that, early in 1916, when thousands of families had been bereaved through the war, Sir Oliver Lodge was encouraged by Raymond to produce a book for their comfort that would show the evidence for survival. The result was published as *Raymond*, a new edition being produced in 1922 called *Raymond Revised* which was enlarged to contain more recent material.

Some of the evidential material can be summarized here, though it will be realized that the part under (2) above is not amenable to summary and in any case depended on recognition by a member of the family. An early and most striking piece of evidence of the living intelligence of Raymond concerned a group photograph taken in France a few days before he was killed. Until it was mentioned no one in the family knew of its existence. The factual record, in which dates are important, runs as follows: extract from an anonymous sitting between Lady Lodge and a medium named Peters on 27 September, 1915. The control is speaking. "You have several portraits of this boy ... one where he is in a group of other men. He is particular that I should tell you of this ... You see his walking stick ..."

Being ignorant of the photo, neither Sir Oliver nor his wife followed up this clue until after 29 November, 1915, on which date they received a letter from a woman unknown to them, a Mrs Cheves, who was the mother of Raymond's battalion medical officer. This lady reported that her son had sent her copies of a group photograph in which Raymond appeared and would the Lodges like one? Lady Lodge replied with a grateful yes, but for some reason the photo did not reach her until the afternoon of 7 December.

Meanwhile, Sir Oliver had had the brainwave of questioning Raymond about it before the copy arrived and on 3 December, in a sitting with Mrs Leonard, he was given the following information through "Feda", her control. There were a dozen or more men in the photo grouped close together, some standing and some sitting. Raymond was sitting and someone was "leaning on him". An officer whose name began with B was "rather prominent" in the photo. Asked whether it had been taken out of doors Raymond replied "practically" and to elucidate this conveyed that there was a dark background with vertical lines on it (Feda thought it might have been a shelter of some kind).

When the photo arrived four days later, it showed twenty-one officers closely grouped, some standing, some sitting on a bench and others cross-legged on the ground, against the background of a military hut darkish in tone with upward sloping strips clearly visible on the roof securing lengths of roofing felt. Raymond was cross-legged, his walking stick (the precursor of the swagger-cane) lying across his feet and the right hand of the officer behind him was resting on his left shoulder. Being in stronger sunlight than the others there was an officer "rather prominent" and his name was established from a key supplied by Mrs Cheves as a Captain Boast.

This was striking evidence but more was coming almost concurrently. At a table session with Mrs Leonard on 28 September Raymond had been asked to name one of his brothers and gave "Norman" which his parents believed they knew to be wrong until, on consulting the family, they found that Raymond used "Norman" as a kind of general nickname when playing hockey with his brothers. At the same sitting he gave details of people he had met in France, unknown to the sitters, which were subsequently corroborated.

Two further examples of such evidence may be quoted. At another sitting Sir Oliver, primed by his sons, asked Raymond what he associated with the word "Argonauts" and the answer came: "telegram". This drew a blank with the brothers, but Raymond's sisters remembered the connection well. On a holiday with his brothers in Devon Raymond had once sent a telegram home to say that all was well and had signed it "Argonauts".

At a sitting between his brother Alec and Mrs Leonard in December, 1915, the question of singing cropped up and Alec asked, "What did you use to sing?" The answer was confused, but sounded like "Honolulu". This, too, was not understood till, months later, an old song sheet was discovered at the family home dated by Raymond "3rd March, 1904", on which he had altered the last verse in pencil to contain the words "Honolulu town". No one in the family knew about this, but on its discovery a further test was arranged by some members. On 26 May, 1916, a son Lionel and Norah, one of his sisters, were due to have a sitting in London with Mrs Leonard which in fact lasted from 11.55 a.m. to 1.30 p.m. On the same day, knowing that the London sitting had been arranged, Alec and two other sisters held a ten-minute table sitting at home, starting at 12.10 p.m., at which Raymond was asked if he would be willing to convey a particular word through Mrs Leonard's control to the party in London. The answer was a vigorous "yes" and the word given was "Honolulu". In the London sitting meanwhile, amid significant pauses, Raymond was talking through Feda about the family dog and then about a boy he had met called Ralph. Then suddenly out of the blue Feda said to Norah, "You could play". Norah: "Play what?" Feda: "Not a game, a music". Norah: "I'm afraid I can't, Raymond". Feda was then heard to murmur to Raymond: "She can't do that", then she said to Norah: "He wanted

235

to know whether you can play Hulu—Honolulu". (Pause). "Well, can't you try?" Another pause, then Feda said: "He is rolling with laughter", which the sitters took to mean that Raymond was highly delighted about something ...

As tests of survival after death, against the background of serious questions concerning human destiny such evidence may be thought trivial. But there is no real reason why we should expect earth-shaking revelations from someone just because he is in another world, and small incidents at least offer evidence which can be examined. At any rate the record of sittings given in *Raymond Revised* seems to show that some entity was eager to partake in such tests with the object, one feels, of satisfying a healthy scepticism, removing barriers to intercourse and finally revealing himself as indeed the living spirit of the Lodges' beloved son. After a time the family got into yet closer touch and one is moved to read, for instance, of an emotional occasion when Alec was sitting alone with Mrs Leonard and Raymond seemed to possess the medium directly, speaking to his brother in his own voice and clasping him with his own hands.

At the same time, there is need for caution. In his book Lodge compares communication of this kind with the vagaries of two inexpert telegraphists passing messages through faulty apparatus, and Raymond himself often referred to the difficulties of getting through without interference or seepage from the subconscious minds of medium, control or sitters. In one case, not connected with Raymond but reported in the book, a medium received a mass of material giving the name and details of the early life of an allegedly departed spirit only to find later that the person was alive in this world and the details, all of them correct, had been obtained without his conscious awareness. As to how this happened, one can answer "by telepathy", but as that is only the name we give to an unpredictable, obscure though potent aspect of extra-sensory perception, that leaves us almost as much in the dark as before. One lesson is clear: to seek advice from the departed, however strong the bond of love, is ill-advised and may be dangerous.

For the same reasons it is necessary to be sceptical about descriptions given in séances of life in another world. Raymond gave some of these, with details of which readers would form their own opinions, though the plausible suggestion did emerge that death is more like changing a suit of clothes than donning a garment of light, and the transition brings wider spiritual possibilities rather than an immediate and automatic enlargement of personality or awareness.

This certainly sounds more likely than a sudden leap from earth to heaven, but without means of verification we cannot judge its truth and Raymond only purported to speak of what he himself had experienced.

Other evidence tending to prove survival is touched on in *Raymond Revised* and one piece, known as the cross-correspondence, is particularly striking. Myers became well acquainted in his lifetime with the pitfalls of psychical research and some years after his death he indicated through a medium who practised automatic writing that he had devised a means to circumvent them. Over a period of twelve years there were then dictated to no less than eight mediums working in several countries separate fragments of a learned puzzle on themes of classical literature is such a way that no one portion made sense on its own. But when all the fragments were finally sent up to the Society for Psychical Research it was found possible, with much labour and erudition, to fit them together into a coherent whole. The cross-correspondences are still considered to be among the best evidence ever obtained of a single discarnate intelligence operating from another world, and one may well ask: if Myers did not dictate those fragments, who did?

Perhaps even on this slight basis we can now form some opinion as to the value of Sir Oliver Lodge's book; we have already indicated the importance of psychical research in general. *Raymond Revised* shows that the Lodge family became convinced that the human personality survives death and love does provide a bridge for communication in a very real and recognizable manner. If this is true, then in the most important respect this and the other world are not two but one and creative co-operation can take place between them. Further, the knowledge gained of the extraordinary scope of telepathy since enlarged and confirmed by other researchers, shows that human beings in this world may be much more inter-dependent and intimately linked than hitherto imagined and are able very specifically to minister to each other's needs through the bond of love.

Surely these insights must be profoundly encouraging at a time when the human race is struggling amid intense confusion towards a sense of common destiny. Surely they give new life to the central theme of Christianity and inspire us to seek a yet more solid foundation for that age-old dream of man, the dream of unity and wholeness within a divine and all-embracing purpose.

Of Saints and a Church

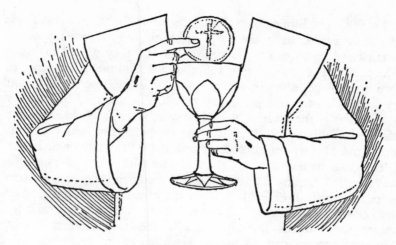

STIG MATA

Christianity, for a religion so non-violent in its essence, is remarkably blood-drenched in its evocations. Sadism is unthinkable—masochism is unbridled.

The immediate result of the Birth of Christ was the Massacre of the Innocents. Thus bloodshed early became established as the accompaniment for His life and for those of his followers for generations to come. The divine footsteps proved a bloody trail. While preaching His gospel of peace Christ continuously spoke of blood. "The blood of Man" ... "This is my Blood" ... "My Blood that will be shed for you". Finally he was subjected to the most appalling suffering and bloody death leaving the legacy "Take up your Cross and follow Me".

The early Christians did not have long to wait. The bloodbath of suffering and persecution soon began and continued throughout the first centuries of the Christian Church. There emerged that most venerated being, the martyr. Martyrdom became not just a fate to be borne with resignation when inevitable, but one to be actually sought out. Thousands went happily to unspeakable deaths when often simple prudence would have sufficed to weather the storm.

Times changed and for reasons, sometimes humanitarian, sometimes political, martyrdom became a glory not so easily attained. Not so easily attained for Christians, that is. For alas, as the Christian Church and its people formed the status quo in Europe they saw to it that many a follower of other spiritual leaders were given the opportunity of a martyr's death.

During the Middle Ages Christians for the most part were free of suffering inflicted on them by others, but did not lose the notion that Christians should suffer simply because they were Christians. The tradition of self-imposed suffering was continued. Suffering by fasting, by flagellation, by acts of humility, by self-mortification and by resignation to affliction. Some practices encouraged fell little, if at all, short of the bizarre. Not a few were given to kissing the sores of lepers. Edifying no doubt for the aspiring saint, but a practice which must have been somewhat startling for the unfortunate leper.

Religious writers were prolific and discussion of religious matters was popular. During the twelfth century among the points debated were the words of St Paul: "I bear the marks of the Lord Jesus in my body." (Galatians vi, 17.) It was held by some that the saint had meant these words literally. Also it was rumoured that some Christian mystics had become so absorbed in contemplation upon the Passion of Christ that they felt physical pain and bore marks corresponding to His wounds.

Then in 1224 a wonder occurred in the Christian world. Rumour became fact. Francis of Assisi, the founder of an order of friars, had a vision. When the vision faded he bore on his hands and feet and side the marks of the wounds of the Crucified Christ.

Francis was born in Assisi in 1182. His father was a rich cloth merchant named Piero Bernardone. His mother was Mona Pica, a knight's daughter from Provence. He was christened Giovanni-Francesco in the church of San Rufino. He had brothers and sisters, but little is known of them.

Francis' childhood was happy, free from want and unremarkable. As well as his native Italian he was taught French by his mother. A priest of San Giorgio taught him his alphabet, sums, and a little Latin. He was slow to learn to write, and throughout his life was never at ease with a pen. In early manhood his father's wealth made it possible for him to indulge in a wayward mode of life common to rich young men at the time.

Not all his pursuits were frivolous. In 1202 he joined in the defence of Assisi when it was attacked by the forces of neighbouring Perugia. He was taken prisoner and was held captive for a year, suffering considerable privation. Regaining his freedom a change came over Francis. He did not immediately forsake his former way of life, but grew increasingly sober-minded and given to spending much time alone. He would disappear for weeks together without explanation.

At nearby San Damiano he came across a small tumbled-down

chapel. A hint of its former glory could be found in a Byzantine crucifix hung over the altar. Splendid art enhancing squalid reality. Francis found this crucifix compelling. For hours he would kneel before it, riveted by the gentleness of the face which had endured so much.

One morning as he knelt at the hour of Prime the sun rose with an unimaginable brilliance. Walls which should have afforded shade were rendered impotent. Francis closed his eyes, but the sun would not be shut out. Just as it seemed that his brain itself would shatter a voice spoke, "Restore My house". For Francis there was no doubt that the voice of God had spoken. He restored the chapel of San Damiano. Forsaking his father's wealth he left home and lived the life of a wandering beggar. When he found a church or chapel lying neglected he repaired it himself or persuaded others either to help or to donate materials.

Soon he had gathered a group of followers, young men also seeking to imitate the Life of Christ. Poverty became their ideal. They had no possessions. They lived entirely on charity. What little money they earned from their labours was given to the poor. As their numbers increased and they could be identified as a community, Francis realized that it was necessary to gain papal recognition of their activities. They had started to preach as well as work, and to do the former without papal recognition could result in a charge of heresy.

In 1210, accompanied by eleven "brothers", Francis travelled to Rome. They were befriended by Cardinal Ugolina who pleaded their cause with the Pope, Innocent III. And pleading was indeed needed, for Francis declared that they had not come for papal "approval" ... they already had approval from Christ ... but for papal "recognition". It is astonishing that he should have "pulled rank" on the Holy Father with this piece of bland self-assurance.

However, Innocent was impressed by the obvious sincerity and goodness of the group, and granted them permission to preach and form an order, which the world later came to know as the Franciscans.

By 1224, two years before the death of their founder, the Franciscans and their spiritual sisters, the Poor Clares, were well established. Francis decided to travel to Monte Verna to keep what he called "Michaelmas Lent", from 15 August, Assumption Day, to 29 September. He was accompanied by Brothers Leo, Angelo and Masseo. On the southern side of Monte Verna Francis drew apart from the others to a small cave. Brother Leo was to bring his meagre rations, a little bread and some vegetables, and even these not every day. He embarked on a period of fasting, prayer and contemplation upon the Passion of Christ.

At sunset on 13 September he left the cave and kept vigil on the side of the mountain. At dawn on the morning of the 14th, the Feast of the Exaltation of the Cross, he turned his face eastwards. The sun rose with a San Damiano-like brilliance. Exalted by the moment, he saw a vision of a seraph flying towards him. The angel's six wings were outspread and shone brighter than the sun. The apparition drew close and hovered above him. He could see that the tips of the seraph's wings were nailed to a cross.

Ecstatic, Francis felt his body wracked with excruciating pain. Pain such as Christ Himself must have endured. As the vision faded the pain subsided. Francis looked down. His hands bore wounds as though nails had been driven through the palms. His feet were mutilated in the same manner. His left side bore a gash as though a lance had been pierced through it to determine death.

The stigmatism of St Francis is considered to be the first case of its kind although the notion of such a possibility was not unknown. Certainly, his is the first that was in any way documented. If no one had borne the stigma since, we would wonder if the accounts were not the testimony of well-meaning but over-zealous followers.

However, Francis was the first of what was to amount to over three hundred cases, the latest of whom have died within the last decade. There has always been someone within living memory claiming or at least reputed to bear the stigmata. Dr Imbert-Gourbeyre, whose book on stigmatism was first published in Paris in 1873, gives as 321 the number of known cases. Of these, 41 are men and 280 are women. A staggering proportion of seven women to one man.

He gives the geographical distribution as follows: Italy 229, France 70, Spain 33, Germany 33, Belgium 15, Portugal 113, Switzerland 5, Holland 5, Hungary 3 and Peru 1. The majority of cases were among members of religious orders. Dr Imbert-Gourbeyre states that in the eighteenth century only two cases out of a recorded thirty were lay people; in the nineteenth century there were nineteen religious to ten lay.

The proportion of seven women to one man must surely indicate that the emotional constitution of women is more likely to produce the conditions necessary for stigmatism than that of men. St Teresa of Avila, herself a stigmatist, constantly warned of the dangers of women dedicated to a religious life being prone to hysterical manifestations. She wisely held that if a nun showed signs of losing the run of herself she should be given some good hard work to take her mind off things.

The geographical distribution of the stigmata seems to follow as definite a pattern as the gender of the stigmatists. The figure of 229 for Italy is staggering. Again the proportion of cases in Italy to cases among other nationalities indicates that there is an emotional climate in Italy conducive to the phenomenon. It could be argued that the Italians are a deeply religious people, and it therefore follows that the proportion of those who will reach a sufficient state of sanctity to be rewarded with the stigmata will be high. This may well be, but it is interesting to note that the Irish who are also a deeply religious people cannot boast of a single case of stigmatism. Indeed, since the fifth century there is an almost total lack of religiously-associated phenomena in Ireland.

There is, however, in Ireland a vast history of allegedly supernatural phenomena, but these tend to be associated with what one might call the spirit-world in general rather than with God or His Saints. This may be because the Irish were well immersed in the belief in a spirit-world long before the coming of Christianity, therefore perhaps their mystical manifestations tend not to be Christian in nature.

I would suggest that countries like Italy, France, Spain and Germany, which have all produced many stigmatists, have a mystical climate firmly allied to Christianity. This is, of course, not to say that they had none before the coming of Christianity, but rather that Christianity was the mainspring of the evolution of their mystical beliefs. Hence their mystical phenomena tend to be Christian orientated.

Art may also have some bearing on the geographical positioning of stigmatas. Italy, France, Spain and Germany have a long tradition of religious paintings and sculptures—many portraying the crucifixion in romantic but lurid detail. These must surely have encouraged and aided deep contemplation of the event. Ireland is totally lacking in any tradition of such paintings—early Celtic Christian representations are symbolic, not material to fire a susceptible imagination.

Imagination plays an important part in the phenomenon. Many persons who have borne the stigmata have had a previous history of nervous disorder. Stigmata are strictly connected with ecstasy, which psychologically is an emotional state. There has been no case where they have occurred independently of ecstasy.

For a well-documented and modern case of ecstasy run riot we need look no further than the case of Teresa Neumann.

Teresa Neumann's life was pious almost from the start. The official records give her date of birth as 9 April, 1898. The Neumanns lived in the small Bavarian village of Konnersreuth, close to the Czechoslovakian border. They earned their living partly by farming a few acres, and partly by tailoring. The ten children, of whom Teresa was the eldest, were given a Christian upbringing, being taught to love and adhere to the Roman Catholic faith. The family home was not a luxurious one, but its inhabitants never knew want.

Teresa could be a nervous and irritable child and had frequent attacks of vertigo. Nothing particularly strange in all that. A hint of what was to come could have been found in her unusual devotion to the Passion of Christ. She would weep bitterly at being told about it or reading of it.

In 1912, when she was fourteen, she was employed as a servant by a wealthy neighbour. She was an industrious girl and did not shrink from hard work. On 10 March, 1918, a fire broke out in a nearby farm. Teresa ran to help. The sight of the fire gave her a severe traumatic shock, but she managed to help control the fire with buckets of water and even later fed the animals in her employer's stable without changing her wet clothes. It was from this date that Teresa Neumann's long history of illness and afflictions began. She suffered extreme pain in her back, had agonizing spasms from the slightest cause, and could eat hardly anything without experiencing severe vomiting. Her sight deteriorated, causing her to fall often—each fall intensifying the pains in her head and eyes. From October, 1918, she was bedridden. On 17 May, 1919, she had a long attack of convulsions from which she emerged totally blind.

Towards the end of 1922 she heard of a student of theology who suffered from an ailment of the throat, as a result of which he was in danger of being dismissed from the seminary. Teresa, as though she didn't have enough troubles of her own, prayed to God that she might suffer in place of the student. Soon after, she experienced a similar ailment in her throat. She felt as if her throat had been wounded, and would sometimes spit blood when coughing. Swallowing became so painful that her sole nourishment was reduced to a few teaspoonsful of gruel or barley mash.

Teresa had a great devotion to Thérèse of Lisieux. The day on which the future "saint" was proclaimed "blessed" in St Peter's Basilica in Rome was 29 April, 1923. That morning Teresa

Neumann opened her eyes and could see for the first time in four years. But though her sight was restored, her many other sufferings were increased in number. Abscesses, ulcers, appendicitis, paralysis of the legs, paralysis of the spine, pneumonia, festering wounds—the awful list reached almost comic proportions.

In 1925, at midnight on 30 September, the anniversary of the death of St Thérèse of Lisieux, Teresa had a vision of a "light". From out this light a voice told her, "Your external suffering will cease, but you must undergo another suffering more cruel". The next day Teresa rose from her bed and went to church unaided. "The suffering more cruel" was not made manifest till the Lent of 1926. On 4 March while resting in bed Teresa suddenly had a vision of Christ in the Garden of Olives. She could see the three Apostles in the background. Jesus was suffering the Agony in the Garden. As she gazed with emotion at the suffering of Christ, Teresa felt a pain in her left side; something warm trickled down her body—it was blood.

The following Thursday night Teresa witnessed the same scene. Early on the Friday morning she saw a vision of the Scourging at the Pillar. Again the wound in her side bled.

The third week she saw the Crowning with Thorns. The fourth, she saw the Journey to Calvary. On the fifth week, on the night of Holy Thursday-Good Friday, she witnessed the entire Passion. She emerged from this ecstasy bearing wounds on her feet and hands.

Teresa Neumann bore the stigmata till her death in 1962. Every Friday in ecstasy she witnessed again the Passion of Christ. Each week it was as though she was watching the scenes unfold for the first time. To her the events were not historic or familiar, but immediate and unknown. So much so that from her reactions to the various incidents it was evident that she thought Christ would be rescued by the Apostles before he died. In time the wounds on her hands and feet ceased to bleed, while those on her head and side continued to bleed during the Friday ecstasies.

Another amazing aspect of her extraordinary story is that from September, 1927, Teresa allegedly fasted permanently. It is claimed that not so much as a drop of water passed her lips let alone food.

Teresa Neumann's stigmatism is an instance, among many, of the phenomenon occurring against a background of physical ailments and emotional disturbance phenomenal in themselves.

Padre Pio of Foggia, a Capucin friar, is an example of the stigmata in a more serene setting.

Francesco Forgione was born in Pietrelcina, southern Italy on

25 May, 1887. His parents, Orazio and Maria were poor. They lived by farming a small plot of land. They had four children in all. It was Orazio's ambition to save enough money to emigrate to America. It was not his plan to take the family with him, but to earn money to send home for his children's education.

Francesco had a deep love of his father, and it is reasonable to assume that the constant talk of the father going away had an unsettling effect upon the child. He also had an unusual compassion for the suffering of others. He had many opportunities to exercise this sensibility, for life was very hard in Pietrelcina. At its best it was a pitiful existence. Winter flooding often caused misery and death. The local priest, Don Salvatore Parrullo, took an interest in the boy, no doubt recognizing a gentler spirit than the harshness of life in Pietrelcina would tolerate.

It is said that Francesco would often play with twigs forming them into the shape of a cross. In view of his later history this may have been recalled by people who gave it more significance than it warranted at the time. Where religion plays a large part in the lives of people many children will imitate what they see in church. However, it is obvious that the young Francesco had an awareness of sorrow which bordered on the morose.

In 1894 Orazio at last went to America. This may have made the family emotionally poorer, but in terms of physical comfort it made them very much less poor. The money Orazio sent from America greatly improved their lot.

Next to the Forgione farmhouse there stood a small hut. Francesco formed the habit of going into it to play after his father had left for America. In time he even slept in the hut and spent long hours in contemplation. It was no surprise to anyone that when asked what he would become when he grew up, he answered, "a monk".

In 1902 Francesco left his home and journeyed to Morcone to become a novice in the monastery there. The work of a novice in the monastery was laborious. Francesco worked by day and prayed long into the night. His health deteriorated. However, on 22 January, 1903 he received the brown habit of the Brothers of Saint Francis. As his name in religion he chose Frate Pio, in honour of the patron Saint of Pietrelcina, Saint Pio.

Frate Pio's health did not improve. His almost frenzied praying increased and, to the alarm of his superiors, he fasted for twenty-one days. The Guardian Brother, Father Agostino, sent for the doctor who advised that Frate Pio be sent home. Orazio happened to be home on a visit from America at this time, and one can imagine the bewilderment that he and Maria must have felt when they learned that their son was being sent home from the monastery.

But the young novice regained his health and returned to the monastery. Shortly after this he was transferred to the monastery at St Elia a Pianisi.

Soon he fell ill again and was sent to the monastery of Verafro. In spite of his ill health he fasted, prayed and endured periods of penance. Again he was sent home. One cannot help feeling that it was with a sense of relief that each Superior saw Frate Pio on his way. Ascetics are all very fine, but they can have a devastatingly disruptive effect on a community's life.

(St Catherine of Sienna fell into a trance during Mass said by Blessed Raymond of Capua. He wrote of the incident later: "My disciples and I were waiting *impatiently* for her to come to herself ...". St Catherine, along with St Teresa of Avila, were cases of invisible stigmatists—they felt pain, but no wounds appeared. St Teresa claimed to feel her heart pierced with a lance, and indeed after her death an autopsy disclosed a scar on her heart.)

On 17 September, 1915, Padre Pio (he was ordained priest in August, 1910) received the invisible stigmata. In the intervening year he was back and forth between monastery and home according to the constant variations in his health. It was during one of his sojourns at home that he received the invisible stigmata in his hands.

He still prayed in the little hut he had used when a boy. His mother went to call him for the midday meal. She found him with his face contorted with pain. Frightened she ran for the priest, Don Salvatore. When they reached the hut they found Padre Pio calm and composed, but his face wet with tears. He explained that his hands had been "burning" in the palms.

In March, 1918, Padre Pio was sent to the monastery of St Mary of the Graces in San Giovanni Rotondo, near Foggia. His life there was somewhat calmer than before. Including him, the community numbered only seven. Among the local people he gained the reputation of being a man of great piety and understanding. The small church would be packed for his mass and long queues formed outside his confessional.

On the night of 20 September, 1918, the friars were startled to hear Padre Pio let out a cry of pain. They rushed to his cell and found him lying on the floor just outside it. He was in a pool of blood. As yet not knowing what had happened, they moved him with extreme care. They soon found the sources of the blood. Padre Pio was bleeding from wounds in his hands, feet and left side just below the heart.

He bore the stigmata for the rest of his life, his wounds bleeding every time he said Mass. He died on 23 September, 1968.

His case is unusual in that he was the only man since St Francis of Assisi to bear the Five Wounds of Christ. Other male stigmatists have always borne only a partial stigmata.

The stigmata of Padre Pio was investigated by the Sacred Congregation of the Holy Office. In 1923 it published its findings. It declared that "after due investigations" the happenings associated with Padre Pio had not been proved to be supernatural in origin. It further exhorted the faithful to maintain an attitude towards them accordingly.

The Holy Office was not making any implications against the integrity of Padre Pio in its declaration; it was merely stating a fact, albeit a negative one—"not proven". It was, however, in its verdict recognizing that the phenomenon could conceivably have had a natural cause arising from the pathological condition of the bearer.

We have already noted that most stigmatists have had a history of nervous disorders. Another factor common to them is that, with few exceptions, they have all been Roman Catholics. A strange exception occurred in Germany in 1935. Arthur Otto Moock, a timber merchant in Hamburg, was involved in an automobile accident in May, 1928. Seven years later the wounds of the Crown of Thorns appeared on his head, shortly to be followed by stigmata on the hands, feet and side.

The phenomenon had no apparent religious significance for Moock had no particular devotion to Christ and, moreover, considered his stigmatism an intolerable nuisance. He is also singular among his fellow sufferers in Europe in being a Protestant.

Stigmatism has also been recorded among Moslem ascetics. They have borne wounds corresponding to those borne by Mohammed.

The stigmata present no problems to those who believe in the possibility of Divine Intervention. For those who believe that the phenomenon must have a natural cause, the problem is unsolved *as yet*, but not perhaps unsolvable. It may be possible that the explanation lies somewhere between the two.

When the woman was cured by touching the hem of Christ's garment He said to her, "Thy faith has made thee whole". He did not say, "Because of thy faith I have made thee whole". Suggesting,

I think, that the woman's mind had played a very large part in the phenomenon.

Are the stigmata this miracle in reverse? Does the intense wish of the stigmatists to share in the Passion of Christ provide the faith to make themselves infirm?

THE BURNT BIBLE
OF BROAD HINTON

It has been rightly said that Wiltshire is one of the loneliest counties in England. In the north is industrial and not very attractive Swindon, and down in the south is beautiful Salisbury with its inspired cathedral; but in between lies a large, sparsely populated territory strewn with monuments such as Stonehenge and Avebury which betoken its association with ancient history. The roads and railways are scarce, the villages few and far between. The land seems to brood still upon time long past.

If you take the narrow road leading north-west across the rolling downs from Marlborough, if you travel some six miles, you will reach the lovely little village of Broad Hinton. This appears, like so many Wiltshire villages, to have sprung up in the middle of nowhere, but it is in fact not more than eight miles south of the bustling complex of Swindon.

There is a fine and ancient church at Broad Hinton, but perhaps its most memorable feature is the most macabre of any village church in Britain. Saints have been butchered in cathedrals, indeed sizeable battles have been fought inside Scottish ones, but the ordinary English village church has its quiet religious festivals, its christenings, its marriages, its funerals, with little more than the very occasional drama of someone objecting loudly after the banns for a marriage have been called, that, yes, he considers there *is* a "just cause and impediment" which would make that marriage a sin. For most villages like Broad Hinton, this sort of drama is about the only untoward happening which takes place in church.

But inside the ancient church of that village there is a statue. This in itself is unusual, for although there are brasses to rub, flat brass representations of great or saintly men and women, set into the floor, there are not many statues to stare at in wonder.

The statue of Sir Thomas Wroughton is one of these.

It has worn the ravages of time since the sixteenth century remarkably well, and one realizes straightway that his hideous deformity was with him in life and has been carefully and accurately depicted. For Sir Thomas has no hands. In every other way, he seems a fine, upstanding fellow, but where his hands should be are only a pair of stumps.

Behind the sculpture is a story, a weird and strange story, which accounts for the gallant knight's deformity. And, if you ask, you will be permitted to see the other, surviving, half of the tale: a large and badly burnt Bible.

Did the good man rescue the book from some fire, and in so doing have his hands burnt off? This seems the most logical explanation, and if true, it makes Sir Thomas a very brave man indeed. Or did Satan himself strike with fire as Sir Thomas was reading the Good Book, and burn both book and reader?

Neither explanation would be correct; and the parish records tell an unlikely but true story of what actually did happen.

Sir Thomas was highly respected, if a little feared, during those early fifteen-hundreds when he was living. He was an absolutely intrepid hunter who would charge a twelve-pointer stag at bay, armed only with a slender pike, would dismount to deal with sometimes as many as three wolves at the same time, rather than have them cripple his precious steed. As for men, it was rumoured that he had killed upwards of a hundred of these in personal combat.

One reason for this "personal combat" to the death, so indulged in during the Middle Ages, may have been Sir Thomas Wroughton's hot temper. He was renowned, admired, despised and feared because of this, and no two people in the neighbourhood seemed to share an opinion about him. Today we would probably call him a bully, but a bully with courage and with a heart of gold, for there are instances of his having shown great kindness to men and women in trouble.

As is so often the case, the bully meets and marries someone he can bully to his heart's content. The pretty young lady from distant parts (perhaps as much as fifty miles away) who succumbed to his charms was a quiet, home-loving and deeply religious person, who was never known to raise her voice. She reared him four fine children—only to have her own devotion coupled with her husband's vile temper turn them into four cripples.

This is how it happened, and deeply religious men and women of Broad Hinton will tell you the story with a shudder.

It had been a cold and wintry day that 16th day of January, 1541, but Sir Thomas indulged his passion for hunting. (Rumour had it that if he failed to encounter stag, wolf, fox or even hare, he would run through the first peasant he came upon during the homeward ride.) Today he had been successful and a great stag lay draped across the fore-part of his horse. He was pleased with himself, and at the same time pleasurably anticipating the meal his wife would have prepared. Not for Sir Thomas some scullion in the nether regions preparing food for the family: he wanted his wife's cooking, and however much she might have preferred to read, or work at her tapestry, the onus was on her to cook all meals for the six members of the family, and have them ready on time.

Ready on time. So it was quite unreasonable, just because Sir Thomas got back early from his hunt and happened to be very hungry, for him to expect a meal ready, or even cooking: it was two hours before the meal was due.

He clumped his way into the big central room where the cooking was done in one corner, over an immense fire, and saw to his annoyance that no one was there, nothing was cooking. Cursing, he went up to the fire and saw that a great haunch of venison had been set on the stone slab, waiting to be spitted. There were vegetables, too, but nothing, so far, was being prepared.

Then his eyes got used to the comparative darkness of the big room with its tiny windows and a few tallow candles flickering in the draught, and he noticed—as he should have done before—that Lady Wroughton was sitting some distance from the great fire, and that she was reading by the light of one of the candles.

"Well, woman," he roared. "Where is my fare? Where is our meal?"

She carefully put down the book on the stone floor beside her and smiled the sweet, innocent smile for which she was well known and loved. "But Thomas, it is a full two hours before the meal time."

"Nonsense. You lie, and my stomach never does. My belly tells me it is meal time. And yet here you sit, not even beginning to prepare my food."

"Had you told me, Thomas, that you wanted food early, I would have prepared it. But you did not. And the children are out, expecting to come back and find their meal ready, too. But in another two hours, at six of the clock. I was about to begin, and I will do so now, but I much fear it will take both those two hours for the venison to cook through and the vegetables to be ready. You dislike your meat 'half-raw'."

"Curse you, woman. My belly screams for food. Prepare it now, I say, prepare it now!"

"Very well, then." Lady Wroughton got up patiently and went over to the stone table where the raw venison was lying.

"And what the devil's the book you've been reading, when you should have been performing your wifely duties?"

"Don't use that language, Thomas. Least of all about that book. It is the Holy Book. And I think it might do you no harm to read a few of its pages, every now and then."

"*What!* You make such a suggestion to me? As if I were some erring child——"

"Yes, Thomas, I do."

"By God, woman, I'll show you." And with one bound the lithe hunter was across into the shadows where his wife had been reading. His strong hands seized the big family Bible, raised it above his head, like an executioner brandishing his axe, and hurled it straight into the huge fireplace where six-foot logs were burning brightly.

His wife screamed.

"Keep quiet. Perhaps that will teach you to prepare a meal for an honest man."

"You—you blasphemous fool!" Lady Wroughton knelt down and plunged both hands deep into the fire, right to the elbow and beyond. It was perhaps six feet from the front of the fireplace to the back (and rather more than that from side to side) and good Sir Tom had hurled it in some distance. It was wedged under a log and she was wrestling with it. He saw the sleeves of her dress catch fire and disintegrate. Fortunately the cloth stopped burning at the armpit, or Lady Wroughton would have been an inferno of velvet and lace. And flesh.

At last Sir Thomas, waking up to the wickedness of his action, dived down on his knees to help his wife. But he was too late, his action was unnecessary; she had somehow retrieved the heavy volume from the fireplace. She was badly burnt, terribly burnt about the arms and scorched on the face, but it was the book that concerned her. It was smouldering. "Get water," she cried, "oh, please get water!"

Sir Thomas, hardly knowing what he did, leapt back across the great room to where a beaker always stood. Another bound and he was back, pouring the water over his wife.

"No, Thomas, *no*! The *book*—see it is smouldering ..."

And Sir Thomas then drenched the Holy Bible till it was a black and sodden mess. But miraculously, only the cover seemed burnt half away, and the Holy Scripture, though scorched as if the devil had licked it with a fiery tongue, was hardly damaged. It was, of course, soaked. But that would right itself.

Sir Thomas was now all kindness and humility—genuine kindness and humility, for as we noted earlier he was almost as renowned for these virtues as for the less attractive attributes of the hot-tempered hunter and warrior. Lovingly he bathed his wife's burnt arms, while she winced in pain, and then, having shouted for a servant to bring cloth, he gently bandaged them up.

One thing was obvious to both. Lady Wroughton had cooked her last meal for several weeks. She was in great pain and heavily bandaged from above the elbow of each arm right to the fingertip.

But she was no coward. She smiled. "Well, the book is saved—and its safe passage through fire may be a good augury for the family of Wroughton. And now, Meg," to the serving wench who had brought bandages, "perhaps you had better begin the preparing of Sir Thomas's meal. It will be some time before I am able to do so."

"Yes, m'lady." It was a polite, two-edged, reply. Of course Meg would do the cooking, and cheerfully. And of course it would be a long time before Lady Wroughton did anything of the sort herself.

She would be lucky if she had any hands left.

"Oh, my dear one, how can you forgive me? I am a vile-tempered fool."

"No, Thomas. You were just hungry. That was all. You were just hungry."

Sir Thomas was silent at the gentleness of the reply. Silent and ashamed.

That night, as they lay together—or more precisely, at some remove—in their big four-poster bed, Sir Thomas was distraught by the subdued moaning of his wife, unable to sleep for the pain. At the same time he was noticing a most unpleasant sensation in both his own hands. They had not been burnt, the Bible had been retrieved by his brave wife before he could do so himself, but they were distinctly painful. He tried to rub one with the other to ease the pain, but that was simply agonizing.

Lady Wroughton stayed in bed all the following day, at her family's request, though she bravely maintained her arms felt better and that within days she would be downstairs cooking again.

The four children, two boys and two girls, ranging in age from twelve to four, had come in for the evening meal and been duly shocked at the bandages on their mother's arms. Meg had managed a satisfactory meal, however, and after they had all washed it down with a little red wine, they retired early.

But in the morning, one of the girls complained of a painful hand. Sir Thomas looked at the small, delicate, hand in question.

"Hmmm," he said.

"Is that all you have to offer, father—hmmm? At least you could say you were sorry my hand was hurting."

"I am, my child, very sorry indeed. But the truth is that both my own hurt so much that I could hardly sleep during the night."

"And yet mother, whose hands must have been so horribly burnt, says she feels no pain at all."

"Your mother, child, is a very brave woman."

That night the girl's hands were both very painful indeed. As for Sir Thomas's, he hardly knew what to do with them. If they hung at his sides the blood flowed in—as after a day's frost-bitten hunting —so he could hardly stop himself from crying out with the pain. Any other attitude was painful, even held directly over his head.

And one of the boys complained of sore hands. The physician was called in.

"Ah, let us see now. Hmmm——"

"See, father: the physician says 'hmmm', too. Perhaps his own hands hurt?"

"No, young lady, my hands do not hurt. Good Sir Thomas, can one of your children, or a servant, bring one of your gloves?"

"One of my gloves? Whatever for, man?"

"I would like you to try it on. That is all."

Sir Thomas roared for someone to bring a pair of his leather gauntlets, which were promptly forthcoming. The physician slipped one on his patient's hand.

"But that is not my gauntlet. Why—it is far too big."

"It *is*, father. These are your favourite pair."

"It is as I thought, Sir Thomas. Your hands are withering."

"Withering? Like leaves in autumn?"

"One might liken it to that phenomenon. Try on the other glove."

It was just the same. "But this is ridiculous. I am no tree, these are no leaves: why should my hands wither?"

"Only the Good Lord can answer that question. Have you affronted Him of late?"

There was deathly silence.

"Yes," said the knight at last. "I have grievously affronted the Lord. In a moment of foolish anger I hurled his Good Book into the fire."

"You hurled the Bible into the fire, man? What in God's name made you do that?"

"To quote from your very words, physician, only the Good Lord can answer that question. I was seized by some demon of rage. And, oh God, if my wicked action has brought down harm on my lovely little daughter—in addition to what it has done to my wife—I shall be unable to live."

The words were prophetic.

The physician was now quite convinced that some law other than natural law was at work. He informed Sir Thomas that his wife's condition had improved to such an incredible extent that he believed her hands would emerge unscarred and sound from her ordeal. But as for Sir Thomas and the child, the disease was so unnatural and without apparent cause that he could only assume it was God's Will. Certainly he could hold out no hope.

The next day all four children were complaining of painful hands, and Sir Thomas could now very easily see that his own were shrinking, shrinking to the size of a child's, but with the skin staying its original size, so that it hung, loose, yellow and hideous about the fingers and across the palm, like gloves made far too large. The children's, too, were withering in the same way. Each day the physician paid his visit, shook his head in dismay, and confirmed that he had no idea when or whether the shrinking, the withering, would cease.

On the fourth day, Lady Wroughton's bandages were off and her hands were perfect, white and unscarred. But she was appalled at what had happened to her family while she lay upstairs, convalescing from what might have been the most serious of injuries.

"Oh," she cried, looking at the youngest girl's withered hands, which were now those of an infant. "Oh, if this could but have happened to me, and not to any of you! How dreadful that five should suffer, and the one who actually came in contact with the flames should recover."

The physician, at the end of his tether, recommended that there should be a ceremony of exorcism. And after some difficulty, for the ecclesiastical community had been deeply shocked at the story of the near-burn Bible, a priest was made available. The solemn exorcism service, however, far from alleviating matters, seemed to make them worse. Within a week Sir Thomas's arms had vanished halfway to the elbow, and his children's were close behind. The young ones were terrified, and wept with pain and fright: Sir Thomas wept with shame; his wife wept with genuine, appalled, distress.

Halfway up to the elbow the disease seemed to die out, for the arms became neatly rounded stumps. The loose skin contracted, like that of any preserved, mummified, body, and the same distressing process took place, one by one, with the four children.

And so people could at last take stock; and every man-jack in the neighbourhood knew that the Lord had taken vengeance on arrogant Sir Tom Wroughton, fearless knight of Broad Hinton. Sir Thomas could obviously never hunt again, but even if his own hands had been spared he would never have had the heart to do so. Slowly the rest of him withered away, though from a different cause, because the will to live no longer activated his once-vibrant body. His children showed a remarkable resilience, according to the parish records, being far more worried about their dying father than the fact that their own lives, however many years might stretch out ahead, had been tragically blighted.

(More than one shocked visitor to Broad Hinton church has come away impressed and moved by the resourcefulness, the courage, of handicapped children through the ages—right up to and through the thalidomide tragedies of the twentieth century.)

The children went on to lead reasonably normal lives, aided by elementary orthopaedic science; spoons, pegs, knives strapped on to pitiful arms; padded, re-inforced gauntlets; and other suchlike items.

Sir Thomas was soon dead.

His heart-broken widow "and grieving children" erected a statue of him, showing the handless arms. This now stands, as we saw at the beginning of this chapter, in the old Broad Hinton church, proof in solid stone of something "supernatural" which really must have happened.

And, as we have also stated, the Bible itself is there, charred, torn and four hundred years old. No man can look at it, then at the handless statue, without a strange feeling, indeed a certainty, that this is not folk-lore. This is fact.

259

War and
The Supernatural

MIRACLE OF THE SWAMP

Ian MacHorton was an eager, handsome nineteen-year-old second lieutenant recently commissioned in a Gurkha regiment when early in 1943 he joined the Chindits. The brain-child of Brigadier Orde Wingate, this irregular force had come into being at a time when the Japanese occupied most of Burma and its object was to penetrate behind the enemy lines, disrupt communications and by proving its superiority over a ruthless, jungle-wise opponent restore British morale, badly shaken after the defeats of the previous year.

In February, seven columns depending on air-drops for their own supplies crossed the river Chindwin to face some of the worst terrain in the world: dense jungle stretching for hundreds of miles interspersed with huge tracts of almost impenetrable bamboo and elephant grass under a burning tropical sun. To move fast, strike suddenly and then vanish again was the essence of the task and so that the column would not be held up the order was given that non-walking wounded would have to be abandoned. Not one of the men thought, of course, that this would ever happen to him.

Ian's column, which was to advertise its presence and act as a decoy, struggled forward for a hundred and fifty miles without mishap till they reached a railway line which they followed towards a depot they were intending to destroy, and there the Japs ambushed them. Many were killed and the survivors, including Ian, were ordered by radio to advance another hundred miles and contact another group from whom they would receive further instructions.

But they now found themselves in serious difficulties. Jap patrols were harrying them and they could not use jungle tracks. Instead, they had to fight their way forward a few feet at a time, taking it in relays to hack at bamboo and dense undergrowth. After days of this some men went mad, while all were reduced to sweat-soaked, near-delirious skeletons.

So they took to the tracks again, to find on reaching the rendezvous that their friends had gone. Then they got the order: "Abandon heavy equipment. Get out of Burma!" But with the enemy closing in on them, the problem was to survive the next twenty-four hours. They were resting on a hill-top when the Japs attacked and young Ian MacHorton was wounded, a long, thin mortar splinter embedding itself a few inches below his left hip-joint, cutting into the muscle—and he realized he could not walk.

The column doctor did what he could; the colonel came to see him, and two friends offered to make a stretcher and carry him at the rear of the column, knowing that with such a burden they could never keep up. This offer, of course, Ian refused. So, heavy-hearted, they carried him down to a shaded spot by a motor road from where he could easily attract the attention of a passing patrol and surrender. Then the column moved away and left him.

Alone now in Jap-infested jungle, Ian felt terror flooding in. Then, after a while terror gave way to bitter resentment at his situation till finally he found his mind comparatively clear.

He began to think how he would give himself up when he sighted the Japs. Should he call out, should he wait till he was found, should he fire a shot to attract their attention? And when they found him, what would they do? Many stories he had heard of their sadistic, inhuman cruelties, their maniacal lust for blood. Would they drag him to a tree, strip him naked, bayonet him to death? Or, little more than a carcass, would he be carted off to some infamous prisoner cage in Rangoon? At these thoughts he shivered convulsively, drew his blanket tighter around him and, too exhausted to dwell on his fears, he slept.

All through the night he slept, to be woken at dawn by the noise of a motor engine approaching from the south on the road below. Peering from his hollow he saw a lorry crammed with Japanese soldiers drive past, then two more, then a fourth which stopped to disgorge ten men under an officer. Gripped with fear, Ian watched as they searched about, obviously for signs of recently made tracks. Then one of them found something and gave a shout, the officer inspected and immediately, gripping his pistol, began to climb quickly to where Ian was lying. Crashing through the undergrowth, closer and closer he came till, hypnotized, Ian registered every detail of his appearance, the drab green uniform, the riding boots, the sword dangling at his side. This was the moment. Now surely the end would come.

But then the officer saw something slightly to one side of the hollow, the tracks made by Ian's friends when they left him, and with a shout to his men to follow him, blind to Ian lying only six feet away, he swerved off in pursuit and away up the hill-side till all of them were lost in the jungle.

Slowly Ian relaxed a little and began to think. God, he felt, must have decreed that the Japs would pass him by. It must be a sign that he would live. Amazingly light-hearted now, he decided he would somehow teach himself to walk and, if only at the rate of one mile a day, cover the hundred miles over the mountains into friendly China. To go with him he chose his water-bottle, hunting knife, compass, pistol, ammunition and other necessities which he crammed into his haversack. Then from a bamboo pole within reach of his hand he trimmed a makeshift crutch, padding the top with a thick balaclava helmet his mother had knitted for him. Then, rolling over and using his good leg as a lever, he tried to stand up—and at once collapsed in searing pain.

Gradually the pain subsided, and deciding to light a pipe he groped in his jacket pocket for matches. There he found a poem, sent in the last batch of mail, against the day, as his mother had written, when he "might need some extra help". It was by Louise Haskins, an unknown writer till George VI had used her lines in his first Christmas broadcast of the war: "I said to the man who stood at the gate of the year: 'Give me a light that I may tread safely into the unknown'. And he replied: 'Go out into the darkness and put your hand into the hand of God. That shall be to you better than a light and safer than a known way'."

Ian read the lines, and re-read them, in his mind a new resolution fighting with despair, till quite suddenly his doubts vanished and he was ready to do just what the poem said. He would try again to walk.

Two further attempts failed in pain-racked nausea as miserably as the first. Then he thought up a better way of getting to his feet. The upper lip of his hollow dropped five feet down into a small clearing. Edging forward on his stomach, he lowered the crutch over the lip and planted it vertically in the ground. Then he inched himself back, away from the lip, into his hiding place, twisted himself painfully round and once more shoved himself towards the lip, this time feet first. Slowly he let himself tip over the edge, clutching a clump of bamboo firmly with his left hand till his right, sound leg was touching the ground, then manoeuvred the crutch under his left armpit, took the strain—and was standing at last.

"China!" He said aloud. "Here I come!"

Paths are not frequent in the jungle and a man might go for days without finding one. But there, miraculously, behind the clearing was a trail worn smooth by generations of bare-footed tribesmen and sideways, right foot first, Ian began to climb it where it led spiralling up the side of a hill. Though in extreme pain and weakness he managed by nightfall to cover about three miles and found a place to rest.

Next day, he had hauled himself to his feet by clinging to overhead creepers and was edging his way, barely conscious, along the path when two men suddenly loomed into view. Instantly Ian drew his revolver and fired from the hip, shot after shot till, still trying to fire, he collapsed into oblivion.

As though transported by magic, he woke to find himself in a friendly Burman village being tended with skill by the headman. Descended from Nepalese, these villagers hated the Japs and the headman himself had served with pride in a Gurkha regiment. This uncanny coincidence gave Ian a strange feeling of awe, for by no means every Burman village would have given him such a welcome. But that was not all. The two men he had fired at—and fortunately missed—had been Shan charcoal-burners, from a tribe traditionally hostile to the Japanese, and on recognizing him as a British officer had picked him up as true Samaritans and carried him to the village.

Well fed and skilfully nursed, he gathered strength in that village for a fortnight, learning to walk with only a stick, then a messenger arrived with news that the Japs were advancing, intending to use the area as a base. The headman had warned him that the mountain passes into China were heavily guarded and escape in that direction would be impossible. There remained the westward route, crossing three hundred miles of jungle, and despite the headman's pressing invitation to stay hidden in the village and become "one of us" Ian resolved to try it.

He was given food for the journey and the whole village saw him off with a young guide who would attempt to put him on the trail of his vanished comrades even now struggling, as Wingate had directed, to get out of Burma. To catch up with them would be essential, for in his present state he could not hope to cross the rivers alone.

Hobbling and in considerable pain, he was led for some days by barely visible game tracks till one never-to-be-forgotten morning his guide suddenly bent down and called: "Come and look, Sahib!" In the soft soil, only a few hours old, were the prints of British army boots with no trace of Japanese pursuers.

Greatly cheered, Ian said goodbye to his guide and followed the trail towards a broad belt of dense and suffocating elephant grass, knowing that he must somehow make his way through it and reach his friends before they crossed the broad Irrawaddy. From the tracks he could tell that they were moving fast, but he would have to move faster, risking delirium under the torrid sun, driving himself to perhaps total collapse. He knew that there were thirty miles at least of this clawing desert, and for sustenance he had only a few handfuls of raw rice left in his pocket and half a bottle of water.

It took him three days to cross that tangling growth of man-high, razor-sharp grasses. Plagued by thirst, flies and the pain in his leg, he was for the most part barely conscious and his mind was filled with nothing but dull suffering and the determination to keep going. Then he staggered out of the grass belt to confront a waste of sand devoid of all vegetation and at the sight of this blazing inferno his resolution failed and he fell unconscious.

Reviving after a while and tottering to his feet, he plodded on, eventually after some hours, as the heat was draining from the sun, coming to scrub, and from there to teak forest where he found water, and from there to the outskirts of a village which he recognized. Close by flowed the mighty Irrawaddy, and on a sandbank preparing to cross the river he found his friends. "By all that's holy, look who's here!" said one of them, having given him up for lost.

They were in mid-stream in boats borrowed from the village when a Jap machine-gun opened up from the river bank ahead, bullets churning the water, whining overhead, slapping into the hulls, killing the men. In a moment Ian's boat had capsized and survivors were thrashing about in the water, while, certain that his leg would not stand up to the hundred-yard swim still remaining, he clung to an upturned side and allowed himself to be carried downstream with the boat between himself and the Japs. Slant-wise as he went he could see some men clambering ashore and dashing for cover.

Somehow he managed to swim the last ten yards, drag himself up the steep river bank and find protection behind a clump of bamboo where he was joined by an unwounded man who had come ashore behind him. At that precise spot all was quiet, but elsewhere in the gathering darkness along the river and back into the jungle they heard the din of a running fight between groups of survivors and the enemy.

Heading westwards by compass they made away from the fight only to come on a group of wounded in a clearing who were on the point of giving up. Ian was faced with a critical decision. To slip away with his companion offered the best chance of survival; on the other hand his duty as an officer was to intervene and saddle himself with this new command of the maimed and the despairing. He decided to intervene.

Ten minutes later, with new heart the men were hoisting their packs once more. Two were unable to walk and had to be carried on stretchers, and in that interval one man had died. They went limping westwards through thinning jungle and over flat ground, each man with only a small handful of rice and when a village appeared ahead they had to take the risk of encountering Japs and went in—to receive a friendly welcome and food. In the village, where the stretcher cases were left, their wounds were bound up and with full stomachs they knew a brief contentment. But they could not wait. They had to move on, and fast, for apart from the Japs the monsoon was now only two weeks ahead and when the rains came all rivers would become impassable.

A guide from the village took them towards a railway line where they managed to avoid two enemy patrols, then for three days they plodded on in suffocating heat, almost foodless, in a daze of near-delirium, till they came to another neat little village which they had to enter, hidden Japs or no, for the sake of life itself. They were in luck once more. In that village they found their friends again, survivors from the battle by the Irrawaddy, haggard and skeletal as they all were, with some wounded but all still able to move.

They bought rice from the villagers, then took up their loads again to cross the next obstacle immediately ahead, the shallow Mu river, two hundred yards wide. All were in cheerful mood. With a wave to Ian, "See you tonight!", an officer friend went ahead with his men—and at that moment the surrounding jungle erupted in the zip and screech of bullets. A Jap patrol had crept up while they rested, and now was pouring in lead from machine-guns and rifles.

In spite of instant casualties, the scream of wounded, the jerk of dying men, there was no panic. Section by section, in extended order, the men dashed for the water and, holding their rifles over their heads, started to wade across, Ian following with his little band, all still alive. Bullets furrowed the water; here and there men tipped forward and soundlessly sank. Ahead, from the very shore they were struggling towards, burst the din of more Jap machine-guns, catching them in cross-fire.

Ian glanced back, but return was impossible. Gasping and floundering through the shallows he yelled to his men: "Keep going! It's the only way!", saw Japs taking aim from the jungle fringe farther off, flopped on to land and found cover under the river bank.

In speed now lay the choice between life and death and soon he was up again, running full tilt for some trees, then falling, almost somersaulting over two Jap machine-gunners hidden in bushes. They were killed by men following behind, then the party sped on towards teak forest which proved sparse, offering little cover. "This way!" yelled his friends, going flat out, Ian pounding after them. "This way!" But suddenly he could not follow. Suddenly he was lying face down on the ground with a searing pain in his right knee—and the next moment all was blackness.

He awoke to find himself behind a rock attended by a single green-clad slant-eyed impassive soldier holding a rifle. Hypnotized he looked at the face, and with a terrible lurch of despair knew he was a prisoner. Pistol, haversack and belt had been taken from him, but his water-bottle was within reach and racked with thirst he took a long swig. Slightly revived he discovered that his right trouser leg, face, beard and shirt were soaked and covered with blood. A bullet seemed to have grazed the bone below the knee and another had gone clean through his hat, then shattered against something, probably a stone, for his face was criss-crossed with gashes. No wound was fatal, but he had lost much blood and already half-starved was now extremely weak. Soon he drifted into oblivion.

He next found himself in a truck being driven along a motor road. Seeing him conscious, the guard laughed at him derisively, later conveying by repetition of the words that he was being taken to a village on the Chindwin river and from there would be transported to the prisoners' jail in Rangoon. The Chindwin was the dividing line between British- and Japanese-held Burma.

Swooning, reviving, jolting along half conscious, Ian was past noting the passage of time, but it might have been three days later that the truck stopped at a small village and he was half dragged, half carried into a squalid hut and left on the floor while the soldier and the truck-driver sat in the entrance as guards. He was now extremely frail and as night came he fell into a strange trance-like state, feeling he had left his body and was young and strong again, able at will to fly across the mountains to rejoin his friends. The sensation seemed so authentic that, a few moments later, when he was drawn back into the body, it was still the only reality and the frame of bone and tattered flesh containing him seemed bound to obey his will. "I will live," he said. "I will cross the Chindwin. Nothing shall stop me now."

He must have said it aloud, for one guard jerked his head up, then let it fall again and slept.

In his new dream of freedom Ian was sleeping too, till he was roused by the sound of an engine roaring outside. It was night still and the moon was shining. Through the doorway he could see a truck standing in a small paddy field beyond the hut with soldiers climbing in. From some distance away came a burst of machine-gun fire answered by rifles, and the next instant an authoritative voice barked out a stream of orders and the two guards in the doorway ran out towards another bunch of soldiers at that moment starting for the jungle in the direction of the firing.

Now Ian was alone, though perhaps only temporarily. The paddy field, about twenty-five yards across and bathed in moonlight was now deserted and beyond that loomed the dark mass of the jungle topped by a hill. The invitation was clear and insistent. This was his moment.

Feeling sustained by mysterious power, he slipped out of the hut, crossed the field and light-footed plunged into the jungle, then started to climb the hill. He had no map, no food, no water, no compass, no weapons, but now he fully realized his good fortune: the Japs had not taken him further from his goal, but brought him nearer, closer to the Chindwin

"I must reach the Chindwin!" he kept saying to himself, ruthlessly driving himself on, the ominous, rumbling thunder of the coming monsoon already audible beyond the mountains.

For two days he kept going, only once finding water, till he came to an escarpment and recognized it as lying some twenty miles east of the Chindwin. Twenty miles—and beyond the river British patrols, safety, sleep. Later he wrote: "I was very conscious at that moment that the hand of God was with me."

But a veritable calvary now began. The escarpment was totally arid, nothing but hot sand, rocks and burnt-up vegetation. Yet this blinding wilderness had somehow to be crossed. Ian trudged on, trusting to instinct to lead him to the river, and like many men in desperate straits before him he started to count his steps, each step an achievement, a triumph of will. To cover twenty miles in a day was impossible, and at some time or other night must have come and he must have slept. But he could not remember.

Later, probably on the next day, he found himself among living vegetation, then saw a stream where he bathed and drank before following it westwards. He was walking on a sandbank round a bend in this stream when suddenly he came on his companions again, no more now than twenty in all. Obviously in the last stages of exhaustion, they were too tired to say more than: "Hullo, Ian. You again." As they talked in desultory fashion, a water buffalo came out of the undergrowth and was shot to provide food. But the shot had alerted other visitors, two Burmese bearing a white flag. The senior officer went forward to talk to them, and came back with calamitous news: the men belonged to the B.T.A., or Burmese Traitor Army, and behind them in the jungle was a Japanese patrol. They were giving the British three minutes to decide on surrender or death.

It took Ian and most of the men exactly two minutes to absorb this news, then they were dashing headlong for the west bank of the stream where there was dense cover. Most, including Ian, got ashore with bullets whining amongst them and eventually came to a clearing where they slept the night before splitting into small groups to cover the last and most dangerous few miles to the Chindwin.

That afternoon Ian was on the east bank of the river, like some modern Moses viewing the promised land. At once he prepared to swim across, accepting a pair of water wings from a friend who intended to search for a boat. With his hat on his head and his boots tied together round his neck, he waded in and soon was performing a sluggish breast-stroke, till the current caught him and carried him towards the west bank at a bend in the river where he waded ashore and at last flopped down on British-held territory.

But the end was not yet. Ian had climbed to his feet again and was happily crossing a paddy field when there came the crack of an unseen rifle and a bullet smacked into the heel of his right boot, throwing him over backwards into a bush. The unexpectedness of the attack just when he felt safe filled him with rage, which grew no less when he saw that not a Jap but a Sikh, a traitor civilian, was pursuing him. As the man loped from the undergrowth he formed a murderous resolve. With no pistol now he looked round desperately for a weapon and found he was almost kneeling on a broken branch from a teak tree. He seized it with both hands and as the Sikh ran up searching for him brought the heavy wood crashing down on his skull. There was a horrible crunch, and the Sikh fell without a groan.

Ian slid the curving knife from the cummerbund, but could not bring himself to take the rifle still gripped in the lifeless hands. Then he staggered on westwards. He had water, but could not remember when he had last eaten. The bullet had grazed his Achilles tendon and walking, mostly in the open under a pitiless sun, was agony. Nightfall brought him to a river which at first he took for the River Yu, a smaller stream well within British territory. Then he recognized the Chindwin: he had been walking all day in a circle.

He slept that night on the river bank, too dejected to stir, but with the dawn he felt refreshed and set out westwards again, resolved this time to make no mistakes. It was fortunate that in a deserted village a young python came his way and he was so hungry by now that he had no hesitation in killing it, cooking portions in a pot which he found and eating python steak. To him it tasted delicious.

He walked for two more days through jungle and paddy fields and was alarmed to find that not even food could do much for him now. What he needed and had to have soon was weeks of total rest. Meanwhile he had sighted no British patrols and he was still alone. But next morning something within him still drove him westward, lucid only in brief snatches, till towards sunset he found himself in a swamp.

It was a sinister place with great shadows looming under the red rays of the dying sun, a fetid atmosphere and great stretches of stagnant water and oozing, treacherous mud. What looked like avenues of undergrowth led in different directions, but none led out of the swamp. He splashed about, clung to branches to prevent himself falling, and felt terror climbing in him. He was irretrievably lost.

In that dreadful situation one decision imposed itself. With darkness falling he would have to spend the night where he was and fortunately there were some mudbanks rising out of the water solid enough to support him. On one of these he slept.

At dawn he found that in trying to get out of the swamp he had lost both his boots. But he hardly cared about that. He staggered to his feet again, but had only gone a few steps when he collapsed unconscious on another mudbank. When he recovered there was an interval of clear-headedness in which, in the teeth of facts, he felt curiously confident that he was going to win through. Without moving he turned his eyes to the left—and came face to face with a lizard. At sight of him it scampered away along the smooth mud-bank, stumbling slightly in a shallow depression near the middle, then vanishing into the undergrowth. Ian's eyes were now riveted on that depression, which otherwise he might not have seen. It seemed to have the outline of a boot.

He crawled over and now he was examining it closely. It was a boot-print indeed, with the thirteen stud-marks of a British army standard issue ammunition boot. Moreover the print was recent. The man, whoever he was, had certainly not been there in strong sunlight, otherwise the minute piles of earth behind each studmark would have crumbled and broken down. Moreover, and even stranger, there were more prints, as he could now see, leading dead straight and diagonally across the mudbank. But they *started* at that spot where the lizard had stumbled, yet there was not the faintest scratch or disturbance to show how the man had got there. But what did that matter to Ian? They were a track and in the word of the poem broadcast by George VI they were "safer than a known way", and he would follow them unquestioningly.

In utter faith Ian followed the boot-prints and they never let him down. Skirting deep pools and treacherous mud, they took him from one patch of firm ground to another till at last, after many minutes, the swamp petered out and he was on solid earth. There he had to rest, for he was very weak.

He leant back against a tree facing the swamp he had crossed and took a long swig from his water-bottle, putting it down beside a boot-print just behind him. Then he looked out ruminatively over the swamp. What a relief to have got clear of that sinister morass! Then he looked again, and again looked with growing amazement: he could see clearly the marks of his own feet as they crossed the nearest mudbank, but the boot-prints had vanished.

Was this some trick of the mind? To make sure, he retraced his steps for over a hundred yards, well back into the swamp, following his own foot marks, but of the boot-prints there was not the slightest sign.

In the presence of this mystery, which he knew he could not solve, he felt profound amazement but no fear. "I will follow and you will lead"—such was the thought that came to his mind and he then went boldly forward, following the prints up hills, along jungle tracks, across paddy fields, light-heartedly singing and laughing with a glorious sense of companionship.

He reached the edge of a stream and there the prints abruptly ceased, but before he could feel anxiety he heard the sound of water flowing ahead and in a few moments he had emerged on to a beach of silver-white sand bordering a river, the River Yu lying many miles west of the Chindwin. Collapsing under the sudden heat of the sun he lay blissfully in the shallows looking out towards the jungle on the opposite bank, when suddenly some men with rifles and bayonets came out from the shadows wearing green uniforms and soft-peaked caps—and his world collapsed in ruins. Only Japs wore clothing like that.

So the Japs had crossed the Chindwin and this river as well, and now must be advancing on India itself. Once more hundreds of miles of perilous jungle lay between Ian and safety, week after week of dodging enemy patrols. That prospect, finally and irrevocably, he could not face. Slowly he rose, from the shallows, drew the Sikh knife and dropped it on the sand, and held up his hands. With total fatalism he stared at the men now crossing the river. One of them raised his rifle, aiming at Ian and he saw an ugly glint of sunlight at the end of the muzzle. At any moment now the man would fire ... the man would fire ... and now the horizontal river and the jungle beyond were swinging up towards the sky ... and back again ... and the sun with its blinding glare was suddenly moving with the speed of a shooting star ... and darkness overwhelmed him ...

When Ian awoke it was night and he was lying on his back beside a camp fire in a jungle clearing surrounded by armed men. Someone handed him a mug of tea.

The men were British soldiers recently issued with jungle-green uniforms, and had been crossing the Yu on a reconnaissance patrol when he had risen unexpectedly from the shallows. Later he learnt that no British troops had been east of the river for many weeks and that patrol had been the only one within a hundred square miles.

With the reaction beginning to work in him, feeling terribly weak and ill, he was taken by ambulance to main headquarters at Imphal, on the way hearing the first downpour of the delayed monsoon, and put into a spotless and almost empty hospital. And there, as he slowly recovered, he began to think.

He thought first of all those friends who had not come back, but had died somewhere lost in the jungle, starved, or shot, or even now were dying as prisoners of the Japs, and he mourned for them and ached for their young lives lost. Then he thought of the extraordinary strokes of fortune which had helped him through, and the more he thought the more certain he became: he had been saved and he now had an obligation to the power that had saved him. What

then should he do? What was now required of him? He could
not tell. He was in darkness again, as the poem said, at the beginning
of another "year" or stage in his life. So once again he must put his
hand into the hand of God and then follow the new path wherever
it might lead. That was his obligation—to God, and to his friends,
and to the living, and to the dead.

THE COLONEL'S
STRANGE GAME OF BILLIARDS

There are many people—officers of standing—who were in the mess
that night, and prepared to vouch for the truth of the colonel's story.
There are many others—including myself—who at this same house,
during the war, encountered the same apparition. I am, therefore,
completely convinced of the truth of the incidents which I now
relate.

But there are people still living to whom the story, being a dreadful, family, one causes great distress. And because of this I have
felt obliged to change the setting, by an English county or two, and
the names of all involved. But if you are old enough and, as we old
gunners maintain, fortunate enough to have served in the Royal
Artillery during the 1939 War, you may well recognize the details
of the tragedy within the next few lines.

It was in 1943 that Lt-Col. Savage was posted to take command
of a regiment of Field Artillery stationed in Kent; that is to say,
three batteries, each armed with eight 25-pounder guns. Like so
much wartime accommodation for a vastly augmented army, Kirkham Place was a large house set in some fifty acres of lovely Kentish
land. It had been requisitioned by the Army; and the 438th Field
Regiment, R.A., were by no means its first military tenants. The
438th had distinguished itself in the North African campaign, suffering in the process many casualties, including the loss, to a German
sniper's bullet, of their much-loved commanding officer.

276

So it was with some trepidation that Lt-Col. Henry Savage was driven from Folkestone railway station the ten miles or so inland to Kirkham Place. He knew from past experience as a more junior officer just how unloved was the "new broom" sent to take charge. He had, of course, no intention of being any such thing, particularly under such sad circumstances as these. He expected to be treated with courteous reserve by the majority of the officers he had been sent to command, with barely-concealed hostility from others, and by gushing delight from those who hoped to gain speedy promotion when the new C.O. had settled in and sorted out friend from foe.

All this, Colonel Savage had experience of. And although it was an honour to be translated from acting C.O. of a training regiment on Salisbury Plain to a very real C.O. of a distinguished fighting regiment which was being re-fitted and brought up to strength for the beaches of Normandy, he had that familiar feeling of butterflies in the stomach as the jeep turned into a long, long avenue of elms.

"It's 'ere, sir," said the driver, brightly, "Not a bad little 'ole, really. Cosier than Alamein. 'A' Battery guns is in that field there, the guns of 'B' Battery, they're kept in the copse behind. And you, sir, 'ave the eight guns of 'C' Battery more or less as a personal bodyguard, sir, as it was found convenient to 'ave them dotted round the garden. Not much of a garden now, sir, with them quad tractors dragging great guns across the beds, but it must 'ave been, well, very salubrious once——"

"I see," said Savage. "And the guns are all out today."

"That's right, sir, a Scheme."

"And Regimental HQ is in the big house, with the offices, RHQ Mess, 'C' Battery Mess, and all that?"

"That's right, sir. And this is such a ruddy *big* estate that the officers, NCOs and men of the other two batteries are all very comfortable in other gardeners' and foresters' houses 'ere and there.'

They had arrived and the driver put on his brakes in mid-sentence, flinging up a spray of the once-lovely gravel which had covered the whole of the mile-long drive, and the turn-round in front of the beautiful old house which was now to be his Regimental Office and his Headquarters Mess.

The Assistant Adjutant appeared, a very young man with one pip on each shoulder, and greeted the new C.O. He seemed a nice sort of chap, neither servile nor hostile, and he confirmed that the entire regiment was out on a manoeuvre led by the 2 i/c. All twenty-four guns, with their retinue of "R" trucks, "G" trucks, "M" and "T" trucks, motorbikes, theodolites and the rest of it were out dealing with some imaginary enemy swarming over Kent and Sussex. Savage was familiar with this sort of thing and he grinned as he pictured the battle, in which the enemy only manifesterd himself in the form of sweating staff officers on motorbikes. "They're still advancing," a typical one would gasp out, "and their leading elements have reached this area here——" pointing with a grubby multi-coloured finger which he'd been using all day to rub off chinagraph crayon markings from this celluloid board. "The Loamshires are putting in a counter-attack, and their C.O. will be along in a moment. Fancy he'll be wanting a barrage——"

And the staff officer would be off. Sometimes, if he had a sense of humour, he might grin and mutter, "Gawd, what a way to fight a war", before he vanished in a blue cloud of exhaust.

It had been late afternoon by the time Savage arrived at his new command, and he gathered from the only officer remaining at Kirkham, this young Assistant Adjutant, that the Regiment would not be back before 22 hours, and would have had their evening meal before then. So—at least as far as Savage could gather—it would be just himself and this Ack-Adj sharing a lonely meal in a banqueting hall where generations of Kirkhams had fed themselves and their guests, and more recently the officers of units going back before the arrival of the 438th had tried to follow.

It was a lovely house, largely Jacobean. The family portraits had of course been taken away for the duration—the marks were clear to see—and their place had been taken by Peter Scott wildfowl and the occasional chilly nude. The whole house was chilly, which was hardly surprising as there wasn't a yard of carpet left (that too had been stored) and the great yawning fireplaces, bereft of logs, were fringed with unlit paraffin heaters.

And yet it was August and really there should be no cause for this rather upsetting chill. Outside, the sun was still up, and the day had been a scorcher.

Henry was introduced to his batman, Higgins, who thoughtfully ran him a tepid bath. The Colonel got through this ordeal as quickly as possible, dried himself in a fervour to warm himself up, and slipped into the fresh underclothes, socks and shirt which Higgins had put out on his bedroll. After these clean items, Savage put on the same battledress tunic and trousers he'd been wearing all day. He could have put on the smarter khaki Service Dress he possessed, but decided to greet his returning warriors later in the evening dressed like one of them.

It was true, though, that he missed the days of peace and the main R.A. Mess at Woolwich where no Officer and Gentleman would dream of sitting down to the evening meal without his "Blue Patrols", with their tight blue trousers and their high choker collar. Sometimes, on greater occasions, it was full Mess Kit. But Savage's Blue Patrols and his Mess Kit were packed away somewhere, he wasn't sure he even remembered where. It hardly mattered: he didn't really expect to see this war out, or have a chance to wear any of that clobber again.

And so it came as quite a surprise when, clean inside and not so clean on the surface, he made his way down the beautiful, uncarpeted spiral staircase to do a little private reconnaissance of the premises, and found himself face to face at the bottom of the stair with a very smartly dressed young officer with a rather comical drooping blond moustache.

And the man—sporting only one pip on each shoulder—wore impeccable Blue Patrols. There was the high choker collar with just a suspicion of the stiff, rather clerical white one which had to be changed after every wearing, the slim-fitting blue jacket with its silver buttons, the skin tight blue pantaloons with the wide red band from hip to ankle, worn over knee-length, paper-thin, spurred boots which had to be inserted and strapped into these trousers before one literally climbed in from the top.

Henry Savage had never paid a great deal of attention to sartorial details, so he was unable to put a finger on the few small points in which this officer's Blue Patrols differed from his own, back in that tin trunk somewhere. Two things were certain: the uniform was quite an old one, of a better material than today's; and the officer had a far better tailor than Henry Savage's.

"Good evening, sir," said the young man who could hardly have been more than twenty-one. "You'll be Colonel Savage, then, sir?"

"Er—that's right," said Savage. "Good evening."

The young man did not volunteer his own name and Savage assumed that the arrival of the Assistant Adjutant for dinner would clear matters up. No doubt there was some good reason for this smart young officer not being out on the "scheme". Perhaps he was a guest from some other artillery unit, in which case it seemed a rather odd night to invite the poor fellow.

"Like a game of billiards?" said the young man.

"Why, yes, I really *would* like a game of billiards. You must forgive me, I don't know my way round here yet: I'd no idea there was a billiard-table."

"Oh yes," said the young man. "We've always had a billiard-

279

table." He looked over at the hideous tin clock on the mantelpiece, obviously standing in for some priceless *ormolu* creation which the house's owners had wisely stored away with everything else. "Yes," he said. "We'll just have time for a game. Before your dinner."

This remark struck Henry Savage as a most unusual one, and a few hours later, when his officers had returned from their manoeuvres and he was talking with them over a glass of whisky, he had occasion to remember the remark which immediately preceded it, as well.

But, for the moment, everything was driven from his mind by the splendour of the room into which he was now ushered. It was true that even here the family portraits had been removed, but the pictures which took their place were attractive, well-framed, suitable, as if the family had substituted them with some care before handing over their precious house.

The real beauty of the room, for Savage, lay in the enormous and superb billiard-table which occupied two-thirds of the floor space. Here was something which the family had chosen not to dismantle and here it stayed like a wonderful ornate throne in an almost empty palace. Along the whole of one wall was an ebony rack with billiard cues, enough for the whole officers' mess to indulge in the sacrilege of "football billiards" or something of the sort. Something, thought Henry Savage with a solemnity approaching the devout, which *he* most certainly would not permit.

His young friend made a little half bow and a wave towards the armoury of cues. Savage selected one and carefully chalked it.

In a moment they were playing, and a rattling good game it was, too. They seemed evenly matched (though Savage once or twice wondered whether the young man wasn't missing the odd shot in deference to the C.O.'s rank). Eventually Savage won, but by only the narrowest of margins.

There was the sound of a dinner gong and he smiled to himself. Every officer but that standard Ack-Adj-cum-teaboy out on some frightful manoevure, and here, not only a priceless billiard-table and fixings, but of all things, a dinner gong too.

"Sounds like dinner," said the young subaltern in Blues. "Thank you for the game."

"I enjoyed it very much," said Colonel Savage, watching in some puzzlement as his recent adversary opened the billiard-room door and went out, closing it behind him.

Still no sign of the Ack-Adj, the Assistant Adjutant, but just as Savage was wondering if the whole thing were a dream and he was in a totally uninhabited house the Mess Bombardier came in. "Assistant Adjutant, Mr Perkins, sends his compliments, sir, but he's had to dash off on one of the D.R.'s motorbikes, sir. Seems the Adjutant himself had a little accident and Mr Perkins has to take over the duty."

"Dear me," said Savage. "I wonder if I ought to go myself?"

"Mr Perkins, Lieutenant Perkins, sir, he said you weren't to worry and he was ever so sorry you'd have to have your first meal all alone, like. I'll just show you the way, sir."

Under the circumstances, Savage had no heart to ask what had happened to the young man with whom he had just finished a game of billiards. He allowed the Bombardier to lead him from billiard-room, via ante-room, to mess. An uncomfortable chair was pulled out, and he sat down.

Dinner was surprisingly good, including even a half-bottle of white wine. But the meal, and the minor emergency involving the Adjutant of his new Regiment, could not drive the nagging question from Henry Savage's mind. Two or three times he was about to ask the Mess Bombardier what had happened to the officer in Blue Patrols, and the same number of times he let the matter rest.

After dinner, being all alone, he wandered back to the billiard-room and switched on all the lights. It was a beautiful room and Savage wandered appreciatively about it.

Then he saw the stain.

It was a black stain running the whole way down the wooden, panelled, wall from roughly six feet up to floor level and then spreading out over the parquet. It was a very big stain indeed, and instinctively Henry Savage knew it had been blood.

A minor pandemonium announced that the manoeuvres were ended and his officers were back. He felt strangely ill at ease, and it was not just the ordeal of confronting these younger men who had come back from what had probably been a hellish day. It was this damn house, the stain, and the billiard player.

Soon the problems of introduction were under control. The Second-in-Command, a great gangling major of about thirty with an engaging personality, soon had everyone sitting happily around a real fire which he himself lit in the enormous fireplace in the ante-room. Drinks circulated, and the muddy, happy, young officers who had just defeated the "enemy" chatted gaily with their new C.O.

After the second glass of whisky, Henry Savage plucked up courage to ask his silly question. There was a convenient hush and he filled it with words.

"I suppose this is an absurd question. But when I came down to dinner, all by myself, I met a subaltern in Blues. And we had a game of billiards together—which he kindly let me win. Since which I haven't clapped eyes on him. Just—just who *is* he?"

There was a long pause. Then the Second-in-Command spoke. "Well sir, in a nutshell, that's the Ghost of Kirkham."

"Tell me more. Nothing would surprise me now."

"Well let's see, it's only half past eleven. I don't think Bateson will have hit the sack yet: no, of course he won't. We'll get him to tell us all the story. Because one or two of the younger officers haven't met our ghost or heard his story. Not yet."

"Fine, fine. Who's Bateson?"

"The old family butler. The Kirkham family's butler. Way up in his seventies, and although we like to persuade him out in his butlering kit for Mess Nights, he's a retiring sort of chap and contents himself with being the best damn cook in Kent. We sort of took him over with the house, and the officers—from all the units since 1939, when the place was requisitioned—have been chipping in to keep him on. So I don't suppose Bateson's left Kirkham Place since he was a young footman in Victorian days. John, just pop out and see if you can persuade him to come and join us in a glass of something."

A young officer jumped to his feet and clumped out in a very muddy pair of boots.

"He was terribly—er—tangible for a ghost," said Savage. "No white sheets, no transparency——"

"That's quite right. He's solid—when he's around. But honestly, sir, I don't think you'll see him again. He turns up, comes back—when someone new arrives. And not always then. And you can wave all your magic wands, mutter all your incantations, but you're not likely to clap eyes on him again."

"Have you seen him?"

"Yes, sir, I have. I arrived alone, like yourself. And I suppose there's half a dozen other chaps in this room (come on, quick show of hands, thanks), yes, five or six chaps who've seen him, simply because he came on them when they were alone. You see, he's not exactly gregarious."

A portly figure who could only have been an English butler in his middle seventies was led in. His uniform of blue shirt and crumpled flannel trousers could not disguise his calling.

"Ah, hello, Bateson. Sir, this is Mr Bateson—Colonel Savage. Glass of whisky? Good. Sit yourself down——" The 2 i/c poured a large whisky, added a drop of water and handed it over.

"Your very good health, gentlemen. And in particular to our new Commanding Officer."

"Thank you," said Henry Savage.

"I gathered, sir," said Bateson, crossing one leg over the other and relaxing, "that you'd met Lieutenant Kirkham—Sir Nigel Kirkham——"

"So I have been told. We played billiards—and then he just vanished."

"Yes sir. He always does. Well it's a very sad story. Sir Nigel was twenty-two when his father was killed in the war; the last war, that is, sir, the 1914 one. And Nigel—and how I admired that young man—inherited the baronetcy. But he was terribly sick, had been sick all his life. Tuberculosis, T.B., it was. They wouldn't let him into the army, not him with a chest like that. He had to stay here, looking after the family interests, when he was well enough. And, oh, how that spirited boy hated that. And this was while his father, Sir Arthur Kirkham, went off to Flanders. And there he was killed. Beginning of '15, it was."

"And Nigel—Sir Nigel, as he'd suddenly become—determined to revenge him. So he managed to fiddle his medical exam. No, I've no idea how he did it, him sometimes coughing blood and all that. But he did. And the next thing we knew (I was butler even then, you know, at Kirkham) next thing we knew he was all dressed up in khaki and heading for Lord Kitchener and those trenches.

"But it didn't work. Starting really vomiting blood—even before he got to Flanders. In Aldershot, it was. So he was re-examined, the M.O. who'd passed him got a real roasting, and back he came to Kirkham."

Bateson graciously accepted a second whisky. "Thank you, sir. Well this, as far as young Master Nigel was concerned—and I still think of him as that, even though he *was* a baronet—this was the end. So he did just what I always said he'd do ..."

The silence could be felt. No one breathed.

"Anyone who really knew the boy could have predicted it. You all know the billiard-room, gentlemen, and the cue-rack. Well, there used to be a gun-rack on the other wall, with all sorts of rifles and shotguns and things. So he merely took a pistol, loaded it, and put the muzzle in his mouth. Standing up against the wall, he was.

'Just blew the back of his head clean out. And the stain, well that terrible, horrible bloodstain, it never went. You gentlemen have all seen it. And Lady Kirkham and the young sisters, they were all heart-broken, and they tried again and again—with me, too, of course—to get that huge stain off. But it's stayed exactly the same, over all those years. No thank you, sir, I won't, if you don't mind, must tidy up the kitchen and get a bit of shut-eye, at my age——"

Bateson got up. "So that's the story, gentlemen. And I've always felt bitter that they never let him go and do his bit in Flanders before death got him one way or the other."

It was rather like a king declaring an audience over. "And Sir Nigel hasn't left the house, he'll never leave Kirkham."

He fixed a not unfriendly look on Henry Savage. "I'll tell you one thing. Because he couldn't do all the outdoor things he wanted to, he became unbeatable at billiards. Never ever lost, from the age of fourteen. Unless, that is, he was being nice to someone. Nobody ever beats Master Nigel at billiards, unless he wants to be polite, because they've just arrived."

Bateson went over to the door, preparatory to making his exit.

"So, that's what I always say: that's the reason no one ever meets him twice at the billiard-table. Master Nigel was a great fighter. He'd let you have one game because you were new; but his natural fighter's instincts, they wouldn't let him lose a second time. So he just saves himself the temptation.

"Goodnight, gentlemen."

Ghosts Benevolent

THE TENNIS COACH

It's strange in a way; although I have known Maurice Pettigrew for nearly forty years, ever since we were at Oxford, and although I have seen a great deal of him at home, in the City, and in the club throughout the whole of that period not devoted to fighting our respective wars in Burma and in Bomber Command, it is only during the last few years, I feel now, that I have really known him at all. Others, of course, have noticed and wondered at the change in Pettigrew, but I am alone, or so I believe, in knowing how that change was brought about. Not because I was especially chosen as his *confidant*, but simply and fortuitously because some years ago he accepted the use of my villa in Spain for a convalescent holiday following a slight cardiac crisis brought upon him by over-zealous involvement in too many boardroom battles.

Both the involvement and the crisis it precipitated were entirely in keeping with the character of Pettigrew as we had always known him; he was the sort of man who is *always* involved in something, and it was simply not in his nature to treat any matter lightly. Only son of a northern industrialist, wealthy rather than rich, the first of his family to climb the steep wall of life on the Oundle-Oxford ladder, he was a born pragmatist determined from the start that his natural attributes should outweigh his natural limitations.

Since the latter were cerebral and the former social and physical, the Oxford of the 'thirties provided an admirable environment for his ambitions, which were even then considerable. Aware that he was intellectually out-gunned by all but the richest of his contemporaries, Pettigrew nevertheless had the native shrewdness not to underestimate the value of a degree—*any* degree, though preferably not an ignominious "Third"—and he worked doggedly towards that end, pacing his academic efforts with the sure sense of judgement and economy that was later to bring him the offer of more City directorships than he could comfortably handle. And in the end he left the city of dreaming spires with just such a qualification as he had determined upon—a parchment testimonial to diligence in acquiring a certain knowledge of a subject to which never again in his life would he devote one single thought.

This was not of course the sum and glory of his university career, but rather the dull academic armour that shielded him from being attacked and stigmatized as a mere "hearty". For Maurice Pettigrew was an athlete of prodigious prowess and versatility, outstanding even amongst that shining band of golden gladiators who bestrode the arenas of university sport between the wars. To catalogue his achievements would be both tedious, and irrelevant; let us say simply that anyone who, at the age of twenty-two, has captained both Oxford and England at rugby football, who has scored a double century against Cambridge at Lord's, has celebrated his boxing blue with the quickest knock-out in the history of university pugilism, and has thrown the discus in the Olympic Games—let us just accept that such a man may be forgiven for regarding athletic ability as an attribute of some basic importance and lasting value. Such acceptance indeed is necessary if, in the light of what happened to him later, one is to regard Maurice Pettigrew as I regard him—as a figure of minor tragedy rather than of fun.

When the holocaust came in 1939 Pettigrew, as was to be expected, did well. Six years later he discarded his uniform with the crown and pip of a Lt-Col. (Acting) and the ribbons of the DSO and MC, and was welcomed with open arms to the boardroom of a City consortium whose letter-headings had hitherto been emblazoned only with OBE's awarded for conscientious clerking in the Ministries of Information and Food.

His progress in the world of business was a steady march onwards and upwards, a march with which his private advancement kept perfectly in step. In 1948 he married the pleasant and decorative if vaguely scatter-brained daughter of an indigent earl, whose poverty was not so dire as to dim the lustre of his title and could in any case be somewhat alleviated by his appointment to one or two not-too-demanding directorships of companies controlled by the consortium. The young Pettigrews bought and furnished at great expense and in execrable taste a Georgian manner in the wilds of Chalfont St Giles, where they enjoyed for several years a life of security and contentment untroubled by problems or passion and entirely in keeping with their prosperity and their position in society.

When their son Simon was born in 1951 their happiness, it seemed, was complete, and the boy's future was, of course, never in doubt. What more could life hold for any youngster than to follow a carefully-cleared path in the footsteps of such a father? And if Simon, when eventually he had passed on from nannie and kindergarten to a carefully-selected prep school—carefully selected for its record of launching a steady stream of young alumni on the rugged road to Twickenham or, at very least, to Iffley Road—if Simon did show a faintly disturbing preference for reading and painting rather than for vingt-et-un (unofficial) or rugby football (very official indeed)—well, surely, it was only a phase and he'd grow out of it all in good time.

Things, however, did not work out like that. As the years passed and Simon moved on from prep to public school his end-of-term reports began to follow an unchanging pattern; a pattern that would have delighted many parents, certainly, but did not delight Maurice Pettigrew. In class Simon's work was excellent without being disturbingly brilliant; in most subjects a place in the topmost quarter of the form appeared to be his for the asking, and with such placings he seemed content, for he was neither a pot-hunter nor a swot. In literature and art he appeared unfailingly at the head of the list, although once again his teachers affirmed that his success stemmed from interest and intelligence rather from assiduous study or driving ambition. All were agreed that Simon Pettigrew was a pleasant, intelligent boy and that only his strange predilection for his own company, civilly but unequivocally made clear to all, prevented him from being one of the school's natural leaders.

This passion for privacy, always alarming in an adolescent, was, the Common Room agreed, the only flaw in young Pettigrew's character—this and, of course, his weird, utterly unaccountable (to all but a few of the younger and less traditionally-minded of his mentors, who had enough sense to keep their heretical mouths shut)—his strange, almost sacrilegious attitude to sport. For it was in attitude, not aptitude, that the trouble had its roots. Had Simon, son of Maurice Pettigrew, been a duffer at games, a physical weakling bereft alike of ball-sense and of biceps, he could have been simply if sadly shrugged aside as a freak, the wry jest of a Creator whose jokes have

289

been known throughout the centuries to include amongst their victims some of the very finest families in the land. But Simon's malady was more serious, more perplexing by far, and headmasters, housemasters, and a whole series of hurt and bewildered games-masters had scratched their heads in frustration and dismay. For Simon, far from being a duffer and therefore a legitimate and natural target for his superiors' scorn and his schoolfellows' wit, was an intelligent and muscular young man perfectly capable of responding to the former with chastening tolerance and to the latter with a resounding clip on the ear. What his mentors could not grasp or would not believe was that team games (whisper it not on Big Side) were, in Simon's estimation, a bore.

He was not in the least aggressive or proselytizing about his belief. When, once or twice a term, the Honour of the House was at stake, he would thunder up and down the rugby field with boisterous abandon, scattering more sophisticated opposition by the sheer animal exuberance of his attack, or, in summer, he would cart a sufficiency of rustic "sixes" clean out of the cricket ground before his eye and his mind began inadvertently but inevitably to wander. But such activities were merely a good-natured acceptance of his civic responsibilities, and with their discharge, felt Simon, the call to duty had been answered.

Nothing, nobody, would persuade him to devote his limited hours of leisure to net-practice or to puntin' a pill about in the muddy twilight while Cézanne or Trollope beckoned him from the warm seclusion of his study. And so things continued until the springtime of Simon's sixteenth year, when he failed to win his colours and his father suffered his first coronary occlusion. To link these two circumstances in any way would of course be both ludicrous and grotesquely unfair—or so I thought at the time.

Maurice's doctor and the specialists were adamant; complete rest for several weeks, a change of scene, a quiet holiday beyond the reach of the telephone, telex, and the turmoil of a shaking stockmarket. Dorothy, Pettigrew's wife told me all this when I called to inquire as to his well-being, and the whole matter was arranged within the hour. My villa in the little village of Cortedia, nestling in the mountains amid groves of almond and orange and commanding a vast sweep of the Mediterranean, might have been specially built and sited for the occasion. It was looked after by a Spanish couple, housekeeper and handyman, who would relieve the guests of all domestic responsibilities, a Renault was there in the garage should they wish to go sight-seeing, there was even a bicycle, bought during one of my fits of determination to stave off the advancing years, that young Simon might use if he felt the call of the sea that lapped the rocky coastline some four miles beyond and beneath his bedroom window. One week later, at the start of Simon's Easter holiday, the Pettigrews set out for the sunshine of the Costa Blanca. Their lives, had they but known it, were never to be the same again.

I did not see them again, as it happened, for more than two years, my business interests having compelled me to spend this period in America, but we did keep in touch fairly regularly by letter. The holiday, it seemed, had been a huge success. Maurice, true to form and taking his enforced idleness seriously, had read his way through the collected works of both P. G. Wodehouse *and* Agatha Christie, Dorothy had endeared herself to the village by her shopping sorties in which she had succeeded in buying exactly what she wanted, and at a fair price, despite her total ignorance of the Spanish language, and—a completely unlooked-for bonus—Simon had suddenly shown a positively passionate interest in sport. Not, to be sure, in rugby or cricket—that was hardly to be expected in such an environment —but in lawn tennis. Hardly the game Maurice would have chosen for his son, but a game for all that, and some of these Aussie fellows who played it seemed husky enough, so he supposed it was all right and certainly better than nothing.

Yet it was this sudden and lasting interest of Simon's, strangely, that wrought the gradual change in the personality of Maurice Pettigrew, that lost him a number of friends, and that brought him face to face, eventually, not only with himself but with something outside himself that he simply could not understand. And it was through me, to my sorrow, that this final confrontation came about.

The first inkling that something was seriously amiss came to me one lunch-time in the Club shortly after my return from the United States. I was passing the time of day with two or three old acquaintances when one of them, glancing towards the door, muttered "Oh my God", and finished off his glass with quite unseemly haste; the others, following his gaze, did likewise, and all three departed hastily, murmuring some fatuous excuses about lunching early before the dining-room became crowded. My astonishment was increased a hundredfold when I realized that the reason for this sudden exodus was, without question, the arrival of Maurice Pettigrew, for whom in fact I was waiting in pleasant anticipation. I shall not dwell upon a matter that even now I find distressing, for I am genuinely fond of Maurice; let me just say that by the end of that luncheon, my first meeting with my old friend for many months, I found myself reluctantly in sympathy with my earlier companions. For Maurice Pettigrew had developed, in the two years since I had last seen him, into a crashing, archetypal Club Bore. And the hobby-horse he rode so mercilessly, so proudly, so interminably was the saga of Simon's sporting achievements; it was sadly ironic that he of all men, who had always carried his own infinitely greater accomplishments with refreshing and wholly unaffected modesty, should now be guilty, as he undoubtedly was, of tedious and immoderate *bragadoccio* on the subject of his son's satisfactory but far from spectacular success at lawn tennis. For it became clear that Simon, though he had won several local tournaments and had been invited to play in the singles at Surbiton, was still a long way short of setting the turf of Wimbledon on fire; he had become, in short, a good club and county player and as yet nothing more.

Listening to Maurice, however, for as long as one could bear to listen to him, one might have been forgiven for imagining the lad to be a prodigy before whom the shades of the immortals would humbly bend the knee. Every point he had ever won, it seemed, every passing-shot that had raised the chalk, every flashing ace that had left the receiver flat-footed and dumbfounded, was lovingly recalled and described in minutest detail; each rally was battled out again stroke by stroke until the mind screamed in protest. But what was worse to one who had always liked and admired him was the gradual and reluctant realization that much of this tinsel glory Maurice was attaching to himself; the talk was all of Simon, but the inference, unmistakably, was that "what's bred in the bone will come out in the marrow". Maurice Pettigrew's son, at last, was living up to his father's lustrous name. I was glad when Maurice excused himself to keep an appointment with a Cabinet Minister and I was free at last to take my leave, accepting because I could not very well decline his invitation to spend the following weekend at Chalfont St Giles, when Simon would be playing in a nearby tournament.

I have often wished since then that I had found some excuse to call off that visit, but in truth there was no excuse that would have been convincing, and in any case I looked forward to seeing Dorothy —and I must confess to a desire, despite everything, to see young Simon in action. Which I did, indeed I did, and more's the pity. He was good, very good, winning the singles with ease and grace and carrying his partner to victory also in the men's doubles, and if the weekend had terminated with the tournament I would have returned to London a happy man and Maurice Pettigrew would have been left to bumble on with his pride and his illusions intact. But the weekend did not terminate with the tournament; it ended instead with a celebration party at which Maurice's extravagant boasting had both the guests and the luckless Simon cringing with embarrassment, and with a furious quarrel between father and son to which I was compelled to add a final cup of weird and eerie bitterness.

The quarrel, which had been simmering beneath the surface of Simon's mental discomfort, erupted suddenly when Maurice, who had perhaps enjoyed one more glass of champagne than was his wont, actually claimed a large share of the credit for his son's sporting success. "Never missed one tournament the boy's played in", was the line he pursued, "watched every stroke and pointed out every mistake. Nothing can compare with the value of really conscientious, *dedicated* coaching." That sort of thing. It was foolish talk, of course, scarcely calculated to endear him to anyone, least of all to his son, but I was totally unprepared for the savage violence of the boy's reaction. His lips were pale, his voice cut like a lash as he rounded on his father.

"*Your* coaching—*your* encouragement ... my God, that's good. You wouldn't know a stop-volley from a hole in the net. And as for your paternal encouragement, why don't you tell them about all the fatherly little talks you used to give me during the school holidays or every time you came to visit the bloody place? Have you any idea just how much I loathed you and your visits, how I used to dread the sight of you striding up and down the touchline like a bloody hero, bravely trying not to show how ashamed you were because I wasn't in the XV? And then the little talks—Christ, how you could lay it on; you sounded like Harry Wharton's uncle. 'Couldn't I be a bit more manly, show a bit of team spirit, forget about books for a while and take an interest in something wholesome, like kicking some other fellow's ribs in?' And then all the blushing, simpering innuendo; was it really right to spend so much time alone in my study? I wasn't ... by any chance, was I? Well I *wasn't*, as a matter of fact, no more often than the other fellows anyway, and just for the record, 'old scout', my *affaire* with Kafka was a damn sight healthier than the rugby captain's with Dingleby minor." And so it went on; bile and bitterness, bitterness and bile —the boy was brimming with it, and he spared his father nothing.

Maurice, to his credit, took it all wonderfully well. The shock of the onslaught snapped him sharply back to both dignity and sobriety, though his ashen complexion and the sudden compression of his down-turned lips gave evidence of what the effort was costing him, and his voice when at last he found it sounded steady enough. "We were talking," he said evenly, "about lawn tennis." But his moderation did not save him: instead it crucified him. Simon's reply was cold with hatred.

"So we were; and more specifically, if I remember rightly, about the value of coaching. Now let me tell you just a little about the importance of coaching. One of the first essentials is that the coach should know what he's talking about. Now I was lucky, I had a first-class coach—but it wasn't you. Christ Almighty, did it never once occur to you that I was a good player from the very moment we came home from Spain two years ago? Not a great player—I'm not that now—but good. And what coaching had you given me up till then, lying around in your deckchair reading penny dreadfuls? Even in my very first competitive season the local pundits were commenting on the quality of my stroke play, the maturity of my courtcraft—where d'you think I learned all that from—listening to you telling me to keep my eye on the ball?"

The boy hesitated, and his voice when he continued was little more than a whisper, vibrant and almost eerie in its intensity. "Listen —I said I had a first-class coach. Well I had more than that; I had a *wonderful* coach, the finest, most inspiring teacher I've ever known in any subject. It just seems funny that *his* subject should be a game, of all things—and yet it's not as funny as all that. You see to him tennis was more than a game, it was an art. It was subjective, if you understand the word, and the aim wasn't so much to beat some other fellow as to create perfection in oneself—to move like a dancer, to understand 'line' as an artist understands it, to use the racquet as a painter uses his brush, producing power or delicacy as the occasion demands. *That* was what he gave me, an appreciation of a sport as something creative, not destructive, something in which it's not winning that really matters but playing—laugh if you like—playing *beautifully*."

When Maurice answered, after a moment's silence, his voice sounded almost humble. "But who was this man? How is it I never met him? Why did you never bring him to the villa?"

Simon groaned, some of the savagery gone from his tone, replaced by a sort of hopeless air of defeat. "Won't you ever understand? I didn't want to bring him to the villa; I didn't want him to meet you. Good God, it would have been like introducing a bull fighter to a bull. Listen, father, this was a great artist, a great teacher, and I was his pupil. Can you try to follow this—during all those weeks

I spent with him, hour after hour and day after day, not once did I play against him, not once did we face each other across the net. When I suggested a knock-up one day, after I had begun to develop some feeling for the game, he just smiled at me and said 'No, Simon; you're not ready for me yet. Concentrate on your own stroke-play, and when you go back to England find opponents of your own calibre. I will teach you all I can; after that you must go out and start learning for yourself. But remember, you will start as literally a flawless player—the other will only teach you to remain flawless under pressure and at a greater pace. One day, when you and I are equal, and only then, we shall play against each other. You will sense when you are ready for that, and I shall be waiting for you, looking forward to the occasion.' "

Simon's eyes were shining now, his audience forgotten. "That's what coaching is all about; that's why I've never wanted to go back and see him again, never even written to him. You see, I *believe* him; one day I'll know without being told that I'm ready for him. *Then* I'll go back; *then* I'll show him his teaching wasn't wasted."

Maurice by this time was wholly won over; no one could fail to be in the face of such enthusiasm, such almost religious faith and fervour. "Just tell me one thing, Simon—how could he possibly teach you so much without ever putting you on the court, putting you to the test as it were?"

"Easily," said his son. "With a green wall and a strip of white paint. Let me tell you how it all started. A day or two after we got to Cortedia I was out for a walk when I came across an old house, a very big house, away out amongst the orange groves and surrounded by a rather broken down brick wall. In fact the wall was so crumbled I thought the place was abandoned, and I decided to go in and prowl around. The garden was vast, but completely neglected, and in one corner of it I saw another wall—but this one wasn't built of bricks; it was concrete, and painted green. I was walking up to have a closer look at it when a twig snapped like a pistol shot under my foot, and a moment later I discovered that the place wasn't deserted after all—in fact the fellow walking towards me had a very distinct air of ownership, of being at home. I was a bit confused, of course, and muttered something about being sorry to intrude, but he didn't seem in the least upset, and in fact he was very pleasant. He said something about being glad to have company and a chance to practise his English. Then he asked me if I played tennis, and I noticed for the first time that he was wearing a white shirt and long white flannels and that he was carrying a racquet in one hand and three balls in the other—I thought even then that he carried them completely naturally, the way a girl carries a handbag. I said no, not really, just pat-ball occasionally for fun, but I followed him around the corner of the green wall just the same, and right away I was fascinated by the way in which he handled the racquet even while he was talking to me.

"We were standing in the middle of a shabby old tennis court with a sagging, ragged net, and as he spoke he kept batting the balls against one of the surrounding walls, always placing the shots just above the level of a white line painted along the wall at the height a tennis net should be. The whole performance was completely effortless, and the power and variety of the strokes was extraordinary. Forehand, backhand drives, volleys and drop shots, all clipping the line and all executed with such ease and grace as you'd scarcely believe. Before long, and almost without thinking about it, I found myself with the racquet in my hand, trying to imitate him in my own clumsy fashion. And that's how it all started. I bought myself some gear the very next day and—well, you know the rest. I've never needed any more coaching, just experience and practice, practice, practice, always up against the training wall at the club, and always imagining Jose Antonio at my side, showing me and telling me quietly how it should be done."

At these last words of young Simon's I felt a chill wrap itself round my heart, and I gazed at the boy in reluctant fascination, knowing that I must believe what reason told me was impossible. I thought of the old mansion on the outskirts of Cortedia, of the crumbling walls and the sadly neglected tennis court in the garden. I thought of the young Spaniard in the long white flannels, and I visualized him and Simon, master and pupil, always side by side, playing their strokes against the solid concrete of the wall. I could see the exquisite artistry of the Spaniard's stroke-play, and I recalled that flawless stylishness as I had seen it reproduced that very afternoon in a neighbouring tournament. I could hear the liquid tones of the teacher as he encouraged his young companion, and I shuddered in horror and compassion as I remembered his promise to Simon that they would play against each other when they were "equal"— a wry jest indeed for a lonely, unhappy creature to make at his own expense. Yes, I could imagine the voice, and I could recognize the philosophical brand of humour, just as I could recognize the name of Jose Antonio and Simon's worshipping description of everything flawless, from his forehead to his flannels. For I had known

Jose Antonio many years before his fateful encounter with Simon, son of Maurice Pettigrew.

Even then I would have remained silent, nursing my strange secret to myself, had not Simon's very next remark forced me to disclose it in order to spare him the unspeakable anguish of facing a bitter and terrifying experience alone and utterly unprepared. For Simon now went on to set a target for himself, a definite time by which he meant to have made himself ready to meet his tutor "on equal terms", and that I knew he must not be allowed in his ignorance to attempt, for who can presume to set limits to the power of the subconscious mind? As Simon talked on about intensifying his training, about setting everything aside but preparation for his long-awaited match with Jose Antonio, I knew I had to speak, to tell him why he must set such an ambition resolutely from his mind.

I made my excuses to the few guests remaining, most of whom in truth seemed glad enough of the interruption, and I asked Maurice and Simon Pettigrew to accompany me to the bedroom that had been allocated to me for the weekend. There I took from my suitcase an old leather album, a sentimental journal that for many years has accompanied me on all my journeyings around the world, and I said to Simon "The full name of your teacher was, I think, Jose Antonio Garcia?"

The boy looked first startled and then delighted. "But of course— I should have realized you would know him, having had your villa in Cortedia. Stupid of me; I just never thought about that. Well, isn't everything I said true—isn't he a magnificent fellow, and a magnificent player?"

I answered slowly and carefully, opening the album as I spoke. "Yes, Simon, I certainly remember Jose Antonio as a splendid young man and a very fine player indeed; in fact great things were predicted for him."

"*Were* predicted? Has something happened to him? For God's sake ..."

"No," I said quietly, "nothing that I know of has happened to him recently; he had his full share of ill luck many years ago, long before you knew him." I handed over the album, opened to display a cutting from a Spanish newspaper faded and yellowing with age; the picture of a young man in white flannels was, however, clear and recognizable. "That is your teacher, isn't it, Simon? Take a grip on yourself, laddie, and I'll read the headline for you." I read the big black print; "Young Tennis Star Killed In Road Accident:

Jose Antonio Garcia Dies At Nineteen." I also read out the date at the top corner of the clipping: 22 April, 1933.

Simon Pettigrew never stepped on to a tennis court again. Some of Maurice's friends teased him at first about the sudden fall of the rising star, but gave that up after seeing the expression on his face. Maurice is no longer the Club Bore: in fact we don't see him in the club very often these days.

THE GREY MAN OF BRAERIACH

The order to strike camp was the signal for immediate and organized activity, for though the climbing party was young it was also disciplined. Kilted figures rose without argument from their hunkered positions around the three peat fires, the fires themselves were doused, ground down, and scattered, the only remaining trace of them a few spirals of aromatic smoke hanging motionless for a few moments in the stilly, frosted, early morning air. Porridge-pots were scoured till they shone, billy-cans rinsed in the stream and sleeping-bags rolled tight in their groundsheets and strapped like huge sausages beneath the aluminium-framed Bergen rucksacks, pup-tents folded and the camp-site cleared of the last trace of debris within thirty minutes of the Scoutmaster's shout. It was seven o'clock on the morning of 21 May, 1935 and the three patrols of the 49th Troop were ready for the mountains.

Twenty-four boys led by two men in their thirties, the party wound its way through the Deeside heather, past Derry Lodge, onwards and upwards towards the foothills of the Cairngorms, the formidable cluster of craggy and rugged peaks that towered in wild magnificence above them. There was little conversation, breath and energy being directed instead to the basic necessity of maintaining a steady, swinging pace, but the climbers, although loosely gathered in a single group, nevertheless split naturally into twos or threes in accordance with personal friendships.

One such pair, at the head of the column, were the Scoutmaster and his assistant, schoolteachers both and firm friends of long stand-

299

ing, linked since their own schooldays by a shared love of the mountains and, in particular, of those stark, beautiful, and sometimes treacherous mountains that now stood rampant before them. This passion apart, they seemed an ill-matched couple. Colin Mac-Dougall, six feet three and broad as a bullock, black-jowled and saturnine with a brooding eye and a lilting voice, could never have been mistaken for anything but what he was, a wild child of the Western Isles. His companion Davie Bruce, by contrast, was almost a caricature of the stock from which the Gordon Highlanders have sprung for centuries in the North-east, in Aberdeenshire and Kincardine. Solid and compact, a muscular five foot three, barrel-chested and bandy-legged, with a ruddy sea-sprayed complexion and a shock of sandy hair as stiff and wiry as a scrubbing brush, Davie was a vibrant bundle of irrepressible energy forever employed to some purpose. A less likely liaison could scarcely be imagined, and yet Davie Bruce and Colin MacDougall understood, liked, and complemented each other, and the combination of their talents and temperaments had shaped and moulded the boys of the 49th Troop into an efficient, happy, and remarkably self-reliant team.

Two members of this team who exemplified these qualities more than most were now striding along together at the rear of the formation, exchanging an occasional remark or merely a companionable grin. Billy Gilchrist and Sandy MacAllister were inseparable; in the same form at school, scrum-half and fly-half respectively in the Colts XV, both members of the Hawk patrol, near neighbours whose parents had long since become accustomed to seeing both or neither at meal-times and in the leisure hours of evenings or weekends, they might best be described—and indeed frequently were—as likeable little devils. Outstanding at games, just comfortably above average at their lessons, often in scrapes but never in real trouble, full of the energy and enterprise befitting healthy fifteen-year-olds, these were the two who, with their teachers MacDougall and Bruce, were destined to make this day memorable—the four of them, that is, and one other.

The heather was sparse and tufted now as the troop passed into the gaping mouth of Laraig Ghru, the rocky, boulder-strewn gully that runs for eighteen miles through the heart of the Cairngorms towards the oasis of Rothiemurchus and thence to Aviemore at the North-western extremity of the range. Past Ben McDhui on their right, the scouts were now picking their way across moon-surface terrain broken here and there by rushing burns that chuckled and sparkled in the morning sun, thankful for the stout climbing boots that kept their feet snug and their ankles secure, and thankful too, though they would not have admitted it, when Colin MacDougall finally called a halt for rest and refreshment on the lower slopes of their objective for the day—Braeriach, four thousand feet and more of heather, bracken, boulders, and loose, leg-wearying scree. To some of them the mountain was already familiar, to others, including Billy Gilchrist and Sandy MacAllister, this would be their first ascent.

MacDougall's briefing was simple and succinct, a mere reminder of rules already well known to them all, right down to the youngest tenderfoot in the troop. For this, strictly speaking, was not mountaineering at all, not climbing as climbers understand the term; rather it was hill-walking, with an occasional and optional pitch of greater difficulty to be tackled if they felt like it by the more experienced. And the ascent was, in the event, in no way out of the ordinary. Sweating and straining, huffing and puffing, plodding here and scrambling there, pausing now and again to gaze out over the awe-inspiring panorama unfolding around and beneath them, the boys toiled their way steadily upwards until at last, one by one, they hauled themselves over the final parapet to flop down in blissful exhaustion on the great plateau that stretches across the tops of Braeriach, four thousand two hundred and forty-eight feet above the North Sea.

Now it was time for food, and soon the camp-fires once again were blazing and the sausages sizzling in the pans while tea as black and strong as tar simmered in the dixies and the cooks' helpers cut wedges of bread the size of cottage doorsteps. The sun was high in an almost cloudless sky, and as they sprawled or squatted or strolled about the climbers drank in the beauty of the highland scenery around them; they could see jagged peaks and rolling mounds like vast purple earthbound whales, deep dark gullies and lochans of sparkling, blue, the long spine of the Grampians and far away, over towards Fort William, the proud pinnacle of the highest mountain in the land, Ben Nevis. They were utterly content.

For an hour or more the boys studied their maps, vying with each other in the identification of distant landmarks and listening to their leaders' enthusiastic descriptions of the many magnificent climbs that lay around them, there for the taking as their skill and experience developed, until eventually Colin MacDougall gave the order that they should unroll their sleeping-bags and take a rest before setting out on the descent and the long trek through the Laraig Ghru to their next selected camping point still miles ahead of them to the north-west. His instruction, like all MacDougall's instructions, was obeyed without questions, and it was shortly after this that he made his only, but none the less inexcusable, mistake. For the afternoon was warm and the Scoutmaster, like his charges, had eaten heartily; within twenty minutes Colin MacDougall, like the others, was fast asleep. His assistant, Davie Bruce, was already snoring; not a single member of the climbing party was awake to watch the weather.

Sandy MacAllister was the first to stir, and at first he could not believe the evidence of his drowsy eyes; indeed the eyes themselves seemed scarcely to be functioning, for instead of vast tracts of mountain and woodland he could make out only dimly the shapes of the boys in their sleeping-bags who were huddled in oblivion only a few feet away from him. Gradually he worked out for himself what had happened: Sandy, like all boys of his breed, had heard of the notorious highland mist that can descend without warning to smother the mountains in a thick grey blanket, chilly, damp, and impenetrable. Now, he realized, he was experiencing it for the first time; and to Sandy MacAllister this spelled not danger, but adventure. He reached out carefully and silently shook Billy Gilchrist by the shoulder, at the same time placing his free hand gently over Billy's mouth. As his friend awoke and slowly took in the changes in his surroundings, the two boys exchanged a series of signals, wriggled quietly out of their sleeping bags, and stole soundlessly away from their unconscious companions.

This was not merely a breach of discipline; it was an act of almost criminal folly and selfishness that might well have cost the lives of others besides themselves, but as the boys later pointed out in a sort of shame-faced plea of mitigation, they did not see it that way at the time. They were being disobedient and they were being irresponsible, but they were, none the less, acting with a purpose; they were conducting a self-devised experiment in scoutcraft. For each had immediately taken out his compass, and as a "safe-guard" they had linked themselves together by their lanyards so that they could not stray more than a couple of yards apart—the mist was so dense that this was, in fact, the absolute limit of their visibility—before setting out on their ghostly exploration of the plateau. What they did not take into account, because they did not know about it, was the fact that the high plateau of Braeriach is liberally pitted with pools and tarns, icy cold and in some cases very deep; nor did they know that at one point the plateau terminates abruptly in a precipice dropping sheerly vertical for several hundred feet. This was the terrain they had set out blindfold to explore.

The boys had been gone half an hour or more before Colin Mac-Dougall awoke with an angry grunt or two, muttering furiously in his shame-faced realization of his lapse from grace; my God, he thought, I'm a fine example—forever drumming safety precautions into these lads' heads and then to go off to sleep without even post-ing look-outs or leaving Davie Bruce in charge ... all this had run burning through his mind before he had opened his eyes. When he had opened them and had felt them itch and prickle in the clammy wetness of the mist, a sudden sickness rose in his throat, a sour and stifling amalgam of fear and self-disgust. But Colin MacDougall, in the right or in the wrong, was not the man to dissemble, and his bellow roused the sleepers from their rest as if they had been tossed in a blanket. No time was wasted on explanation or apology; "Patrol leaders—check your numbers and call in a report. Now everybody in the meantime sit still; don't move about at all."

He heard the cries of his patrol leaders and the muffled re-sponses of the scouts hidden from him in the soft, motionless mist, and it seemed an eternity before the first of the senior boys shouted out his report—"Owl patrol all present and correct". Moments later came the second call—"Beaver patrol all present and correct". Mac-Dougall began to breathe more easily; so long as the troop was in-tact there was no danger—discomfort, certainly, but no danger, and the discomfort could be swiftly assuaged with mugs and mugs of scalding, sweetened tea. But why was there no response from the Hawk patrol? There had been plenty of time for even the most careful and meticulous head-count. At last the voice of the patrol leader came floating through the mist, and every emotion but pure fear drained out of Colin MacDougall as his mind took in the im-plications of the message: "Hawk patrol—two scouts absent, Gil-christ and MacAllister."

The scoutmaster thought of the pools, of the steep corries drop-ping away without warning from the summit of the mountain, he thought above all of the terrifying precipice that turned the plateau into a death-trap, a trap waiting for the unwary, only a few hundred yards away in the deep grey silence. The dangerous act of disobedi-ence was the work of young Gilchrist and his friend MacAllister, but the responsibility for it, and for their safety in this wild mountain country, rested squarely on the shoulders of their leader, Colin MacDougall. The big man groaned inwardly and tried to figure out as coolly and rationally as possible the best course of action.

The patrol nearest to him was set to work re-kindling its camp-fire and the entire troop ordered to gather around it, bringing with them all the twigs and brushwood readily at hand. One of the big dixies was suspended above it for the inevitable and now very necessary brew of tea. MacDougall next instructed the scouts to bring their whistles from their shirt pockets and, with himself acting as conductor, to blow in unison the "recall" signal; as the final long blast eerily pierced the mist he cut his arm sharply downwards in the firelight and all listened anxiously in the sudden silence. Nothing; there was no answering call. Keeping his jangling nerves under strict control, the scoutmaster forced himself to space out the signals at two-minute intervals and to maintain absolute silence between the calls; Davie Bruce, fully aware of the mental torture to which his friend was being subjected, said nothing—there was in fact nothing to be said. Time after time the call went out, the notes dwindling into the far distance, muffled and distorted in the grey dampness, and time after time there was no response, only silence, until at last MacDougall knew that he must change his tactics, that he must do something more positive than whistling in the dark, if indeed it was not too late—and his heart contracted at the thought—to do anything at all.

"You take over here, Davie," he said to his assistant. "Keep up the signals, and make sure nobody moves. I'm going out to have a look around; I'll be back in an hour. If these little blighters turn up, hang on to them but don't strangle them—that's a treat I'm saving for myself." Davie Bruce's grin was weak and unconvincing; neither man had ever felt less like joking. He nodded, and said tersely, "I'll look after things here, and—good luck, Colin. We'll have three mugs of tea waiting." MacDougall returned the nod in silence and vanished into the mist, taking his compass in his hand and following, as luck would have it, a course sixty degrees divergent from the route the two boys had taken.

It was typical of MacDougall that the area he chose to explore first was that in which the going was roughest and the hazards most frequent. "To have a look around"; he smiled grimly at the recollection of the words he had used to Davie Bruce. There was precious little "looking around" involved in this lonely, fear-ridden journey across the rocky plateau; all his concentration was centred upon the ground a few feet in front of him and even he, for all his care and his long experience of the mountains, came close to disaster on several occasions when the earth yawned open beneath him and he was forced to edge his way around the lip of a corrie from which he heard with a shiver the receding rattle of the small stones dislodged by his heavy boots. Every hundred yards or so he stopped and blew a few sharp blasts on his whistle, and every time his heart sank as the call went unanswered.

Before long, sooner than he had expected, he found to his dismay that he could no longer hear the recall signals being sent out by the troop; the mist, obviously, was smothering the sound in its choking thickness and the two missing boys were hopelessly cut off from their companions and from the safety of the troop's rest site. MacDougall himself became more meticulous than ever in the use of his compass, checking his bearings before and after the slightest digression from his original route; he was not in any fear for his own safety, for he knew himself to be well capable of handling his problems on the hill, but he knew also that these mountain mists may lie for many hours, and he realized that if he were to fail in his promise to return within the hour the effect on the scouts' morale would be disastrous; they were good lads, tough and self-reliant, but they were, after all, only youngsters, and the fog-bound tops of the Cairngorms make an uncomfortable bivouac for climbers already troubled about the safety of their friends. Colin MacDougall checked and whistled, moved forward now only fifty yards at a stretch, and finally, sick at heart, turned round on to a reciprocal bearing and began to make his way back to the troop.

One look at Davie Bruce's expression was enough to tell him on his return that there had been no sight of Billy Gilchrist and Sandy MacAllister, and MacDougall was hard put to it to disguise his feeling of utter dejection from the anxious boys around him as he squatted down wearily beside the blazing fire and silently accepted the big mug of tea that one of the patrol leaders handed to him. He swallowed down several long draughts of the steaming hot liquid and knew that sooner or later he must break the tense and frightened silence; the boys were huddled as closely as they could be at the fire-side, and Davie Bruce, he was glad to see, had had the good sense to issue rations and set the scouts to fixing up their own meals individually; elbowing each other good-naturedly they were taking turns at grilling sausages on sticks or thrusting billy-cans of soup or stew into the glowing edges of the fire. That's it, Davie, he thought, keep the little devils busy and don't let them just sit there getting more scared every minute. But he, Colin MacDougall, was the leader of this ill-starred expedition, and now was the time for him to prove his capacity for leadership. He took a deep breath and finally broke the silence.

"Well, lads," he began, "this is a worrying situation and I'll make no bones about that. But don't you be getting daft ideas and deciding something dreadful has happened—for all we know, Billy and Sandy may be as safe and sound as we are. If they've shown any sense they'll most likely have huddled down in a corrie as soon as they realized they were lost, and they'll just be waiting like the rest of us for the mist to lift. That's all we can do for the moment. I'm going out again in the opposite direction, and maybe this time I'll be lucky."

Davie Bruce was about to protest that it was his turn to leave the comfort and security of the camp fire, but glancing at MacDougall he wisely and tactfully held his peace. The scoutmaster's face was taut with anxiety; nothing would do for Colin MacDougall, and Davie realized it, but to continue the search on his own—he was, after all, the leader. There was another thing to be considered too, reflected Davie Bruce; of the two of them Colin, brought up almost since babyhood with the Cuhullins as his playground, was unquestionably the better and more experienced mountaineer. If there should be an emergency, if Gilchrist and MacAllister had been involved in an accident, Colin was better equipped than himself to handle it; it was impressive, thought Davie, remembering other and more arduous expeditions, to watch Colin MacDougall in action; in the Cairngorms or in the Black Cuhullins of his native Skye, in the mountains of Wester Ross or the peaks of the Dolomites, the big islander seemed to move like a dark shadow, swift, sure and nimble for all his bulk. Yes, thought Davie Bruce ungrudgingly, if young Billy and Sandy were in trouble, Colin was the man to get them out of it.

Davie Bruce was to learn within minutes, and so were the others, that on *this* mountain, Braeriach, there is someone infinitely better qualified than Colin MacDougall to come to the aid of climbers in danger or distress.

The scoutmaster was just finishing his second mug of tea and munching a bar of chocolate before setting off to resume his search when one of the patrol leaders, Iain Campbell, said excitedly, "It's beginning to lift". MacDougall looked around him, and sure enough the grey blanket was becoming threadbare and starting to rise like a curtain of gauze; already he could see on the far side of the camp-fire scouts who only a few moments before had been invisible. His feelings at that moment were a strange, uncomfortable mixture of eagerness and dread. From long experience he knew the pattern of behaviour now to be expected from the weather; the mist, now it had begun to rise, would rise swiftly, and a glance at his watch told him that it was still daylight. Very soon now, perhaps within minutes, he would know whether Billy Gilchrist's and Sandy Mac-Allister's escapade had been merely a misdemeanour—or a tragedy. Silently and without affectation Colin MacDougall bowed his head in prayer.

As if in answer came another excited voice, and this time it was an exultant shout: "There they are—they're all right." The big scoutmaster jerked his head upwards, and his gaze followed the outstretched arm of one of the scouts who had leapt to his feet and was pointing out into the now swirling mist. Walking steadily towards them, several feet apart but still linked at waist level by the lanyards looped around their belts, came Billy and Sandy, their faces showing all too clearly their awareness that a far from friendly reception awaited them; the two boys, in truth, had realized a long time ago just how badly and how stupidly they had behaved. It was not at their nervous, frightened faces, however, that Colin MacDougall, Davie Bruce, and the other scouts were staring, nor was it even at the two wanderers themselves. The figures suddenly standing stock-still and silent in the flickering light of the camp-fire were gazing in stark disbelief at the enormous bulk of the man who was guiding Billy Gilchrist and Sandy MacAllister firmly and unhesitating across the rocks and heather.

Never had they seen such a giant; towering high above the two youngsters, this lofty, broad-shouldered Colossus made Colin Mac-Dougall himself look like a pigmy. And yet, as they all agreed afterwards, there was nothing in any way frightening about his appearance. He seemed, on the contrary, almost to radiate an air of gentleness and goodwill, of immense strength tempered by simple compassion. Appropriately enough, he was dressed in the clothing of a shepherd, a loose grey cloak as voluminous as a bell-tent covering him almost completely from neck to ankle and a long crook with a ram's horn handle dangling from one massive shoulder. His weather-beaten face was fringed by a bushy grey beard, and a shock of thick grey hair surmounted his wrinkled forehead. In one so obviously powerful, moving with the tireless grace of the mountain man, it was hard to assess his age—he might have been anywhere between sixty and eighty. Two great hands like legs of mutton poked out from the sides of his cloak and rested on the shoulders of his young companions, neither of whom, however, was paying the slightest attention to him. Billy and Sandy were gazing fearfully in the direction of Colin MacDougall, puzzled and only half-thankful that for some reason he had not yet unleashed the raging hounds of his inevitable anger.

The blast when it came did not take the form they were expecting. For all MacDougall's pent-up wrath suddenly released itself not upon the boys' folly and lack of responsibility, but upon their inexplicable lack of gratitude and common courtesy. The two scoutmasters and the rest of the troop had watched the huge shepherd, with a gentle push on the shoulders, thrust Billy Gilchrist and Sandy MacAllister right up to the fringe of the group standing silently around the fire; they had seen him wave, they had seen him smile, and they had seen him, before any of them could speak, turn and vanish into the thinning mist as silently as he had come out of it—and neither Billy Gilchrist nor Sandy MacAllister had so much as looked at him, let alone attempted to thank him for bringing them back to safety through heaven knew what difficulties and dangers.

For one long moment Colin MacDougall remained speechless in his indignation and shame, and when at last he did utter a shout of welcome to the unknown benefactor, urging him to the warmth of welcome of the fireside, the huge figure had disappeared entirely, and there was no answer to his call. The scoutmaster rounded furiously on the two boys standing in front of the fire, and all the anguish and anxiety of the past few hours rasped in his usually soft and musical voice as he told them in graphic terms and at considerable length exactly what he thought of them and of their behaviour. It was not until he had at last run out of both breath and adjectives that it dawned upon him that the faces of Billy Gilchrist and Sandy MacAllister were expressing not merely guilt, though guilt, understandably, was there in plenty, but also sheer, bewildered lack of understanding. It was young Billy who finally answered him, and the boy's voice was faltering close to a sob as he said quietly:

"Colin—Sandy and I know what we've done and we'll never forgive ourselves. It was silly and it was selfish and we want our backsides kicked. We know how angry you are and how worried you must have been, and we know we've asked for it if you turf us out of the troop—but Colin, what's all this about bad manners and lack of gratitude? Please, Colin, what on earth are you talking about?"

MacDougall stared down at the wide-eyed, unhappy youngster in front of him, and then at the face, equally woebegone, of Sandy MacAllister, and his heart lurched with something more than sudden pity and relief. They looked so very small and vulnerable and contrite—but more than that, they looked, they *were*, as he knew, so patently, innocently honest. Generations of Hebridean blood stirred in Colin MacDougall's veins and passed its message with clarity and with certainty to his brain—these lads really *didn't* know what he was talking about; they and they alone of all the members of the climbing party were and had been totally unaware of the presence of the big shepherd who had steered them to safety past all the pitfalls and hazards of the Braeriach plateau. MacDougall shifted his gaze to look at Davie Bruce, and he found that Davie Bruce was already looking at *him*, the light of comprehension slowly dawning in his eyes. "Good God," breathed Davie, and not even by the strictest standards of Scouting was there a trace of irreverence in the words, "you know who that was, Colin, don't you, without me telling you?"

"Aye, Davie, I know all right," replied the big man from the Western Isles, "we've just had a visit from the Grey Man." His voice was little more than a whisper, but it was a whisper that carried to the ears of every one of the scouts gathered around him, and MacDougall knew that they must be told, and told immediately, the meaning of his words. And so he made them sit down, these twenty-four healthy, practical, extremely rational young men, reminding them first and quietly that not one of them had experienced any feeling of fear, and he explained to them simply and without melodrama that they had all, all but two, that was, just seen what ordinary mortals choose to call a ghost.

He told them, and Davie Bruce corroborated his story, how years and years ago in their childhood their fathers and grandfathers had thrilled them with tales about the Grey Man of Braeriach, a wandering shepherd who, as far back as men then living could remember, had been known to appear from time to time, sometimes at intervals of many years, but always on this one particular mountain of the Cairngorm range and always at times of desperate danger. Dour, unimaginative, rock-steady north-eastern farmers, men not given to flights of fancy, had told of receiving his timely aid, and always the description had matched that of just such a man as the one who had come so dramatically to the rescue of Billy Gilchrist and Sandy Mac-Allister. These two would have something to talk about for the rest of the lives so miraculously saved that day on Braeriach.

Miraculously? Lives saved? Is that not perhaps to exaggerate the danger into which these boys had blindly wandered, and the power of the presence that guided them safely through it? Well, it might be fair to regard those words as something of an over-dramatization of the circumstances—had it not been for the Celtic mysticism of Colin MacDougall who, having thus found himself confronted by irrefutable evidence of the supernatural, was determined to explore the experience to its limits.

By the time yet another dixie of tea had been brewed up, and with his tongue-lashing of the two wanderers now over and done with, Colin had decided upon his next move in examining the mysterious incident. The mist had now cleared, giving visibility of several hundred yards, and Colin had not forgotten what the boys had told him about their use of compasses to check their route; it was on this matter that he framed his next questions. What route had they in fact followed? What bearing would enable him to re-trace their journey? What, in particular, had made them decide at some point to halt and to start heading back for the camp-site, for they must have realized that they could not expect to cover exactly the same ground and that every movement, therefore would carry them into the unknown and once more into danger? It was this question, and the boys' reluctant answer to it, that led Colin Mac-Dougall to the most blood-chilling moment of the whole weird episode.

"Well, Colin," began Sandy MacAllister, glancing miserably at his companion-in-crime as if to say "aren't we in bad enough trouble already?" but deciding that the least they could do was to own up to the truth, "suddenly, for no special reason, we both began to feel awfully scared. It was a queer feeling, horrible, like a cold hand grabbing the back of your neck, and it stopped us right in our tracks; dead still, just like that. In fact we said to each other how queer it was, both us checking so simultaneously we didn't even jerk the lan-yards linking us."

Sandy hesitated, stealing another unhappy look at Billy Gilchrist, and then plunged on with his story. "We were so scared we felt we wanted to smoke; I had just two fags in my pocket, so we had them, and when we were smoking them we both agreed we'd gone far enough and decided to turn back right away. And so we did. Sorry, Colin; we seem to have let you down all over the shop today." He fell silent and waited with Billy for the next manifestation of their leader's disappointment and disapproval. They were not in the least prepared, despite the Boy Scout motto, for Colin MacDougall's rejoinder. There was a gleam in his eye, certainly, but it did not look like a gleam of anger.

"You say you had only two cigarettes; what did you do with the empty packet?"

Billy and Sandy stared open-mouthed at the scoutmaster; they had expected a brief homily on the evils of tobacco, but not an inquiry into the tidiness of their habits. Colin, however, was clearly waiting for an answer to his question. It was Billy who gave it to him. "Sandy kicked it down into the turf with his heel; it would scarcely show, even if there was anyone there to see it."

"Scarcely," repeated Colin MacDougall thoughtfully, "but it *would* show, if only we could find the exact spot."

"Well yes, I suppose so," said Billy, thankful but utterly mystified by the turn the conversation had taken, "but what on earth ...?"

"Interest, laddie," answered Colin MacDougall laconically, "just put it down to insatiable curiosity. Plus the fact of course, that I'd like to know whether your talents for scouting extend beyond smoking and silliness to include some ability in following a compass bearing. Come on," he added, hoisting on his rucksack and flashing the boys a grin that took the sting out of his rebuke, "let's all spread wide on each side of you and see if you can lead us to the scene of the crime."

Minutes later the scouts of the 49th Troop were plodding steadily across the plateau in a long line that took its dressing from the tight little group in the centre formed by Billy and Sandy and, close behind them, Colin MacDougall and Davie Bruce; they had marched for perhaps twenty minutes, making a good pace in the clear sunlight, when Billy looked first at Sandy, who nodded in silent understanding, and then up at the two leaders." Allowing for the way we were crawling along this afternoon," he said, "I reckon we couldn't have come much farther than this. We'd better start looking for the packet. It was ..." He hesitated, and then gave a lopsided, in-for-a-penny-in-for-a-pound sort of grin, "it was a Player's—a Twenty". He saw the grim look on MacDougall's face, and he felt his flippancy had been misplaced. In this he was quite mistaken; Colin at that moment would not have noticed if Billy had said they were looking for a casket of a hundred Havanas. Colin MacDougall was looking bleak because what had been born in his mind earlier as a mystical, almost whimsical suspicion was now growing into a cold and terrifying sensation of near-certainty.

Turning first to his right and then to his left, he called out to the line of scouts; "Stay right where you are, all of you; sit down and sit put. No one is to move until I get back. You chaps," addressing Davie and the wanderers, "you come along with me, but come carefully, and Billy—you and Sandy get round behind Davie and me and watch every move we make. When we stop, you stop—don't move a muscle, got me?" The boys nodded, let the two scoutmasters pass through between them, and followed in silent wonderment as they made their way slowly across the heather. They hadn't far to walk; with a sudden shout of "Stop" Colin flung one arm in the air and told his three companions to sit down. He then moved forward for only a few paces before dropping to his knees and starting to crawl from side to side on all fours. In less than two minutes they heard him shout again and saw him rise from the heather about forty yards away to their left, waving something high above his head; "Here it is, lads, here's your guilty secret. At least I have to give you credit for using your compasses properly. Now listen; come on along here, but keep between me and rest of the troop. Understand, Davie? Don't get ahead of the line you're on now whatever you do. Okay —come on then."

As they approached they could see the strange blending of fear and excitement in Colin's expression, and as they came slowly forward in response to his beckoning hand all three of them suddenly sucked in their breath in a choking gulp of pure horror. They stopped dead in their tracks, and they stood staring as MacDougall, his dark eyes shining with an almost religious fervour, said to Billy Gilchrist and Sandy MacAllister, "Well, my bonnies, here's where you suddenly felt you had to stop and turn back. You didna' have the chance to say thank-you in person, but I think maybe now you've seen this you'll be saying thank-you to Someone tonight for your meeting with the Grey Man of Braeriach."

The two boys and Davie Bruce were listening to the scoutmaster's words and agreeing with them from the bottom of their hearts, but it was not at Colin MacDougall they were staring. They were staring at the yawning chasm where the plateau ended not four feet behind his back, and at the rolling slopes of the foothills stretching away hundreds of feet beneath them from the base of Braeriach's great precipice. They stood silent for a moment, all four of them, and then, still silent, they made their way back across the heather to the waiting troop.

Ju-Ju and Voodoo

AFRICAN MAGIC

In the days before the sun actually set on the British Empire, it was the custom of His Majesty's colonial servants in tropical climes to send their children, for reasons of both health and education, back to the mother country as soon as they were considered ready, as it were, to leave the nest.

For this reason, although I was born in Uganda, I left it when I was six years old and did not return to East Africa until I was seventeen. It was a time of change and restlessness, shortly before Mau Mau, that horror which based its power on the Africans' firmly ingrained belief in the supernatural, broke loose.

I was driving one day with the local police inspector, Monty Locke, through banana plantations dotted with the huts of the Africans who owned them, on the way down to Lake Victoria to sail. In the middle of the narrow dirt track, firmly planted in the earth, stood a slender pole about five feet long. Tied to it was a dead snake, by string threaded through its eye sockets.

Monty bumped his way round the obstruction, half in the ditch, narrowly missing the banana trees, and back on to the track. Somewhat surprised by these antics I asked why he had not simply stopped and removed the pole. He told me that it was a magic talisman of some kind, probably placed there to prevent evil attacking the village. Had he removed it we ourselves could have been in danger, perhaps from a magic spell, or even from an actual physical attack by the villagers. Twenty years in Africa had taught him a healthy respect for the powers of the African witch-doctors and a firm belief in a magic that, despite the efforts of the police, was still so widely practised that he reckoned that there was at least one ritual murder a day in Uganda alone.

Much impressed by this revelation, I told my parents of the incident when I got home, and for the first time I then heard the strange story of the African nurse, the ayah.

When I was born my mother, in the way of mothers with a first child, went to great care to choose for me a suitable ayah, with first-class references. In those days the household of the average European family included six or seven servants—a cook and kitchen-boy, two or three house-boys, two garden-boys and casual labour which came in to do the washing and sewing.

Most of the servants lived in the compounds behind the houses, in a row of small single rooms built for the purpose and screened by trees and bushes from the rest of the garden. There they cooked their own meals and led their own lively, sometimes quarrelsome lives. Some of them had wives and families living in the native quarter whom they would periodically visit, but most of their time was spent ministering to the needs of the Bwana and his Memsahib.

To my parents' house was added Sala, the ayah, who had come with impeccable references from a family returning to England on leave. She settled down happily enough and proved as devoted an ayah as even a new mother could wish: indeed Africans generally are fond of children. A year or so after her arrival my mother also acquired a new cook. Good cooks were hard to come by and the Memsahib usually had to train them herself, but this boy was unusually well experienced and my mother counted herself lucky in having three key servants, the cook, ayah and head houseboy, Fesito, all of whom were of first-class calibre.

Soon after the cook's arrival, however, the ayah began to behave in a strange and alarming manner. She made extraordinary mistakes: the drinks she gave to my one-year-old self were scalding hot; she forgot to put the mosquito net over the cot; she left the pram in the full heat of the tropical sun and she was often found fast asleep when she should have been alert to prevent her charge wandering into danger.

Every time an incident of this kind occurred the wretched Sala wept with shame and remorse. My mother could not understand it and the ayah herself could give no reason for her lapses. But despite her genuine efforts her mistakes continued until eventually my mother was obliged to dismiss her. African servants always took the keenest interest in the affairs of the Europeans, knowing everything that was going on in their family, and as soon as the cook heard that Sala was to go he suggested that my mother should employ his newest wife in her place. She had had no experience, he said, but she would very soon learn. My mother, however, had already engaged another ayah, who had been highly recommended to her, and she firmly resisted the cook's importunities.

The new ayah came to our household and Sala managed to find herself another job—where she showed no sign of the strange irresponsibility which had led to her dismissal. But my mother was as unlucky with the new ayah as she had been with Sala. Within a few weeks she came to beg the Memsahib to allow her to leave. She had been warned, she said, by magic signs that she was in danger if she stayed in the house. My mother reacted as most Europeans would, and scoffed at the superstitious nonsense. She succeeded for a while in persuading the girl that magic had no power to hurt her, but a few days later the ayah came to her grey with fear. (And, my mother said, it is difficult to believe unless you have ever seen a really terrified African, that their faces really do go grey.) Now the ayah told her that outside her hut in the compound she had found the sign of very bad magic indeed. If she did not leave at once she would die.

Accompanied by a group of excited servants, my parents went to investigate. The terrifying sign seemed to them to be just a heap of small sticks, laid across one another. But to the natives it meant that someone was trying to death-wish the girl. Once more my parents tried to persuade her that she would only die if she actually believed she was going to die; but when, the following morning, the ayah woke to find her hut surrounded by leaves she gathered her belongings into a bundle and fled, leaving the other servants to tell my mother of her departure.

In despair—for she had not been very well for some time and to be without an ayah was a disaster— my mother listened again to the cook's representations on behalf of his wife and agreed, finally, to see her. The next day the cook, grinning from ear to ear brought her to the house. She was a young woman, about twenty-seven years old, called Ndula, who quietly answered all my mother's questions, seemed intelligent and respectful, and amiably inclined towards myself.

She greeted with calm satisfaction the news that my mother would give her a trial—indeed, mildly to my mother's annoyance she had brought her bundle, all ready to move in. Ndula turned out to be a reasonably efficient ayah, but within two weeks of her arrival my parents' previously well-ordered household began to disintegrate. The quietly respectful young woman turned out to be rowdy and over-bearing, continually stirring up trouble between the other servants. Her husband was completely under her thumb. While she screamed and raved at one of the other boys, he stood grinning; while she flirted with them he sulked.

Since the kitchens and servants' quarters were situated away from the house my parents were not at first aware of what was going on, beyond the fact that there was occasionally some unseemly noise from the compound. One night, however, the head boy ran into the house begging the Bwana to come quickly. Outside the native quarters my father found the cook and one of the house-boys fighting while Ndula looked on with a derisory smile.

My father quelled the riot and, ignoring the explanatory streams of Swahili from a dozen excited Africans, told the head boy, Fesito, to follow him into the house.

"Bwana," said Fesito earnestly, "if you do not send Ndula away she will cause more trouble. She is a bad woman. I myself even will leave and nobody will come to work here because of her."

"If Ndula goes the cook must go too," said my mother. "I cannot risk any more trouble."

"*Ndio Memsahib*, I agree," said Fesito, "but they won't like that. They make a lot of money here. It is very important for them."

My mother promised to think about it. She and my father had, in fact, decided that, because of her health she should return to England soon, taking me with her, although my father was not due for leave for more than six months. They now determined that my mother should leave as soon as possible, and proceeded to make arrangements.

Of course the boys soon knew all about it, and within forty-eight hours Ndula had heard that my mother was taking me away. Knowing that this meant she would quite likely be out of a job—at least until my mother returned—she stormed in and more or less demanded to know what my mother meant by it. Since the problems she and her husband had caused were by now well known throughout Jinja another job would be hard to come by and this was, for them, a serious matter for any other kind of work was scarce. A shattering scene followed to which my father put a peremptory end, demanding the departure of both Ndula and her husband within the hour. Ndula's shouts turned to wails and pleading and, when my father remained adamant, to a stream of abuse in Kikuyu. This,

318

perhaps fortunately, my father did not understand, but it caused the house-boys, eavesdropping as always, to break into excited chatter.

Nevertheless within the hour the couple was gone and my mother fell back upon the help and hospitality of her friends until the time came to board the train for the two-day journey to Mombasa and the ship for England. She was fortunate : a passage was available within three weeks and meanwhile my parents were invited to stay with friends, Molly and Roland Buchan.

While she made arrangements for her voyage and her arrival in England, my mother also looked about for another boy to cook for my father. She made the usual inquiries, but could find no one. This was surprising because the job of cook to a bachelor or grass widower was a popular one. The fact that, in the absence of the Memsahib, they could safely be fed on "mincey-mincey" night after night was a standing joke, and there was usually a number of second-rate cooks only too anxious for such a position. Fesito had promised to remain with my father with one of the house-boys, but when she consulted him on the question of a cook he merely looked embarrassed and shook his head. Two days later Roland Buchan told my parents that he had heard from one of his boys that "in the market" they were saying that a curse had been put on my parents' house and all those in it, and that it would be dangerous to work there.

Naturally my parents scoffed at this but, eventually, my mother was obliged to leave for England without having found a cook, while my father returned to his own house, relying for his meals on the efforts of Fesito. Fortunately this boy came from a tribe known as the Masai, much sought after as servants for their reliability, and he seemed unperturbed by the threat of Kikuyu curses.

So while my mother and I sailed for England my father returned to a house which, although he refused to believe it, had in fact been cursed. The boys knew, because they had seen the signs—the bones, the crossed sticks, the ashes of roots and leaves that had been burned outside the door. They were afraid, but so far nothing seemed to have happened to them. They needed the money so they decided to stay on.

The night my father returned to his house, he was woken by strange nightmares. Something seemed to be crawling over him, nipping his flesh. In Africa one is always alert to the possibilities of scorpions, or soldier ants or similar unsociable insects, but when my father cautiously turned on the light, afraid to move too fast in case something really should bite him, there was nothing to be seen.

319

Nor were there any marks on his body. Yet when he turned the light out the whole performance started all over again. By the morning he was rather exhausted from lack of sleep. During the following weeks this happened several times. My father, however, was the kind of man who refused to admit that he could be prey to such fanciful delusions, and so he never told a soul. Then he began to suffer from splitting headaches—which he put down to being the result of sleepless nights, but which no amount of aspirin contrived to alleviate.

On top of this everything began to go wrong for him. When he went out on safari to pay his men on the roads—my father was a civil engineer—his car would break down drastically, his office boy would forget vital documents or a rock fall would make the road impassable. Out on the actual job unforeseen incidents would delay the work for weeks—the foundations of a road built across a swamp would suddenly sink; and expensive and, in Uganda, almost unique pieces of machinery would meet with such untoward accidents as rolling over a precipice.

As the weeks passed my father began noticeably to lose weight, and to look as ill as he often felt. Sometimes, after an unusually sleepless night, he would sleep far into the morning, undisturbed by the faithful Fesito who—though reviled for having allowed the Bwana to sleep late—was perfectly sure that he was under some kind of spell but, knowing my father's character and his reluctance to admit that such things could happen, did not dare say anything.

Finally, and this was a drastic step for a character like my father, he decided that he must go to the hospital and seek advice. But all he could tell the doctors was that he was suffering from continual nightmares which kept him awake and all they could tell him was that he appeared to be anaemic, run down and under weight. He went home again and during the next three days and nights, he said, it seemed to him as though some kind of leech-like power was slowly and inexorably sucking the life out of him—and my father is the least imaginative man you could meet.

At the end of those three days he was so weak that he could barely move. Fesito, deeply concerned, came to him once more and said that he was sure that my father was the victim of some powerful curse and that if he did not get help he would die. By this time my father was past arguing and it was apparent, even to him, that help was needed. His friends arranged for him to go into hospital. Various tests were made, but still nobody could diagnose the mysterious sickness from which he was suffering. He spent a week in hospital, and during that time his health improved and he suffered no more nightmares. But once he returned home the nightmares started all over again, and this time even more vividly.

Eventually, and against all rational arguments, my father was obliged to believe that he might indeed be the victim of black magic. At last he agreed to allow Fesito to help him. Persuaded by the head-boy, my father agreed to visit an *nganga*, a witch-doctor, who told him that among other things, he was probably the victim of a magic medicine buried at the entrance to his house. Every time my father walked over it the evil would affect him, bringing sickness and weakness and the influence of malevolent spirits on anything he did.

The witch-doctor, an evil-smelling, aged character dressed in a weird assortment of ancient animal skins, failed to impress my father but he agreed, with some scepticism, to let him try to exor-cize the evil spirit. Later in the day the *nganga* arrived at the house to carry out various rituals which seemed to involve (said my father) "the swilling and spilling of a good deal of corn beer and goat's blood" all round the house. Despite his scepticism, my father slept peacefully in his own house for the first time in weeks. He decided that this was due purely to the power of suggestion, but resented intensely the fact that he should be subject to it.

A week passed and life seemed to be back to normal. The fifty pounds that he had paid the witch-doctor appeared to have been well spent on the luxury of unbroken sleep. And then, suddenly, he was attacked by crippling pains in the chest and abdomen. At the time he was out inspecting work being carried out on the roads, and it was his men who loaded him, incapable of protest, into the back of a car and drove him to the hospital. Once again the doctors were unable to diagnose his illness, but by now, the story of his dealings with the witch-doctor had got round, and one of the doctors at the hospital, who had spent many years in Africa, sent for Fesito.

"I know," he said, "that you think the Bwana has been cursed, and that you have helped him in the past. Will you tell me why you know this and what you think has happened. Personally," he said as he saw Fesito hesitate, "I think you are right. Unless you help us I think he will die."

And so Fesito told the story of Ndula and her husband, and how Ndula, ambitious, greedy, determined to have nice things for her-self, had decided she must have the job of ayah in my parents' house so that she and her husband could earn what was, for an African couple, an unusually high wage. Ndula's mother, he said, was a witch : she had helped her daughter by putting a spell on Sala and then on the ayah who had succeeded her, so that she could get the job. But when Ndula had been dismissed the witch had revenged the slight put upon her daughter by cursing my father.

"What, then, can we do?" asked the doctor.

"If you will permit me," said Fesito, "I will go to the *nganga*. It seems that the curse is no longer just upon the Bwana's house but upon the Bwana himself. If I go quickly with enough money I think he will be able to help."

"I will drive you there," said the doctor, "because I believe you are right."

There is little more to tell. The doctor and Fesito visited the witch-doctor and, on his instructions, obtained various objects including some of my father's hair and some of his blood. From these and various other strange ingredients, the *nganga* made an amulet. It took him nearly twenty-four hours and during this time my father's condition grew steadily worse. When the amulet was placed under the pillow of his hospital bed he was barely conscious. But from that moment he began to recover. The doctors, of course, said that it was a result of their treatment—although they never knew what it was they were treating.

As for my father, he was inclined to believe the doctors. Witchcraft was not a thing that he *could* believe in. But my mother says that, during all the rest of his time in Africa, he carried the amulet everywhere he went.

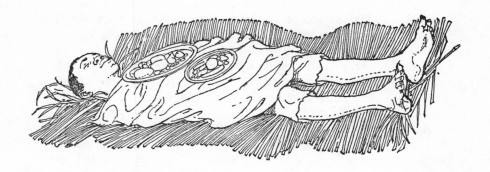

OF ZOMBIES AND SPELLS

"Voodoo"—what images that word can conjure up: drums in the night; devil worship; possessions by spirits; the "living dead"; and rituals involving animal, and even human, sacrifices. Over the years writers about the Caribbean have devoted reams of paper and gallons of ink to describing these magic arts of the Negro population. Undoubtedly a lot of what has been written has a strong basis in fact, but much also can be said to have been subject to that exaggeration which is often deemed necessary to produce "a good story".

Just what is this cult, and how did it all start? Voodoo owes its origin to the slave trade. The first European settlers in Haiti—the centre of the cult proper—were quick to notice how much hardier and more suited to hard agricultural work were imported Negroes than the local Indians. The result of this observation? A flourishing export trade in human flesh from North-west Africa, and extinction for the native population of the Caribbean.

Naturally, the slaves brought with them their own religions. The governments of the slave-trading countries often insisted that all captives should at least be baptized as Christians, but they were not so particular about following up this initiation with instruction in the faith. In fact, in Haiti a too-avid slave interest in Christianity was often discouraged—it wouldn't do to have a slave population learning too much about a doctrine preaching equality in the sight of God. Thus, though formal gatherings of the black population may have been prohibited by law for fear of rebellion, it was still possible for the traditional ritual to take hold on the other side of the Atlantic Ocean.

When missionary zeal eventually attempted to introduce the slaves to orthodox Catholicism little resistance was found. There was little trouble attached to accepting the new saints—they were simply identified with African counterparts and incorporated in the existing rites.

It was not only Haiti that took delivery of West African human beings, of course. Countries on the Eastern seaboard of both North and South America as well as the Caribbean islands soon became densely populated with black people.

As the local conditions varied, so did the physical and spiritual lives of the slaves. In Brazil, for example, the Portuguese settlers were much more ready than their Spanish and French neighbours to interbreed and even inter-marry with both the local Indian population and the Negroes they had imported. Thus the white man's Catholicism and the black man's spirit-worship blended early on in the nation's history. In fact, the white man added some spirit influences of his own in the nineteenth century by importing the fashionable French craze of Kardecism: and the Umbanda cult, which currently holds sway in the neighbourhood of Rio de Janeiro, is a mixture of all three.

Whatever the local variations though, the central point of all voodoo ritual is possession by spirits of some of the worshippers. The typical meeting is conducted in a large bare building having at one end an altar decked with flowers and statues of saints, and in the centre of the room a bare space big enough to dance in. Spectators line the sides of this dance-floor while the centre of the stage is occupied by the priest or priestess; several female initiates dance to the rhythm provided by three or so drums.

As the excitement induced by the beating of the drums increases, each of the women becomes "possessed" by a member of the spirit hierarchy. The mortal host takes on the attributes of the god who has occupied her body; for example in the Haitian cult the chief of the gods is Damballah, the snake, and those possessed by him creep about hissing and flicking their tongues in a snake-like manner. Considerable use is made of animal sacrifices—usually either chickens or a goat—but human sacrifice is considered to be a thing of the past, if it existed at all. As for Devil worship, the Brazilian Umbanda ritual goes so far as to make specific provision to keep him out of their ceremonies by confining him to a small house outside the main meeting-hall.

The associated Quimbanda sect, though, actively encourages him (*Exu*) to be present at their ceremonies. The differences between the two approaches are very marked. For example, the benefits of Umbanda intervention such as healing or spiritual well-being are meted out free of charge, but for inciting the aid of *Exu* through Quimbanda ritual one must often pay dearly. There is little attempt made to avoid making this payment—the defaulter is only too aware of the havoc that a cheated spirit could wreak.

Magic lies at the centre of all voodoo lore, and in the vast majority of cases it is white magic. But it is the black variety which has consistently hit the headlines through the years.

One of the more disturbing manifestations of this nature to capture foreign imagination is that of the zombies, the "living dead", who have been raised from their tombs to work for ever for their masters. Surely, one thinks, these must be an invention of black-magic fiction. And yet there are many Haitians who would strenuously disagree—their folk-lore abounds with tales of the living dead. One of the more famous stories concerns a young girl who was foolish enough to refuse the advances of the local voodoo priest (or *hungan*). She fell ill and eventually died to the great sorrow of her family and friends. The usual wake was held to pay the last respects to the body, but unfortunately one of the guests was not quite respectful enough as far as his lighted cigarette was concerned —it fell on the girl's foot and caused quite a burn. That was not the only misfortune to befall the cadaver either, for when it was time to place the body in its coffin it was found that the box was rather too short and as a result the head had to be bent to one side to fit it in.

The remainder of the burial proceeded normally and the coffin was interred under the customary mound of earth. The attractive young girl who had so fatally attracted the *hungan*'s attention was no more, but several people later remarked on a speechless idiot who was seen to take up residence at the priest's house shortly afterwards —a female idiot who had a bad burn scar on her foot, and whose head was always permanently slumped to one side!

Such occurrences are greatly feared by the simpler folk, and it is far from unknown for families to ensure that their dead loved ones are not condemned to perpetual slavery by "killing" the corpse a second time by strangling or shooting it. The legend goes that a corpse can be raised only if it can answer when its potential master calls its name. Thus there has grown up a practice of sewing up the mouth of a body to prevent it talking itself into an unwelcome job contract.

Simple superstition? The island's legislature saw fit to write laws against the practice anyway. "Raising from the dead" they did not necessarily believe, but they knew it was possible for someone skilled in herbal medicine to discover a mixture of drugs which could induce a state of catalepsy in a victim with such effect that the rest of the world would think him dead. Because of the climate, burial in Haiti usually follows quickly after death, so the potential master of the zombie has usually only to wait one night until he is able to disinter and revive his victim. In all cases, though, it would appear that revival can only be partial, and a state of dumb idiocy is all that the "once-dead" can look forward too.

The malevolent *hungan* is by no means the only source of black-magic. Feared at least as much by ordinary people is the threat of the secret society of black witches. Each member of this sinister organization has at some time availed himself of his own personal spirit which undertakes to serve him by looking after his material welfare in return for receiving payment of its own choosing—often human sacrifices. The crimes committed in the course of keeping these spirits satisfied bind the society together, and its members are reputed to wander abroad at night searching for luckless travellers to serve as victims. Not every stranger caught in this way is killed—some are given the choice between death and joining the band—but as the latter course of action involves sacrificing someone they are fond of, it is not the easiest of decisions to make. The imagination of generations of peasants has imputed many fearful attributes to these sects. By day a member is indistinguishable from anyone else, but you can never be sure what your closest neighbour does after night-fall. How do you know that he doesn't follow the call of the secret drum which is inaudible to the innocent ear, but which is able to summon initiates to a sabbat to commit their terrible crimes?

The traveller by night must beware, and not only of parties of people on foot. There are tales in the area of Port au Prince, for instance, of a motorized version of the secret society which drives a ghostly car around whisking likely victims into the back seat. Beware of lifts from strangers if you don't wish to finish up transformed into an animal in the slaughterer's yard—one of the more picturesque ways of dispatching victims.

The members are also credited with being able to change their own appearance at will, and are reputedly quite fond of becoming animals themselves—though one imagines they are careful to avoid the slaughterer in that condition. The purpose of this transformation seems to be to annoy and terrify the innocent passer-by by appearing in front of him on a lonely road and blocking his path. There are remedies for being pestered in this manner, though, and the wise voyager may well take with him some such safeguard as a whip which has been blessed by his local *hungan*. Alfred Metraux in his authorititative book *Voodoo in Haiti* recounts the tale of such a traveller who was annoyed one night by a large cow which persistently blocked his path on the road. Presumably as much in fear as annoyance he proceeded to belabour the obstructive animal with a blessed whip he had on him. To his surprise the cow reverted to the human form of none other than the local chief-of-police, who pleaded with him to keep the incident dark, and then limped home to bed. Apparently black voodoo spirits cannot always save those whom they possess, for the policeman never rose from his bed again but wasted away and died—his body covered with weals.

Perhaps the most feared of these animal/human forms is the peculiary female werewolf, or *loup garou*, who feeds nightly on blood sucked from the necks of children. Again, by day there is no way of distinguishing these fiends, but by night they are capable of changing themselves into all sorts of animals or insects to get near to their sleeping sources of food.

The *loup garou* can feast off a child only if it has been "given" by its mother. As one would expect, most mothers do not readily consign their offspring to such a fate, so some form of trickery has to be employed. A favourite device involves creeping stealthily to a potential victim's house at dead of night and softly asking the sleeping mother if she will hand over her baby. If the semi-conscious woman agrees, the child is lost and the werewolf has a feast on her hands. The same objective can also be achieved by appearing to the sleeping mother in a dream and offering a present at the same time as mentioning the child's name; if the mother accepts the gift the werewolf dines well and the child wastes away until it finally dies. But even its death is not the end of the little one's plight, for some insist that the werewolf will later dig up the body from the cemetery and take it away as a gastronomic treat.

It is with reason then that the werewolf should be feared. But not all magic is on its side. The pregnant woman can protect her baby from such an attack by drinking black coffee laced with petrol and bathing in a special herbal bath. If the baby is bathed in a similar infusion soon after birth its blood will be "spoiled" for werewolf purposes, and if the *loup garou* attempts to drink it she will be seized with a fit of vomiting and be forced to rush home leaving a trail which anyone can follow.

The worst and most feared of all the black-magic practices is that of "sending the dead" upon someone. Disease and death always follow for the victim unless the trouble can be diagnosed and exorcized by the appropriate authorities. In Haiti the person wishing to invoke the aid of the dead in destroying an enemy must first gain the assistance of the King of the Dead, Baron Samedi. Once his aid has been secured through a nocturnal visit to a cemetery, handfuls of earth and stones must be gathered from graves to be put in the victim's path. With this accomplished the victim is surely doomed unless a *hungan* intervenes with rival magic, which might involve nothing more complex than a course of herbal baths, but on the other hand could entail making pacts with Baron Samedi himself to accept an alternative life such as that of a plant or an animal.

To people outside the voodoo influence the way the curses work seems obvious. If a superstitious peasant can be convinced that the powers of evil are seeing to it that he will waste away and die, then sure enough he will waste away and die. Convincing someone of the seriousness of the spirit threat is not difficult when the victim has been raised in a background of voodoo folk-lore. You wouldn't expect it to work so well in a modern city, though, and certainly it wouldn't work on someone brought up in the materialist atmosphere of present-day Europe or North America. At least, that is how the critics rationalize it.

American journalist and author David St Clair spent several years in Brazil travelling widely and writing on subjects ranging from the country's mightiest river, the Amazon, to the religious life and beliefs of its people. His career there wasn't without its successes, for he soon found himself able to afford all the trappings of middle-class life in Rio de Janeiro—trappings which included a well-appointed flat and a living-in maid.

It seems that even in South America the servant situation is not without its problems, and a succession of people had to be found to cover these domestic duties—that is until one particular Negro girl arrived. She was more than efficient—the house was spotless and became renowned for its cuisine, and what was more she showed no sign of leaving in a hurry like so many of her predecessors.

Naturally, the man of the house made every effort to keep her and accommodate her idiosyncrasies, one of the chief of which was the exception she took to her employer's study of the primitive religions of her people. Statues of local gods which he brought into the house for decoration or study had a habit of disappearing or being broken "accidentally", and she was continually warning him against getting mixed up with the Umbanda and Quimbanda cults. However, the minor irritation caused by the disappearance of a few ornaments was far outweighed by her prowess in other areas, and an excellent master/servant relationship developed and flourished for some considerable time.

Business for the journalist continued to be good and showed signs of being even better with the completion of a book which was likely to make its author a considerable sum of money. Maybe it was time to move on from Brazil; Greece seemed as though it might be a good place to try. Money from the book would help with the cost of removal, and furthermore there was word of a legacy which was due to materialize. It could be just the right moment to try pastures new. As for the maid, loyal service had to be rewarded, so he proposed paying her a year's salary, which should have gone quite a way to buying herself a small house and providing her with some security. Unfortunately she didn't seem at all pleased at the prospect of his departure. St Clair, however, considered he had done more than was strictly necessary to make sure she was adequately provided for; after all, she was only his maidservant, not his mistress.

She would soon get over it, he reasoned, once he was really out of the country. But suddenly it seemed that the day of departure might not be as sooon as he had expected. The book didn't sell; not only were publishers not falling over themselves to pick it up, but they didn't seem to be too enthusiastic about even giving it a reading. The manuscript became used to spending long months in "in trays" only to find itself in "out trays" accompanied by rejection slips. To make matters worse the inheritance ran into legal snags, and funds really began to look dangerously low, so that instead of being in a position to bow gracefully out of Rio St Clair was actually facing eviction for failing to pay the rent of his flat.

Financially he was certainly having a run of bad luck but the troubles weren't confined to his bank balance. A lightning trip to Buenos Aires to keep a lovers' tryst ended in disaster with the loved one fleeing into the arms of another the moment our hero landed in Argentina. And to make matters worse, the loan which he had relied upon getting to finance this whirlwind trip was very firmly not forthcoming.

There was nothing for it but to return to Brazil, sadder and poorer than ever. Then he caught malaria.

Shortly after these events he met a spiritist friend in the street. With misfortunes of this magnitude lying on his shoulders it would presumably not have required any great powers of divination to see that all was not well with the struggling author. This friend did indeed see just that, but she saw more too, and offered a diagnosis of the problem: someone was putting the evil eye on him.

As it turned out this was not an isolated warning. Another friend called on him shortly after saying that a message had come through from the spirits at a Umbanda meeting proclaiming that a journalist, David St Clair, was in deadly peril from the deeds of a woman living in his flat. Then a spiritist actor friend came to stay. He could hardly wait till the maid was out of the room to convey the warning which he had received from the spirit world that she was attending Quimbanda black-magic sessions in order to put a jinx on her employer.

As unlikely as this seemed to St Clair three independent warnings were a lot to ignore completely, so he resolved to tackle his maid on the subject by indirect means: he asked her to take him to an Umbanda meeting the following Saturday, to ask the spirits the source of his misfortune. Reluctantly she eventually agreed to do so, and late that Saturday night found him in the company of his maidservant and two of her relations, standing on the cold beaten-earth floor of a large hut in the outer suburbs of Rio.

Eventually at midnight the ritual began. This was orthodox Umbanda. Thirteen female acolytes entered the hut, dressed in gowns of pale blue and white and danced in the bare central space to the beating of the drums. The priestess then made her appearance also in a white ensemble, but one which far outshone those of her attendants, and proceeded to call for the blessing of God and the saints—both catholic and voodoo—on the night's proceedings. Then followed "routine" possessions; but instead of going on to answer the questions of the members of the congregation, the priestess concluded the ceremony. Then she left.

This was indeed the end of the Umbanda service, but it was far from being the end of the evening's ritual. The drum rhythm changed and the priestess made a second entrance. But no longer was she in pure white. The costume had changed with the change in the general atmosphere; she was now clad from head to foot in vivid red. The remainder of the evening was not to be spent with God and the saints but with *Exu*—the Devil.

After much unladylike conduct involving smoking cigars (sometimes the wrong way round) and copious drinking of rot-gut alcohol, the woman (who was of course no longer a female priestess but "an embodiment of the Devil himself") got around to the question-and-answer session.

Working through the oracle of two possessed acolytes, one of whom was the maid's cousin, it was learned that St Clair was indeed the victim of a black-magic curse which had been placed by none other than the maid herself. The motive? She did not want her master to leave, and had thus asked a black magic priest to concoct a spell that would dog him with bad luck until he either married her or bought her a small house.

The maid was furious at this exposition. However, she was sent away from the meeting by the priestess, and a start was made to rectify the damage she was alleged to have done. In her absence St Clair was told that the trouble wished on him would now be doubly visited on the person responsible. He went home in a state of mind which was a mixture of emotional misgiving and disbelief.

Three days later, however, a telegram arrived from an American magazine commissioning him to write a long article and sending him the expenses in advance. A week after the midnight visit the inheritance came through, and a few days after that a letter arrived from the Argentinian loved one offering an explanation for the recent misunderstanding.

What happened to the maid? She fell ill with a stomach complaint and the doctor was called. Apparently there was nothing for it but to operate. This was done at her boss's expense, but nothing was found. Shortly after her return from hospital he found her packing to leave, and then she confessed—all the accusations had been true. She had indeed sought the aid of black magic to prevent him leaving without either marrying her or buying her a house. The Quimbanda priest had told her to steal articles of her master's clothing—she chose socks—and put a special pepper in his food. The treatment was obviously effective. But so had been that meted out by the rival Umbanda representative on her employer's behalf: she was now far more cursed than her master and would remain so until she left his house for ever.

And leave she did, amid much regret on both sides. What happened next the author doesn't relate, but at the conclusion of his account of that episode in his book *Drum and Candle*, David St Clair confesses that he had to change his attitude to the Brazilian spirit world. It seems that the recognition of the powers of voodoo is by no means confined to the Negro peasant.

Messages from Another World?

THE VOICES OF ROSEMARY BROWN

What would the world have heard if Mozart or Schubert had not died so young? What would Beethoven's next symphony have sounded like? This form of idle speculation is often indulged in by musicians. But is it actually so idle? If the experience of a South London widow can be believed we may yet hear Beethoven's Tenth, though the first ears it will fall on will not be those of critics in a concert-hall or of professors in a conservatoire, but those belonging to neighbours in a very ordinary suburban street.

For the past ten years or so Mrs Rosemary Brown of Balham has been writing music—not her music, but music which she affirms is dictated to her by a group of composers ranging from Monteverdi to Stravinsky.

In her book *Unfinished Symphonies**, she tells how, when she was seven years old, she was visited by the ghostly shape of a very old man in a cassock who told her that he had been a pianist and a composer when he was alive, and who promised one day to return and give her music. Over the years she had many more meetings with this "visitor", whom she later recognized as Liszt; but it was not until 1964 that the business of transmitting music actually began.

One day as she was housebound, recovering from an accident at work, she sat down at the piano to pass the time. Suddenly she was

* *Unfinished symphonies, Voices from Beyond,* by Rosemary Brown. Published by Souvenir Press, price £1·75.

aware that the now-familiar form of the composer was standing beside her, but this time it was different. He took hold of her hands and started to guide them over the keys of the piano: he had come to fulfil his promise of all those years ago. Thus began a process of musical communication that continues to this day.

She liked the pieces that she was being made to play, and it soon occurred to her that it might be nice to write some of them down. This she started to do, but with difficulty, for she had only a scant knowledge of musical notation. However, she struggled on. Liszt was delighted, and soon brought other dead colleagues to visit her; musical transcription from someone or other became a daily occurrence.

For a long time the story of the visitors and the new music was kept to family and friends, but gradually it leaked out. Eventually it leaked as far as a local newspaper, and then to a radio programme. Now the public had a chance to hear what had been going on and they liked it. In fact they liked it enough for the street to become a thoroughfare for journalists from the world's leading newspapers. But this wasn't all: there followed an offer to publish her autobiography, the issuing of a gramophone record of some of the compositions, and television interviews and concerts both at home and in America.

Today a considerable number of deceased musicians are regular visitors to the Brown household, but Liszt has always remained the chief of the group. He has produced by far the greatest quantity of music through her, and enjoys the attention it is getting. He certainly seems ready enough to help things along in that direction, even when public demonstration of the "communication" process is required.

One of these public occasions occurred when the producer of a forthcoming radio programme asked Rosemary Brown if she could produce anything from her composers there and then. Liszt delivered the goods. First he dictated a few bars of the left-hand part of a piece in 3/2 time, which she wrote down. Then came the right-hand part—in the completely different time signature of 5/4. With her limited technique she could not at first play it on her piano, but the producer (who was a talented pianist) could, and was impressed with what he heard.

He was not alone in this, for when the piece in question—*Grubelei*—was shown to the composer Humphrey Searle, who is one of the world's leading authorities on Liszt, he was very interested. "It is the sort of piece which Liszt could well have written," he said. "Particularly during the last fifteen years of his life when he was experimenting in new directions." He felt that the complex rhythm was particularly remarkable, for while it is not really strange in our day it would have been very unusual in the nineteenth century when Liszt was alive. He was also impressed with the Lisztian quality of the design of the form of the piece, and found the harmonic style and the language of the score markings consistent with the composer as well. Furthermore, he drew attention to the resemblance between one bar of it to a bar in the cadenza of the famous third *Liebestraum*: at this point the notes in the two pieces are identical though they are written at a different pitch.

Other scholars have been impressed with this piece too, and Professor Ian Parrott of the University College of Wales at Aberystwyth thought that it did indeed sound like what Liszt "was going to write next".

Liszt has also produced non-musical demonstrations to help his twentieth-century friend get her point across to potentially sceptical interviewers. When she was being interviewed by a German magazine, for instance, the Hungarian photographer asked Liszt, whom Rosemary Brown had said was present, a question in German which produced the reply "*Ja*" from the composer. Liszt then disappeared, but shortly returned with a female companion. When Rosemary Brown described this woman in detail the photographer nodded approval. He explained that he had asked the composer if he would fetch his mother who had recently died: Rosemary Brown had just described her perfectly.

Liszt has had a hand in other things too. On one occasion he helped find the best-buy in bananas in the supermarket, on another he provided assistance with the youngest Brown's homework, and twice he has helped the family to win modest sums on the football pools.

Chopin, who after Liszt is the next most frequent visitor to the South London living-room, has also been known to concern himself with domestic matters. The most notable of these events was his timely intervention which saved the house from flooding. Mrs Brown's daughter had begun to run a bath one day when her mother was deep in conversation with the composer. Suddenly he stopped short and cried: *Le bain va être englouti!* It took a few moments for the full meaning of the message to sink in as French is not a common language in the house, but eventually his earthly partner realized what all the fuss was about and ran upstairs just in time to avert a very messy accident.

Most of his contact though, even if it is less spectacular for the Browns' daily life, is likely to be more interesting to the world at large. He has dictated a considerable amount of music (mostly for the piano of course) including a *Fantasie Impromptu*, which has impressed Leonard Bernstein among others. Chopin prefers to work with his translator sitting at the piano, so that the music can be played as it evolves. Mrs Brown likes this method too, even though the difficulty of much of the writing stretches her limited piano technique to its limits.

She also gets on well with Schubert who, like all the composers, was first introduced by Liszt. On that occasion he was wearing spectacles as in most of his portraits (possibly as an aid to recognition, she supposes) but once he became a regular visitor he left them off. So far his musical donations include several songs, mostly with German words, and portions of string quartets and orchestral works though none of these is finished. However a lengthy C major piano sonata which runs to about forty pages of manuscript has been completed, and work is progressing on an opera which has "life after death" as its main theme.

What of the quality of the Schubert music? Well, it has impressed many Schubert experts including the pianist Louis Kentner, who thinks that this composer would be one of the hardest to forge. Will he finish the *Unfinished Symphony*? Apparently it is completed, and Rosemary Brown had heard it "by telepathy". She was very impressed with it, particularly the first subject of the last movement. Unfortunately though, she did not write it down when she heard it, and it is now forgotten: the world must wait for it to come through again. And why didn't he finish it in the first place? It seems he just ran out of inspiration in that direction.

He has also been able to resolve some of the other major controversies which have raged among Schubert scholars. One of these concerns the famous *Grand Duo* for the piano, which many have insisted is really a piano-reduction of a lost orchestral work. Mrs Brown was asked to inquire of the composer as to the truth of the matter. He replied that it was not a reduced orchestral score, but a true piano composition. And was it true, she asked, that there were many of his compositions still to be found like the lost symphony he was supposed to have written at Gastein? There were many more pieces, he said, especially in Vienna.

Then there is the incident when he helped Rosemary Brown to win special attention in a score-reading class which she was attending. The work being studied was Schubert's Ninth Symphony, and students were asked a question concerning the structure at a certain point. Schubert, being at Rosemary's side, pointed the answer out to her—and she was the only one to get it right. This didn't surprise her—after all he had written it in the first place, so he should know —but it did give a bit of a jolt to the teacher. The question was not at all easy, and she was by no means one of the brightest students in the class.

Other composers have solved musical puzzles too. Debussy, for instance, was able to clear up doubts for a recitalist over the interpretation of one of his pieces. The British composer/pianist Richard Rodney Bennett commented to Rosemary Brown one day that he was having trouble with a Debussy piece which he was due to play shortly at a recital, though he did not specify the piece. She relayed his difficulties to the composer, and received back instructions to vary the tempo and the use of the pedal in a way that could only apply to the composition in question.

Debussy's image seems to be changing: he is now clean shaven and is fond of wearing sheepskin jackets and straw hats. He is still concerned with music, of course, and has dictated several piano pieces, the beginning of a septet for wind and strings, and is working on some songs with new words by Lamartine. But his latest departure —painting—is taking up much of his time.

On the other hand there is no change of purpose for Beethoven who, now freed from his deafness, says he has much music to give the world. Apparently there is a Tenth Symphony, but it is taking a long time for Mrs Brown to get it on to paper. Even though many people have been impressed with the speed with which she transcribes the notes, it can be a long and arduous process for both her and the composer, working with more than two staves at once, as is necessary with an orchestral score or a string quartet.

Quartets have been transcribed for Brahms, though, and one of them has been performed and broadcast. This composer has shown himself to be particularly adept at psychic communication, and has handed on many pieces—most of them for the piano, as one might expect. Rosemary Brown finds Brahms particularly difficult to play, mainly because of his liking for making the hand stretch a tenth— two more notes than an octave. She has small hands herself.

Some of the spirit visitors are doing their best to improve her skill at the keyboard. Liszt is particularly good with interpretation, but it is Rachmaninov who is the main master of technique. He, of course, was a virtuoso pianist of the highest rank, and some of the fingering which he suggests are rather unorthodox.

339

Naturally, he also dictates music. One morning he was particularly insistent that she should take down a large portion of a new piece—a complicated concert study and take it with her when she went out that evening. At that moment she planned nothing for the rest of the day but to stay at home. However, she learned later that that evening she was to have a surprise meeting with Leonard Bernstein. As instructed she took the new Rachmaninov piece with her, and the American played it with *brio*, seemingly very taken with it. That is, he liked all but one bar of it—Rachmaninov has since revised the bar in question.

Not all the composers communicate with the same facility. Berlioz, for example, tends to appear for only a short time and has not so far succeeded in getting through a whole piece. Of course with him there is the added difficulty of trying to transcribe a complete orchestral score. He seems ready enough to advise on the performance of his existing music, however. David Cairns of Philips Records recalls that when Colin Davis was recording *The Trojans* for that company, a discrepancy was noticed between the speeds that Davis was using for parts of the Septet and the Love Duet and the metronome markings that Berlioz had written into the score. The problem was mentioned in passing to Rosemary Brown, who in turn asked Liszt to take the matter up with Berlioz. He reported back that the metronome markings were indeed wrong, and suggested alternatives which were much nearer the tempi being used by Colin Davis.

Other musical spirits visiting the Brown household include Bach, who is currently fascinated by styles more modern than his own, Mozart, the Schumanns (Robert and Clara, though not together), and Grieg. Stravinsky seems to have lost little time in taking up his pen again, for he too has already attended several sessions of score-writing and left some music.

All of which raises the question of "Why are they doing it?" The answer, as one might expect by now, comes not from Rosemary Brown, but through her: the originator is the spectral musicologist Sir Donald Tovey, who died in 1940. He got Mrs Brown out of bed one night to dictate to her an explanatory sleeve-note for her record which was about to be published. In rolling prose, which some scholars have accepted as being typical of his style, he explains that the composers are communicating to try to let the world see that "physical death is a transition from one state of consciousness to another wherein one retains one's individuality". He tells us: "The knowledge that incarnation in your world is but one stage in man's eternal life should foster policies which are far more far-seeing than those frequently adopted at present, and encourage a more balanced outlook regarding all matters."

So the idea is not so much to entertain with the music itself, but to get people thinking and talking about the whole phenomenon of its appearance. The music's "live" debut at London's Wigmore Hall certainly got people talking, but it could not be counted an unqualified success, at least from the point of view of the notices it received. The programme had been arranged at short notice, and as Mrs Brown herself was to be the pianist her self-confessed lack of technique meant that many of the more complex and interesting pieces had to be left out. Critics, especially London critics, are however not ones to make allowances. They pounced.

The Financial Times found the pieces "Pointless, worthless and trivial", and went on to declare that: "Most of them are laughably bad; none of them is good enough to merit the title of pastiche." The *Daily Telegraph* thundered: "Not one work could have been written by the composer when alive. The superficial aspects of style, the mannerisms were sometimes present, but what was missing in all cases was the hard creative thought that makes cogent syntax from vocabulary and that indicates the presence of a master." *The Times* wasn't any more convinced and maintained: "Any sensitive competent student of music can improvise pastiche; these pieces could be taken to suggest a limited and rather naïve gift of that sort"; while *The Sunday Times* was kinder, but still not convinced: "Her degree of musical sensitivity is unquestionable, but I personally doubt the supernatural flow of musical pastiche."

"But," say her followers, "isn't it always like that with music critics? Most of these composers didn't have a particularly good relationship with them in their lifetime anyway, so what does this present outburst prove?" Certainly, response from other musicians has inclined to be far more favourable. In a television programme in 1969 Richard Rodney Bennett said: "The music so far is fairly slight. It is all typically early music of each composer with no stunning intellectual constructions, but it seems to have the right definable quality by which one recognizes each composer. As music it is not terribly interesting, but the way we have come by it is fascinating."

Later, he went further, saying: "We can all imitate Debussy at the piano, but to create a piece of music that is coherent as a piece and which seems to go straight to the heart of the composer's style is much more complicated. You couldn't fake music like this without years of training. I couldn't have faked some of the Beethoven myself. Even if some of the pieces are bad, that doesn't mean anything. I produce lots of lousy pieces."

Professor Ian Parrott is prepared to vouch for the genuineness of the pieces, too. As to the possibility of their being faked—"Faked?" he says, "In twenty years as Professor of Music I have met only one student who might have been able to achieve some small part of it and then I am sure he would not have wanted to do it." Likewise, the *Gramophone* magazine in reviewing the record declared: "Mrs Brown appears to be no hoaxer, but even if she were it would take infinitely greater insight than she possesses into each composer's harmonic idiom, keyboard style and so on to create 'her' music by pastiche".

Could she have faked it? A music teacher, who gave her a thorough series of musical ear tests and examined her capability for playing music at sight, found that she didn't appear to have as much basic musical ability as one would expect to find in the average music student. Certainly students of composition would normally score far higher. Also her local piano teacher had not been particularly impressed with her pianistic abilities when she went to him, finding that she couldn't play properly the pieces that she had written down.

Still, whatever her merits as a student, the possibility of conscious fraud is soon dismissed by anyone who meets her. "But," say the sceptics, "she must then have had some musical education in her childhood which either she has forgotten about or has kept a secret from the world." At one stage she went to Holland to the University of Utrecht to be examined by the Institute of Parapsychology. The process was long and searching but at the end of it, Professor Tenhaeff, the Institute's Director, was able to report: "The result shows that here is a woman of sound mental balance who is not in the least anxious to occupy the limelight. My colleague —an asylum psychologist of many years' experience—was unable to find a single aberration, neither did our psycho-diagnostic examination give reason to conclude any deviation whatsoever."

Anyway, as Mrs Brown points out, there was never any spare money in the house for music lessons, secret or otherwise. The lack of cash also prevented her from attending concerts and recitals, so she could not have stored up the music in her subconscious. Moreover, there wasn't even a radio in the house when she was a girl, and when one did arrive access to it was strictly rationed to conserve the life of the batteries. Her parents were not ones to tune into classical concerts either—variety shows and news broadcasts were more the order of the day. But even she herself never particularly liked the music of some of the composers she "works" with—Bach being a case in point.

"Well then," the argument runs, "she must be picking up the thoughts of some nearby musician by a process of telepathy." But are we not now beginning to reach a level of "explanation" which is about as far beyond the "normal" twentieth-century mind as that offered by Mrs Brown herself?

Does the answer lie in the music itself? Wherever it comes from, many people have found it very interesting. As Humphrey Searle has said of the Liszt piece, *Grubelei*. "We must be grateful to Mrs Brown for making it available to us."

However the arguments may range back and forth, to many people the voices of Rosemary Brown are a fact—and one, moreover, which has successfully resisted the challenge of the cynics.

For those who wish to see her music, *The Rosemary Brown Piano Album* is published by Novello.

BRIDEY MURPHY

It had been an ordinary enough day in Pueblo, Colorado. Now as it was drawing to a close, local businessman Morey Bernstein was relaxing after dinner with his wife and their guests, Mr and Mrs Tighe. Tonight they were going to try another of their experiments. Bernstein was something of an amateur hypnotist, and had found on several occasions that Virginia Tighe was a very good subject for his powers.

This time they planned to take a further look at "age regression", a process in which a subject is encouraged to "re-live" experiences from his, or her, past life. The woman was duly put into a deep hypnotic trance, and a start was made by getting her to recall her experiences at junior school. Next, Bernstein took his subject back to her kindergarten days; and then he told her that she was only one year old. Did she have any toys? Yes, she had some blocks and a doll. What did she say when she wanted a glass of water?—"Wa ... wa"; and a glass of milk?—that she couldn't say. So far so good, but nothing essentially new had been established; Virginia had "been one year old" before. The next few moments, though, made this particular night very different from all the others.

"Now," said the hypnotist, "go on even further back ... back ... until, oddly enough you find yourself in some other place, in some other time ... What did you see?"

In reply came a tiny (could it be Irish?) voice "... scratched the paint off all my bed. Jus' painted it, n' made it pretty. It was a metal

344

bed, and I scratched the paint off of it. Dug my nails on every post and just ruined it. Was jus' terrible."

Somewhat non-plussed at this unexpected reply to his command, Bernstein was at a loss for words. "Why did you do that?" he eventually asked.

"Don't know," said the strange voice, "I was just mad. Got an awful spanking."

"What is your name?" he ventured tentatively.

"Bridey ... Bridey Murphy."

So began a phenomenon that was to capture the imagination of the world, provide the basis of several best-selling books, and form the subject of a film. It was also to launch a controversy which continues to this day.

What was pieced together in the Colorado living-room on the evening of 29 November, 1952, and in the five subsequent question-and-answer sessions of the hypnotist and his subject, was the life story of another woman, an Irishwoman (neither Bernstein nor Virginia had ever been to Ireland), and what was more an Irishwoman who had died nearly a hundred years previously. It appeared that the age regression technique had been successful not only in taking this twentieth-century American housewife back to her own American infancy, but also in going beyond to a previous "existence" in another continent.

Under hypnosis Virginia Tighe told the world of Bridey Murphy, who was born to barrister Duncan Murphy and his wife, Kathleen, in Cork in 1798, and who died in Belfast in 1864. The paint-scratching episode had occurred when she was four years old. At the age of eight she remembered playing with her elder brother Duncan, and living in a white, two-storey, "wood" house in an area of Cork known as "The Meadows".

At fifteen she was a pupil at Mrs Strayne's school in Cork studying "house things and proper things", and at twenty she married the son of another local barrister in a protestant ceremony in Cork, though the husband, Sean Brian Joseph MacCarthy, was himself a Catholic. The couple subsequently moved to Belfast travelling in a "livery carriage". In the north the husband completed his studies, and eventually he too practised as a barrister, later teaching at Queens University. The couple lived near St Theresa's church, whose priest Father John Gorman performed a second private marriage ceremony for them in his house.

The marriage was childless but very happy. It ended when Bridey died at the age of sixty-six as the result of an accident in which she had broken bones in her hip and which had rendered her helpless. She was able to remember details of the day she was buried, or "ditched" as she put it, managing to read the inscription on her own tombstone and to identify the people present at the graveside as her husband, the priest Father John, and her friends Mary and Kevin Moore.

Throughout the sessions of hypnosis Bernstein constantly asked his subject for details which might be corroborated. Could she remember any Gaelic words, for instance? Bridey promptly replied that Gaelic was the language of the peasants, but she could recall such words as "colleen" and "banshee". There was also "tup"— a sort of ne'er-do-well—and "brate", which she maintained was a small cup. She volunteered the grace that the family used to say before meals: "Bless this house in all the weather, Keep it gay in springy heather. Bless the children, bless the food. Keep us happy, bright and good." And a song which she particularly liked ran: "Father's girl's a dancing doll, Father's girl's a dancing doll, Sing around and swing around, Father's girl's a dancing doll." A rather more spontaneous colloquialism was heard when the hypnotized woman sneezed suddenly and asked for a "linen" to wipe her nose.

Reasoning that one of the most convincing demonstrations of a second entity inhabiting his sitter's body would be to find some ability that Bridey had but which was not shared by Virginia, Bernstein began to ask Bridey about her pastimes. Could she play chess, for instance? She could not, but she could remember playing with her brother a game called Fancy which involved using a squared board and cards. She had a passion for dancing though, and had particularly enjoyed dancing "The Morning Jig", so it was put to her that after she woke up she would be able to dance it again. In due course she was woken and the assembled company waited. Sure enough, when it was suggested that she might be able to remember the steps, she neatly performed a dance which ended with the gesture of raising her hand to her mouth. Why did she do this? "That's for a yawn", was the automatic response. Later the fully conscious Virginia was able to remember little of the dance and nothing of these remarks.

As for geographical memories, Bridey recalled that she had passed through Carlingford, Bailing's Crossing and Doby on her way from Cork to Belfast, and had vivid pictures of the white cliffs and black basalt rocks of Antrim where she had been taken on holiday as a girl. Of her everyday life in Belfast she remembered food being bought from two shops—Farr's and Carrigan's—that ladies' things could be obtained from Cadenn's House, and that Brian enjoyed eating "Irish dishes" like boiled beef and onions and potato cake.

After six sessions the series of experiments was stopped for good —the Tighes were not particularly happy with the idea of repeated hypnosis. Bernstein himself, though, felt that he had sufficient material to publish his results as a book, and soon managed to interest a publisher in the project.

The first version of the story came not in this book but as a series of newspaper articles in the *Denver Post* written by William Baker, one of the journal's feature writers; but it was the publication of the book itself (*The Search for Bridey Murphy*) which really captured the imagination of the public at large. In fact it captured it to such an extent that Hollywood was soon fighting over the film rights, and records of the edited tapes of the sessions were selling in their thousands.

Of course, not everyone was convinced by Bernstein's story, and the Irish searches for supporting evidence commissioned by the publishers before the book's publication had not really given much support to the story. The job had turned out to be more difficult than had been thought at first, for there were no official records of birth, marriages or deaths kept in Ireland before 1864, so concrete evidence of the existence of Bridey or her family and friends would have to be found elsewhere. The most common source of family records at that time was the front page of the family bible (Bridey actually referred to this practice herself), but tracking down the Murphys' (or the MacCarthys') family possessions would not be easy.

Better luck had been had with some of the more circumstantial evidence. Perhaps the most startling discovery involved finding a copy of a Belfast Directory for 1865 which showed both a Farr's and a Carrigan's among the list of Grocers. Bridey had got the name of the newspaper right—the *Belfast Newsletter* was being published in the first half of the nineteenth century—and her talk of the coinage current at the time was accurate too; the pound, sixpence, twopence and halfpenny were all in circulation. (The twopenny-piece was in circulation only between 1795 and 1850!) Agricultural information was also accurate, and the hay, corn, flax and tobacco that she mentioned her family growing when she was a child in Cork were all held to be crops typical of the area, though tobacco was grown only in small quantities.

With the book's publication, however, other organizations put their minds to investigating the possible truth of the Bridey story.

The American newspapers got into the act. The *Denver Post* sent William Baker to Ireland to see if he could do any better than the investigators hired by Bernstein's publishers, while the staff of such journals as *Life* and the *Chicago American* set to work digging in other channels. Not all these searchers after the truth were working for the same purpose—some were out to substantiate any possibility of reincarnation, but it seemed that many more were determined to discredit the Bridey Murphy record altogether. A welter of conflicting articles resulted.

The "metal bed" episode came in for some heavy criticism. Basically it was said that Ireland did not catch sight of a metal bed till well on into the nineteenth century, but if Bridey was to be believed she was sleeping in a metal bed in 1802 at the age of four. However, according to *Encyclopedia Britannica* metal beds were introduced into England in the eighteenth century and as at that time (and indeed today) Cork was a port with a flourishing English trade, it would not have been at all impossible for the little Irish girl to have slept as she claimed. Certainly by 1830 a local Cork iron works was advertising the sale of metal beds of its own manufacture.

Now that the heat was on, people were listening and re-listening to the recordings of the original sessions in the hope of catching any extra evidence or inconsistency. Some careful ear was struck by the pronunciation of the word "metal". Was Bridey in fact saying metal at all or had listeners been mis-hearing it all along and she was really saying "little"? Yes that was it. People eventually decided she was talking of her little painted bed, so that though it was not impossible that the child's bed could have been of metal, now no one was claiming this to have been the case.

A re-interpretation of the tape-recorded words proved significant in settling another argument too. A *Life* magazine article took the record to task for claiming that the Cork family had lived in a "wood" house. There was a great timber shortage in Ireland at the end of the eighteenth century, affirmed the magazine, so a two-storey wooden house was not exactly a likely object to find. Again the keen-eared tape listeners picked up the fact that the hypnotized woman was not using the disputed word after all. In this case instead of "wood" she was saying "good", they maintained. And anyway didn't people think that "It's a good house" is a much more likely thing for anyone to say than "It's a wood house"? In the latter case one would say wooden rather than wood, went the argument.

348

The manner of its construction wasn't the only criticism the childhood home had to face, for there was also the question of its address, given by Bridey as "The Meadows". There is no record of any house of this name, claimed the sceptics; but, retorted the supporters, she didn't say that was its name—that was just its location. Indeed, during his searches in Ireland, Barker came across a map of Cork dated 1801 which shows clearly an area marked as Mardike Meadows outside the main town, where Bridey said it was, and which contained several houses. A print of 1805 shows the Meadows to have been a peaceful and pleasant spot where cattle grazed, and was apparently an area where it would have been quite possible to spend a happy childhood.

However, not all the statements of the young Bridey could be corroborated so satisfactorily. No trace has been found of the school which she said she went to, run by a Mrs Strayne whose daughter Aimée later became the wife of Bridey's brother, Duncan. The subjects which she is supposed to have learned, "house things and proper things", on the other hand, were thought by Irish scholars to have fitted in with the pattern of Irish middle-class life of the times.

The critics didn't accept that the young Bridey could have been read to by her mother from a book called *The Sorrows of Deirdre*, as she claimed. The first mention of this title in a catalogue came with the publication of a play by Synge in 1905, they maintained. But somebody else found a record of a paperback book published in 1809 which bore the title *The Song of Deirdre and the Death of the Sons of Usnach*; so again there was no reason to suppose that the ten-year-old girl could not have been referring to this story. Bridey was certainly fond of Irish legends and outlined the Deirdre story accurately enough, even if she credited Dierdre's elderly suitor with being the King of Scotland and not the King of Ulster as in most versions. However, even here researchers have found accounts of the story which include a King of Scotland episode. No such quibbles have been found with her description of the legendary hero Cuchulainn, though, for whom she confessed to having a soft spot.

Bridey was aware of the legend of the Blarney stone, but makes no reference to ever visiting Blarney Castle even though it is not far from Cork. Some scholars have said that the practice of kissing the stone did not begin until about 1840, but on Bridey's side references were discovered which showed it to have been practised at least in 1820. As she herself never visited the place it is reasonable to suppose that the custom was not in full swing at that time, though it is interesting that she does refer accurately to the way the stone had to be kissed: Today one leans through a hole in the parapet to reach it, but in the last century it was necessary to be suspended over the parapet with one's legs firmly held from behind.

Of the places referred to on her journey to Belfast it was easy enough to find Carlingford and Lough Carlingford on any map, but Bailing's Crossing and Doby proved more elusive. However, people came forward who could vouch for the former, even though it was too small to be found on any map; and several theories were advanced as to the real identity of Doby.

Place names in Belfast were not so easy. No trace could be found of the Dooley Road near which Bridey and Brian were supposed to have lived; nor of St Theresa's Church nor of Father Gorman. On the other hand, there was that record of her neighbourhood grocer shops, and there were tobacco and rope factories operating at the time as she said there were.

Queens University records showed no trace of a Sean Brian Mac-Carthy ever having been on its teaching staff, but they did contain the names Fitzmaurice and McGloin—Fitzmaurice and McGlone had been cited by Bridey as two of her husband's colleagues. Could be that her spelling was at fault again?

Then there was the question of the particularly "Irish" phrases that Mrs Tighe used under hypnosis. "Colleen" and "banshee" are well enough known to surprise nobody; but what about words like "tup" and "brate", the habit of calling a handkerchief a "linen", and Bridey's referring to burial as "ditching"? In fact, authorities were found who were prepared to testify to the authenticity of "tup", which she used as a synonym for rascal, and of "linen". "Brate" proved more difficult, the nearest anybody getting to it being a corruption of the Scottish "quaich" or of the Irish "breach"; but as for "ditched", it has been suggested that she might have been referring to the days of the Great Famine when the dead were simply buried in trenches, as coffins and money were in very short supply.

Great efforts were made to find inconsistencies in Bridey's story; for example, it was maintained that Queens University did not exist at the time; but it was subsequently shown that the first students started attending in 1850. On the whole the story seemed to stand up remarkably well in this regard.

What could have been a much more crushing blow to the pro-Bridey camp was dealt by the newspaper the *Chicago American,* which had turned its attention not to Bridey's Ireland but the America of Virginia Tighe. The whole story was simply a dredging up of facts from Virginia's own past, the paper maintained, and she learned all her Irish lore not from a previous existence but from the lips of a favourite Irish aunt. In defence, Virginia herself said that the aunt in question, who had been born in New York and had spent most of her life in Chicago, had never been particularly interested in Ireland and had had little to do with Virginia's family until she came to stay with them when her niece was about eighteen.

The Chicago paper also stated that it had found the source of Bridey's Irish brogue and jig-dancing ability. They had located an elocution teacher who, they said, had taught Virginia Irish monologues. The *Denver Post*, being kindly disposed to the deceased Irish woman, countered by reporting that when they found this elocution teacher she hardly remembered the girl and had no memory of her ever learning any Irish items.

Other things were pointed out too. The *American*'s reporters discovered that Virginia had spent her early days in Wisconsin in a white frame house like the one which Bridey described; but as Virginia observed, many Americans live in white frame houses. The attacking reporters also reported that less than two blocks from this house was a park or "meadow" in which the young girl must have played many times. This received a similar answer, this time from Bridey's protector William Barker of the *Denver Post*. In essence he too pointed out that many Americans had parks near their houses, but added that the Bridey records say nothing of *playing* in a meadow; rather it was an area where she lived outside the town.

Then there was the question of Cadenn's House, the shop which Bridey had said sold ladies' things and of which searchers in Belfast had managed to find no trace. Very near Virginia's home in Chicago, said the newspaper from that city, there was a store called Kaden's which the girl must have passed every time she went to the cinema. Virginia had no recollection of such an establishment, and added she was rarely allowed to go to the cinema anyway.

Undoubtedly, however, the paper's biggest bombshell was its discovery of a Mrs Anthony Bridie Murphy Corkell, who lived across the street from the young Virginia, and whose children and Virginia used to play together. Here was the original Bridey Murphy, the paper affirmed, and what was more she was alive and living in Chicago. So what, retorted the Bridey Murphy loyalists, what's in a name? Bridie (or Bridey) Murphy wasn't exactly an uncommon name—the Chicago directory for the period listed seven Bridget

Murphys for example—and if the newspaper reporters had been able to find one name from the Bridey Murphey story linked to Virginia's past there was no trace of any of the other names which had been mentioned in the trances.

In any event the Mrs Corkell unearthed by the paper came from County Mayo, whereas all the dead Bridey's experiences were linked either with Cork or Belfast. Virginia could not actually remember ever meeting the woman, though she said she had known the children; also she could not recall ever having heard her first or maiden names. How likely is it, asked William Baker, that one knows the maiden name of a neighbour anyway? Might it be significant that Mrs Corkell refused to be interviewed by the pro-Bridey *Denver Post* reporter?

For many people the Chicago newspaper's story was the end of the Bridey Murphy mystery. But does it explain everything? Even if Virginia Tighe's memory has given a twentieth-century name to a nineteenth-century personality, does that explain how an American housewife knew the names of two grocer's shops in the Belfast of a century ago, or how she knew so much of the habits and customs of bygone days in a country she had never seen?

Perhaps it was all a coincidence. But what of another coincidence in the affair—the *Chicago American*'s Bridey Murphey Corkell turned out to be none other than the mother of the editor of the Sunday *Chicago American*. Just what is the sceptic supposed to make of that?

Curses

THE TICHBORNE CURSE

Throughout the ages cursing has not only been intended to bring harm to one's enemies, but has also been an accepted way of ensuring that an obligation is kept. For some reason cursing also falls into certain well-defined categories.

Many famous jewels—sometimes because they are said to have been stolen—have carried curses or been credited with evil powers. The Koh-i-noor, which is believed to date from the time of the Great Mogul, appeared to carry evil with it and bring only harm to its Indian owners until the East India Company eventually acquired it and presented it to Queen Victoria. Although the Punjabis were convinced that it would attract nothing but disaster until it was restored to their ruling family, the Koh-i-noor's powers seem to have waned since it joined the crown jewels in the fastnesses of the Tower of London. The Hope diamond, acquired—some say nefariously—by the French traveller Tavernier in the eighteenth century, has carried with it a long trail of misfortune, up to the present day, as it has passed from hand to hand and country to country.

The disturbers of tombs have been the subject of curses since the days of the Pharaohs and one of the most famous of English curses is to be found on Shakespeare's tomb in the parish church of Stratford-upon-Avon.

Good friend for Jesus' sake forbear
To dig the dust enclosed here

355

Blest be the man that spares these stones
And curst be he that moves my bones

Despite this an American, a believer in the theory that Bacon wrote Shakespeare's plays, sought permission some ten years ago to open the grave in the hope of finding some proof of his theory. Permission was refused and so this curse at any rate has not yet had the chance to prove its effectiveness. There is, however, a generally accepted superstition that no good can come of disturbing a grave for any but the purest motives.

Another common curse is that placed on families—usually eminent landowners of ancient lineage, the threat being that the family would die out. These curses were often placed by people on their deathbeds, who had nothing to gain or lose one way or another. Many of these curses have come to pass, and those families who still remain under the shadow of such a curse—and there are several in Scotland and England—take the greatest care to see that their obligations are fulfilled.

One of the most famous curses, and one of the most ancient in English history, is that of the Tichborne family. The curse, of the type to ensure that an obligation was fulfilled, was placed by Lady Mabell Tichborne in the twelfth century.

The Tichbornes were a very ancient family who owned the manor of Tichborne two hundred years before the Conqueror came to England. This latter event caused a considerable upheaval among the landed lords of the period, and William was ruthless with those who would not swear fealty to him. The Tichbornes, situated as they were close to the ancient capital of Winchester, no doubt considered it politic to keep on the right side of the king. In any event, a hundred years later, when William's great grandson Henry II was on the throne, the Tichborne family was rich and prosperous.

Some of this wealth could be ascribed to the fact that Sir Roger had improved the family's fortunes by marrying Lady Mabell, or Mabella, who was the daughter and sole heiress of Ralph de Lamerston of the Isle of Wight. Lady Mabell, as was the custom of the day, would have brought with her a substantial dowry in money, goods and clothes; but all that she possessed—including her inheritance on the death of her father—became the property of her husband to administer as he pleased.

History does not relate whether the marriage had been arranged by the de Lamerston and Tichborne families; it is not unlikely as arranged marriages were frequent among the upper classes of the day. But at least it would appear that there was no great disparity between the ages of the couple—arranged marriages sometimes resulted in a girl of twelve being married to a man of forty-five—for Lady Mabell died "worn out with age and infirmity" (to quote a hundred-year-old account by a member of the Tichborne family) before her husband.

The medieval husband was very firmly the head of his household, and women were kept strictly in their place. They were rarely allowed, for example, to join the men at the communal meals in the great hall where the lord of the manor sat on a daïs, with the huge open fire, its smoke escaping through louvres in the roof, burning on the floor before him. There were few comforts. Even in the royal castles living conditions were austere. The floors were strewn with rushes which were rarely changed and among which all kinds of filth accumulated. Benches, which converted to beds for those who slept in the great hall, trestle-tables and chests constituted most of the furniture. The lord and his wife, however, would have a bed of wood and hides, with some privacy in the solar chamber built out from the hall. And although the lord might have a chair, this was a mark of his rank rather than a concession to his comfort.

The wife of the lord of the manor was, however, expected to play her part in the running of the household. She was required to have a knowledge of all her husband's manors and tenants. If her lord was absent she must take full responsibility for the welfare of the peasants and the household servants and train them in their duties. She must ensure that the villeins' tributes were paid, and she must buy goods for the household in an economic way. She was also often an adept in various crafts and industries, and was expected to be able to diagnose and treat diseases and, if need be, act as midwife. She might even be required—as some ladies of the time successfully did —to conduct a siege in the absence of her husband.

One of the most important duties of a lady was the distribution of alms to the poor, in both money and kind. Every large household had a coffer for alms-money, so that anyone in need who came to the door could be given help. Poverty in those days was no crime, it was even a virtue, and alms were never given in a spirit of patronage. On the contrary, they were given in a spirit of humility and charity, and all the great households, from the king's downwards, paid for the feeding of poor people.

It may be assumed that Lady Mabell was assiduous in her care of the poor of her husband's manor. Being rich she would not have been expected to contribute much to the houshold work, in the way

357

of time spent at the loom or in the still room, and she would have had plenty of time to get to know the problems of the peasants, whose miserable huts provided even less in the way of comfort than did the manor itself.

It may also be assumed that Sir Roger Tichborne was a man not only of unpleasant but also of parsimonious character. One may imagine that, unlike more charitable lords of the period, he was unlikely to excuse a peasant who had fallen upon hard times from the payment of his dues, although he could surely have afforded to do so.

When Lady Mabell, who had been an invalid and virtually bedridden for many years, felt that her end was approaching, she therefore pleaded with her husband to allow her to endow an annual dole of bread, to be given to the local poor people each Lady day. No doubt in assuming that he was pretty safe in so doing, Sir Roger immediately promised her that he would give to the poor the produce of as much of his land as she could walk over. Another version of the story says that he snatched a brand from the fire and told her that this would apply to as much land as she could encircle while it still burned.

However, Lady Mabell, despite the protests of her retainers, insisted on being carried from her deathbed to a corner of the estate where, to the astonishment of her household—and no doubt the annoyance of her husband—she summoned up some strange reserve of strength and tottered and crawled round no less than twenty-three acres. (The fields which were the scene of this remarkable feat are known to this day as "The Crawls".)

Her strength at last failing, Lady Mabell had herself carried back to her chamber and, no doubt distrustful of her husband's intention to keep his promise, had the family summoned to her bedside whereupon, in God's most holy name, she then laid the famous curse upon the Tichborne family. The annual distribution of the dole, she said, must continue in perpetuity, the prosperity of the family thus being assured. If it should cease, however, there would be a generation of seven sons, followed immediately by a generation of seven daughters, and thereafter the family name would become extinct.

With such a threat hanging over their heads, the Tichborne family religiously carried out the promise. Every Lady Day a dole of nineteen hundred loaves of bread was handed out to the poor, and the 25th March became the family's festive day. The family prospered and the famous dole became so treasured that pieces of the bread were often kept as talismans against sickness. Gradually, however, the news of the dole began to spread and to attract the poor from far and wide. By the eighteenth century vagabonds, gipsies and other undesirable characters took to descending upon Tichborne as Lady Day approached, causing trouble and doing damage, and the annual distribution of the dole became nothing more than a civic nuisance. Eventually after strong representations from the local magistrates and gentry, the baronet of the day, Sir Henry Tichborne, agreed in 1796 to end it.

Although Sir Henry arranged instead to give an equivalent amount of money to a charity for the poor of the neighbourhood, this was apparently not good enough for the shade of Lady Mabell. Sir Henry, the eighth baronet, could be considered to be somewhat rash—or at least unimpressed by the family curse—for he had married, in 1778, and by the date that the dole was ended he and his wife Elizabeth must have produced a goodly number of the seven sons with which they were ultimately blessed. The eldest of these seven sons, another Henry, married Anne, daughter of Sir Thomas Burke, and they had seven daughters. Thus there was clear warning that the curse would take effect.

The estate was inherited by Edward, brother of the eighth baronet. To a certain extent the curse was fulfilled, for Edward had assumed the name of Doughty upon inheriting an estate in another part of the country, and Tichbornes no longer lived at the manor.

What exactly induced the Tichbornes to reassume the name and to reinstate the dole is not known. Certainly the family had problems—including the heavy cost of fighting the case of the well-known Tichborne Claimant (who pretended to be an heir lost at sea). In any case, in the 1860s the dole was resumed, although now it is distributed in the form of flour instead of loaves of bread.

THE GLENLUCE DEVIL

In 1654, there was living in Glenluce, near Newton Stuart, in Gallo-way a weaver called Gilbert Campbell and his family. One day, Alexander Agnew "a bold and sturdy beggar", called at Campbell's house and it was Campbell himself who opened the door to him.

"Alms, master!" Agnew pleaded. "I have eaten nothing these two days."

"I notice," replied Campbell, "that you have not said you have had nothing to drink, either."

"Nothing but water, master weaver," the beggar assured him.

"You are a liar, man. The reek of spirits on your breath confounds you. Be off, beggar!"

"Spare a coin for a loaf, I beg you."

"No man deserves bread who does not work for it," Campbell re-torted piously. "If you are hungry, work for your bread. If you will not work, you must expect to be hungry. Be off, I say!"

From pleading, the beggar became menacing.

"Give me a coin for bread," he threatened, "or I will place on this house and the family who dwells in it the curse of the Devil."

"I am not impressed by your threats," shouted Campbell. "Shall I summon the constable?"

"On your head be it," replied Agnew. "You will soon rue the day you treated me in this manner!"

And turning away, he ambled off muttering imprecations.

During the last exchanges, Mistress Campbell, who had been

made curious about what was keeping her husband at the door, had come to his side.

"Husband," she said. "Was it wise? Some of these vagrants have the power ..."

"Nonsense, wife!" Campbell interrupted her. "What powers? All powers come from God."

"Some from the Devil," Mistress Campbell reminded him.

The weaver, discomfited by the reminder, retorted, "Tcha, woman! Believe in God, and the Devil is powerless."

But he was wrong; perhaps his belief was not strong enough.

Not long afterwards, strange noises began to be heard, and strange commotions to occur, in the Campbells' house. The first manifestation was a shrill whistling, "such as Children use to make with their small slender Glass Whistles", which was heard inside and outside the house. Then Mistress Campbell, while going to fetch water from the well, "was conveyed with a shrill whistling about her ears", which made her exclaim that "she fain would hear it speak as well as whistle". To her surprise, it spoke, declaring in a threatening manner that it would cast her into the well. A neighbour who was accompanying her, heard both the whistle and the voice.

"I do wish, husband," Mistress Campbell complained, "that you had given the beggar the alms he asked for."

About the middle of November the demon began to play new tricks, in the best poltergeist tradition.* Stones were hurled through doorways, in at windows and down chimneys, "which were of great quantity and thrown with force". Naturally the neighbours learned of what was going on, and this necessitated the weaver, against his wishes, to reveal all to the minister. But this only served to provoke the demon further, "for not long after, he (Campbell) found oftentimes his Warp and Threads cut as with a pair of Sizzers, and not only so, but their Apparel were cut after the same manner, even while they were wearing them, their Coats, Bonnets, Hose and Shoes, but could not discern how, or by what means".

At nights they were prevented from sleeping by "something"

---

* The word *poltergeist* to denote *a spirit which causes a commotion* has been used in Britain only since 1848; but such manifestations as comprise poltergeist phenomena – noises or knockings that have no apparent natural origins, the uncontrolled movement of small objects, the disappearance of small objects, later discovered in unexpected hiding-places, and a rare major disaster nearly always originating with fire – have been referred to by writers on the supernatural from the earliest times. Between 1450 and 1750 the activities of poltergeists were naturally associated with witchcraft, and the poltergeists themselves reckoned as demons.

pulling their bedcovers and nightclothes off them, "leaving their Bodies naked". Their chests and trunks were opened, and the contents strewn about the room. Their tools, which escaped damage, were spirited away and deposited in hiding-places about the house. Any cloth that was in the house was so cut and torn that the weaver had to remove what was undamaged to a neighbour's house, and he had to give up working.

Despite all this Campbell refused to surrender to the demon by quitting the house. However, he did listen to the advice of some "not very judicious" people, who advised him to send his children away, suggesting that each child should be sent to a different place, "to try whom the trouble did follow, assuring him that this trouble was not against the whole Family, but against some person or other in it".

After the children had gone, there was no trouble for four or five days. But when the minister heard what Campbell had done he pressed him to call the children back on the grounds that it was sinful to split up the family in this way. If he persisted in their evacuation, the minister assured him, he could not expect "his trouble would end in the right way".

Campbell agreed to call the children home. No trouble followed until one of the sons, Thomas, who was at the grammar school in Glasgow, came home. On the following Sunday afternoon the house was set on fire and would have been burned down if neighbours returning home from kirk had not helped to put the fire out. Next day the Campbells prayed and fasted all day, but on the Tuesday, at about nine o'clock in the morning, the house was set on fire again. Once more, however, the neighbours prevented it from being badly damaged.

This time, Gilbert Campbell's patience was exhausted by being "this vexed and wearied both day and night", and he went to the minister and asked him to let Tom stay with him for a time. The minister agreed, but assured Campbell that he "would find himself deceived". And the minister proved right, for though Tom was absent from his home, the family was much disturbed not only during the day but the night as well, so that they were often kept awake until midnight, and sometimes all night. Their clothes were slashed, clods of peat were hurled about the house, turf and straw were pulled from the roof and walls, and sometimes their clothes disappeared completely and they were "pricked of their Flesh and Skin with pins".

News of what was happening began to spread throughout the

whole town, and the neighbouring countryside, and a number of ministers, after consultation among themselves, decided to try the effect a Day of Humiliation might have. But they stipulated that before they convened Tom should be brought home from the Glenluce manse. When he arrived home, he declared that a voice had told him not to enter his father's house, or workshop. However, he did enter and was "so sorely abused" that he had to return to the manse.

On 12 February the other members of the family began to hear the voice. Mistress Campbell believed it to be the voice of Alexander Agnew, the beggar, but Campbell told her to hold her tongue. "It is the voice of the Devil," he told her. "Set on us by the beggar," insisted his wife.

Instead of ignoring the voice, "From evening till mid-night too much vain discourse was kept up with Satan, and many idle and impertinent questions proposed, without due fear of God, that should have been upon their Spirits under so rare and extraordinary a Trial". This bred a familiarity among the members of the family and they were no more afraid of talking with the Devil than they were with one another. "This pleased him well, for he desired no better than to have Sacrifices offered to him."

When the minister heard of this he went to the Campbell's house accompanied by James Bailie of Carphin, Alexander Bailie of Dunraged, Mr Robert Hay and a Mistress Douglas, who was chaperoned by the minister's wife. As they entered the house, the voice spoke to them saying *"Quum Literatum* is good Latin". As a contemporary scholar noted, "These are the first words of the Latin Rudiments which Schollars are taught when they go to the Grammar School".

The voice next exclaimed, "You are a dog, sir", and the minister, thinking that he was being addressed, retorted that he did not mind being reviled by Satan, since his Master Jesus, had "troden that way before him".

"It was not you, sir, I spoke to," the voice replied. "I was speaking to that dog there," whereupon the minister turned and saw a dog at the back of the room.

The minister then led the company in prayer, and when he had finished they heard the voice, which appeared to come out of the ground under the bed, say in perfect local dialect, "Would you know the witches of Glenluce?" and proceeded to name four or five notorious persons. Campbell pointed out that one of those named had been dead sometime.

"It is true," the voice agreed, "but her spirit is living with us in the world."

Though he hesitated to do so, "for it was not convenient to speak to such an excommunicat and intercommuned person", the minister felt that he must say something to the voice.

"The Lord rebuke thee, Satan," he said, "and put thee to silence. We are not to receive information from thee, whatsoever fame any person goes under. Thou art seeking but to seduce this Family, for Satan's kingdom is not divided against itself."

After this passage the minister once more led prayers, and this time the voice remained silent, but as soon as the praying stopped, it rounded on the boy Tom, and so terrified him, threatening to set fire to the house if he did not go back to the manse, that he pleaded to be allowed to do so. The minister tried to intervene, but the voice told him that if Tom did not go freely, he would drive him out and pursue him "to the ends of the earth". Again the minister prayed. Then the voice made a proposition.

"Give me a shovel and spade and depart from the house for seven days, and I will make a grave and lie down in it, and shall trouble you no more."

Rejecting the pleading of Mistress Campbell, whose constant reminder of his treatment of the beggar was more and more causing his natural stubbornness to assert itself, the weaver refused to accept terms, saying that he would not give so much as straw, even though that would put an end to his troubles. The minister approved of this attitude, and added that in time God would drive the voice out.

The voice then changed tactics. "I will not remove you," it said. "I have my commission from Christ to tarry and vex this family."

"A commission thou hast indeed!" the minister exclaimed. "But God will stop it in good time."

"I have, sir, a commission," the voice repeated, "which will perhaps last longer than your own. I have given my commission to Tom to keep."

They asked Tom if he had anything in his pocket, and he told them that something had been put there, "but did not tarry".

The company now decided to try to locate the spot from which the voice appeared to be coming, but the most diligent search revealed nothing. One of the gentlemen suggested that it was speaking through one of the children, but the voice resented this, and exclaimed, "You lie! God shall judge you for your lying, and I and my father will come and fetch you to hell, with warlocks and thieves". He would not bandy words with them, but would speak only with the minister "who hath a Commission, for he is the servant of God".

There then followed an exchange of texts between the minister and the voice, until the minister asked, "Tell me from whence you come."

"I am an evil spirit, come from the bottomless Pit of Hell, to vex this house. Satan is my father," was the reply.

At this point there appeared a naked forearm and hand which beat upon the floor until the house shook.

VOICE: Come up, Father, come up! I will send my Father among you. See, there he is behind your backs.

MINISTER: I saw indeed a hand and an arm, when the stroke was given, and heard a voice.

VOICE: Saw you that? It was not my hand, it was my Father's. My hand is more black in the loop.

GILBERT CAMPBELL: O that I might see thee, as well as hear thee.

VOICE: Would you see me? Put out the candle and I shall come butt the house among you like fire balls. I shall let you see me indeed.

ALEXANDER BAILIE: Let us go ben, and see if there is any hand to be seen.

VOICE: No. Let him (Campbell) come in alone; he's a good honest man; his single word may be believed.

But the minister forebade Campbell to enter the house alone.

Then the voice rounded on Robert Hay, "a very Honest gentleman", and began to abuse him calling him witch and warlock. Just as suddenly he switched his attention elsewhere, and cried out, "There's a witch sitting on the ruist. Take her away." But all that the company could see was a hen sitting on the gable.

After another period of prayers led by the minister, the voice declared that he had plans for the Campbell children.

"I will have Tom a merchant, Rob a smith, John a minister and Hugh a lawyer," it announced.*

Then it said to Jennet Campbell, a daughter, "Cast me thy belt!"

"What do you want with it?" she demanded.

"I would fain fasten my loose bones together with it," it told her. But she refused to part with her belt.

Mistress Campbell, the practical housewife, now brought some oat cake, and was breaking it to give everyone a piece, whereupon the voice cried, "Grizzel Willie, Grizzel Willie, give me a piece of

---

* The children did eventually follow these callings.

hard bread, for I have gotten nothing this day but a bit from Marrit (Margaret, the Campbell's servant)".

The minister warned Mistress Campbell not to give it oat cake, for that would be sacrificing to the Devil.

Margaret was called, and when asked, denied that she had given anything to the voice. "But," she said, "when I was eating my due piece this morning, something came and snatched it out of my hand."

By this time, it was getting late, and it was decided that everyone should go home.

"Let not the minister go," the voice cried. "I shall burn the house if he does."

Campbell pleaded with the minister to stay, and he agreed, but the others left.

"Ah, you have done my bidding," the voice exclaimed, guffawing.

"Not thine," the minister retorted, "but in obedience to God I have returned to bear this man company whom thou dost afflict."

And he prayed again. When he had finished he told Campbell and the family to say something to "the Devil, and when it answered they were to kneel and speak to God. The Devil then roared mightily, and cried out, What? Will ye not speak to me, I shall strike the bairns and do all manner of mischief. But after that time no answer was made to it, and so for a long time no speech was heard. Several times hath he beat the Children in their Beds, and the claps of his hoofs upon their Buttocks would have been heard, but without any trouble to them."

While the other gentlemen were at the door taking their leave of the minister, the voice said to Mistress Campbell, who was in the house with the minister's wife, "Grizzel, put out the candle".

"Shall I?" Mistress Campbell asked the minister's wife, who told her not to, as that would be obeying the Devil.

Twice more it cried out for the candle to be extinguished, but "no obedience being given to him, he did so often reiterate these words and magnify his voice, that it was astonishment to hear him, which made them stop their ears, they thinking the sound just at their ears".

Eventually, however, the candle was put out, and the voice promised, "I'll trouble you no more the night".

Before they slept Mistress Campbell put a new suggestion to her husband. "Do you not think," she said, "that we should find the beggar and make amends? He might then call off his curse." Her answer from the weaver was a curt No.

Next day, the minister and others—there were five, though many had been summond—met outside the Campbell's house, and discussed what should be done. They decided on two things: not to use conjuration, that is, to call upon the voice in God's name to tell them where it came from, or to leave the family alone; and second, that when the voice spoke, no one should answer, but continue with their prayers and worship of God.

So they went into the house, and when all of them had prayed in turn, and three of them had spoken words from the Scriptures, they prayed again. During all this time the voice remained silent.

Tom Campbell now left, but he had not gone far when Hugh Nisbet, one of the company, caught up with him and asked him to return, as the whistling had started again. But Tom angrily refused.

"No," he said firmly. "I tarried as long as God called me, but go in again I will not."

This seemed to take all the heart out of the company, and they also left. The record then continues:

> After this the said Gilbert suffered much loss, and had many sad nights, not two nights in one week free, and thus it continued till April; from April to July he had some respite and ease, but after, he was molested with new assaults; and even their Victuals were so abused, that the Family was in hazard of starving, and that which they ate gave them not their ordinary satisfaction they were wont to find.

Almost at the end of his tether, Gilbert Campbell decided to appeal to the synod of Presbyters, for their advice whether or not to leave the house. The synod convened in October, 1695, and after some discussion appointed a committee to meet at Glenluce in February, 1656, to conduct a Solemn Humiliation throughout all the area controlled by the synod, "and among other causes to request God in behalf of that afflicted Family".

The reason for the delay in holding the Solemn Humiliation is not explained. However, after it, the Campbells' troubles grew less until April, and from April till August they were altogether free.

In August, the Devil began new assaults upon them. Food disappeared from the house and was sometimes found hidden in holes by the door-posts, and at other times under the beds, or among the bed clothes. On occasions it disappeared altogether, leaving the family with but bread and water.

The family was also physically attacked, and at night the "presence" moved through the house making a terrible noise. This lasted throughout August, and then grew worse. The Devil roared, threw stones and beat the Campbells with staves when they were in bed at night. On 18 September the voice informed them that it intended to burn down the house, and three or four nights later one of the beds caught fire. Happily, it was soon put out, and no damage was done except to the bed.

Some months later, the beggar Alexander Agnew was arrested in Dumfries and hanged for blasphemy. The main charge against him was that when he was asked if he thought there was a God, he had replied: "I know no God but Salt, Meat and Water."

After the death of Agnew, the Campbells were troubled no more.

Spirit Healing and Psychic Surgery

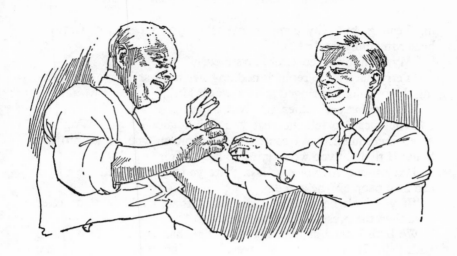

THE HEALINGS
OF HARRY EDWARDS

One evening three years ago I chanced to drop in upon some
friends, Leon and Terry, and found them, much to my astonishment preparing to visit a faith healer.

"A faith healer?" I said incredulously, "what on earth for?"

It transpired that the healer, Mrs Wrighton, was a friend of
Leon's mother. She had persuaded her son into the visit in the hope
that something could be done about the migraine from which Leon
had now been suffering for almost three days.

Intrigued by the idea of meeting a real faith healer I begged to
be allowed to accompany them and so off we set, thinking it was all
a bit of a joke, to the small terraced house in Balham where Mrs
Wrighton lived.

We were shown into a bright, cheerful room decorated in white
and blue with several modern paintings on the walls. It was not at
all the dark, over-stuffed, bead-curtained house I had expected; and
Mrs Wrighton, in dress, deportment and manner might have been
any youngish housewife.

The only detail of her dress which clashed with this image was
an enormous gold ring, set with a lapis carved in the form of an
Egyptian scarab—obviously very old and valuable—which she wore
on the little finger of her left hand.

Quite suddenly Mrs Wrighton said, "I can understand you wanting healing, but why come to me when you have so powerful a healer in your friend?"

"My friend?" asked Leon, mystified.

"Terry here," she replied, nodding her head at Terry and holding the palm of her ringed hand towards him.

We gazed at each other, totally at a loss.

"You mean to tell me that you didn't know?" Mrs Wrighton asked incredulously. "I sensed it the moment you came into the house. I thought you were trying to hide it from me."

Terry found his voice at last. "Are you trying to tell me that I can heal people?" he asked.

"If you have never tried," she said, "there couldn't be a better time than the present. Look at Leon."

We both looked at him. He was paler than ever, his face drawn with pain. He had closed his eyes, resting his forehead against the wing of the chair, taking no notice of what was going on around him.

Briefly Mrs Wrighton explained to Terry that he could be a source of healing. Whether the power came from within him or merely passed through him he would never know. But it was there, and extremely strong. There were many ways of using it. At first it could be concentrated through the hands, by passing them slowly over the source of the illness or by touching the sick person. Later he might be able to use it at a distance, without the physical contact.

Leon seemed to hear nothing of this conversation. Following Mrs Wrighton's instructions, Terry and I sat with her for a while in silence, trying to relax and will ourselves open to whatever influences there might be in or around us. Then, as if he judged the time to be right, Terry slowly, and with great seriousness, walked behind Leon's chair. Later he told me that his heart was nearly jumping out of his chest. He passed his hands three times over Leon's head in a circular movement, as if he were outlining the lobes of the brain. Then he rubbed his hands together and shook them, like someone shaking off drops of water.

His actions had authority. They seemed decisive, practised, purposeful and not at all theatrical. Afterwards he told me that he had had no idea what he was going to do when he rose from his chair: the actions seemed to come to him naturally. When he rubbed and shook his hands it had seemed to him as though some sticky, rather dangerous fluid was leaving his fingertips, but he had no real sensation.

In five minutes Leon's migraine had disappeared. The colour had returned to his cheeks, he was cheerful and lively. Terry was exhausted. Not, he said, because he felt something had been taken from him in the healing, but purely through the excitement of his discovery. Later he told Mrs Wrighton that he had often been depressed and irritable, feeling that life had no meaning.

"Now," said Mrs Wrighton, "you know why. It is because you were not using that thing in yourself which is of the highest value. A gift of healing is a gift of goodness for other people, ignore it or keep it to yourself and you bring a spiritual sickness on yourself."

All this happened some time ago and Terry still uses his power, but he does not practise publicly. To preserve his privacy I have changed the names of the people involved. The location, however, has not been changed and it was also in Balham that another man, who has become a legend in his own lifetime, first discovered *his* remarkable power.

This man, Harry Edwards, faith healer extraordinary, has fought many battles with the medical profession in his efforts to substantiate his cures; he has not obtained anything but the most grudging approval. Either, it is argued, the cure is scientifically explicable and so has nothing to do with intercessionary healing, or the doctor must suspect that the diagnosis is wrong. Otherwise he offends against that basic scientific belief that every event has a specific cause.

It is certain, however, that a scientific explanation of faith healing is out of the question. Science does not admit of supernormal powers that can influence anything from a pimple to cancer or psychosis—and often from a distance, sometimes without even the patient's knowledge and thus without any co-operation from him.

Perhaps the most famous—and one of the earliest—examples of faith healing, is the story in the New Testament of the woman who had suffered from haemorrhages for twelve years and who had unavailingly spent all she had on medical treatment. Hearing that a crowd had gathered to greet Jesus, the man whose miraculous cures had become famous, she pushed her way through, telling herself that if she could touch even His clothes she would be cured. She reached out and touched His cloak and immediately the haemorrhage stopped. Despite the people pressing round Him Jesus, "aware that power had gone out of him", turned round in the crowd and asked: "Who touched my clothes?".

Nobody knows just what this mysterious power is. Some believe it comes from the spirit world, others from God. Others call it radiesthesia (defined by the British Medical Society for the Study of Radiesthesia as "the name given to human sensitivity to and perception of radiation"), and believe it is akin to the power which enables diviners to find water or metals—many diviners indeed do have the ability to heal or to pinpoint a source of illness in the body.

Most healers agree that they are merely the medium through which the power, whatever its source, flows. Some spiritualist healers are "guided" by medical men who have died, but who wish to continue to help mankind from the spirit world. Others, sometimes assisted by helpers who join with them in concentrating upon the wish to heal, merely allow the power to flow through them.

Harry Edwards himself summarizes the forces involved in spiritual healing thus: "That consequent on the emission of a thought appeal by a human instrument, a discarnate mind is able to receive the request, and is then able to apply the correct quality of force to the particular disharmony in the body of the patient", and points out that one has either to accept these conclusions or assume that healings are the result of the personal intervention of God on behalf of one favoured individual.

Whether or not one believes that human beings can be healed through intercession with the spirit world, there is no doubt that Harry Edwards has brought comfort and relief to many people in his lifetime, but it was not until he was more than forty years old that, almost by chance, he discovered his great healing gift.

Harry Edwards was born in 1893 and, as the son of a London compositor, was apprenticed to the printing trade. At an early age he became interested in public work, pioneered a Boy Scout Troop and became involved in Liberal politics. When the Great War broke out he enlisted in the Royal Sussex Regiment and was sent to India. In Bangalore he established and edited a battalion magazine and brought trouble on himself for writing outspokenly about the poor reception given to the men of the Royal Sussex by local residents. The article brought Harry Edwards before a court-martial, from which he escaped unscathed; but it also improved the lot of his fellow soldiers—his lively concern for others was already bearing fruit.

As a qualified engineer he was sent to Persia, a country which at the time was in great civil disorder, to build roads and bridges. Thousands of people were dying of starvation, or roaming the country having fled before the advance of the Turks. Now a commissioned officer, Edwards had a considerable part to play in administering the region, and was made Director of Labour over an area of a quarter of a million people. It is said that when he had to return to England he had won so much friendship and gratitude that many wept to see him go.

Back in England Harry Edwards married and bought a small printing press and a stationery shop. His business, however, did not prosper, and the next fifteen years were a continual struggle. Meanwhile, however, he worked hard for the Liberal party, standing as a candidate for North Camberwell in 1929 and in 1935. His rationalist, liberal philosophy also prompted him to work for the League of Nations and to interest himself in local affairs.

Another of Harry Edwards' interests during the thirties was magic. As a member of the Magic Circle he learned many of the tricks of the game and developed the magician's eye for sleight of hand. Confident that this training would enable him to see through the illusions—as he then thought them—of the mediums, he went to a spiritualist meeting in Ilford. He was so impressed by what he saw that he left the meeting determined to make further investigations.

Accompanied by his wife and a friend, he attended a Balham spiritualist church in 1934 where he was told that there were spirit guides who would like to work with him, and was given many spirit messages. He was sufficiently convinced to join a development circle to see if he really possessed psychic powers.

In the circle he had some disturbing experiences, and was convinced finally that he should continue with his training. He saw visions, found himself involuntarily making speeches in voices not his own, and soon fully believed in the truths of spiritualism. Gradually he learned to allow the spirit world to take over without resistance and was, in particular, guided by the spirit of a Red Indian called White Feather.

Instructed by White Feather, Harry Edwards set up a home circle, The Fellowship of Spiritual Service, and began his service to the sick. He also worked closely with Jack Webber and Arnold Clare, two well-known mediums. His own healing powers, however, soon caught the attention of the local press and the spiritualist paper, *Psychic News*.

He held healing sessions every Tuesday in his own home. There he would see the patients, record their illnesses and follow up their condition from week to week. Every evening he interceded with the spirits for help for his patients, by concentrating his thoughts on each case and asking for the spirits' co-operation. As his work grew, Edwards set aside a second evening each week and this he devoted entirely to "absent" healing—asking for help for patients who might be miles away from him. He was helped by a team of sympathetic workers who supported him in his prayer for healing and assisted him in routine clerical work. During these sessions Harry Edwards often experienced spirit journeys into the rooms where his patients were lying. It seemed that there he could watch the healing take place. The accurate descriptions that he brought back from these "journeys" were later checked with his patients and confirmed that, in the spirit, he really had visited his patients' houses at the relevant times.

Maurice Barbanell, ex-editor of *Psychic News*, in his biography of Harry Edwards, describes one of the first important cases. This is an example of healing at a distance, and also without the patient's knowledge.

The patient—let us call him Smith—was a Balham man who had been forced to give up working because of increasing weakness, stomach troubles, dizzy spells and a disturbing loss of weight. Examined by a specialist he was found to have a weak heart and a shadow on his right lung. Mrs Smith was told the bad news and advised to persuade him to go to hospital for treatment, or to make him as comfortable as she could at home; his condition was serious.

Mrs Smith knew Harry Edwards—after all, he had been a public figure in Balham for many years—but she did not know of his spiritualist activities. Shortly after the chilling diagnosis she followed a friend's advice and attended a spiritualist service, where she was surprised to hear Edwards address the meeting. Coincidentally she met Edwards again in a local shop the following week and, summoning up her courage, approached him and told him her problem. Edwards thereupon offered to mention her husband during the next intercessionary meeting.

In order not to worry her husband Mrs Smith had kept the news of his condition a secret from him. Nor would Mr Smith have welcomed the assistance of a spiritualist, so Mrs Smith never told him that his name was being put forward and she did not herself attend the intercessionary meeting. During the night following the meeting Mrs Smith was attacked by severe cramps. Her distress wakened her husband who, to her surprise, got out of bed and filled a hot water bottle for her. More surprising still, next morning he rose early and brought her a cup of tea. His whole complexion had changed; he no longer looked tired. It was obvious to all his family that his condition had dramatically improved.

From that day Mr Smith began to put on weight and within five weeks he had gained several pounds. The next time he saw a doctor the specialist was so impressed by the improvement that he thought he had completed a successful course of treatment. That intercession took place in 1937. In 1943, when Edwards lost contact with him, the man was still alive and working.

Another case quoted by the *Psychic News* was described by a doctor, who notes that it was "most unpromising from the medical point of view", and is also one of absent treatment. In this case the patient had, three years previously, contracted a skin disease known as Sycosis Barbae, an intractable and distressing complaint. For various reasons there was considerable delay before the patient could obtain expert treatment and then because of this delay he was told that the prospects of a cure were remote and, as one physician said, "Having had no treatment for nine months, he will be fortunate if he is cured in nine years". For nearly two years he attended the skin department of various London hospitals, but the sores on his face did not heal and the area they covered slowly increased.

Then Harry Edwards was asked to treat the case. Within about three months the patient's face had entirely healed, nothing remaining but the pale scars showing where the sores had been. As in many cases treated by Edwards the cure was gradual, only a slight improvement being observed during the first few weeks then suddenly the healing process accelerating until the sores disappeared.

"Incurable" diseases can also respond to the ministrations of a spiritual healer. In December, 1952, the father of a boy pronounced hopelessly incurable since he was found to be suffering from chronic myeloid leukemia approached Harry Edwards and treatment began. Three months later the boy went back to school, and continued active and well.

Growths also will respond to healing. In his book *The Science of Spirit Healing*, Harry Edwards describes that: "The healer puts his right hand around the growth and as he does so he is conscious of a vibratory movement pulsing down the arm to the fingers. Sometimes this is so strong that the hand and arm can be seen to vibrate violently and at times ache as a result."

Despite the fact that many doctors were witness to these remarkable cures, the attitude of the medical profession in general appears to be that their diagnosis must have been wrong or that the cure is, for some reason, spontaneous. Harry Edwards's healings have always been the centre of controversy. Nevertheless over the years his "practice" has grown enormously. By the early forties he was interceding for several thousand patients a year, most of his treatment being absent healing with intercession taking place at a time agreed with the patient. By then he had thrown over all the trappings of passes, trances and special lights, and by just relaxing his body and concentrating for a few moments he could prepare himself for the spirit's use.

When in 1944 his house in Balham was destroyed by V1 rockets, Edwards continued interceding for his patients although all the records of his treatments and the agreed timings for intercessions had been destroyed. Despite the impossibility of co-ordinating the times of intercession the rate of healing improved.

Reports in the press of his increasing successes brought Edwards an even larger flood of requests for help and he set up a healing centre in the house in Ewell, Surrey, to which he had moved. In 1946, when his brother returned from the war and took over the running of the printing business, Harry Edwards was able to devote all his time to healing. He had always refused to charge any fees for his work, but voluntary donations from grateful patients enabled him to move to a large house, Burrows Lea, at Shere in Surrey where there was more room for his helpers and the mechanics of administration.

In one year only at Burrows Lea some 126,000 letters arrived. In the same year 5,000 sufferers visited the house and 4,600 were personally treated by Edwards. Eighty per cent of his patients reported their health improved, and thirty per cent reported a complete cure. In the same year 20,000 people attended 21 healing sessions given in public by Edwards, for after the war he had begun a series of public healing sessions in large halls throughout the country.

At these sessions Harry Edwards treated hundreds of people suffering from arthritis, muscular dystrophy, disseminated sclerosis, curvature of the spine, deafness, blindness and many other afflictions. At many of these meetings members of the medical profession who declared themselves sceptical at the beginning were invited on to the stage to witness the cures. They were allowed to examine the sick, and to keep their hands over the twisted limbs and displaced bones as the healing took place. All had to agree that in some way the sick and disabled were being helped on the way to health.

The late Beverley Nichols described in his book, *Powers That Be*, his own experience as a patient in unorthodox circumstances. He had had a motor accident in which his right hand had been badly damaged and the bones improperly set. For two years he had suffered continuous pain and been unable to play the piano. Finally, he visited a "faith" healer, a Dr Ash, a man of impeccable medical record, after the efforts of Harley Street specialists had failed to improve his condition.

On the second visit he made to Dr Ash, Beverley Nichols took with him a friend as an independent witness to what took place. He describes how he took off his jacket, rolled up his shirt sleeve and sat with his arm before him on a table while Dr Ash stretched out his arms towards him, making no physical contact whatsoever. After about fifteen seconds, during which Nichols was concentrating on not helping, since it was very vital that there should be no question of self-hypnosis, things began to happen which he could not possibly have achieved of his own volition.

"An unseen force," he said, "was compelling part of my body to react in a manner so physically unmistakable that those reactions could be analysed, measured and, if necessary, photographed ... The skin was vibrating like a cord of elastic after you have stretched it and let it go ... My fingers were doing a sort of supersonic trill." After six minutes Nichols found that he was becoming physically exhausted, and that his whole arm from shoulder to fingertips was aching almost unbearably. He asked Dr Ash if they could stop now, and as the doctor dropped his arms to his side Nichols's hand gave one last flutter and came to rest "as though somebody had switched off the electricity".

It felt, said the author, as though his hand was protesting at what the bones and muscles were being made to do. But it was his friend who found the right words for it. "To me," she said, "it was like the casting out of devils."

Perhaps this is one way to describe the treatment which Harry Edwards continues to this day in his "sanctuary" in Surrey. People who come for help are not asked to believe in any creed nor pay any fees, and the work continues to be financed by voluntary donations. Medical opinion tends to assume that Harry Edwards works on the minds, emotions and beliefs of his patients—although this hardly explains cures made without the patient's knowledge. Even if this limited view, that his power is purely an ability to call up the patient's own strengths, is accepted, then Edwards possesses a gift which is not only beyond the reach of most of us but, in natural terms, totally inexplicable.

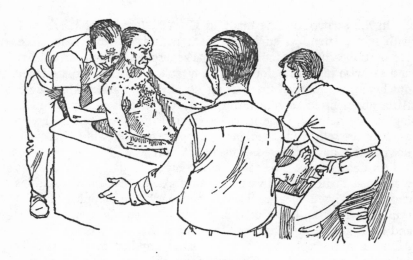

LOURIVAL

Where would you expect to find a needle, some cotton, a razor blade, a kitchen knife and some nail scissors? In the back of an old kitchen drawer? Possibly. More or less anywhere really, except in a surgeon's "little black bag". But these are the very tools of the trade of a remarkably successful surgeon, whose skill with the knife and the needle has cured conditions ranging from cancer to nervous depression—that is when he has not been broke and earning money as a part-time taxi driver.

Lourival de Freitas was born at Coroa Grande, Brazil, in 1929. Orphaned by a fire when he was very young, he was brought up by his gipsy grandmother who had built up quite a name for herself in the locality as a herbalist and healer. The young boy must surely have picked up many of his grandmother's skills at concocting and prescribing remedies for all sorts of ills; certainly by the age of nine he was showing that her gift of healing had been handed down the generations. He cured a surprised visitor of a stomach ulcer.

As the child grew through his teen-age years so did his healing reputation, till by the time he was twenty his fame had spread far outside Brazil. One of his cures was performed on the wife of an English businessman domiciled in Rio. For the woman it was the end of an age of suffering, for Lourival it was the beginning of a new era for his healing powers. The woman's husband was so impressed with the young man's powers that he became his business administrator and advisor. The world would now hear about these gifts.

380

Not everyone was as enthusiastic about his achievements, however. The law in Brazil took a dim view of them for a start, and he was actually prosecuted in 1962 for illegally practising medicine. Part of the defence consisted of a demonstration cure, and an operation was duly performed on a cancer victim. It was successful. The surgeon received a six-month deferred prison sentence.

His first healing manifestation in London took place true to form, not in a sterile operating theatre or even a lecture-hall, but in the living-room of a house in a quiet respectable suburb. The patient was a six-year-old girl who for eighteen months had been suffering from a chronic chest complaint which left fluid on the lung. She also had a heart murmur. Doctors had tried orthodox remedies with little success and now it was recommended that the only course open was an operation to remove the lower part of the afflicted lung.

This session had been arranged by the little girl's uncle who was none other than Lourival's business mentor, but not all those present had such a belief in his talents. (Like his counterpart in a teaching hospital the Brazilian operates surrounded by on-lookers, though in his case they are very rarely medical students.) On this occasion the assembly consisted mainly of friends of the family but their attitudes to the phenomenon they were about to witness ranged from complete faith, through curiosity to outright scepticism.

What they saw that evening was an operation which in its outward physical form was simplicity itself. The child's wasted body was held in her mother's arms while an ordinary whisky tumbler with its rim covered by cotton wool was applied, rim downwards, to her skin just over the afflicted portion of the lung. The surgeon did not hold it himself which, said eye-witnesses, ruled out the possibility of his putting anything inside the glass. Instead he summoned the child's grandfather, who was one of the more sceptical people present, to perform this particular task. With this man's hand, covered by that of Lourival, firmly holding the vessel in place the company watched and waited.

At first nothing happened, then suddenly through the transparent tumbler they could see something "growing out of the girl's back" even though there had been no sign of any incision made. The thing continued to grow until it finally became detached inside the glass, leaving no mark whatsoever on the skin. And that was it. The child was packed off to bed while the grown-ups continued the party.

The next day the child "raided the fridge" and began to exhibit something which her parents had never seen in her before—a healthy

381

appetite. Her father later reported in the journal *Light* that from that moment on there was a sustained improvement in her general condition, and what had been a pale sickly invalid rapidly grew into a normal healthy child. A subsequent medical examination showed that the lung had been cleared of fluid and that there was no trace of the heart murmur.

The glass was the major surgical instrument in another British lung operation, though on this occasion the subject of its attack was not fluid but a cancerous growth. It happened at a party. Nearly all his healing is done in a party atmosphere—curing someone is a happy-joyous occasion after all, he says. This time is was a party for people in England to meet the man they had heard so much about. He was tired, having just rushed from Brazil to Belgium to treat some people there, and was in England for a rest. There was to be no healing on this occasion. But it didn't turn out quite like that. One of the guests at the party was a young woman who had many problems on her mind, the most significant of them being the tumours she had on her lung which were claiming ninety per cent of her vitality and energy, and threatened quite shortly to claim much more.

Few people at the party knew the cause of her malaise, but the entranced Brazilian found it. He decided to operate. The proceedings began with his making a small incision with a razor blade on the patient's chest just above the site of the tumour. The surgeon placed a needle across the wound and began a lifting motion, but all was not well. The atmosphere in the room was not right. There was a hiatus—someone fainted—and in the confusion the identity of the spirit controlling the surgeon's trance changed.

The new "entity" demanded a change of technique. The needle was discarded and a glass found. As before the rim of the vessel was covered with cotton wool, and a hand other than Lourival's held it rim downwards over the trouble spot. This time, under everybody's eyes, the glass misted up and filled with a liquid. In due course this solidified to an evil smelling piece of tissue about one and a half inches in diameter and half an inch thick, which was left in the glass. An ex-nurse who was present and who knew nothing of the patient's complaint, recognized the offensive odour from her days in the cancer ward.

As for the patient, who all this while had felt nothing except "something leaving my body", she went back and joined in the party. And afterwards? Instead of thinking twice about picking up an ashtray because of lack of energy, running up the six flights of stairs to her top floor flat held no difficulties for her.

Lourival maintains that in nearly all of his operations it is not he, the Brazilian taxi driver, who is in charge but one of the twenty or so "spirit guides" who take over his body when he is in a trance. The major influences are Nero, the Roman emperor, and Naor, his own great-grandfather who is said to be particularly good at handling children. Others who may make an appearance range in personality from Messalina, his only female spirit, to German and French doctors.

One of the rare occasions when Lourival has actually healed in his own right without the aid of one of his "guides" was also in England. The spot was Brighton, and the patient a local vet. This man had been stricken with polio as a child and as a result had been left with very much weakened muscles. Deterioration over the years had led him to spending the last eight of them in a wheel chair, and worse still, had finally made arm movement so difficult that it was almost impossible for him to lift them above his head. Brushing his hair was certainly very difficult.

Through the connivance of friends Lourival was brought to this man's house one Sunday afternoon, and through an interpreter— the Brazilian speaks only Portuguese—they chatted. Lourival was anxious to demonstrate what he could do for the stricken man. He passed his hands over the upper half of the withered body then suddenly found the spot he had been looking for. One arm shot over his head high into the air—a feat that he hadn't been able to accomplish for years. The procedure was repeated with the other arm. Then came an even greater test. The wheel-chair victim was to stand up and walk towards the healer—he managed half a dozen or so steps. But this was only the demonstration session. Would he be allowed to go further, Lourival asked.

He was back in two or three days laden with a bundle of Brazilian herbs, which were to be boiled up to make an infusion. This was then to be added to his patient's bath water. The boiling and mixing completed the victim was lowered by the hands of friends into the strangely coloured liquid. Could he move his legs? No. There was then an explanation, in Portuguese, that a psychic shock of about 250 volts was about to be administered. It was. The effect was no less than one would expect. The patient shot to one end of the bath looking dazed. But could he move his legs now? This time the answer was most definitely affirmative. Ten minutes later the company in the living-room were aware that the wheel-chair victim of eight years' sitting had just walked the twenty feet from the bath-room unaided.

The jubilation was general. Lourival and his spirits were pleased too, and a proclamation was issued to fill the place with all and sundry to take part in general rejoicing and general healing. In the event, a goodly proportion of fashionable Brighton turned up—and was cured. A woman, crippled since she'd been buried by a building which collapsed because of war-time bombing, emerged from the treatment-room pushing her wheel-chair. Another woman was found with the surgical collar she had worn for years perched jauntily on her head as a hat. A stroke victim had movement restored to a paralyzed side, and a cyst was removed from behind someone's eye-ball with a pair of nail scissors borrowed from another visitor.

The most dramatic event of that day, though, was a "psychic heart transplant". After most of the guests had gone home, one of those remaining was summoned to the side of his brother who was not expected to last the night because of a worsening in the already bad condition of his heart. The brother went to the bedside—and so did Lourival and the assembled company.

They found the ill man apparently unconscious, and very weak indeed. The surgeon looked around for the strongest male in the party. No, it was not to be a family man because there was an ele-ment of danger in the process. The "donor" was eventually chosen —a famous anthropologist—and he was asked to remove his shirt.

Two tumblers were then called for and one was placed over the heart of each of the men.

The man on the bed was motionless, apparently feeling nothing. The other felt nothing either—at first. Then things began to hurt a little, then they hurt a lot. The next thing he knew he was coming round after passing out and slumping in a chair. Meanwhile, how-ever, the once unconscious eyes had opened and he who had been at death's door was talking. He was made to sit up, a prayer was said, and the party left the room. He lived, and continued to do so for another eighteen months.

The mentally ill have benefited from the Brazilian treatments too. One of the first English patients to be helped in this way was an autistic child with whom conventional therapy had proved of little use. His mother took him to Brazil with her on holiday with the thought that maybe that country's unusual unofficial medicine would be able to find something to help him. After a long search she con-tacted Lourival who suggested that a brain operation might help the boy. A healing party was duly arranged.

This time the patient was laid face down on a bed while his mother was compelled to photograph the whole operation. It began with an incision at the base of the skull of the fully-conscious child —with a pair of nail scissors. After considerable prodding with the unsterilized instrument and much drawing of blood, some tissue was removed which was said to be the "materialized form" of the obsessive entity which was responsible for the boy's condition. The photographs show the entire operation sequence with the exception of the extracted tissue. The negatives of this stage of the proceedings show the surrounding activity clearly enough, but in place of the tissue there is a blank area in the centre of the picture looking for all the world as though someone had shone a bright light at the camera. Throughout the boy lay quietly sucking his thumb. Finally the wound was bound up with sticking plaster and the child joined in the remainder of the party which continued until the early hours of the morning. He was then taken down to the sea shore, and amid much protesting was told to cover himself with the radio-active mud to be found there.

This he did. The dressings were then removed from his neck and everyone saw—nothing but a fully healed thin red scar.

This was not the end of the treatment though, for the child then remained in Brazil for about a month having herbal treatments and leading a back-to-nature existence with the healer. When the boy finally returned to England friends and neighbours were immediately struck by the change in his condition. Here in the place of what had been a withdrawn 12-year-old who had to be taken to school and who was incapable of so much as tying his own shoelace, was a healthy boy who would think nothing of running errands by himself to the local shops.

Lourival's skill as a herbalist came to the fore in the treatment of the mental affliction of another English child. His trouble of brain damage at birth was diagnosed psychically by the surgeon as soon as he met the boy. He prescribed a series of herbal treatments. The parents were sent a collection of Brazilian herbs which they were told to divide into batches, and over regular intervals to cook a batch in water and douse the child with the resulting mixture immediately after his bath. After the second application, bed wetting stopped, and the general improvement in the child's condition was soon being commented on by the staff at his special school. Anxious to see what his son was being given to take, the boy's father took some of the herbal mixture prescribed for the boy to drink to a homoeopathic firm for anlysis. Their verdict? Not exactly what we would have prescribed (one of the ingredients could be very poison-ous in some circumstances) but in that particular case it looked appropriate enough.

Not all mental cases receive the same amount of herbal treatment though, for in some treatments surgery is much more important. Such an operation was done on an English woman who had been suffering from depression for many years. In her case, Lourival showed that passing a needle through one's flesh could be absolutely painless by threading a needle through his own cheek. He then set out to "realign" his patient's nervous system by passing two threaded needles through chest, two through the flesh in her back and one through her neck. Members of the on-looking congrega-tion were then asked to take hold of the bloodied cotton, now securely threaded through the woman's body, and pull with all their strength.

This was done, and eventually the threads were withdrawn. The patient, who claimed that she had felt no pain throughout the entire process returned to her seat laughing—according to her sister, the first time she had laughed for many years. The mood continued and though recovery was not a hundred per cent she has maintained a substantial improvement.

But what does it feel like to be one of the man's patients? Not many have recorded their experiences under the knife, or razor blade. One who has, is the English journalist Anne Dooley. Accounts of her experiences in Brazil have appeared in various national news-papers and in her own book *Every Wall a Door*. She was a victim of bronchiectasis—the same complaint as the young girl who was Lourival's first patient in England. British medical experts had been able to give her little lasting relief.

When given an assignment to follow up the story of the Brazilian healers for her newspaper, she availed herself of the opportunity to experience a psychic cure first hand. In her case, some days before the actual operation the surgeon marked out the area on her back in which he could operate by scratching it with the sharp blade of a reed. She was then told to cut down her smoking until after the treatment and to take daily doses of specially prepared herbal remedies.

The operation itself was again a social affair but this time was in a farmhouse in the mountains, in an atmosphere which was a far cry from the English middle-class living-room. Lourival, or rather his spirit guide Nero, treated several patients; but then the surgeon's mood changed. He was seized by another "guide" whose personality was much more violent, and he started the treatment of his English patient at once.

His immediate area of concern, though, was not the lung but the woman's throat. Her tonsils must be removed, he said, and set about them with an ordinary pair of scissors. After digging about in her throat for some time—a process which caused her considerable fear and pain—he told her to spit hard into a tumbler. A mass of tissue and blood was ejected.

The operation on the diseased lung came next. An incision was made with a razor blade at right angles to the scar left by the reed and Lourival applied his mouth to the wound. He sucked very hard and eventually withdrew a dark mass about an inch long. It was placed in the woman's hand and the wound sewn up again—with a sewing needle and ordinary thread. No attempt was made at sterilizing the area.

The treatment had been rough and painful, and the pain continued for the next day or so, especially in the throat. But she found that she could breathe better than she had done for years, and her whole general level of health improved. As for the tonsils, a later medical examination showed that they had indeed been removed.

Not all his healing sessions have ended with success, however, and not all have been held in a friendly atmosphere. His very first visit to London almost ended in disaster through a public meeting. Last-minute changes to the timing of the session had upset the emotional balance, and the continual flashing of flash bulbs in Lourival's face as he worked did not help matters. A woman was operated on for a cataract and something, said to be a lens, was removed from her eye. Her subsequent history, though, reported no improvement in her condition—indeed the diseased lens was found to be still in place. Another operation did not appear to be too successful either, though this one was interrupted before its close. The patient in this case was a man fatally ill with cancer. Lourival operated on his throat and removed some growths, but the man died a few months afterwards anyway. He might well have recovered if the operation had been allowed to continue, say some of Lourival's followers. Indeed he might have done—other cancer operations have been successful in other places at other times. Would this one have been too? One will never know. As it was, it finished in an emotional scene with the surgeon throwing his operating knife into the floor, and storming from the building.

Most of his healing sessions are very different affairs, though, with much music and laughter. In fact music plays a very important part in the proceedings. Soon after the group is complete, Lourival goes into a trance and one of his spirit guides takes over. Music is then used to monitor the mood of the company—if the atmosphere is a little sad he will sing a cheerful song accompanying himself on the guitar. Too boisterous a mood is quelled with a more wistful melody.

Many of those who have been present at one of these meetings have been struck by the insight the man appears to have into their personal lives and problems—an insight which he is able to demonstrate through two or three simple sentences uttered through an interpreter. The whole process, according to an eye-witness seems to generate an atmosphere of mutual trust and affection. It is in this highly charged emotional atmosphere that the operations are actually done.

Like the Shamans of central Asia, Lourival uses stimulants to heighten his trance state. In his case the stimulant is alcohol and it is far from unknown for him to drink half-a-bottle of whisky without coming up for air—a feat which could well kill an ordinary man. There is never any trace of the smell of alcohol on his breath though, and out of the trance he is strictly teetotal.

What does he get out of it? It is certainly not material wealth. He has never been known to take money for his treatments, professing himself scared that if he did so his gift may leave him—if he needs money he drives his taxi.

When not operating he is shy and self effacing. He never guarantees to cure anybody, and will say outright if he feels himself to be unable to help a patient. Sometimes he will cure one patient of a particular malady while turning away another suffering from the same complaint saying that there is nothing he can do for him.

Medical genius or charlatan? Will we ever know? Official assessments of the results of his work are difficult to arrange, for he is operating outside the law and already has a suspended prison sentence hanging over him in his native country. Detailed medical examination of any removed growths is difficult too, because he says that his "controlling spirits" insist that all such matter is destroyed at the end of every session to prevent the evil in it from spreading.

If he is a charlatan, he is a charlatan with a success rate which would do credit to most orthodox surgeons. Whatever he is, one thing is certain ... Lourival de Freitas is no ordinary man.

Practitioners and Prophets

DANIEL DUNGLAS HOME

The latter half of the nineteenth century can truthfully be called the heyday of the medium. Tables turned, spirits rapped out messages, flowers fell from the air, unearthly music was played, bells rang of their own accord and ghostly visitors arrived.

Victorian society loved spiritualists and flocked to séances. The fame of well-known mediums was international, and they were welcomed in the homes and courts of the great. Many were fakes, of that there is no doubt; and there is also no doubt that many who did have some inexplicable powers gave the spirits a little help when they failed to come up to the expectations of the sitters. Gadgets and wires which would produce spirit raps and turn tables were openly advertised, with the result that the whole fraternity came under suspicion and every successful medium was the centre of controversy. (The Society for Psychical Research, the first body to undertake research into various supernatural phenomena in a thorough and scientific fashion, was not founded until 1882, and The Society gradually developed more and more stringent and foolproof methods for testing the genuiness of various phenomena: it is an interesting fact that there are comparatively few mediums active today.)

Despite the doubts and scandals that periodically rocked the faith of the spiritualists, many mediums continued for years to confuse their critics and delight their supporters. One of these, and perhaps the most famous of the Victorian era, known as the King of Mediums, was Daniel Dunglas Home. Like most other mediums he had his supporters and detractors—men of science such as Faraday and Huxley denied that he had any supernatural powers, others of almost equal eminence such as Crookes and de Morgan believed in them; Home caused some noisy (the neighbours heard them) matrimonial tiffs between the celebrated Brownings—Elizabeth, who stoutly supported him, and Robert, who angrily scoffed. But he was a welcome guest in the courts of Europe and the perpetrator of one of the most famous and remarkable acts to be performed by a medium—levitation.

Levitation has always been one of the supernatural phenomena reported as having been achieved by mystics and mediums throughout history. Saint Francis of Assisi and Saint Teresa are both believed to have levitated, but perhaps the most famous of all was the monk, Saint Joseph of Copertino, who was born in 1603 and whose "flights" were witnessed by hundreds of people from villagers and monks to the Pope himself.

St Joseph's story is worth recording briefly since it is both colourful and supported by a wealth of evidence. Joseph was a notable ascetic, who indulged in extreme mortification of the flesh. When he was only about twenty-five, stories of his supernatural powers led to his examination by the Inquisition, and it was then that his first recorded levitation took place.

He had been given permission by the Holy Office to say mass in the Inquisition's own church. When it was over he retreated to a corner of the church to pray and then suddenly rose into the air and, upright and with his arms outstretched as though he were on a cross, flew over the heads of the astonished congregation to land on the altar. There he remained for a few moments, unscathed by the flames of the candles, before flying back to his corner, this time in a kneeling position.

The Inquisition fortunately decided that his gifts came from God and not from the Devil, and he was sent to Rome where he had an audience with the Pope. Gripped by pious excitement as he stood before Urban VIII, Joseph drifted upwards and remained suspended in the air in an attitude of respect and prayer for more than a minute. The Pope, much impressed, promised that he himself would testify to the truth of the incident.

Joseph was then sent to Assisi where, however, the abbot was not so impressed and warned him not to get up to his tricks. Joseph became so wretched that his plight came to the ears of the Superior of his Order who sent for him. When Joseph got back to Assisi after a short stay in Rome, he found a large crowd waiting to greet him in the basilica of the monastery. Delighted to be back in his beloved church, Joseph uttered a loud cry and rose from the ground alighting gently after a short flight.

During his flights, which were watched, usually unknown to Joseph, by numerous royal and eminent persons, Joseph appeared to go into an ecstatic trance. There are records of him landing on laden tables or altars without disturbing the things which lay upon them, and of once perching on a branch which would not bear the weight of an ordinary man. The numerous tales of his levitations are incredible, but it is impossible to assume that they were all the result of mass hallucinations; nor, as has been suggested, that Joseph was simply an outstanding athlete whose leaps caused such excitement that they were magnified to extremes—Joseph's already delicate health must have been considerably undermined by the mortification he continually practised. The evidence of scores of (often sceptical) witnesses was given to the truth of Saint Joseph's levitations on some sixty occasions, but it all happened three hundred years ago and there is a tendency to treat the credulities expressed by our ancestors with some indulgence.

Daniel Dunglas Home's levitations were by no means so spectacular and were witnessed by a handful rather than hundreds of people, but the evidence has been examined and sifted over and over again by all kinds of people—and still no satisfactory conclusions have been reached.

Daniel Dunglas Home was born in 1833 in a small village near Edinburgh of working-class parents. He claimed, sometimes, that his father was a natural son of the Earl of Home (whose second title was Baron Dunglas) and his name was often pronounced (and spelt) Hume in the style of that family. When he was a child he was taken by his mother to America, where he lived with an aunt in Connecticut. As a youth he had one or two "visions" or presentiments which proved correct and which included that of the death of his mother. But when the house began to resound with mysterious raps his aunt, much annoyed, sent for a clutch of local clergy to exorcize the devil or whatever it was which possessed the boy.

Their efforts, however, failed and the aunt, tired of what she insisted were the boy's tricks, turned him out of her house. He was then about nineteen years old and was fortunate enough to be taken into the home of a Mr and Mrs Hayden, who ran a thriving business as fully fledged mediums. The spiritualist cult was then just beginning to get under way in America—its birthplace—but

393

Daniel's talents proved even greater than that of his benefactors and the business throve even more. It was during this period that a sitter at a séance gave the first account of him being lifted up in the air. The account was ecstatic and far from well authenticated, but it brought publicity in its wake and started Daniel Home on his life's work.

During the whole of his career Home never accepted money for demonstrations of his psychic or spiritual powers, relying on gifts and the generosity of friends with whom he lived to provide for his needs. He was never physically robust and when he was twenty-two years old he developed a mild form of tuberculosis and was told that he must go to Europe for treatment. Friends raised money for him, but he arrived in London to find himself without friends and almost penniless. Luck, or the spirits, directed him to a hotel in London the proprietor of which was interested in spiritualism. When Daniel demonstrated his powers his host was so delighted that he invited Daniel to remain at the hotel as a guest and introduced him to London society.

At this time spiritualism had only fairly recently arrived from America and was still a new and fashionable "religion". Daniel was immediately in demand; his powers attracted the attention of all kinds of people among society and the intelligentsia, and he was invited to live with a lawyer and his wife in Ealing.

Like all mediums before and since, Home was the centre of controversy between, on the one hand, convinced believers who enthusiastically described the way he had made tables float about, bells ring, flowers land on people's heads and an accordion play, and on the other hand sceptics who pointed out that popular conjurors like Maskelyne, who was a current favourite, could do exactly the same thing. Some, including Robert Browning, claimed to have detected Home in actual fraud; others declared it was impossible. Home himself, like most mediums, accepted all this as an inevitable adjunct to his powers and remained for the most part calm and aloof, only occasionally protesting at some particularly unfair attack.

Home continued to refuse to take money for his séances and allowed certain conditions to be imposed when he worked. His popularity grew: he visited Paris (where he met Madame Blavatsky who worked with him for a while) and became a favourite of the Empress Eugénie, making many visits to the Tuileries palace. He left Paris under a somewhat mysterious cloud—although the Empress continued to show him favour on later visits—and travelled through Europe.

In Rome he met the daughter of an aristocratic Russian family and, despite his delicate health, lack of family and money, was allowed by her family to marry her. The success of the séances he held at the Tsar's court ensured his welcome there, and his wife's income ensured a new pecuniary independence for Home—who was also by now possessor of an impressive collection of jewellery, given to him by grateful clients. Eventually Home returned to England with his wife and their child and again settled down in London. However, by now there was a good deal of competition from other mediums and Home's own fame was given a much-needed boost when, once again it was reported that, at a séance, he had been levitated.

According to a witness he had risen from his chair to a height of four or five feet above the heads of the people in the room and floated to and fro. Meanwhile an accordion also floated about on its own, playing unearthly music.

This report, published in a soberly Victorian magazine, immediately aroused the usual burst of controversial argument, while some witnesses pointed out that the room was in almost total darkness and others busily explained just how the trick was done. The editor of *Punch*, a determined sceptic, published a poem of which the first verse ran:

Through humbugs and fallacies though we may roam
Be they never so artful, there's no case like Home,
With a lift from the spirits he'll rise in the air
Though as lights are put out, we can't see him there

and Thackeray, the editor of the journal which published the account of the levitation, was much berated.

Home's fame, however, continued, and his supporters remained staunch. The spiritualists continued to flourish although Home among the others suffered set-backs, sometimes being caught out in minor frauds, and refused the serious attention of such bodies as the Royal Society which Home had invited to investigate his powers. Home's wife, always delicate, died and her family refused his claim to her income. Home took to lecturing and poetry reading to make money, and for quite a while gave very few séances. He found himself in real trouble when a rich and elderly lady, having been instructed (via Home) by the spirit voice of her dead husband, to hand over considerable sums of money to the medium, thought better of the idea and successfully sued for the return of her gifts on the grounds that she had been unduly influenced by Home.

Regardless of these unpleasant events Home's friends continued loyal, among them being one who became a witness of the most famous of Home's phenomena—which is always mentioned in connection with his name—a levitation par excellence. This incident took place in 1868, and has generally been accepted as being proved without doubt since "the three witnesses were of high social standing". (A fact which would have considerably less significance today!)

For some time Daniel Home had been a friend of Lord Adare, son of the Earl of Dunraven, whom he had met in Paris. Adare, and a friend Lord Lindsay (who later became President of the Royal Astronomical Society and a Fellow of the Royal Society), spent a good deal of time with Home, and the two young men—Adare was twenty-seven and Lindsay only twenty-one at the time of the levitation—with a Captain Charles Wynne, a cousin some five years older, of Adare, often sat in at the séances with Home. Adare and Lindsay went to considerable trouble to record their experiences during these séances, and after the remarkable levitation both wrote separate accounts of the incident.

One evening, according to the account of Lord Adare, he and Charlie Wynne went round to the house where Home was staying and there found him with Lord Lindsay. Home proposed a sitting. Adare reports that they all sat round a table in a small room. "There was no light in the room, but the light from the window was sufficient to enable them to see each other and the different articles of furniture."

At this period the spirit of Adah Isaacs Menken (a staunch spiritualist who, as "Mazeppa" riding the Wild Horse of Tartary had been a star of Astley's Circus and who had recently died in Paris) often visited the séances held by Home. On this particular December night Home went into a kind of trance and walked about uneasily. According to Adare he was both "elongated and raised in the air" (phenomena which, apparently, were not unusual). He then said to his friends "Do not be afraid, and on no account leave your places", and he went out into the passage.

Lord Lindsay then suddenly said, "Oh good heavens! I know what he is going to do; it is too fearful. I cannot tell you, it is too horrible."

However at this point Adah's spirit took a hand, and Lindsay reported that she had told him to tell the others, "He is going out of the window in the other room and coming in at this window."

Adare continues: "We heard Home go into the next room, heard the window thrown up and presently Home appeared standing upright outside our window; he opened the window and walked in quite coolly. 'Ah,' he said, 'You were good this time', referring to our having sat still and not wished to prevent him. He sat down and laughed."

Charlie asked why he was laughing, and Home replied that he had thought how astonished a passing policeman would have been if he had looked up and seen a man turning round and round in the air, along the wall. He then told Adare to shut the window in the next room.

"I got up, shut the window, and in coming back remarked that the window was not raised a foot, and that I could not think how he had managed to squeeze through. He arose and said 'Come and see,' I went with him: he told me to open the window as it was before, I did so: he told me to stand a little distance off; he then went through the open space, head first, quite rapidly, his body being nearly horizontal and apparently rigid. He came in again, feet foremost, and we returned to the other room. It was so dark I could not see clearly how he was supported outside. He did not appear to grasp or rest upon the balustrade, but rather to be swung out and in. Outside each window is a small balcony or ledge 19 inches deep, bounded by stone balustrades, 18 inches high. The balustrades of the two windows are 7 feet 4 inches apart, measuring from the nearest points. A string-course, 4 inches wide, runs between the windows at the level of the bottom of the balustrade; and another, 3 inches wide, at the level of the top. Between the window at which Home went out and that which he came in the wall recedes 6 inches. The rooms are on the third floor."

As so often happens in these cases there are irritating, inexplicable and often quite irrelevant discrepancies in the accounts given of the event at the time and later. Adare contradicted himself over both the date and the venue of the séance; and although at the time Adare got his friends to read his account of the event and agree that the details were accurate, when Lindsay and (many years later) Wynne described the levitation the details given again did not tally in such matters as the light in the room, the position in which the men were sitting, and so on.

However, all three of them agree in the fact that Daniel Dunglas Home floated in and out of the windows three storeys above the ground. Investigation into the mystery has continued enthusiastically ever since, and various explanations of it have been put forward (for as someone pointed out, man would rather believe in a lie than a miracle). The house was placed by later investigations in Ashley

Place, near Victoria (although there is some slight doubt even as to this), and the stone belconies described by Adare have vanished, being replaced by wrought iron after bomb damage during the Second World War. It has been suggested that Home, who is known to have had a good head for heights, could have climbed from one balcony to another, edging along the string course, or that he could have previously fixed clamps to the wall which he later removed. It has also been suggested that, over a long period he had conditioned his observers to believe what they saw that December night by discussing with them the whole question of levitation, by forecasting a levitation, and on one occasion by standing outside the window at Ashley House—which had given his friends considerable concern for his safety.

Nobody, however, has ever explained why Home should have carried out such a dangerous trick, for he obtained no pecuniary benefit from it. Adare and his friends were merely puzzled and intrigued, and not long afterwards the association between Home and Adare gradually became less close. Another incident of levitation was reported soon after the one at Ashley House, when at a luncheon party given by Lord Carnarvon Home was said to have levitated himself again, floating out of one window and in at another and "alighting breathless and trembling". The story was told by a guest at the luncheon in a letter to a newspaper, but no other witness ever came forward.

Home meanwhile went on with his routine life, with increasing competition from other, often fraudulent mediums. He took to his travels again and married another aristocratic Russian lady. Eventually, when his tubercular lungs gave him cause for alarm, he left England for the sake of his health. He eventually settled in Switzerland, where he lived in a modest *pension* with his wife. His powers gradually failed, and he held fewer and fewer séances. He made a little money from literary work and wrote another volume of his reminscences, *The Lights and Shadows of Spiritualism* (in which he considerably annoyed fellow mediums by exposing many of the tricks of the trade).

But his health grew considerably worse. Somewhat belatedly his wife took him to Paris to consult a specialist and there in 1886 he died, and was buried in the cemetery of Saint Germain. On his gravestone was inscribed: "Daniel Dunglas Home. Born to earth life near Edinburgh (Scotland) March 20, 1833; born to spirit life June 21, 1886". Faithful spiritualists still visit his grave, and within it still lies the secret of the famous levitation.

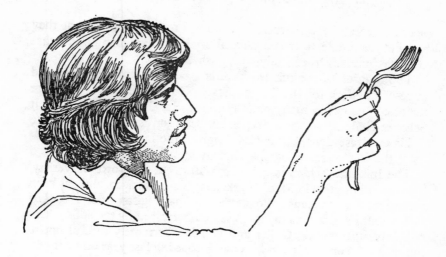

URI GELLER

Uri Geller: showman-magician or miracle-worker?

That is the conundrum posed to scientists by public performances and private examinations of his powers which seem to be out of this world. Geller became a widely-discussed figure in Britain and the United States after giving TV demonstrations of his ability to bend at will metal objects like teaspoons, forks and keys without touching them, as well as stopping and re-starting wrist watches although the wearers were many miles away from him.

Geller is twenty-seven years old, handsome and quick to smile: he favours the current long-hair style but is clean-shaven. He has no precise explanation for himself but thinks he may be an avatar from outer space, a sign to us earthlings from the world of flying-saucers. He is aware of certain similarities with Jesus Christ, but does not claim to be His re-incarnation. Once, he says, he changed a thin rosé wine into one resembling a rich burgundy. In a magazine interview he remarked that the Israelis put Jesus's date of birth as 20 December, which happens to be Geller's birth-date too.

"Possibly just a coincidence," he said. "I believe that Jesus had powers and so did Moses—and all those other wise men of history."

It is, however, doubtful if Jesus would have become a paratrooper in the Israeli Army, as Geller did. It is also doubtful if Geller would have won such instant recognition in the western world had not the highly-respected scientists of the Stanford Research Institute decided to investigate his powers and, having done so during five weeks of carefully constructed laboratory tests, admitted that they had not been able to find a normal scientific explanation and that Geller requires further study.

The Stanford Research Institute is a large organization engaged in research work for the United States Government as well as for major companies in many parts of the world. The statement that it believes Geller deserves a deeper investigation is not only a tribute to his manifestations, but is also a sign of the increased respectability of the whole area of parapsychology in our Space Age.

The Institute, which is quite separate from Stanford University, has its headquarters in Menlo Park, near San Francisco, and has been testing two Americans who appear to have gifts similar to Uri Geller's. It has been, to say the least, embarrassed by the subsequent publicity surrounding Geller and is being extremely careful not to jump to any conclusions in his case. Reporting last year on its investigations into Geller and one other (unnamed) person, the scientists Dr Harold Puthoff and Mr Russell Targ said: "We do not claim that either of these men has psychic powers. We draw no sweeping conclusions as to the nature of these phenomena or the need to call them psychical. We have observed certain phenomena with the subjects for which we have no scientific explanation. All we can say at this point is that further investigation is clearly warranted. Our work is only in the preliminary stages."

A film was made of the Geller experiments by SRI and here is a summary of the Institute's account of three tests:

DICE BOX: A double-blind experiment was performed in which a single die was placed in a closed metal box. This box was heartily shaken by one of the researchers and placed on a table. The subject (Geller) then had to look at the box without touching it and call out which die face he believed was uppermost. He gave the correct answer each of the eight times the experiment was performed. The probability that this could have occurred by chance is approximately one in a million.

PICTURE DRAWING: In this test simple pictures were drawn on 3-by-5 cards at a time when Geller was not at the Institute. The pictures were put into double-sealed envelopes by an outside assistant not associated with the experiment. The subject made seven almost exact reproductions, with no errors.

HIDDEN OBJECT: Ten identical aluminium film cans were placed in a row by an outside assistant not associated with the research. The experimenters, who were not themselves aware which can contained the object, would then enter the room with the subject, who would either pass his hand over the row of cans or simply look at them. He would then call out the cans he felt confident were empty, and an experimenter would remove them from the row. When only two or three cans remained, the subject would announce which one he thought contained the target object. This task was performed twelve times, without error. The probability that this could have occurred by chance is approximately one in a trillion.

The researchers say they "have no hypothesis at this point as to whether this is a heightened sensitivity of some normal sense, or whether it is some paranormal sense that Geller possesses". They are convinced that the experiments they conducted were virtually fraud-proof but they add, cautiously: "A film never *proves* anything. Rather, this film gives us the opportunity to share with the viewer observations of phenomena that, in our estimation, deserve further study."

A second group of tests was carried out in the field of psycho-kinesis and included Geller's apparent facility in bending spoons, nails and other metal objects although he apparently performed less well in laboratory conditions than he does in public. He did, it seems, bend some spoons and buckle some rings, but not until he touched them.

Two of his manifestations did impress the scientists: in one he succeeded in moving the needle of a magnetometer, which measures magnetic fields, without touching it at all; in the other he is said to have raised and lowered a scale which was completely enclosed inside an aluminium can and a glass cylinder.

The scientists reported that, in several experiments, Geller improved his performance as he went on. With the film containers, for instance, he had to pass his hand over them before making his selection but he did this less and less.

Conditions for these tests were made as rigorous as possible, indeed several experiments were eliminated because it was felt that trickery could have been possible. The most important aspect of the Stanford investigation was that it was, unlike a public performance, always under the control of the scientists who had worked out several devices to eliminate any chance of Geller's cheating.

Geller was by no means an easy subject and did not fit easily into the bare, clinical conditions of a laboratory but, once a rapport had been established, he appeared to co-operate to the satisfaction of the scientists who are keen that he return for a further series of tests at Menlo Park. Every time he was put to a test, they reported, he was reluctant to involve himself completely and do what was asked—

he had to be coaxed. When it turned out that he had succeeded he seemed genuinely delighted at his performance—even surprised.

The Stanford scientists concede that, first and foremost, Geller is a showman, an entertainer, and he may very well use some tricks of that trade to put himself over to his public. But this does not mean that he does not also have the special powers which he claims —even if they do not always work with the same force.

Dr Harold Puthoff, one of the two investigators, twice allowed Geller to drive him blindfold. Neither drive, of course, qualified as a controlled experiment. Nevertheless Dr Puthoff was impressed: Geller drove so fast along winding roads that a following car could not keep up with him. Dr Puthoff points out that some people are extremely good at "seeing through blindfolds"—unless an opaque bag is placed over the subject's head and tied at the neck, Dr Puthoff says, you can't be one hundred per cent certain that the subject is not "cheating".

Geller was first spotted when giving a "party turn" in Israel by Dr Andrija Puharich, author of *The Sacred Mushroom*, who has now written a book about Uri's powers. "It is a fact," says Puharich, "that there is an outer-space intelligence that exists independently of any form we know. This intelligence operates through Uri and around Uri. That is the bare truth. My problem is to define this intelligence."

That is why he has written the book which makes some remarkable claims for Geller—one theory it advances is that Uri managed to avert a third world war. "I can't substantiate that fully," says Puharich, "because it involves so many people in Washington, Cairo, Tel Aviv, Moscow and elsewhere. But a good case can be made."

Dr Puharich who claims that he "wouldn't put his seal on anything that wasn't true", declares that Geller often causes things to materialize and claims that he once travelled to Brazil by astral projection while lying on his bed in Puharich's home in Ossining, near New York, and as proof he brought back a 1,000 cruzeiro note. He and Geller have apparently seen many flying saucers and have had many conversations (in English) with the occupants of the saucers which Puharich calls "IS"—short for Intelligence in the Sky. In his book on Geller, he quotes some of these talks verbatim, including one in which he was told that he and Uri had been chosen by IS computers as "the perfect and ideal men" to do IS's work on earth. (IS claims to have been the force behind Moses and Jesus.)

Another strong supporter of Geller is Captain Edgar Mitchell, who went to the moon with Apollo 14 in 1971. He caused something of a sensation by trying out a number of psychic experiments in outer space. He has no doubts at all about Uri's gifts and, indeed, believes that they are an extreme example of capacities that exist to a greater or lesser extent in everyone. Here, argues Captain Mitchell, is a whole new area of human consciousness which had long been unrecognized and now needs thorough exploration.

But the most effective of Geller's supporters is Judith Skutch, president of the Foundation for Parasensory Investigation which is based in her large New York apartment. That is where Geller gives most of his private demonstrations, and it is this foundation which has put up the money to pay for Stanford's further study of Geller.

Mrs Skutch admits that Uri has marked show-business impulses. She herself lays no claim to psychic powers. But she makes this point: "I don't know why everyone assumes we are the centre of intelligence in the universe. Flying saucers to me make absolute sense."

How did it all begin? Uri Geller was born in Hungary, and apparently became aware of certain powers when he was three years old. "I could guess the numbers on playing cards," he has said. At school four years later he could make the hands on his wrist watch move simply by concentrating on them.

His father died when he was nine and his mother, Mrs Margaret Geller, decided to make a new life for herself and her son on a kibbutz in Israel where Uri went to a boarding-school. There, according to fellow pupils, he "kept dabbling in magic". After school he did his army service as a paratrooper. That over, he earned a living in Tel Aviv as a male model, his speciality being modelling underwear.

The breakthrough came for him when he decided to go on the stage. He asked the Israeli trade-union group, Histadrut, for a contract to entertain at their social centres. They sent him to an astrologer and student of the occult, Mrs Aviva Stan, who was a Histadrut lecturer. At her home in Tel Aviv Uri gave a demonstration to Mrs Stan and four of her friends. That was in the autumn of 1969. Mrs Stan's verdict? "He was a thoroughly charming young man, handsome and well mannered, but his demonstration, we thought, was pathetic. He could see we were not impressed by what he was doing, so he asked one of the girls present if he could borrow her ring, saying he could snap metals. Then he went into the kitchen for a glass of water and when he came out he had snapped the ring. We all suspected he had used a small pair of pliers. I felt sorry for him, but I recommended that Histadrut should not offer him a contract."

However, soon after this unsuccessful audition, a theatrical manager, Mickey Pelect, decided he had what it takes to charm audiences so he took Uri under his wing, polished up his act and hired a publicity girl to promote him. This girl, Mrs Miri Zichrony, has said recently: "I always thought he was using trickery, but Uri himself believed absolutely that he was a superman. Knowing his confidence in his own powers I found it much easier to 'sell' him to people as a man in touch with supernatural influences."

Geller got his first show business break through Shmuel Shai, usually described as Israel's David Frost, who first gave him a spot on his stage show at the Sheraton Hotel in Tel Aviv then later featured him on his TV and radio shows. According to Shai he "went across so well that, in no time, everyone here was talking about Uri Geller".

This popularity, of course, brought him plenty of space in the newspapers. Geller had made around one thousand appearances in Israel when American tourists saw his act and brought him to the attention of Captain Mitchell, the sixth man to land on the moon, who sent a scientist to check him out. That led to appearances in the United States.

Geller made his first public appearance in Britain on a David Dimbleby TV Talk-in show on 23 November, 1973. Millions saw him break a steel fork just by stroking it, and will a broken watch to mend itself. The following day the whole country was agog with his feats. He became a five-day wonder for the national newspapers which vied with each other to take him up. And he sparked off a fascinating correspondence in *The Times*. One reader wrote:

Uri Geller has demonstrated in public that he has unusual powers to bend metal by thought. Now that there is a trend for people to go back into history further than ever before, surely it will soon be realized that these powers are only lost and waiting to be rediscovered?

Take, for instance, the tradition among Easter Islanders that their fantastic statues "moved into place of their own accord". To King Arthur's so-called wizard Merlin was ascribed power to move standing stones. Again, when are scientists going to solve the mystery of "perpetual light"? Plutarch wrote in the first century AD that he had seen a "perpetual lamp" in a temple of Jupiter and that the priests assured him it had burned continually for many years. Neither wind nor water could extinguish it.

Or the cold jungle lights seen by natives in the lost cities of the Matto Grosso jungle who related the circumstances to Colonel F. P. Fawcett— where did they come from? Again, what was the source of the incandescent spheres discovered in a jungle valley in New Guinea populated by Amazon women?

Numa Pompilius was credited with the ability to light altar fires without aids. Elijah also did this in the famous passage in I Kings: This fascinating character also had foreknowledge of his own disappearance from the earth when he was removed from it by some sort of aircraft, and his successor Elisha declared it was no use sending out a search party of 50 men to find him. They searched fruitlessly for three days and Elisha simply remarked: "Did I not tell you not to go?"

The world is packed with clues. Surely it is time our society took these things seriously and started to explore the massive evidence existing of incredibly highly evolved technological societies existing in the very long ago past?

This letter was followed by one from Lord Corvedale writing from Christ's Hospital, Horsham, Sussex:

There is a time for scepticism, and there is a time for sense. I might argue, if I choose, that Antarctica does not exist. I have not been there. I have met no one who has been there (if I did I should not believe him). The sagas we have been told, the maps that have been printed are part of a gigantic mistake, or a dark conspiracy. I shall wait for more solid evidence.

I shall wait in vain. So too will the men of science who chase the rainbow's end, devising ever more foolproof tests for such as Uri Geller. For them no evidence is going to be enough. At the moment when we may be on the verge of some of the most exciting discoveries about the nature of mind and matter ever made, it is disheartening to see many who by training are best equipped to investigate such happenings looking so resolutely the other way, convinced, presumably, of their intrinsic impossibility.

Too many promising investigations have now been snuffed out, or have died from lack of support or fear of ridicule. Galileo's discoveries were embarrassing at the time, but they did not put an end to the activities of good scientists ...

If Uri Geller is indeed able to make broken watches tick again, might he not, as others have shown they can, succeed in doing the same for human beings? In the face of such possibilities it is high time to temper scepticism with a rather keener spirit of scientific adventure.

Geller, of course, has plenty of detractors. Chief among these is *Time* magazine which summed him up as "a questionable nightclub magician". Leon Jaroff wrote the *Time* article apparently to make the Stanford Institute look foolish for being so gullible. Jaroff argues that there has never been "a single adequately documented psychic phenomenon". Many people believe in things like this, he writes, because they need to. From the moment Jaroff heard of Geller's supposed powers, he knew Geller had to be a fake, so he set about collecting evidence to support this view.

"At first (in 1970) he was widely acclaimed," said the magazine.

"He came under suspicion when a group of psychologists and computer experts from Hebrew University duplicated all of his feats and called him a fraud. He eventually left the country in disgrace."

But Benjamin Ron, Israeli vice-consul for scientific affairs in Washington, says that no scientific testing on the scale of the SRI experiments was ever done in Israel and adds: "There is no question in our minds from a scientist's viewpoint that there is something in this man." And he dismisses the *Time* account as "over-blown".

Professor Kelson, a physicist at Tel Aviv University and himself an amateur magician, is on record as saying that, after much observation, he is convinced that Geller is "an established fraud". But he has never done any laboratory testing.

Perhaps the last word should be left with the British weekly, *The New Scientist*, which has set up an informal committee including two members of its staff, a psychologist, a professional magician and an independent journalist and has issued a challenge to Geller to appear before this group and demonstrate his powers. Everything, the magazine promises, will be recorded on video-tape and all results will be published.

"With a cautious approach of this nature," concludes *The New Scientist*, "it could be that parapsychology will finally undergo a genuinely disinterested study of its validity."

A DIVINE GIFT?

Of all the powers which are regarded as supernormal, perhaps the most readily accepted is that of divining or, as it has been called for centuries in the West Country, dowsing. The existence of this power is, in some people, so well proven that diviners have been employed by organizations such as government departments and businesses—which are not normally given to gullibility.

Divining is also a relatively common gift. I once had the opportunity to try it for myself, when my uncle, who needed another water supply on his land in Devonshire, sent for the local dowser in much the same way as you or I might send for the local electrician. He took it for granted that the dowser would find any water that was there: the only concern was whether it would be in a suitable place.

Amused by the fascination with which I watched him quartering the fields, the Y-shaped twig he carried occasionally twisting in his hands as it reacted to the pull of water, the dowser invited me to "have a go". He searched the hedgerows for a stout and suitably shaped twig—hazel is the conventional wood used, but it is not necessary—cut it to size for me, and I walked over the field beside him, the twig held out before me. Nothing happened: when my friend's twig dipped, mine remained inanimate, but when he put his hands over mine my twig reacted too.

Seeing my disappointment the dowser explained that the water he could "feel" was apparently both scanty and deep. He led me across a couple of fields and told me to try again. This time he walked beside me, merely watching, and soon I felt the twig move and then jerk and twist so strongly in my hands that I almost dropped it. It was impossible to hold it still, or to control it in any way.

The dowser was much entertained by my excitement. He had known that there was water there—plentiful and not very deep but unfortunately inconveniently situated for my uncle's purpose—and not wanting to influence me in any way had let me try for myself if I could "find" it. He told me that in fact about three people out of ten could dowse, and that if I developed the gift I would become more sensitive to the existence of water and perhaps other things. He knew when his twig was reacting to some substance that was not water, and he made me hold one fork of his twig while he held the other, so that I could feel for myself the difference between the pull of water and of some other influence (but to tell the truth, I couldn't). He himself never knew what other things he could feel below the ground, for he was a countryman, who appreciated the value of water and who had no more ambition than to put his gift at the service of others for a modest fee. He found water in three or four places on my uncle's land, and at the most suitable a shaft was sunk. A little windmill atop its steel tower is still pumping up the water to this day.

Divining is an ancient art, widely practised throughout Europe. Marco Polo met diviners during his travels in China in the thirteenth century. It was probably introduced into England, according to a book entitled *The Divining Rod* which originated from an investigation made by the late Sir William Barrett on behalf of the Society for Psychical Research, by German miners who were brought over in the latter part of the sixteenth century to work the tin mines of Cornwall. The local dowser is still more commonly to be found in the West Country than in other parts of Britain.

Water, however, is by no means the only substance a diviner can find. Coal, various metals, oil and even missing objects or persons have been discovered by diviners, some of whom specialize in one or more of these fields. Conventionally, as we have seen, a forked hazel twig was used as a divining rod but, as the art has progressed, a variety of appliances have been developed for amplifying what are, basically, the diviner's natural reflexes. They include a pendulum, an angle rod, and a "motorscope", a curved double angle of thick wire with a pointer. Many other devices are also used, every diviner having his preference, while some are able to work only with bare hands—a more exhausting method, however.

There is no real explanation of this strange power in some people.

Scientists and others who have investigated the subject have come to the conclusion that there is no physical theory to cover the facts. In some manner the diviner receives a suggestion, perhaps a form of radiation, from the buried substance, which indicates its presence in the physical reaction of the appliance he carries. Dowsers work in many different ways to suit themselves. But there are certain phenomena which are common to all. For example, as he approaches the object of his search the diviner experiences a feeling of strong attraction towards its source; also a dowser can usually transmit his gift to another person by touch, or by allowing that person to use his rod. Atmospheric conditions, changes in the earth's magnetic fields, interruptions which distract the diviner's concentration, and even the wearing of rubber boots can inhibit the sensitivity of the diviner and the reaction of the appliance he carries.

Contrary to popular belief, dowsing for minerals was known long before dowsing for water. Diviners often carry a small "sample" of the particular metal for which they are searching, and if they change from one type to another they have first to wash their hands—either in reality or by gestures—to rid themselves of the influence.

Dowsing, however, is not confined to water and metals. Many oil companies have employed dowsers and it is said that coal miners have been known to produce a divining rod to follow a seam. More extraordinary is the dowser's ability to find lost objects or people. The dowser is given some object owned by the person and, holding this, he is attracted to another object owned by that person. The same method is used to find missing people. The late John Clarke, of Leicestershire, was enormously successful at finding drowned people. Between March and May, 1933, he traced the whereabouts of six bodies, five of which were later recovered. With an object belonging to the missing person the dowser can follow his trail in much the same way that a dog follows a scent.

The same techniques can be used in all kinds of fields. Dowsing has helped archaeologists by outlining the limits of a buried building or of a Roman ditch. It has also been used to diagnose disease and pinpoint the actual source of the trouble. It can indicate whether a person is allergic to certain substances. Given the right conditions, the divining rod can be put to any number of purposes.

Another remarkable aspect of dowsing is the ability of some dowsers to find metals or water simply from a map. The Reverend H. W. Lea-Wilson, who had the gift of dowsing, describes (in *Practical Dowsing: A Symposium*) how he had heard of this method but was completely sceptical. However he and his nephew, who had just learnt to dowse, decided to try it. They made a rough plan of the tennis court, following instructions in a book, and pinpointed reactions which they got from it. They then went outside to check their results, and found that there was underground water in the exact places marked on the map. "We couldn't understand it," said Mr Lea-Wilson, "but it worked."

Many dowsers, do, in fact, use this method and neither they nor anyone else have been able to explain it. It is obviously of considerable practical value, and the dowser usually employs a pendulum instead of the conventional rod since it leaves one hand free to mark the areas where some reaction is found.

This method of dowsing from maps is one which has been used frequently by Evelyn Penrose, a well-known English diviner whose gift has taken her to many parts of the world and led her into a number of strange adventures. She was born in Cornwall and inherited the gift of dowsing from her father, who in turn inherited it from his mother. He was a big powerful man, Evelyn Penrose says in her biography, *Adventure Unlimited*, and used a thick strong rod. The rod would often skin the bark off itself and sometimes twist itself into a sort of rope in his hands, but nothing would stop it turning. He delighted in taking guests out into the grounds of their Cornish house to try for themselves if they had the power of dowsing—and was undeterred by the disapproval of a severe bishop who, much to his own annoyance, could not stop the rod turning with great violence in his own hands.

Evelyn Penrose inherited her father's gift in generous measure, but it was not until after the deaths of first her father and then her mother that she set out on her travels and started to use her gift to earn her living. Her first trip was to America where she stayed with relations in California. She was taken by her host on a visit to the oil-fields, and at her instigation he asked one of the managers whether Evelyn might be allowed to discover whether she could find oil by divining. The manager entered into the spirit of the thing and took her to a group of producing wells. She found that the reaction she got was stronger than any she had previously experienced and when she was tested—without being told—on a dry well she got no reaction, thus proving to everyone's satisfaction that she could find oil. At the end of the day, however, she was completely exhausted, for she still had to learn that oil divining produced a severe reaction—an experience shared by many other diviners.

In California Evelyn Penrose met an Englishman who knew the manager of a large sugar plantation in Hawaii. The latter, it seemed, had been looking for a dowser. It was arranged that she should go to work for this man, so off she set, having been promised by cable her fare and a fee for each well developed. She found several good wells for the plantation manager, but she was eventually cheated of the money due to her and discovered that a contract made by cable could not be enforced.

So, cutting her losses, Evelyn sailed for Canada. She left the ship at Vancouver Island and, armed with many introductions from friends, travelled round British Columbia. The main subject of conversation at the time was the terrible drought, which was then in its seventh year. When local fruit-growers learned that she was a dowser they approached her. But even if she did find water, she asked how could they, ruined by the drought, find the money to develop the wells? So an appointment was made for her with the Minister of Finance—who fortunately also happened to be the district representative in the Legislative Assembly—whom she managed to persuade that it would be to his own interest to do something for the fruit-growers. And thus she found herself appointed as official Water-Diviner to the Government of British Columbia.

Evelyn Penrose was a tremendous success in the drought-stricken valleys, earning herself the title of "Divine Lady" among the fruit-growers and a reputation for independence of character. Her work took her on to looking for oil and gold in addition to water, and her adventures included meeting a grizzly bear and being affected by a curse which Red Indians had put upon an area from which the white men had evicted them, so that she could not work there.

During her stay in British Columbia, what she described as "a great event" in her divining career happened to Evelyn Penrose. This took the shape of a letter from the President of the English diviners' society, accompanied by a book giving an account of a Congress in Paris which had met to study the claims of diviners. It was from this book that Evelyn first learned of the idea of divining from a map, and it struck her "as being far-fetched and wellnigh impossible" for she felt it was totally inexplicable that there could be some contact between a printed map and the ground it represented. Various experiments indicated without a doubt, however, that she could indeed divine from maps; but she found the discovery so alarming that she decided to go to France and England, as the diviners' associations of both those countries were holding congresses that summer and she longed to discuss the matter with her fellows.

At the Congress in France, Evelyn was the only woman among

411

some five hundred delegates from all over the world. She had hoped to remain inconspicuous but in conversation with another delegate mentioned that finding her hands became so torn and blistered from using a forked stick, she sometimes used her bare hands. Soon she was the centre of an interested group—but she found it impossible to teach any of them how to work without apparatus. At the end of the Congress she was made a *Maitre Sourcier* (Master Diviner), the first woman ever to receive the honour. She also learned a great deal about divining from maps, and this is how she describes the system she worked out for herself, using bare hands and no tools.

"I get Government survey maps of one inch to the mile, which in most countries are about 27 in. x 27 in. I do all my preliminary work with my eyes shut which necessitates having an assistant to listen to what I say—as I have taught myself to talk aloud—and notice where I receive the strongest reactions. I start by rubbing my hands over the map until it seems to turn into something alive. I get the same sensations and shocks from the map as I would from the actual ground. Every mineral gives its own special sensation.

"Sometimes the map becomes alive instantaneously, irrespective of distance; at others I seem to meet a curious barrier or antagonism and the map remains dead. Then it takes great determination and concentration to make my contact with the area, but once it is made I have no further trouble. I start the actual work by rubbing the tips of my fingers over a small area and waiting. If I am looking for oil and my hands rest immobile I known that there is no oil there. If my hands are over oil they start to rise alternately. Where the oil is very rich my arms and hands are thrown back with such force that I think they would be torn out of their sockets if I were not double-jointed. All this is done with my eyes shut ... My assistant then takes the maps and numbers the area according to the violence of my reactions."

After her return to England, Evelyn Penrose tried her hand at finding tin and wolfram in her native Cornwall and coal in Scotland. In Bath she undertook what she describes as perhaps one of her oddest jobs, the search for the body of the goddess Minerva whose bronze head was discovered in the remains of a temple near the Pump Room.

Since it was impossible to get a "sample" of the goddess to keep her tuned-in to it and enable her to make contact with the remainder, she was obliged to make do with a handkerchief, and had to keep returning to the Museum to rub it over the head to get the vibration. She explored the site of the temple and the area all round the

Pump Room, but got nothing except a continual pull in one direction which eventually led her to the middle of the main street. Since it was a busy street it was arranged that at midnight the police should divert the traffic from the area in which Miss Penrose wanted to work. This time the pedestal with the head of the goddess was brought out, so that she could pass her hands over its head to get the vibrations.

Watched stolidly by the policemen and a slowly growing crowd of astonished citizens, Evelyn Penrose set to work. She had arranged with two members of the Pump Room Committee that if she found anything she would drag her heel along the road : they would follow, and chalk in her marking. Soon she discovered something round. The two committee men went to work with the chalk, and when they had finished became most excited, for although it was probably not the body of the goddess it had very much the shape of a shield. They begged her to continue, and this time she found something long, which could be a spear. The next day the City Fathers met to decide whether to dig up the road in order to recover the objects, but in the end they decided that, since it was not the body, they would not grant permission.

To escape from the attentions of the Italian government, then at war with Abyssinia, who wished to employ her to search for water thirty miles *in front* of their advancing troops, Evelyn Penrose set off again on her travels, via Jamaica and Chile to South Africa. When the Second World War broke out she felt it wise to leave Africa and was offered a job in Australia, looking for oil and water. However on her arrival Evelyn found that there had been a change of government and nobody now in office would employ her. Finding that a drought was threatening to devastate large areas of Eastern Australia she offered her services to the Graziers' Association and was gladly accepted. During this period she found opportunities, too, of successfully testing her theory that by hammering the ground above it was possible to clear blockages on underground streams which had caused wells to run dry. She also did some prospecting for gold, with considerable success; but alas, when the government was approached for a mining permit the farmer was told that the area had been made into a national park and no mining leases could be granted in any circumstances.

The scope of a diviner's power varies considerably and can change from one day to another. Evelyn Penrose once found water from a map which later turned out to be hopelessly inaccurate and, from a diviner's point of view, theoretically useless. How this happened she never understood, but incidents of this kind are by no means uncommon in the experience of a diviner. Evelyn Penrose once spoke to Paul Brunton, one of the most advanced European Yogis, about the "great force emanating from the earth, which governs diviners at their work and asked him, should they become really angry when divining, could they use this force for evil, even to the extent of killing someone?" She showed him a quick but simple gesture with one hand, by which she believed this to be possible. Astonished, Brunton asked her where she had come by this knowledge. It was perfectly correct, he said, but she had no right, unless she had studied the highest aspects of yoga, to the power such knowledge gave. Hastily Evelyn assured him that she had never put the knowledge to the test on man or beast, nor even wished to.

It is generally accepted that the diviner's power is very strong and that it can be exhausting to the user and even, if it is used too continually, harmful to him. Nobody knows whether the power comes from outside the diviner or through him, or whether it emanates from within him.

The British Society of Dowsers, which was founded in 1933 and has about seven hundred members, has come to the conclusion that the cause of the dowsing phenomena is not a radiation of some kind, referred to by some as radiesthesia, but is probably due to a subconscious appreciation on the part of the dowser. Scientists have certainly never been able to detect or measure any rays reaching the dowser. If the subconscious is responsible then this mysterious gift becomes even more inexplicable, leaving one only with the knowledge that man still has a great deal to learn about himself.

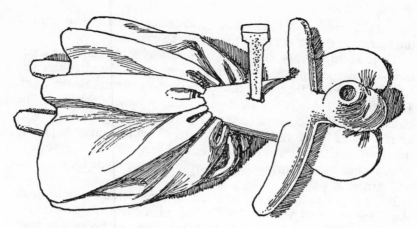

FAMOUS MAGICIANS OF HISTORY

Throughout the centuries men have sought knowledge and power —knowledge of the meanings and secrets of life which might give them power over their fellow men. This delving into the unknown, with all its implications, caused such fear that the pursuit of secular knowledge was condemned by the early church as part of the devil's domain.

Such scholars were credited with powers that were, on the whole, totally without foundation and with carrying out experiments which, largely because they were incomprehensible, were regarded as evil. Scientists and philosophers who did, perhaps, succeed in learning more about the way the universe or men's minds worked, were feared and misunderstood to the point at which they were accused of being in league with the devil. Men who, through experiment and self-discipline, developed certain powers were suspected of having sold their souls to the devil in order to obtain this superior knowledge and to be able to call strange forces to their command.

Sometimes these men did indeed discover some of the secrets of nature and manage to achieve feats which even today would be remarkable. Among them a handful of names stand out—Faust, the necromancer, Cagliostro, the diabolist, Dr Dee, the astrologer, and Nostradamus, the soothsayer.

Faust has now become virtually a legend, but there was indeed a Dr Johann Faust who lived from about 1488 to 1541 in Swabia. He is reputed to have studied necromancy—the raising of the spirits of the dead—in Cracow, and to have been a famous astrologer, diviner, medium and alchemist. The first history of Dr Faust appeared at Frankfurt in 1587 when it was declared that he had learned the secrets of the future from the spirits he evoked.

There is little doubt that Johann Faust was something of a charlatan—a wandering conjurer taking every advantage of a superstitous age. Modern mediums, however, raise the spirits of the dead, and astrology today is a perfectly respectable subject. Alchemy, the basis of our modern systematic chemistry, was most commonly known for its belief in the transmutation of metals—most hopefully into gold—and it still has its twentieth-century adherents, reports of alleged successful transmutations having recently come from France and Armenia.

Faust made such an impression on his sixteenth-century compatriots, and legends grew so rapidly around his name, that the true story of his life has become buried in fiction. At about the same time, however, there lived in Europe another notable magician whose life story is not only well known but who has left behind him a remarkable document the effects of which will survive for centuries —Nostradamus.

He was born Michel de Nostredame (or Notre-Dame) in St Remy, Provence, in 1503 and was the son of a notary. He studied arts at Avignon, and philosophy, medicine and probably astrology at the University of Montpellier. This was the period at which Europe was ravaged by a series of plagues and, even before he qualified as a doctor in 1529, Nostradamus became well known for his successful treatment of its victims. The grateful city fathers paid him for his services and gave him a pension, and Nostradamus settled down to general practice in Agen. But he could not save his own young wife and two sons from the Black Death and, shattered by his loss, he wandered through Europe for many years before he finally settled down in Salon de Craux and, in 1547, married again.

During his years of wandering several incidents had shown that he had clairvoyant gifts, and after his second marriage he decided to begin the task of writing down some of the events which, to him, the future plainly held. He wrote all his prophecies in quatrains and the first of the seven volumes, called *Centuries*, appeared in 1555.

The prophecies soon became famous, although they were by no means easy to understand. Nostradamus knew perfectly well that prophecy was regarded as a gift of the devil and so he made them as difficult as possible for all but the discerning reader to understand, "so as not to scandalize their fragile hearing". He used what he himself called "abstruse and twisted sentences", and wrote everything down "under a figure cloudy rather than plainly prophetic".

After the publication of his second edition Nostradamus was sent for by Henry II—probably at the instigation of Catherine de Medici, who was deeply interested in the occult arts. He soon became a favourite at court, a rosy-cheeked, hard-working old man in a long black gown, who slept only four or five hours every night and was eagerly sought after by all the courtiers to foretell their future, as well as by every man of learning in Europe.

Nostradamus foresaw the death of Henry II in one of his quatrains, which reads:

> *The young lion shall overthrow the old*
> *In war-like field in single fight*
> *In a golden cage he will pierce the eye.*
> *Two wounds one, then die a cruel death.*

Henry was in fact killed during a tourney, riding against the captain of his Scottish guard. The point of the captain's lance pierced the gilded, cage-like vizor which the king wore. His eye was pierced and a splinter entered his throat.

Nostradamus continued in favour, and when the boy king Charles IX succeeded to the throne he visited Salon, while on a "progress" through France. He made Nostradamus his Physician in Ordinary and gave him the title of Counsellor. Nostradamus cast the horoscope of the young brother of the king and foretold that he would one day be king himself. Henry of Navarre, then a child, was also in the royal party and to him Nostradamus prophesied that he would one day become heir to the whole of France. In 1565 Nostradamus, prosperous and a respected citizen, died of dropsy.

He himself said that his prophecies covered the years 1555 to 3797 and some of them are remarkably accurate, while others are so obscure as to be virtually incomprehensible; he went, one feels, a little too far in his attempts not to upset those of "fragile hearing". The quatrains and the sixains in which he later wrote are full of metaphors, allegories and allusions. He used anagrams continuously, and just to confuse the issue still further he often changed the letters in the anagrams, or omitted one altogether. Thus "Rapis" is a simple anagram for Paris, but "Ergaste" was his anagram for "Estrange" (foreign), by which name he called Marie Antoinette.

Nostradamus foretold many events of the French Revolution, which would not take place for more than two hundred years, and his prophecies were not confined to his own country. One of his more precise quatrains—he did not often give exact dates—refers

417

to Elizabeth I, and was made while Mary Tudor was still on the throne.

> *The rejected one shall at last come to the throne*
> *Her enemies found to be conspirators.*
> *Her period shall triumph as never before*
> *At seventy she shall die, in the third year of the century*

(Elizabeth died, in her seventieth year, in 1603.)
Another precise forecast referred to the fire of London, of 1666.

> *The blood of the just shall be required of London*
> *Burned by fire in thrice twenty and six*
> *The old dame (Nostradamus's term for a cathedral) shall fall from*
> *on high*
> *An many edifices of the same belief shall be destroyed.*

He foresaw Napoleon's end:

> *The captive prince, conquered and sent to Elba*
> *He will sail across the gulf of Genoa to Marseilles*
> *By the huge efforts of foreign armies he is overcome*
> *Though he escapes the fire he shall yield blood by the barrel.*

and the coming of three anti-christs. The first two, Napoleon and Hitler, the third presaged for nineteen hundred and ninety nine years and seven months.

Nostradamus's prophecies are quite fascinating: what else but a bombing raid can he be referring to when he speaks of:

Living fire and death hidden in globes, will be loosed, horrible and terrifying. By night enemy forces will reduce the city to powder. The fires already burning being favourable to the enemy.

And considering their remarkable accuracy he was fortunate—perhaps due to his care in not revealing unpleasant futures to those in power—to die in prosperity and his bed.

A contemporary, Dr John Dee, who was born some twenty years after Nostradamus, was not so fortunate although he was perhaps the greatest of all English magicians and also for a time enjoyed the favour of Queen Elizabeth and her court. Like others who experimented and sought knowledge he was also feared and reviled. He was accused of practising witchcraft and necromancy, and of causing the death of children by magic spells.

Queen Elizabeth, however, had such belief in his powers that when a puppet, made in her likeness, was found with a spike driven through it and left to rot away in Lincoln's Inn Fields, she at once sent for Dr Dee to ward off the magic. Despite the Queen's patronage Dee feared that he might be accused of devilish arts and insisted that Mr Secretary Wilson should accompany him to the spot in order to see for himself "that I only do it by godley means".

On this occasion Dr Dee, having looked at the waxen image with considerable care, decided that it was all a practical joke and there was no threat to the Queen's life since there were no indications that the doll had been made by a skilled magician. When he reported his opinion to the Queen she, having such faith in her court astrologer that she rarely undertook any major venture without consulting him, was quite happy to accept his advice.

Dee's life, however, was not always so easy. He had a good education at Chelmsford Grammar School and then at St John's Cambridge, and in 1547, when he was twenty years old, he went to Louvain in Belgium to study the arts and sciences. He very soon became known as a scientist, mathematician, geographer and astrologer and returned to England in 1551 with his reputation made.

Edward VI, that unusually percipient boy king who might have done much to enlighten his age had he not died so prematurely, gave John Dee a pension, but after Mary Tudor's accession in 1553 things changed. Mary was much displeased by Dee's "occult practices"—no doubt annoyed by his uncompromising disapproval of her activities—and he was for a while actually imprisoned: indeed, he was fortunate to escape with his life. However he had cast Elizabeth's horoscope and foretold that she would become queen, and as soon as this was fulfilled all was well. Dee was even asked by Robert Dudley to choose a propitious date for the Queen's coronation.

Thereafter Nostradamus became a familiar figure at Court, on easy terms with the great and often visited by them in his own home at Mortlake where he lived with his wife and three children. There he proceeded to study astrology, mathematics, optics and alchemy. But he still had his enemies and despite royal protection a fearful and superstitious mob, aroused by his enemies, broke into his house while Dee was away on a visit to Germany and destroyed many of his four thousand books together with his "magical" instruments.

He continued, however, to dabble in the occult, basically because he was obsessed with the idea of finding a source of cosmic wisdom through which the purpose of human life would be revealed. He had some psychic powers and was given to crystal gazing. (He wrote in his diary, in 1581: "I had sight in Christallo offered me and I saw." Unfortunately he does not relate what it was he saw.) Nevertheless he apparently felt that his limited powers were holding up his experiments and after advice from "the angel Annael, through a preacher called Barabbas Saul" he conducted an experiment with a young man named Edward Kelly. Kelly set the crystal on the table before him and fell to prayer and entreaty, while Dee retired to his oratory to pray. After a quarter of an hour a vision of the angel Uriel, the Spirit of Light, ordained that Dee and Kelly should work together.

Despite Kelly's undoubted powers as a seer—through the medium of Uriel he had foreseen Mary Queen of Scots kneeling on a scaffold, and had described the Armada, seven years before it gathered "against the welfare of England"—he was in fact a minor crook, having been pilloried for forgery and also charged with digging up a dead body for the purposes of necromancy.

When Dee eventually discovered all this there was quite a scene but Saint Michael, conveniently for Kelly, appeared to tell Dee that he must continue to employ Kelly. The association continued, but it was always a troubled one for Dee was a truly learned, otherworldly man, while Kelly was neurotic, even violent and quite prepared to cook the evidence to his own advantage. Nevertheless there is no doubt that the two men together produced a great deal of genuine psychic phenomena.

Eventually Kelly went too far. Dee, with his wife and family, and accompanied by Kelly and his wife, had accepted an invitation from the Count Palatinate of Siradia in Poland. Unfortunately the Count was enthusiastic but poor, and their attempts to interest other great men in the attempts of Dee to find the philosopher's stone through the medium of Kelly and the crystal failed. Kelly threatened to return to England and quarrels abounded.

The group had settled in Bohemia under the patronage of Count Rosenburg when Kelly announced that a spirit called Madimi had announced that they must share everything including wives. Unlike Kelly, Dee was devoted to his wife and she to him and the suggestion caused a good deal of alarm and many prayers for guidance. When a second consultation of the crystal confirmed the instruction, Dee decided to take the order as intending mutual love rather than physical action and Kelly, furious and frustrated, took his threatened departure.

John Dee with his family returned to England and to his experiments, but he was still troubled by the superstitious fears of the ordinary people. After the Queen's death James I dismissed him from his post as Court Astrologer on the grounds that he was "an ally of Satan". Dee was furious and, although he was eighty, insisted on being tried for witchcraft. James, perfectly well aware that any such hearing would only establish Dr Dee's innocence, retracted. And when John Dee died, a year or so later, he was indeed described by a neighbour as "A mighty good man".

Over a century later, however, superstition was still rife and it was easy for the unscrupulous to prey on the beliefs even of the well educated. Giuseppe Balsamo, better known as (probably self-styled) Count Alessandro di Cagliostro, was a grocer's son who spent his early years wandering around Europe as a jobbing artist. He always had a genuine interest in alchemy, astrology and various forms of magic, and although he was undoubtedly also a cheat, ably assisted by his beautiful young wife, one story that is told of him is said to be well authenticated.

Visiting an independent principality south of the gulf of Riga, he used the younger son of the principality's Chamberlain, Count van der Howen, as his medium in a demonstration of "scrying", or crystal-ball gazing. A globe-shaped carafe was filled with pure water and placed between two candles. Gazing into it the boy saw his sister clutching her breast as if in pain. Then he saw the girl embracing her soldier brother. At the time the Chamberlain's daughter was in excellent health and his son was away on active service. But when he got home Count van der Howen found that his son had unexpectedly come home on leave, while at the time of the "scrying" the girl had suffered a severe pain in her chest.

It is also said that Cagliostro made many true prophecies, including the death of Marie Antoinette and, in detail, of her companion, the Princess de Lamballe. Like Nostradamus he too predicted many of the horrors of the French Revolution, and the eventual rise of Napoleon Bonaparte.

Other tales are told of Cagliostro's powers, but since much of his reputation can be traced to the gullibility of fashionable society, while he made a fortune in selling his elixir of immortal youth, many of these can be discounted. His luck didn't last. He was involved in the notorious Diamond Necklace scandal in 1785 and was thrown into the Bastille. England offered him no haven for he was imprisoned in the Fleet, and he eventually ended his life in the fortress prison of San Leone in Italy, where he was incarcerated for life for being a freemason.

Cagliostro, perhaps, brings the reputation of all these wise men into disrepute, but it is probable that he did indeed have some super-normal powers which he bolstered with a great deal of conjuring. Others, however, despite the overlay of superstition and ignorance of their times undoubtedly possessed strange gifts and were adepts in the magic arts.

PROPHETS AND DOOM

The ability to foresee the future is a fact. There is no question of illusion or coincidence; there is as yet no known explanation as to why some people can see into the future at will, why others have occasional, involuntary, glimpses and others never "see" at all. Premonitions, precognition, prophetic dreams are all a form of divination which centuries ago was taken for granted, and which today is once again recognized as a science and a fact for which modern experiments have as yet provided no answer.

"The facts of prediction of the future," said the late Dr Alexis Carrel, Nobel prize winner, physiologist and biologist, "lead us to the threshold of an unseen world. They seem to point to the existence of a psychic principle capable of evolving outside the limits of our bodies."

It is, however, an inexact "science". Why some people should have the power more than others, or why the power cannot be turned on or off at will, or even be guaranteed to work properly, nobody knows. However parapsychological research has established without doubt that some kind of extra sense does exist in man, which cannot be measured nor limited by the ordinary laws of space and time.

The use of the word "prophet" to describe a person who foretells the future is, in fact, incorrect, for the ancient prophets were, actually, interpreters, who revealed or explained the meanings of the word of the gods or of God. However, the utterances of these prophets included so much that predicted the future that the meaning of the word eventually became changed.

There are various means by which divination is carried out. By the use of a crystal ball or mirror, through the casting of a horoscope, or through dreams or omens. Sometimes the future appears as a vivid picture, sometimes it is formless, a vague precognition of disaster. Although it has been recognized that the more one can eliminate the interference of the conscious mind the more one can achieve the necessary rapport with the subconscious, or the mysterious "sixth sense", many experiments have failed to reveal just how or why this happens.

Throughout history there have been famous soothsayers. The ancient Egyptians, Romans and Greeks believed wholeheartedly in soothsayers and oracles and, it would not be too much to say, ran their lives round their advice. Wherever a civilization has been interested in magic and religion of any kind there has been a firm belief in the powers of those who could see into the future.

The stories of correctly fulfilled prophecies are so numerous that they would fill many volumes. One of the greatest diviners, Nostradamus, whose life is detailed in another part of this book, first became aware of his gift for prophecy through odd incidents which occurred when he was a young man. In Italy, for example, he encountered a young monk, Felice Peretti, son of peasant parents from a neighbouring village. To the amusement of the onlookers, Nostradamus fell to his knees in the dusty road, greeting him as "Holy Father". Forty years later Peretti became Pope.

The most commonly experienced glimpses into the future usually arrive in the form of warnings. For some reason, perhaps because the power of the unconscious force is not urgent enough, one rarely hears predictions of happy events or of such useful items as to what will win the Derby. On the other hand premonitions of disaster have saved lives on many occasions.

One of the best known modern predictions is that made by Mrs Jean Dixon, an American who has had the power of "seeing" since she was a child. Mrs Dixon foresaw some years before the events took place the election of a Democrat in the 1960 election and his assassination, her prediction being published in an American journal in 1956. After the election she "saw" Kennedy's coffin being carried in to the White House, and during the three weeks or so before President Kennedy was killed she had repeated warnings that the President was going to be shot. Three days before he died she knew he was to be shot in the head and she begged that a message should be taken to the President warning him of his danger. On the day of his death she "saw" the White House shrouded in black, and knew that this was the day of the murder and that nothing could avert it.

Mrs Dixon has made many other prophecies—she told Winston Churchill that he would lose office after the war but come back to power again, and she predicted the date of his death. She foresaw many international events, and many tragedies, including the deaths of Dag Hammarskjold and Marilyn Monroe.

In the past there seem to have been many more dedicated prophets than there are now—or perhaps the stress of modern life distracts too much the contemplative mind. One of the most famous British prophets was Coinneach Odhar Fiossaiche, who became known as the Brahan Seer and who was a Highland Scot. His gift of "the sight" was widely known even among a people to whom second sight is not unusual and he foretold many strange things, such as the coming of railways—"long strings of carriages without horses"—which, in the seventeenth century he could not possibly have imagined.

Coinneach Odhar, a farm labourer, was said to have used a small round stone, with a hole in it through which he "saw" the future. He was continually consulted by all around, including the gentry, and it was his famous prophecy concerning the noble Seaforth family, which has become known as the Doom of the Seaforths, which made him famous.

It is said that the Countess of Seaforth, a jealous and domineering lady, sent for the Seer to find out what her husband, the third Earl, was up to. He had ostensibly gone to arrange some business in Paris, but nothing had been heard from him for some time and his visit was being unduly protracted. Coinneach Odhar, having put his stone to his eyes, "saw" the absent Earl in a richly furnished room in which was sitting a beautiful young woman. The Earl, on his knees before her, was plainly begging her favours. The Seer, being no fool, and mindful of the traditional fate of the bearer of bad tidings, decided to say nothing. He reassured the Countess that her husband was perfectly well and happy, but his visit was likely to be even further prolonged.

More he would not say, but the Countess, no doubt sensing that he was hiding something from her, insisted, and finally goaded Coinneach by her suggestions that he could not in reality see anything at all, into describing the scene in the room to her in detail. Unfortunately he did not have the sense to insist on speaking to the Countess alone and his revelations, eagerly absorbed by the bystanders, would be common knowledge within hours. Furious, the Countess called him a liar and a cheat who had sullied the name of the Earl, and insisted that he be arraigned for witchcraft. Such was the power of the Seaforth family that nobody could prevail against the Countess, and the wretched Coinneach was executed by one of the means of dealing with witches, by being forced head first into a barrel of tar.

Before he died, however, the Seer pronounced the famous Doom of the Seaforth family. "I see," he said, "into the far future and I read the doom of the race of my oppressor and die mourning. The long-descended line of Seaforth will, ere many generations have passed, end in extinction and sorrow.

"I see a Chief, the last of the house, both deaf and dumb. He will be the father of four fair sons, all of whom he will follow to the tomb. He will live careworn and die mourning, knowing no future Chief of his clan shall reign at Brahan or at Kintail.

"He himself shall sink into the grave and the remnant of his possessions shall be inherited by a white-coifed lassie from the East, and she shall kill her sister.

"A sign by which it may be known that these things are coming to pass shall be given by four great lairds in the days of the last deaf and dumb Seaforth. They shall be Gairloch, Chisholm, Grant and Ramsay, of whome one shall be buck-toothed, another hare-lipped, another half-witted and the fourth a stammerer. These shall be the allies and neighbours of the last Seaforth, and when he sees them at his side he may know that his sons are doomed to death, that his broad lands shall pass away to the stranger and that his race shall come to an end."

The Seer died, but when the Earl returned soon afterwards he told his wife that every detail of what the prophet had seen was correct. In the sumptuous Paris house he had been accompanied by the mistress of Charles II, Lucy Walters, the mother of the Duke of Monmouth. The pictures on the wall, the ornate, gilded furniture, were all as the Seer had described.

The Earl of Seaforth, himself lived to a ripe age and died in 1678. His wife, however, for whom the condemned man had foretold nothing, threw herself to her death from the tower of Brahan Castle. Several generations passed before the Doom of the Seaforths began to be realized.

In 1754, the man who was to be the last of the Seaforths was born. At the age of fifteen an illness left him deaf and later he also became dumb. The Doom had not been forgotten and the omens were looked for. Four Scottish lairds lived nearby, and of these Sir Hector Mackenzie of Gairloch was buck-toothed, the Laird of Chisholm had a hare-lip, Grant was half-witted and MacLeod of Ramsay had a pronounced stammer. But Lord Seaforth had six daughters and four sons, and if the signs of impending doom were present there was little he could do, in any case, to avoid it. The Earl raised a regiment which fought in the French revolutionary wars, and went about life in a normal way. Then one of his sons died in childhood. Two others died later. When the last boy who had a "wasting" disease, fell ill the fears of the Seaforth family became a reality and he was sent to the south of England to be treated by a specialist. Daily news of the young man's progress were brought north, but to the superstitious Scots there was no hope for his life, whatever his parents might believe, for all the portents foretold by the Seer were there. Sure enough the boy died.

In 1815 the Earl himself died, and the rest of the Doom inexorably was fulfilled. The Earl's eldest daughter had married an Admiral, Sir Samuel Hood, and had gone with him to the East India Station where he was in command. He died, however, at about the same time as the Earl, and his widow returned "from the East", wearing the white cap decreed by the conventions of the time. Lady Hood continued to live at Brahan Castle and she eventually married again. Her husband, a Stewart, took the name of Mackenzie since there were no males left in the Mackenzie family, but much of the estate was sold for one reason or another and the family's property much reduced.

One would imagine that, with so much of the Seer's prophecy fulfilled, Mrs Stewart-Mackenzie's sisters would have given her a very wide berth indeed. But the final and perhaps most tragic part of the prophecy was to be duly completed. One day Mrs Stewart-Mackenzie was driving her sister Caroline through the grounds of the estate in a pony carriage when, for a reason which was never discovered, the ponies took fright and bolted. The carriage overturned and although Mrs Stewart-Mackenzie was merely badly shaken, her sister was so seriously injured that she died.

Two hundred years after Coinneach Odhar Fiossaiche had foreseen it, the broad lands of Seaforth had indeed passed away to the stranger and his race had come to an end.

Another family came to an end over centuries in a manner foretold by a seer called Thomas the Rhymer. He predicted its end during the twelfth century. The prophecy is described by Sir Bernard Burke in *Ulster King at Arms*, which was published in 1853. Thomas the Rhymer thus addressed the Earl of Mar:

"Proud Chief of Mar: Thou shalt be raised still higher until thou sittest in the place of the King. Thou shalt rule and destroy and thy work shall be after thy name; but thy work shall be the emblem of thy house and shall teach mankind that he who cruelly and haughtily raises himself upon the ruins of the holy cannot prosper. Thy work shall be cursed and never finished, but thou shalt have riches and greatness and shalt be true to thy sovereign and shalt raise his banner in the field of blood. Then when thou seemest to be highest, wher. thy power is mightiest, thou shall fall; low shall be thy head among the nobles of thy people. Deep shall be thy moan among the cauldren of sorrow. Thy lands shall be given to a stranger and thy titles shall be among the dead. The branch that springs from thee shall see his dwelling burnt, in which a king is nursed, his wife a sacrifice in that same flame, his children numerous but of little honour and three born and grown who shall never see the light. Yet shall thine ancient tower stand, for the brave and true cannot be wholly forsaken. Thy proud head and daggered hand must dree thy weird until horses shall be stabled in thy hall and a weaver shall throw his shuttle in thy chamber of state.

"Thine ancient tower, a woman's dower shall be a ruin and a beacon until an ash sapling shall spring from the topmost stone. Then shall thy sorrows be ended and the sunshine of royalty shall beam on thee once more. Thine honours shall be restored. The kiss of peace shall be given to thy Countess though she seek it not, and the days of peace shall return to thee and thine. The line of Mar shall be broken, but not until its honours are doubled and its Doom ended."

Three hundred years later the Earl of Mar was appointed Regent of Scotland and guardian of the young King James I. He was a proud and domineering man who unscrupulously used his position to further his own ends and destroy his enemies. He began to build himself a palace in Stirling which was locally known as "Mar's Work". It was never finished.

A descendant who fought for the Stuart cause had his lands sequestered and his titles stripped from him after the Pretender was defeated. Alloa Tower, a property brought into the family as the dowry of one of its brides, was burned down in the time of that Lord Mar's grandson, James Francis. His wife died in the fire and he had three children all of whom were born blind. The tower fell into decay, and during the French war scare horses were stabled in the hall and a weaver made a home in the ruins; while under-growth, including an ash tree, grew out of the stones.

At last, in 1882, George IV restored the earldom of Mar to the original owner's descendants and bestowed on them the title of Earl of Mar and Kelly. As for the kiss of peace, it is said that Queen Victoria, meeting Lady Mar by chance in Stirling Castle, kissed her in a friendly manner.

Such resounding prophecies are not made today, but there is no lack of modern seers. Their predictions present a depressing similarity to the reader.

Nostradamus in his *Centuries* predicted the coming of the third Antichrist in the last years of this century, during a troublesome period which would be followed by peace. Jean Dixon, too, has foretold the appearance of an evil man, born in the Middle East in 1962, who by force of arms will dominate the world in the last decades of the twentieth century. Mario de Sabato, an Italian astrologer, predicts the dominance of Eastern races during the same period.

From 1973 onwards numerous seers have foretold an increasing chaos in the world, a breakdown of the civilization we know, the disintegration of Europe and invasion by Eastern races. The Papacy will be overthrown, the Pope will die a prisoner, and in the last decade of the century there will be a final war. By 1999, however, the epidemics, wars, natural catastrophes and other cataclysms which are to plague the world will come to an end and there will be the dawn of a new age of world peace, well-being, prosperity and brotherly love.

Let us hope that the prophets have lost their touch. For if they are right we are in for a most uncomfortable quarter of a century.

Supernormal or Supernatural ?

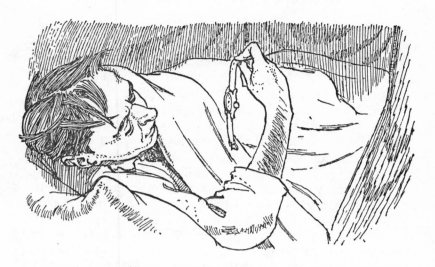

THE STRANGE WORLD OF DREAMS

Ever since his point of origin in pre-history man has been a dreamer. There seems little doubt that this awareness of a "phantom" self which became active during sleep, and sometimes even when awake, produced the first concept of a soul and the various associated religious beliefs, pagan or otherwise. This soul or ghost was something quite separate from the normal human body; indeed, it could leave the body during dreams and perhaps survive the ultimate blankness of physical death. Thus, as Sir James Frazer mentions in *The Golden Bough*, if life is explained by the soul's presence in the body, then sleep becomes the temporary absence of the soul and death its permanent absence.

One of mankind's oldest beliefs is that dreams can foretell the future, and in the ancient world the Assyrians, Egyptians, Greeks and Jews, for example, believed that dreams were messages from the deities indicating the future. The Bible is a prolific source of dreams, especially the Old Testament, while the New Testament also has its share of prophetic dreams (thus, in St Matthew's gospel Joseph is told in a dream that his wife is pregnant, and later the life of the Holy Child is twice saved because of "visions of the night").

Seers were important people. It was for them to translate the obscure imagery of most dreams into understandable prophecies. Such interpretations were later set down in writing to form the original "dream books"—for which, like astrology, there is a steady

433

vogue, even today. Thus, according to one such book, to dream of a fire signifies the arrival of "hasty news". Prevision in dreams nevertheless has its serious side, and a multitude of well-documented records are held by the Society for Psychical Research in London and the American equivalent in New York, though whether such previsions come under the headings of telepathy, clairvoyance or extra-sensory perception in general is a matter for debate.

With the increase in materialism in the later years of the nineteenth century, the mystical attributes of dreams became subject to more and more scepticism until, finally, at the beginning of the twentieth century the whole question of the interpretation of dreams was revolutionized by Sigmund Freud. Freud, a professor of neurology at Vienna University, specialized in the treatment of hysteria and neurosis, and it was the publication of his book *Die Traumdeutung* (dream interpretation) in 1900, with its emphasis on sexual symbolism, which indicated to the medical world the extent to which dream analysis had become a foundation stone of his psychoanalytical techniques.

Partly because his ideas outraged the public morality of the day and partly because he had elevated the dream to the stature of a science, he was subject to a storm of scepticism and ridicule—as are so many innovators. Nevertheless, his ideas persisted, and other psychologists began to regard dreams seriously and scientifically while rejecting the cryptic sex imagery which dominated Freud's own theories.

Today, Freud is respected for his pioneering work and his influence persists, although the sexual aspects of psycho-analysis have been largely discounted. During the past decade the dream has moved into the world's electronics laboratories where scientists, using electroencephalographic techniques, can now tell those who are interested the frequency and duration of dreams by measuring brain waveforms and eye movements of sleepers.

For the record, sleep is cyclic in nature, taking the form of long waves lasting an hour or more, descending deeply into unconsciousness then surfacing to near consciousness. The deepest sleep wave is the first one, the rest becoming progressively shallower throughout the night. It is at the crest of each wave that dreaming takes place, and such dreams may last from ten minutes to half an hour. As four or five waves occur during undisturbed sleep we each experience four or five dreams throughout the night—indeed, some twenty per cent of our sleeping life is spent in dreaming.

So far, so good, but meanwhile the question of prevision or foreseeing the future has fallen by the wayside. Perhaps it is regarded as unscientific. Nor do we know, even today, precisely what dreams are, where the images come from, how they are blended and integrated and, indeed, why we should dream at all and spend so much time in this apparently irrational and pointless activity when our waking lives are busy enough.

All of which brings us to the work of J. W. Dunne, a highly original theorist and experimenter, who alone devoted much of his life to the practical analysis of dreams and prevision and in so doing inadvertently created a new science of time, space and consciousness which he named Serialism and which, when first published in the 1920s, created quite a sensation. Today in retrospect, alas, his remarkable efforts have been sadly overlooked and no longer appear to carry any weight—a failing which is difficult to understand since he set up positive indicators to mass experiments which could be easily carried out to check the validity of his conclusions.

Dunne was an engineer (actually an aircraft designer in the very early days of aviation) so that, not being a professional psychologist or acknowledged philosopher, he was perhaps taken less seriously than his work merited. Additionally, his theory of Serialism came into conflict with the accepted scientific methodology of the day in a world which was struggling to comprehend Einsteinian relativity and other new concepts in physics. He wrote four books, the first of which was entitled *An Experiment with Time*, and gave many lectures on his controversial subject which began with experimental proof of prevision in dreams and ended with evidence of immortality and the existence of a universal spirit or "god" which animates all living matter—but all couched in the language of mathematics and science and not a word about religion or mysticism.

It began when Dunne, accepting that some recorded dreams were acceptably prophetic, questioned the abnormality of such prevision. Why should it be the prerogative of a privileged few? Suppose it were a normal function of the dreaming brain unrecognized by the multitude who, in any case, invariably forget their dreams within a few seconds of awakening. He decided that dreams might consist of a blend of past and future events and set out to devise a practical experiment to check such a strange hypothesis, using himself as the subject and unaware initially of the arduous nature of the task he was to undertake. Even Dunne himself concedes that "the task which had to be accomplished was the isolating of a single basic fact from an accumulation of misleading material. Any account of any such process must contain, of course, some description of the stuff from

435

which the separation was effected. And such stuff very often is, and in this case very largely was, rubbish."

In his first book Dunne relates a considerable number of dreams, some of undoubted prevision significance, others less so. He also ran into certain practical difficulties which he describes in detail. In the space available here it is not possible to outline every dream, but the more important ones are summarized and the reader may, if he wishes, refer to *An Experiment with Time* for the full narrative (it is available in libraries). Dunne, incidentally, as an engineer and mathematician, always evaluated the probability factor of what might appear to be prevision in a dream; thus, to dream of a relatively commonplace event could be ascribed to coincidence and would carry low or zero prevision probability. To qualify, a dream would need to be of an unusual character and (very important) unrelated to any similar event in the past. The constraints imposed were therefore quite formidable.

The first two "incidents" were not quite of the nature one might look for, though they fit well into what later took shape as Dunne's explanatory theory involving Serialism. The first occurred in 1899 while staying at a hotel in Sussex. The dream was of an argument with a waiter as to the correct time, Dunne asserting that it was 4.30 in the afternoon and the waiter insisting that it was 4.30 in the middle of the night.

"With the apparent illogicality peculiar to all dreams," the dreaming Dunne concluded that his watch must have stopped and on checking it found that this was so—it had stopped at precisely 4.30. With that he awoke. Out of curiosity he got out of bed and lit a match to look at his watch which was lying on a nearby table. In fact, it *had* stopped and the hands stood at 4.30. He assumed that the watch must have stopped on the previous afternoon, anyway, and he had failed to notice or had forgotten. Not knowing the exact time he merely rewound the watch, leaving the hands as they were.

The following morning he checked the time by the nearest hotel clock, fully expecting the watch to be out by several hours, but "to my absolute amazement I found that the hands had lost only some two or three minutes—about the amount of time which had elapsed between my waking from the dream and rewinding the watch". How then, did he come to see in that dream that the hands stood, as they actually did, at half-past four?

The incident was trivial enough and could perhaps be attributed to some form of clairvoyance—seeing across space through darkness and closed eyelids—but Dunne was in no sense a "seer". Some time later in Sorrento, Italy, lying in bed half awake beneath a mosquito-net and wondering what the time might be, he idly tried to repeat the effect. He continues: "A moment later I found myself looking at the watch. The vision I saw was binocular, upright, poised in space about a foot from my nose, illumined by ordinary daylight and encircled by a thick whitish mist which filled the remainder of the field of sight. The hour hand stood at exactly 8 o'clock; the minute hand was wavering between 12 and one; the second hand was a formless blur.

"To look more intently would, I felt, wake me completely, so I made up my mind to treat the minute hand as one treats the needle of a prismatic compass and to divide the arc of its swing. This gave the time as two and a half minutes past eight. That decided, I opened my eyes, reached out under the mosquito curtain, grabbed the watch, pulled it in and held it up before me. I was wide awake, and the hands stood at two and a half minutes past eight."

Dunne then lists a number of dreams experienced over a period of years which "foresaw" future events of a unique nature, thereby rating a high probability factor in terms of prevision. One was the arrival of the *Daily Telegraph*-sponsored Cape to Cairo expedition at Khartoum, one of the white members of the party having died en route. The story appeared in full in the issue of the *Telegraph* on the day following the dream, the death of one of its members having been unknown up to that point due to poor communications (the year was 1901). Others included a prevision of the volcanic disaster in the West Indies island of Martinique with a loss of 40,000 lives (in the dream the figure was 4,000), a big fire in a rubber factory near Paris in which many of the female staff were suffocated before they could be rescued, the derailment of the Flying Scotsman on an embankment near the Forth Bridge in 1914, and various dreams of a personal nature selected from a group of about twenty which had been carefully remembered.

So far Dunne had largely been relying on memory. Many of the dreams concerned events of a trivial nature, the prevision occurring merely a day or two before the reality. Dunne himself observes: "These dreams were not percepts of distant or future events. They were the usual commonplace dreams composed of distorted images of waking experience, built together in the usual half-senseless fashion peculiar to dreams. That is to say, if they had happened on the nights after the corresponding events they would have exhibited nothing in the smallest degree unusual, and would have yielded just as much true and just as much false which had given rise to them as does any ordinary dream—which is very little. They were the ordinary, appropriate, expectable dreams; but they were occurring on the *wrong nights*."

He adds: "Even the watch dreams were merely the dreams I ought to have had *after* seeing the watch. No, there was nothing unusual in any of these dreams as dreams. They were merely *displaced in time*. That, of course, was staggering enough, but I felt, nevertheless, that it had been a great advance to resolve all these varied phenomena into one single class of incident—a simple, if mysterious, transposition of dates. But in all this speculation I was still a long way from the truth."

So far Dunne had been relying on memory, working on an *ad hoc* basis in what he describes as a "hopelessly unscientific fashion". It was not until 1917 that he posed the question: was it possible that these phenomena were not abnormal, but *normal*? That dreams —dreams in general, all dreams, everybody's dreams—were composed of images of past experience and images of future experience blended together in approximately equal proportions? That the universe was, after all, really stretched out in time, and that the lopsided view we had of it—a view with the future part unaccountably missing, cut off from the growing "past" part by a travelling "present moment"—was due to a purely mentally imposed barrier which existed only when we were awake? So that, in reality, the associational network stretched, not merely this way and that way in space, but also backwards and forwards in time; and the dreamer's attention, following in natural unhindered fashion the easiest pathway among the ramifications, would be continually crossing and recrossing that properly non-existent equator which we, waking, ruled quite arbitrarily athwart the whole?

The supposition (for it was not seen as a possible explanation) was immediately rejected by Dunne, for it seemed to him "absolutely inconceivable that a thing of this sort, if true, could have managed to escape, through all these centuries, universal perception and recognition". The seed had nevertheless struck and begun to germinate; it was the starting point of the true scientific experiment with its rigid and tiring disciplines and the beginning of a new theory of time and space which was to take Dunne much farther than merely establishing the normal nature of previsional dreaming— indeed, into those esoteric areas normally considered the province of theologians and mystics.

A year went by before any practical steps were taken. Dunne recognized that dreams were only too easily forgotten; nine mornings out of ten there would be no recollection of having dreamed at all because one forgets the dreams at the very instant of waking, and even the details of a remembered dream will generally not survive the time taken to wash and dress. It was therefore necessary to write down a remembered dream immediately on waking, recording as much detail as possible, and to establish a method of recalling the more elusive forgotten dreams. Furthermore, since this was to be a daily routine of recording and retrospective checking, a time limit was considered desirable. Dunne set this at two days, with the proviso that it might be extended in ratio to the oddity and unusualness of a given incident. (He cites one instance of a prophetic dream which occurred twenty years before the waking event!)

Another factor was the nature of one's life and work. A dull, monotonous life with every day exactly like the last would hardly be likely to produce identifiable prevision in the short term. Variety and change offered much better odds; in practice Dunne found that such simple matters as a visit to a theatre or cinema, or even reading a novel, could prove to be a lucrative source of advance dreaming data. Also, one had always to guard against mere coincidence (i.e., low prevision probability).

That the experiment proved to be a success goes without saying, otherwise Dunne's books would never have been written. To prove that there was nothing abnormal or "sensitive" about himself he was able to persuade friends and colleagues to try to experiment for a period; the results were generally comparable. There were snags, however. Most of the foreseen events were of such a trivial nature that one might well disregard them. Also, "the dreaming mind is a master-hand at tacking false interpretations on to everything it perceives"; for this reason the record of the dream should describe as separate facts (a) the actual appearance of what is seen, and (b) the interpretation given to that appearance. Thus, in one example the waking event of a dense shower of brilliant sparks produced by blowing a red-hot wood fire with a pair of bellows was "previewed" in a dream as a crowd of people throwing cigarette ends.

Finally, Dunne found in practice that the waking mind refuses point-blank to accept the association between the dream and the subsequent event, for the association is "the wrong way round" and no sooner does it make itself perceived than it is instantly rejected— "the intellectual revolt is automatic and extremely powerful". This is understandable because there is no conscious memory of a future event as opposed to a past event with which a dream can be readily linked. Even when checking written records after the two-day time limit one is apt to read straight on through the very thing one is looking for, without even noticing its connection with the waking incident. There is an unacceptable lack of cause and effect.

One way of overcoming this rejection is to pretend that the records you are about to read are those of dreams which you are *going to have* during the coming night, and then to look for events in the past day or two which might legitimately be regarded as the causes of those dreams. This is a device which Dunne found most useful.

The dodge for recalling forgotten dreams is quite simple, he states. A notebook and pencil is kept under the pillow and, *immediately* on waking, before you even open your eyes, you set yourself to remember any detail, however tiny, of the rapidly vanishing dream. Ignore the rest and concentrate on that single point of detail, attempting to amplify it. Like a flash a large section of the dream in which that incident occurred comes back, and, more important, usually an isolated incident from a previous dream or dreams. Write them down briefly, then concentrate on them one by one. Most of the dream stories will unfold themselves gradually; write them down and do not attempt to simply remember them. Finally, take the abbreviated record thus made and write it out in full.

Dunne stresses, however, that the whole of the practical experiment is a fatiguing chore so that one is inclined to give up after the first couple of days. With persistence and discipline it becomes easier over a period of time. Even so, it explains why the experiment has never been widely taken up. For most of us life is busy enough with day-to-day practical problems to allow for a regular long-term essay in dream recollection and recording immediately on waking from sleep. In later mass experiments Dunne took this factor into account and did not demand too much dedication from his co-operative subjects.

★   ★   ★

There is little space left for an exposition of Serialism, nor is this book a proper medium for a somewhat advanced scientific discussion, but it is necessary to outline the basic principles if the dream phenomena are to be properly explained. The full theory is explained in Dunne's remarkable book *The Serial Universe,* to which the interested reader is referred.

Basically Dunne starts with the accepted picture of the physical universe, including the physical body, as a four-dimensional continuum occupying the three familiar dimensions of space (length, breadth and height) extended (i.e., enduring) in the fourth dimension of time. All these dimensions are at right angles to each other, but the human mind is capable of observing only the three spatial dimensions and is unable to visualise any other direction at right angles to all three. The *passage of time*, however, can be measured by means of a clock. To the observing mind time consists of a now-point of immeasurable and probably zero duration whose motion separates a growing past from a diminishing future.

So far we are not with Dunne alone, but in the good company of the Relativists and modern physicists. Sir Arthur Eddington in his book *Space, Time and Gravitation* writes: "An individual is a four-dimensional object of greatly elongated form; in ordinary language we say that he has considerable extension in time and insignificant extension in space. Practically he is represented by his line—his track through the world."

Along this bodily lifeline, from birth until death, travels the observing mind (referred to by Dunne as the Observer), with attention while awake rigidly glued to the moving "now". Note that *now* is the only point at which the environment can impinge upon the Observer via the bodily senses, and the only point at which the Observer can interfere or experiment with (or even observe) his physical environment. A mere fraction of a second ago is already too late and a fraction of a second in the future is too soon. The body can be regarded as an instrument which, through the senses, produces electro-chemical changes in the brain, and these are read and interpreted by the travelling Observer. They are his only form of contact in building up a subjective picture of the external environment, and this picture contains many qualities which do not exist in the physical world, e.g., colour, sound, smell and taste which, in the outer environment, are mere frequencies or particles or both.

Dunne demonstrates that the now-point moves at the speed of light which is why, from the Observer's point of view, the dimension in the direction of motion shrinks to zero so that the four-dimensional universe is seen as three-dimensional (this is one of the odd effects of relativity and can be demonstrated both mathematically and experimentally). We have therefore a four-dimensional physical lifeline along which a travelling Observer (or self) moves at the speed of light from birth until death following a now-point which presents events in succession.

This we call time, but the perceptive reader may already have anticipated Dunne's next point, namely, that any form of movement or progression, even along a timeline, of necessity takes time—in this case of a higher dimensional order. Dunne designates the motion of the Observer along his life track as Time 1, which itself is measurable in terms of a fifth-dimensional Time 2 moving at right angles to the other four dimensions, and the motion of Time 2 in turn is measurable in terms of a sixth-dimensional Time 3. We are at the beginning of a series which continues indefinitely and is known as an infinite regress. It is the bane of physicists and mathematicians who avoid it like a plague. It constitutes Dunne's "serial time". Sir Arthur Eddington himself, in a letter to Dunne, wrote: "I agree with you about serialism; the 'going on of time' is not in Minkowski's world as it stands." (Minkowski's world referred to is the space-time world adopted by Einstein for the purpose of his theory.)

There is one other point of importance. Each higher level order of time calls for its own higher level Observer. Thus, it is the motion of Observer 2 along Time 2 which activates Observer 1 in Time 1, otherwise Observer 1 would co-exist, without moving, along the whole of his lifeline from beginning to end. Consequently, in addition to serial time we also have a serial Observer extending in infinite regress to infinity, each Observer by his own motion activating and concentrating on the lower-order Observer down the line to Observer 1.

This, according to Dunne, accounts for man's "self-consciousness". As might be expected, there are certain novel conclusions to be drawn from serialism. Thus, the only Observer with finite limits to his observing capacity is Observer 1; it starts with birth and terminates with death. All other Observers are boundless, their horizons stretching to infinity. Even Observer 1 continues to exist after death although there is nothing to observe but the past experiences of the extinct body. This multiple self is therefore eternal, regardless of whether the physical body exists or not.

Dunne goes further by regarding the human race from its point of origin as a family tree, ever growing and expanding in physical terms. He postulates that it is animated in time by the infinite ultimate Observer or Universal Self which differentiates downwards into individual Observers moving in Time 1. Although he avoids any religious connotations, it is a fact that many Eastern religions are based on the pursuit of the 'self' or 'I' through higher and higher levels of meditation until the self as such disappears and blends with the Universal Spirit—whatever name they may call it.

Paul Brunton, for example (referred to elsewhere in this book) records a dialogue with a Holy Maharishee in India who says: "The first and foremost of all thoughts in the mind of every man is the thought 'I'. It is only after the birth of this thought that any other thoughts can arise at all. If you could mentally follow the 'I' thread until it leads you back to its source you would discover that, just as it is the first thought to appear, so it is the last to disappear. This is a matter which can be experienced."

Brunton: "You mean that it is perfectly possible to conduct such a mental investigation into oneself?"

Maharishee: "Assuredly! It is possible to go inwards until the last thought 'I' gradually vanishes. A man will attain that consciousness which is immortal, and he will become truly wise when he has awakened to his true self, which is the real nature of man."

In the light of the above, dream prevision falls naturally into place. During periods of sleep and unconsciousness when Observer 1 is freed from the exacting discipline of concentrating attention on the travelling now-point, he is free to spread both forwards and backwards along the four-dimensional lifeline, producing blended images which combine and integrate elements from both the past and the future. The process is perfectly normal and to be expected if one accepts Dunne's theory of serialism, even though practical tests and experiments at Observer 1 level are arduous and difficult.

Dunne continued his experiments, sometimes on a mass basis, for many years and in the end was satisfied on statistical grounds alone that dream prevision was not simply the art of a sensitive minority, but generally universal even if difficult to recognize as such without long training and experience. That he only wrote four books on the subject is a pity, since serialism is at least worthy of a more detailed examination. Today it is virtually a forgotten science in a world which seems more concerned with the conquest of space rather than of the mind.

CHARLES FORT
AND THE UNEXPLAINED

Fish don't drop out of the sky—at least most people would say that they don't. Occasionally, however, events do occur which confound common sense and standard scientific explanation. For example, not so long ago a British housewife was astounded to find a goldfish flapping unhappily about in her hearth, apparently having just fallen down the chimney.

Such events are deemed newsworthy by bored sub-editors, and often get prominent display in the newspaper columns. They become universal talking points for a few days, and experts are called upon to submit explanations for them. The explanations are unconvincing, but in a very few days the event has been replaced in the public eye by the birth of quintuplets to a grandmother in Bolton, or by a gruesome murder on Clapham Common.

The expert might be heard breathing a sigh of relief that nobody is going to ask any more awkward questions about airborne aquatic life, and he is not likely to bring the subject up again of his own accord. So the world forgets about the mother and professes itself equally amazed when some time later a postman in Toronto is hit by a shoal of herring.

One man, though, did make a positive attempt to catalogue events that baffle scientists. In fact he devoted his life to it. His name was Charles Fort; he was born in the USA in Albany, New York, in

1874 and he died in New York City in 1932. Materially his life was not of the easiest. From a middle-class childhood he got off to a reasonable start as a newspaper reporter, and things went well enough to take him off on a "world" trip. However, on his return to New York City luck was not so good. Married now, work didn't come so easily. He tramped many miles on the streets of the city in search of a job. He tried his hand at being a novelist; many books were finished but only one was published. He did get the odd free-lance commission, but poverty was never far from the door until he was left a modest legacy. This was a great turning-point, for not only was he assured for the first time of enough money to keep him and his wife housed and fed, but he was able to devote more time to indulging in the occupation which fascinated him most and for which we remember him—collecting facts which embarrassed the scientists.

For years he could be found in the New York Public Library, assiduously sifting through piles of books and journals, making notes of any event which he considered to have been ill-explained by the scientific establishment of the day. Gradually the facts mounted up —enough to fill four published books (*The Book of the Damned, New Lands, Lo, Wild Talents*), and many reams of unbound note-paper—more than enough to keep the astronomers, zoologists, botanists and geologists supplied to this day with nagging questions.

Falls of fish? Yes there were many. The most widely publicized occurred in Wales, at Mountain Ash, Glamorgan in 1859. One February day in that year the property of one Mr Nixon was deluged with four-inch-long fishes. Many of these unfortunate animals were alive, and some survived to be exhibited at the London Zoo where they were identified as minnows and sticklebacks. Apparently not all the fish fell at once. Two inundations were reported about ten minutes apart, but both were concentrated in the twelve by eighty yard plot of Mr Nixon.

What did the scientists think? One of the most popular explanations was that a playful neighbour had emptied several buckets of pond water—minnows, sticklebacks and all—over Mr Nixon's land. Others favoured the explanation often invoked to account for showers of unusual objects—they had been taken up and dropped by a whirlwind.

Wales was by no means the only fishy spot. India did well with these phenomena too. In 1850, after one of the region's heaviest ever rainfalls, the ground at Rajkote was covered with fish, but this could not be accounted for by supposing that a local stream had overflowed in the deluge as some of the fish were discovered on top of haystacks! Earlier in 1839 a similar fall had been reported near Calcutta, only in this case the witness was struck by the pattern in which the animals hit the ground—they were all in a straight line. In these two happenings the fish had been alive; but in Futte-poor in 1833 there had been a fishy shower which was dead and dry, while three years earlier a mixture of wet and dry dead fish had rained on Fridpoor.

Were these all the results of the pranks of jesting neighbours? Unlikely to say the least. What about the whirlwind theory then? This is often used to explain why only objects of similar size and density are found together—the wind separates them from the other debris, it is said. In several of the Indian manifestations, though, the descending fish were of differing size and shape, as Fort points out. Moreover, some were shrivelled and dry while others were fresh. And in the case of the Welsh happening, two falls occurred at almost precisely the same spot ten minutes apart. Surely, Fort maintained, that was odd behaviour for a whirlwind.

There were frogs too. In 1804 large numbers of small toads were seen to fall from a thick cloud near Toulouse; in 1873 a shower of frogs darkened the sky and then covered the ground in Kansas City; in 1838 tiny frogs were found in London after a storm; and toads were found in a desert after rain. Frogs and toads everywhere, but where were the tadpoles, Fort asked. He never found a single mention of a deluge of these creatures. Yet records of snails, shellfish, lizards and snakes were there in abundance.

The orthodox explanation in all these cases is that a whirlwind or some such phenomenon snatched the contents of a pond, drew them high into the air and then let them fall back to the ground. If it is a question of "what comes down must have first gone up", then, Fort asked, where were all the other contents of the pond, the weeds, the other animals? Also, shouldn't one expect to find as many records of things rising into the air? They were very few. There was the case of a Wisconsin tornado lifting a horse and a barn right up into the air, but no trace of either was ever seen again.

The sky holds many secrets. Fort found many assertions that "phantom soldiers" had been seen in the heavens. They were witnessed by 27 people in Scotland in 1744: a mirage of British troops rehearsing for the rebellion of the following year, said the sages. Soldiers were seen in Silesia in 1785: also a mirage, it was said, this time of troops at the funeral of a general. They were seen later in the same spot, though by this time the general was long dead and buried.

Similar manifestations were reported in 1848 from Lough Foyle where the sky seemed to open to a reddish interior in which were a regiment of soldiers, warships under full sail, and a man, a woman, a swan and a peahen. Other sightings followed in 1850 and 1854; and then in 1858 Lord Roberts saw aeriel Hindu troops in India.

There were cities, too. In 1846 one appeared over Liverpool. This was said to be a mirage of Edinburgh—a panorama of that city being on show in Liverpool at the time. In the summer of the following year a French traveller reported seeing a vast and beautiful city adorned with monuments, domes and steeples on what was, before and after, a gently rolling hillside. The following year over Vienne in France there was seen, not just a city and an army (usually dismissed as mirages wherever they occurred), but also enormous lions. Could these be mirages? If so, where in France can one find enormous lions?

If not mirages, then of course one can always suppose that the observer was either mistaken, drunk, suffering from hallucinations, or lying. Drunkenness was the accusation levelled at one Lee Fore Brace who, along with the captain and the third officer of the steamship *Patna*, claimed to have witnessed two enormous luminous wheels in the sea while the ship was steaming up the Persian Gulf. It was May, 1880, when at about 11.30 at night a vast wheel-like shape about 500 or 600 yards in diameter appeared on either side of the ship. They were rotating horizontally so that the spokes seemed to "brush the ship along". The phenomenon lasted for twenty minutes.

Drunkenness? What do we find elsewhere in Fort's notes but that in 1879 a Commander Pringle of HMS *Vulture* had seen a similar sight. Submerged on either side of his ship were large wheels rotating in opposing directions, the waves of light forming the spokes extending from the surface well down into the water. This manifestation lasted about thirty-five minutes. And where did it happen? In the Persian Gulf.

The submarine wheels made their appearance elsewhere. Fort has records of them in the China Seas in 1891, 1907, 1909 and 1910. In the last instance the wheel was reported as being above the water, much to the distress of the captain, the first and second mates, and the first engineer of the Dutch ship, *Valentijn*.

Of course there were things in the air too. The inevitable unidentified flying objects long before the days of flying saucers. In Fort's notes, however, there is little mention of anything which approximates to the saucer shape. There was a spate of UFO sightings in 1898. On 8 July in Kiel an object "broad as a rainbow" was reported in the sky. It was red in colour due to the reflection from the sun which had just set. For five minutes it hung in the air shining brightly; then it began to fade, finally disappearing about eight minutes after it had first been sighted. In October of the same year people in County Wicklow in Ireland saw a golden-yellow object looking like a three-quarter moon appear in the early evening sky. It stayed in view for about five minutes before disappearing behind a mountain.

Could these have been balloons? Fort took the trouble to check through *The Times*, the *New York Times* and the aeronautical journals for mention of escaped balloons in England, the USA or Canada for the summer and autumn of 1898. He could find none.

There were other shapes. In the summer of 1762 two independent observers working in the vicinity of Lausanne in Switzerland saw a vast spindle-shaped body slowly cross the surface of the sun. So slowly in fact that it took a month to complete its passage. What was more odd was that the two observers, though only fifty miles apart on the earth's surface, did not see the subject at the same spot of the solar disc, and another observer working at the same time in Paris found no trace of it. The strange body must have been some considerable distance from the sun.

It seems reasonable to suppose that such odd phenomena have been occurring throughout history. Why haven't we heard more of them, and why haven't scientists investigated them more fully? Ah well, says Charles Fort, that is because of the way the scientist works. He forms his theories and then observes things to fit in with them. He denies the truth of an observation which contradicts his doctrines.

In *The Book of the Damned* (the title refers to the data which is cast out by the established authorities because it does not allow for explanation in terms of their theories), he cites the following examples of how authority protects itself from any necessary changes to its beliefs. In 1772 the French Academy received a report that a stone had fallen from the sky at Luce. The Academy knew very well that there were no stones in the sky and therefore they could not fall. They only seemed to fall, and if they were hot and perhaps showed signs of melting, well then they had merely been struck by lightning. In the case of the Luce object the Academy sent Lavoisier to investigate. He "absolutely proved" that this stone, which showed signs of fusion, was one such—it had been struck by lightning.

The necessity of not conflicting with a known scientific law causes the experts to cling to all sorts of tenuous explanations which may ignore many observations completely. One windless summer night in Nova Scotia a load of yellow substance fell upon a ship. It was reported as having given off nitrogen and ammonia and as having had an animal smell. A sample of the substance was sent to the editor of the *American Journal for Science*, who found pollen in it. This is hardly surprising, Fort points out, remembering that the time was June and the place Nova Scotia, bristling with pine forests. The trouble was that it was thus stated that the substance was pollen. No more mention was made of ammonia or the animal smell as it would have been too difficult to explain.

It wasn't science or even scientists in general that constituted the problem, rather it was scientific dogma. Some sciences were worse than others, and the one to get the roughest edge of Fort's observation was astronomy.

How was it that astronomers could seem to be so good at predicting events? By the simple expedient of predicting all sorts of conflicting possibilities and in the event remembering only the one that was correct ... thus spake Charles Fort. In support of this assertion he quotes by way of example the prediction of the discovery of the planet Neptune: according to Leverrier there was but one planet beyond Uranus in our solar system; Hansen had said there were two, and Sir George Airy had said there was none. One of these three was more or less bound to be right.

In the event Hansen was right (Pluto was not discovered until 1930), but it was Leverrier who received the initial accolade, even though he had been wrong about the planet's distance from the sun and the time it took to complete its journey round the sun.

The discovery of the asteroids is supposed to represent another great triumph for astronomy's great powers of predictive calculation. What was the reality? According to Fort's catalogue it all began with Piazzi, the discoverer of the first asteroid, not looking for a body whose presence in the heavens had been deduced from Bode's Law, but charting stars in the constellation Taurus. On seeing a light which he thought had moved he told the world, not that he had found the asteroids, but that he had discovered a comet. History claimed the former on his behalf.

As for the comets themselves, the Fort notes abound with incidences of unfulfilled prediction. (One can imagine how he would have revelled in the recent Kohoutek saga!) Suffice it to quote only one such occurrence. In 1892 Edwin Holmes discovered a comet and wrote that others had produced calculations which showed values for its distance from the earth which ranged from 20 million to 200 million miles, while for its diameter answers ranging from 27,000 to 300,000 miles were obtained. Three learned professors maintained that it was approaching the earth, one specifying that it would touch the earth on 21 November. The comet was in fact receding from us, and continued to do so.

Did Fort have explanations of his own for his establishment-defeating events? He certainly did, though it seems he regarded them no more seriously than he did science's most rigid dogmas.

Where did all those fish, frogs, stones and odd substances come from? He postulated that high above our earth there exists an area where gravitation does not apply, but from which objects sometimes descend to our level. This he called the Super-Sargasso Sea—a sea loaded with all kinds of flotsam including horses and barns sucked up in whirlwinds.

The sea has islands in it too, islands with strange names like Genesistrine and Monstrator. On these there were, among other things, ponds. And from time to time the bottom would fall out of one of these ponds, showering us with minnows and sticklebacks, or frogs, or toads. Because these islands float relatively near to the earth's surface and do not move very rapidly, when things fall from them they tend to land on one spot on the earth. Hence all the fish-falls in Aberdare, for instance, can be concentrated on one man's plot of land.

Fantastic? Of course it is. But then is it any more fantastic than some of the official explanations meted out to us—explanations which don't even fit the observed facts anyway?

The point about Fort is not so much that he wanted to explain the so-far inexplicable—he himself said, "I believe nothing of my own that I have written"—but that he wished to provide the world with ammunition to keep the scientists in their place.

Maybe there is a lot we could learn from him. Though today it tends to be the technologist rather than the astronomer who we allow to run roughshod over our judgment, the consequences of submitting uncritically to the opinion of the "expert" are at least every bit as dangerous as they ever were.

Crank or prophet? The world in general is only now beginning to let itself be aware that it is possible for technological advances to have adverse effects on our daily lives which can far outweigh any improvements they are supposed to bring. This is what Fort had to say on the subject: "Whoever discovered the uses of coal was a benefactor of all mankind, and most damnably something else. Automobiles, and their seemingly indispensible services—but automobiles and crime and a million exasperations. There are persons who think they see clear advantages in the use of a telephone— then the telephone rings."

Fort died in 1932.

MRS METHUEN'S EXPERIENCE

One spring afternoon in 1936, Mrs Richard Methuen was returning from luncheon with a friend, recently returned from India. They
had not met for several years, and they had so much to tell one
another that, after the other guests had taken their leave Mrs
Methuen had stayed on. Only a reminder by her chauffeur, conveyed
to her by the friend's parlourmaid, that she was entertaining guests
for dinner herself, eventually persuaded her to tear herself away
from her friend.

"This is really quite terrible of me, Ethel," she apologized. "Coming to luncheon and staying for tea, but it has been so wonderful
to see you again and we have had so much to say to one another."

"My dear Margaret," her friend smiled. "I did so want to have
you to myself. I thought the others would never leave. And what
are the social niceties between friends. When are we going to meet
again?"

"It's such a bore being twenty miles apart. Couldn't you and
John come over for a weekend soon?" Mrs Methuen suggested.
"Not a house party, just the four of us, and we can talk our heads
off. Richard is very anxious to see John again. They always got on
so well. I've stupidly come without my book. May I telephone you
tomorrow and let's arrange something."

"That would be lovely," the friend agreed, and as they embraced
at the door, "It is so good to see you again."

In the drive, Evans, Mrs Methuen's chauffeur, was inspecting the car's engine. Mrs Methuen, who knew nothing of the mysteries of the internal combustion engine, always grew apprehensive when she saw the car's bonnet raised, though Evans had often told her that the bonnet had to be lifted to check such things as the oil level and the battery, which signified nothing alarming at all. But this time, as Evans lowered the bonnet and came to open the door for her, she saw that he was looking slightly worried.

"Nothing wrong, I hope, Evans," she said.

"Nothing serious, I'm sure, mum," the chauffeur said. "But when we get to Taunton, I'll stop at a garage and get them to check the leads. I've had a look at them myself and can't see anything wrong, but to make a thorough check would be rather a dirty job, so I'll leave it to a mechanic, mum."

"But we shall get home, Evans?"

"Leave it to me, mum," the chauffeur reassured her, though feeling far from sanguine about their chances unless they could make it to Taunton, some twelve miles away.

As Mrs Methuen entered the car, a large spot of rain fell on her face.

"Oh dear!" she said. "Now it's going to rain. Look at those black clouds! Shall we be driving towards them?"

"Afraid so, mum," Evans replied. "But it will probably be a short sharp storm. Nothing to worry about, mum."

"I do hope so," Mrs Methuen sighed. Though she had often been told that the odds against lightning striking a fixed object were several million to one, and against striking a moving object even greater, she did not like motoring in a storm.

"It's all that metal," she would explain to her husband. "My father often remarked that metal is a great attractor of lightning, and one feels so shut up in a motor. I know you say, Richard, that one is safer in a car than almost anywhere except the cellars, because of the rubber tyres doing something or other which prevents the lightning from being effective, but you've never been able to tell me of a single case of a motor being struck by lightning and no one was hurt."

"Only because, my dear, I have never heard of a moving motor being struck by lightning. You worry about it quite unnecessarily."

She wound down the window to say goodbye to her friend, who called to her, "Wouldn't you like to wait until the storm has passed?"

"I'd love to," she called back. "But I must be home before dinner. Goodbye, and thank you for a lovely day. I'll telephone tomorrow and we'll arrange a weekend."

As Evans started up the car, it spluttered and the engine almost stalled. The chauffeur cursed under his breath and prayed they would make the twelve miles to Taunton. As though his prayers found favour immediately, the engine pricked up, and as he slipped into gear and released the brake, the car glided forward as though nothing at all were wrong with it.

Before they reached the road, the rain was falling heavily. As they passed through the drive gates, a vivid streak of lightning zig-zagged across the sky. It was followed by a longish pause and then a tremendous peal of thunder which sounded as though a mountain-side were cracking, making a river of reverberating, frightening noise.

Mrs Methuen pushed herself into the corner of the car, as though hoping she would become invisibly part of the upholstery. She began to tremble a little. Unclasping her handbag, she fumbled in it for the vial of smelling-salts which she was still old-fashioned enough to carry with her everywhere. The sharp pungent scent of the salts in her nostrils, made her draw in her breath with a gasp, but she felt stronger for it.

The rain was falling now in a solid sheet. Once again the light-ning flashed, and was followed by a gargantuan rattle of thunder. The windscreen wipers were incompetent to deal with the volume of water, and for safety's sake, Evans changed to a lower gear, re-ducing speed so that the car just kept moving.

The road was lined along one side by splendid oaks, whose leaves were just breaking bud, and whose branches overhung the road.

Seeing them, Mrs Methuen muttered to herself, "Whatever hap-pens we must not stop under the trees!"

She unhooked the speaking-tube and said to the chauffeur, "You won't stop under the trees, will you, Evans?"

The chauffeur shook his head. He was not all that fond of storms himself, and had no desire to be struck by lightning. Like his mis-tress, he heaved a sigh of relief when the parkland gave way to open, ploughed fields. But the rain now seemed to be falling with greater density than ever, and visibility was even more curtailed. Slowly he edged forward.

There came a sound that made it only too clear to him that his prayers had not found the favour he had at first believed they had. But this time the spluttering of the engine had become a coughing, and the car almost stopped. Frantically, he change down once more, double declutching, and to his relief the engine kept turning.

The storm, however, showed no sign of abating. Indeed, it now seemed to be directly overhead, for the flash of the lightning seemed scarcely to have disappeared before the tempestuous roll of the thunder deafened them. To Mrs Methuen cowering in the rear seat, it seemed that the gods were directing their assault at her. Again and again she steadied her wavering nerves with a whiff of smelling-salts. "But if it doesn't stop soon," she told herself, "I shall be reduced to a gibbering imbecile."

Pulling herself together, she unhooked the speaking tube again.

"Evans," she said into it, "will you, please, stop at the first house or cottage, and I will ask them if we may shelter until the storm is over."

"Very well, mum," Evans replied, knowing how upset she was being in the car in a storm, but doubting the wisdom of stopping, fearing the engine might not start again. He would stay in the car, he decided, and try to keep the engine ticking over. They had plenty of petrol.

A few minutes later they came to tall gates at the entrance of a long drive. Beside it was a small lodge. Evans saw the cottage at the same moment that Mrs Methuen tapped on the glass partition, and pulled into the approach to the gates. Without waiting for the chauffeur to open the door for her, Mrs Methuen let herself out and ran the few yards to the cottage. She had no thought for Evans, nor for the niceties of social behaviour. As another tongue of lightning forked across the sky, without knocking, she lifted the latch of the door and literally fell into the small, neatly-kept living-room. An oldish woman in a full black skirt down to her ankles, a white blouse smocked with black, and a white mob cap perched on greying hair, who was bent over the fire, looked round startled.

"Do forgive me for bursting in like this," Mrs Methuen said, closing the door behind her and standing with her back to it. "I am caught in the storm, and I am afraid of travelling when it is lightning. May I shelter with you until the storm has passed?"

The woman smiled and dropped a curtsey.

"Why, of course, m'lady," she said, gesturing to an armchair by the fire. "Sit here, m'lady, and warm yourself. Your coat and hat are wet, let me dry them for you."

"You are very kind," Mrs Methuen smiled back, and taking off her hat and coat passed them to the woman. "I wouldn't have thought it possible to have got so wet in such a short distance."

"It is certainly raining cats and dogs," the woman remarked, placing the hat on a stool by the fire, and draping the coat over the back of an upright chair. "Can I offer you some refreshment, m'lady?"

"No, no!" Mrs Methuen exclaimed quickly. "It is very kind of you, but I have just taken tea."

"Very well, m'lady. Will your ladyship excuse me for a moment? I have the cat in the scullery."

"Of course," Mrs Methuen said, and when the woman had left the room stretched out her hands to the fire, half-musing. "Why did I say I had 'taken tea'? I have never said that in my life before. But she is such an old-fashioned body. Her clothes are positively archaic. I shall be telling her that my coach and coachman are without, next."

The woman came back into the room.

"I would not be mistaken, would I," Mrs Methuen said to her, "if I thought that this is Burton Pynsent?"

"You would not, m'lady."

"Who owns the house now?"

"It used to belong to Sir William Pynsent, as you probably know," the woman said. "They say he was a great lover of the countryside. At any rate, he engaged Mr Capability Brown to plan the park and lay out the gardens. Mr Brown planned the drive, and designed the gates and this cottage. Sir William only lived in the house for a few years before he gave the whole of the property to Lord Chatham, whom he greatly admired. Are you sure I cannot offer you a glass of cowslip wine, m'lady?"

"Thank you, no," Mrs Methuen declined, and asked again, "Who lives here now?"

She did not hear the answer that would have surely surprised her, for at that moment Evans knocked on the door, and as she was speaking, the woman moved across the room to open it.

"The storm has passed, mum," Evans said. "I think we should go on."

"And the car? Is it behaving itself?"

"For the moment, mum. But don't worry. We shall get to Taunton."

She turned to thank the woman.

"It was kind of you to let me shelter," she said. "Thank you."

"It was my honour, m'lady," the woman smiled, and bobbed another curtsey.

As she walked across to the car with Evans, Mrs Methuen paused for a moment to look down the splendid drive, at the far end of which stood the gracious country house, reputedly one of the most beautiful in the West Country, glowing in the clear post-storm atmosphere.

"Isn't that perfect, Evans?" she said.

"Yes, mum. It certainly is. Who lives there?"

"I asked her twice, but she never told me. Never mind, perhaps the master will know."

Evans closed the door after her, went round and climbed into the driving seat. With symbolically crossed fingers, he put the car in gear and took off the brakes, and the car moved forward with its customary assurance, all signs of its spluttering hesitation gone.

Surprised and relieved, Evans told himself, "I'll keep my fingers crossed a little longer, though." But the farther they went, the more certain he became that whatever the trouble had been, it had passed.

* * *

One day, two years later, Mrs Methuen was glancing through the advertisements of properties for sale, and came upon one announcing that Burton Pynsent was on the market. For some time, she and her husband had been considering buying a larger house, and when she read the particulars of Burton Pynsent, even allowing for the estate agent's customary exaggerations, she believed it was what they were looking for.

When she showed the advertisement to her husband, he agreed that it would be worth looking at. So he telephoned the agents, and made arrangements for a representative to call for them two days later, and they would go together to Burton Pynsent.

As they approached the house, the agent instructed Evans to take a route that would bring them to the entrance to the drive leading to the house.

"I didn't know there were two drives," Mrs Methuen said, when she realized that they were not on the road which they had taken during the storm.

"There aren't," the agent replied.

"But this isn't the way to Capability Brown's drive, is it, Evans?" she insisted.

"No, mum, it isn't!" Evans confirmed.

"I was born and brought up in the next village, Mrs Methuen," the agent said, "and man and boy I have known Burton Pynsent. During all these years I assure you there has only been one drive, and this is it."

"How very strange!" Mrs Methuen commented, and as they

drove up to the house, she related what had happened on the day of the storm.

"I have a plan of the house and grounds here" said the agent. "Let's try and identify where you were on that day."

After a few minutes study of the plan, it was Evans who pointed out the spot.

"But these are the tennis courts," the agent said. "And they were laid down oh—ten years ago at least."

"I don't understand it!" Mrs Methuen was indeed bewildered. "I went into the cottage, the woman dried my hat and coat, and I spoke to her and she told me about Capability Brown's drive. Evans saw her, too and the gates and the drive didn't you, Evans? Two of us couldn't imagine it!"

"There's another thing, too, mum," the chauffeur said. "There's a wing of the house missing. It was here." He pointed to the plan.

"I didn't see that," Mrs Methuen admitted. "But I could have missed it because I was so taken with the beautiful drive."

"The house has been the same ever since I've known it, and that's forty odd years," the agent assured her.

The house was what they were looking for, and Mr Methuen opened negotiations. About a week later, the agent called to discuss one or two points in the contract, and he could scarcely restrain his excitement.

"I've had a search made, Mrs Methuen," he said, "and you are quite right. Capability Brown did make a drive where you said you saw it, and there were some gates and a lodge cottage. But a new drive was made seventy years ago, and the gates and cottage were removed, and the old drive allowed to become overgrown. There used to be another wing to the house, too, but it got into a bad state of repair and was demolished over forty years ago."

"But how could two people see what wasn't there?" Mrs Methuen demanded. "One person I could believe might imagine he or she saw something, but not two—and certainly not see exactly the same things that weren't there."

"Perhaps they *were* there that afternoon," suggested the agent, and when he saw Mrs Methuen's incomprehension, he went on, "There are many things that happen in this world we don't yet understand."

As Mrs Methuen pondered over it later, the only conclusion she could reach was that that afternoon, she had journeyed back in time. The woman's dress and mode of speech could be confirmation of that.

BLACK BOXES

The human animal is never more susceptible to superstition than when he is dealing with the mysteries of the way his own body functions. Modern western man hasn't really come very far since the days when he rushed to the local "cunning woman" for a potion to cure the pain in his leg.

The medicine-show, with its fast talking salesman and his bottles of sugared water, was as much a part of the history of the American West as the wagon-train and the stage-coach. And even today, sellers of biochemically worthless elixirs wax rich over sales of their products in herbalist stores and health-food shops.

If the authorities of orthodox medicine do not like this state of affairs they have none but themselves to blame, for the medical profession is among the worst for keeping its secrets from its customers, thus promoting an attitude of magic towards the curative process. Can one blame the layman for pinning his faith in the smart new remedy in the well-packaged container to that prescribed by his general practitioner if no attempt is made to tell him how either does, or does not, work?

Not that modern medicine has all the answers as research workers will readily admit. New breakthroughs often come from amazing quarters: who would have thought that a substance extracted from an ordinary-looking mould would have revolutionized the world of antibiotics, yet that is exactly what happened in the case of penicillin.

And what of the Chinese science of acupuncture? It certainly seems to work, though few in the west can tell one how.

The public may like the unorthodox nostrum, but the medical establishment hates it. The only thing it finds worse is unorthodox equipment; and inventors, especially amateur inventors, of curative devices can be sure of rough treatment.

Whatever else he may have been, Albert Abrams was certainly no amateur. He was an academic success in that he had gained a very respectable degree from Heidelberg, and was the author of about a dozen respected medical textbooks. His achievement wasn't solely theoretical either, for his activities in general practice in California earned him a much more than comfortable living. It was in the course of these therapeutic activities that he became convinced that the human abdomen had a vital role to play in diagnosing diseases.

One day while he was tapping a patient's stomach someone switched on the X-ray machine in the consulting-room. The sound produced by the tapping changed. Was there a connection between the two events? The process was repeated and the same result obtained, but only when the patient was facing east or west. This phenomenon fired the scientist's imagination. Could it be of use in diagnosis? After much painstaking research he came up with his first diagnostic invention—the Dynamizer.

This amazing instrument was not the simplest of devices to set up and use. It consisted in the main of a box filled with wires, one of which was connected to a source of electrical power while another was attached to the head of a normal healthy human being. The only contact required between the box and the patient whose ailment the apparatus was to identify was the placing inside the box of a filter paper carrying a drop of the patient's blood. The doctor would then begin to tap the stomach of his healthy assistant, listening intently for clues which would help him to label the patient's illness.

The diagnosis achieved by this method was remarkably specific; for not only did Abrams claim to identify an illness being suffered, but also the part of the body afflicted, and the age, sex and even religion of the sufferer.

How could it all work? The good doctor explained that though conventional medicine recognized that disease was the result of changes in the cell structures of the afflicted part, the real source lay at a much more fundamental level in changes in the structure of the electrons of the atoms making up the cells. These changes caused variations in the radiation given off by the body, and it was these fluctuations that were being picked up by his invention.

He later discovered that it wasn't even necessary to have a sample of the patient's blood for the box to do its work—a specimen of handwriting would do equally well. This opened up vast possibilities of cataloguing the maladies of the famous dead, but it was with the living that most of his followers were concerned.

With success in diagnosis, it ought not to be a big step to invent a device which could heal. Sure enough in due course a further instrument, the Oscilloclast, was developed and produced in commercial quantities for leasing to practitioners throughout the USA. This device was said to use vibrations to combat disease employing, according to Dr Abrams, the same principles as drugs in destroying harmful bacteria.

The theory may have appeared a little vague, but the apparatus made a lot of money for its owner. Was the world witnessing a revolution in medicine? Naturally the American Medical Association was interested. This body decided to test the process by the ruse of sending an Abrams practitioner a blood sample of a healthy male guinea-pig, saying that it came from a human female. They received back a doom-laden diagnosis involving cancer and gynaecological complaints. A similar daunting list of ailments was produced when another orthodox medical man sent Abrams some chicken blood passing it off as human. In this case the diagnosis involved not only cancer and venereal disease but also malaria. This did not daunt Dr Abrams's more ardent followers though, after all, what had been shown was that the blood of these animals produces vibration patterns similar to those of humans suffering from the diseases mentioned.

Towards the end of his life Abrams paid a visit to England. His techniques gained immediate success as talking points for fashionable conversation, but he was after something more—recognition by the British Medical Association.

Eventually a BMA committee was set up to investigate Abrams's claims, and here the doctor received rather more initial success than he had had at the hands of his native professional watch-dogs. Contrary to widespread expectation the members of that august British body, which included no less a dignitary than the King's physician himself, found the diagnostic claims made by its inventor for the equipment to have some foundation—two of the medical men reporting that they had felt their abdominal muscles contract at the appropriate point in the proceedings! However, the mechanism by which the process worked was far from clear and the BMA found itself unable to recommend that doctors should use the method.

Abrams died shortly afterwards. It was the early 1920s. Since that time black boxes have always been somewhere on the medical horizon, but not many have attracted attention from the orthodox practitioners. One that did belonged to a Dr Drown of Los Angeles. This lady had so impressed certain of her patients with her invention that they persuaded the University of Chicago to investigate her methods. This they did by arranging for a demonstration in which the doctor was to use her own apparatus to make diagnoses from ten blood samples. The attempt was abandoned after the third sample because of the doctor's lack of success. Certainly diseases were being found—there were rather too many in fact—it was just that the correct specific disease was not discovered. The investigating committee concluded that the doctor owed her success rate to postulating trouble in so many organs that she was bound to be right somewhere.

Even though it is America which has produced most of the samples of black box inventions, it is Britain which has come nearest to taking the "black magic" out of them. This was due largely to the activity of one man—George de la Warr, a civil engineer of the City of Oxford.

Early in his life he had been impressed by the success met with in treating illness by homoeopathic methods. In this form of treatment the practitioner attempts to cure his patient by feeding him doses of drugs which if administered to a healthy subject would produce symptoms similar to those being suffered by the patient. De la Warr concluded that this method of treatment worked by virtue of something which he thought of as a "life force", and he spent much time and energy in trying to detect the presence of this in plants and animals. Early experiments ended in failure, but when he began to turn his attention to producing his own modification of the black box principle for detecting this natural energy he felt that his luck had changed.

De la Warr's box did not have to have the human abdomen attached to it—a modification which immediately made his invention much more probable. In place of the human sounding-board a rubber pad was built into the surface of the instrument which also housed a collection of dials, graduated in divisions from one to ten. Inside the box was a collection of wires and spaces for housing the blood samples to be analysed.

The Englishman found, like Abrams that his apparatus was sensitive to the "vibration patterns" produced by blood samples from diseased patients; so sensitive in fact that it produced a different "reading" for each disease encountered.

How did it operate? The operator, after having loaded the blood samples into the central well, proceeded to stroke the rubber pad while he altered the setting of the first of the dials. Eventually he would find that his finger would stick on the pad. At this point he would note the dial setting and then repeat the process with the next dial until another "stick" was obtained. This dial reading was noted and so on ... The final result was a many digited number which was the code number of the disease under investigation. Seven thousand such numbers were listed in the Book of Rates which de la Warr compiled: for example 07752 showed that the patient suffered from a bacterial condition, while a reading of 6435 showed him to have an inflamation of the lower intestines.

Physical conditions were not the only things the box was good at detecting though: it was also quite proficient at sorting out mental states. The Book of Rates lists numbers for conditions ranging from "self indulgence" to "acute persecution complex".

How did it work? The lack of an external source of power baffled many investigators. The dials were variable rheostats which were connected in series to the metal plate under the rubber pad. In other words altering the setting of the dials altered the length of the circuit. Could this affect the friction of the finger on the pad? According to de la Warr the "stick" occurred because at that moment the operator's thoughts changed the signals on his skin.

Again this does not look to be a very easily understood mechanism, but did it work? Apparently so, at least enough to set its inventor trying to apply its principles to a curative box. This had the dials of its diagnostic brother, but no rubber pad. All one had to do to work it was consult the accompanying table to find the dial setting for the complaint one wished to be cured, and make those dial settings. The box would then happily broadcast the curative radiation to the patient no matter where he was. What is more the patient need not know that he was receiving such treatment. This made the therapy particularly good for use with animals— de la Warr considered them to be among his best patients—and did much to give the lie to theories that the apparatus worked by a process of auto-suggestion on the part of the patient.

Things didn't stop here though—there was more to come from de la Warr's laboratory. The next product involved the use of photographic principles, but not with an orthodox camera. Again the major component was a box with dials, but this time it was used to contain photographic plate as well as the patient's blood sample. The box was closed and the dials set to the appropriate illness reading. The result? A "photograph" of the pattern characteristic of the diseased blood sample and its associated force fields. This box could also be used for diagnosis.

One of its more spectacular successes actually saved life; not, however, the life of a man or woman, but that of a cow. This poor animal had been in a bad way for some time and was causing considerable anxiety to both its owner and its vet by its refusal to respond to treatment. A sample of its blood was sent to de la Warr who placed it in his new photographic analyser. The resulting print showed a section of the animal's stomach, but showed it to be containing some foreign body with a long irregular shape. Could it be a wire? An operation was recommended anyway, and foreign bodies including a length of wire were indeed found and removed. The animal subsequently recovered.

Dr Christopher Evans in his book *Cults of Unreason* recounts how this same box also produced interesting results with substances other than blood. On one occasion it was used to analyse water samples. Oxford tap water showed a pattern distinctly different from that produced by water from a spa, while holy water which had been blessed by a priest produced a print showing a large white cross.

The apparatus read thoughts too, and one day its inventor sat in front of it thinking of his wedding day, having first fed it samples of the blood of both him and his wife. The resulting print showed a wedding group.

The novelist Beverley Nichols describes in his book *Powers That Be* how another piece of de la Warr apparatus showed its prowess at thought-reading. He was treated to a demonstration of the "Multi-Oscillator Unit and Detector", which he describes as looking like "the sort of thing one finds in the control room of an ultra-modern television studio".

It was suggested that he should feed this monster a thought which the operator would then try and decipher by the usual method of setting the dials and consulting the code-book. The thought he chose was not easy. Cats came to his mind, but not any particular cat, rather he concentrated on "the quintessence of felinity". The rubbing of the control pad began and continued for more than a quarter of an hour. However, during the course of this time the machine narrowed down the field from all animals to non-human animals, then to cats, then to the abstract. Nichols was convinced.

De la Warr techniques could perhaps also help the fishing industry, that is if they were able to repeat another experience also recorded by Beverley Nichols. In this case a de la Warr disciple was holidaying in Ireland having taken his box along with him. He reckoned to have evolved a technique for tracking the movements of herring shoals by taking a few scales from a live fish, putting them in his box and returning the fish to the sea. One night he went to work with some freshly found fish scales, his box and a large-scale map, and by manipulating his dials located very large shoals. The following day the newspapers reported the finding of gigantic herring shoals in just the positions he had predicted.

In 1956 de la Warr retired from his job with the Oxford County Council to devote his energies to the products of his Delawarr Laboratories and the private treatment practice which he ran with his wife. The boxes of various kinds were put on the market and sold well. Unfortunately for the de la Warr's not everyone was as delighted with their purchases as was, for instance, the finder of the fish.

The most sensational discontent was registered by a Miss Catherine Phillips, and her sister, a Mrs Holdsworth. She sued de la Warr for fraud on account of the claims he had made for his boxes. The case was heard before Mr Justice Davies in the summer of 1960. All hung on showing that the science of radionics (on which de la Warr said his boxes were based) was nonsensical, and that the inventor was not honestly convinced of the truth of his own claims.

The prosecution produced a series of expert witnesses to testify to the impossibility of the black box being anything but a sham; but the defence found its own share of expert opinion, too, including a high-ranking Royal Air Force Officer and a respected Minister of the Church.

In his summing up the judge found that any dispute over the inner workings of the box was irrelevant, for no one had claimed that they understood the mechanism; rather, all they had said was that they had found it to work. He took notice of the fact that there was a great body of opinion which believed in radionics, and found himself convinced of the sincerity of de la Warr. The judgment went in the defendant's favour and costs were awarded against the plaintiff.

Unfortunately for the Delawarr Laboratories, however, they received not one penny towards meeting their expenses of over

£10,000, even though they had been awarded costs, because of a technicality in the British legal system. It was a financial blow from which the company never fully recovered, and at de la Warr's death in 1969 it was a mere shadow of what it had been ten years previously. However, his wife continues in private practice as do many box owners, confident that one day the inventor's true genius will be recognized. The products themselves? They continue to bring comfort to many people—and to cows too.

MYSTERIES OF SPACE-TIME

All the various religions of mankind postulate the presence in each of us of a non-physical element which is usually known as the soul, psyche, self or spirit. Followers of most religions find little difficulty in accepting that this invisible entity is indestructible and survives physical death by transference to another unseen world or "plane of existence" (in some cases after undergoing many cycles of reincarnation on earth). Ask them to concede, however, the possibility that an entire human being, body and soul, can be transferred while alive to such an unseen world and eyebrows will be raised in scepticism.

There is, nevertheless, the tacit admission that such an unseen world does exist. Indeed, there may be more than one—undetectable to human senses and scientific instruments, and separated from our own familiar world by dimensional barriers which, on rare occasions throughout human history have, either by accident or design, been penetrated. Alternatively, real worlds in alien planetary systems millions of light years away may be in virtual contact with our earth through space-time channels as yet unsuspected by scientists. After all, it is only recently that the famous and sinister sounding "black holes" were discovered in outer space—but more about those later.

One can, therefore, legitimately ask whether it is possible for human beings to be snatched out of this world to some other planet or plane of existence—or, conversely, for people from other worlds to visit us under conditions which would allow of no other explanation.

Take the case of David Lang, a Tennessee farmer, extensively reported in the newspapers of the day but never explained. On the afternoon of 23 September, 1880, Lang, whose farm was twelve miles from the township of Gallatin in Sumner County, spoke to his wife and two children on the veranda of their farmhouse and, in their sight, walked across a 40-acre field—and was never seen again.

As Lang was walking across the pasture-field of close cropped grass, his brother-in-law was driving an attorney in a buggy towards the farmhouse. The attorney saw Lang in the middle of the field and was about to shout to him—there were no trees, hedges, fences or boulders near the spot—when Lang vanished from sight as if the earth had suddenly opened and swallowed him up ...

The two men rushed to the spot, where they were joined by Lang's wife, but they found no crack in the turf or soil and nothing whatever to indicate what had happened or where Lang had gone. One moment he was seen to be there, the next he was no more!

Every inch of that field was subsequently searched by the police without result. A geologist was called in and he said that limestone bedrock lay a few feet under the soil but no crack or fissure could be detected in it. The search for David Lang went on for a month, but in vain ...

Ten months later, in the early August, 1881, Lang's son and daughter were walking over this same 40-acre field when they noticed that the grass at the spot where their father had disappeared showed a 20-ft.-wide circle of high, uncropped grass—all outside the circle had been well grazed, but no cow, sheep or horse would venture within that circle. For some reason the girl felt impelled to shout: "Father, are you anywhere around?" She repeated the cry four times and the boy joined in. They were about to leave the spot, thinking how stupid they were, when, on a sudden, they heard a voice call for help. It seemed far away in, but not of, this world ...

When they told all this to their mother she ran to the spot in the field and called. She swore her husband answered and she went back for several days: each day the voice grew fainter until it was heard no more.

A scientist speculating about such a weird incident might suggest a "hole in the wall" (i.e., a breach in the dimensional barrier) dividing our world from another—a hole through which people may involuntarily and unexpectedly pass or be drawn, with perhaps no possibility of a return to our own world. Or such a return might be accompanied by total amnesia obliterating all that happened just before, during and after the phenomenon.

Or, again, a victim might need to possess some psychological or psychic quirk or twist in the mind which, like a key in a lock, would open the door in the barrier. Such an individual would inadvertently fall through the gap or be swept through a space-time vortex as a swimmer might be carried away by a current under, say, an ice-flow. If he could not rediscover his point of entry the world from which he vanished may know him no more.

Of course, such phenomena can be two-way. For example there is the extraordinary episode of the two "green children" which for centuries has been a folk tale around Bury St Edmunds although the happening was in the twelfth century and referred to in the medieval chronicles of that era as *de Viridibus Pueris*. The tale concerns the appearance of two other-worldly children, a sister and a brother with green skins at a place today known as Woolpit, but then called "Wulpets" in the hundred of Thedwardsty, Suffolk.

The place-name Woolpit is said to signify a wolves' den. One Jacobean writer, Burton, author of *The Anatomy of Melancholy*, gave it as his opinion that the two green children "either fell from the sun, or were dropped from the moon". Lest it be thought that we have made giant strides in scientific explanations since those days, it must be pointed out that, in the years 1955 and 1956, the police of half-a-dozen mid-Western towns in the United States received many reports from motorists that, when driving along lonely roads at night, they had seen manikins with green skins standing in the highways near strange blazing discs in fields or near woods. Some reports had these little creatures wearing green dresses.

The earliest known chronicler of the green children phenomenon was William of Newburgh, a learned Augustinian monk who was born at Bridlington around 1136. In his *Historia Rerum Anglicarum* he wrote that "it is well known that it occurred in the reign of King Stephen" and went on:

"Although the thing is asserted by many, yet I have long been in doubt about the matter, deeming it ridiculous to credit a thing supported by no rational foundation, or at least one of a mysterious character; yet, in the end, I was so overwhelmed by the weight of so many competent witnesses, that I have been compelled to believe and wonder over a matter I was unable to comprehend and unravel by the powers of my intellect ..."

"The place is called Wolpittes after the ancient cavities or pits for wolves near it. The boy and girl were completely green in their persons, and wore garments of strange colour and unknown materials when they emerged from the pits. They wandered through the fields in astonishment, and were seized by reapers who took them to the village. Here they were for some days kept without food and gaped at by persons from far and near. By degrees, after many months of food and bread, they gradually changed their colour and became like ourselves and learnt our language. The boy was the younger of the two but died first. They said they had lived in a twilight land, not warmed by the beams of the sun. 'A certain luminous country is seen not far distant from ours and divided from it by a considerable river.' "

Another who wrote positively on the phenomenon was Ralph of Coggeshall who, in 1207, was abbot of the reformed Benedictine Abbey which once stood in the picturesque village of Coggeshall in Essex. He puts the happening in the reign of Henry II (1154–89) and reports that he was told the story by Sir Richard de Calne, in whose house at Wykes the two children are said to have resided. If this were so then Abbot Ralph heard the tale later than William of Newburgh, presumably 35 to 40 years after it happened, whereas Newburgh appears to have questioned many eye-witnesses about the affair, being contemporaneous with it. The story goes that the green girl gradually became white and lived as a domestic servant for some years in de Calne's house, later marrying at King's Lynn in Norfolk.

Coggeshall writes thus of the episode in his *Chronicon Anglicarum*:

"This boy and girl, brother and sister, came out of holes at St Mary de Wulfpetes, next the edge of a pit found there. They had all the members (limbs) like those of other men; but in the colour of the skin they differed from all other mortals of our earth. For all the surface of their skin none could understand.

"At that time, weeping inconsolably, they were taken, out of astonishment, to the house of Richard de Calne at Wikes. Bread and other food was placed before them but they would not eat it and, indeed, with great hunger from fasting, they were a long time tormented because, as the girl afterwards confessed, that all that food could not be consumed by them. However, at last beans cut off or torn from stalks were brought to the house and they fell on them with great avidity. So now those beans were given to them and they broke open the beanstalks, not the pod or shell of the bean, evidently supposing that the beans were contained in the hollows of the stalks. But, not finding beans within the stalks, they again began to weep which, when the bystanders noticed, they opened the shells and showed them the beans themselves. Whereupon, with great joyfulness, they ate beans for a long time, entirely, and would touch no other food.

"The boy, however, almost always weighed down with sickness and debility, grew weaker and weaker and died in a short time. The girl, indeed, always enjoying good food and growing accustomed to whatever food one was pleased to set before her, completely lost the green colour of her skin and by degrees assumed a normal red-blooded condition of the body (like our own). And, after being regenerated by the holy waters of baptism, for many years remained in the service of the soldier, aforesaid, as from the same soldier and his family we often heard. She showed herself very wanton and lascivious. Indeed, asked frequently about the men of her own country, she affirmed that all who dwelt in her land, or had lived there, were coloured green, and no sun was perceived there, but that a brightness or shining such as would happen after sunset was seen there.

"Asked in what manner she had come from the land aforesaid, with the boy, she replied that they were following sheep or small cattle, and arrived at a certain cavern. On entering it they heard a certain delectable sound of bells and, in trying to reach the sweet sound, they wandered for a very long time through the cavern until they came to its end. Thence emerging, the excessive brightness of our sun and the unwonted warm temperature of our air astonished and terrified them. For a long time they lay at the mouth of the cave. When overcome with anxiety they wished to flee but they could not in the least find the entrance to the cavern, until they were seized by the people of the countryside."

The interesting feature of these two accounts of the emergence of the green children is that no scintilla of doubt is thrown on the fact: each writer is satisfied that two such children did appear and dwell among the inhabitants of our own physical world. Abbot Ralph's narrative seems to hint that the world from which they came was subterranean or that their other dimensional world existed side by side with ours—a "twilight world".

Gervase of Tilbury who was probably a contemporary of Ralph de Coggeshall wrote that the green children were sitting in the pits weeping when the beans were brought to them. This suggests that the children went back to the pits to seek the "hole in the wall"— the point of re-entry from the third to their trans-dimensional plane so that they might be transferred back to the world from which they had so mysteriously come to twelfth-century England. According to Gervase the girl married a man at Lynn "where she was said to be living a few years since"—that is, at the end of the twelfth or in the early years of the thirteenth century. When asked whence they had come Gervase reports the children as replying:

"We are folk of St Martin's Land, for he is the chief saint among us. We know not where the land is, and remember only that one day we were feeding our father's flock in the field when we heard a great noise like bells as when, at St Edmunds (Bury St Edmunds, Suffolk) they all peal together. And on a sudden we were both caught up in the spirit and found ourselves in your harvest-field. Among us no sun rises, nor is there open sunshine but such a twilight as here goes before the rising and setting of the sun. Yet there is a land of light to be seen not far from us, but cut off from us by a stream of great width."

The reference to St Martin's Land is curious—Martin's mass was the time of death, or killing. St Martin's Land, or Merlin's Land, was the land of necromancy, a twilight land to which the old gods were forced to descend after a cataclysm which sank an ancient continent. Beans were considered by some ancient cultures to contain souls in a state of change offering a mystic link with the dead. There was also much speculation among the ancients that the way to the Antipodes was through a series of vast subterranean tunnels and caverns.

*　　*　　*

Certain scientists and researchers of our own generation have put forward the hypothesis that mankind's development throughout history has been significantly influenced by visitors from extra-terrestrial civilizations. Much of the evidence for this appears in Erich Von Daniken's controversial book *Chariots of the Gods?*, which includes such inexplicable curiosities as the strange, immense statues of Easter Island, the mathematical singularities of the structure of the famous Pyramid of Cheops and the criss-cross of "air-field runways" with strange marker symbols on the plain of Nazca in Peru which can only be seen and identified from a very high aircraft altitude.

The Bible itself contains passages which can be interpreted as referring to the intervention of beings from outer space. Take, for instance, the description of the destruction of Sodom and Gomorrah, in Genesis XIX, 27–28: "And Abraham got up early in the morning to the place where he stood before the Lord; and he looked toward Sodom and Gomorrah, and toward the land of the plain, and beheld,

and lo, the smoke of the country went up as the smoke of a furnace."
The account could well fit that of an atomic explosion.

Then how about visits from alien spacecraft? According to the
prophet Ezekiel, "I looked and, behold, a whirlwind came out of the
north, a great cloud, and a fire unfolding itself, and a brightness was
about it, and out of the midst thereof as the colour of amber, out
of the midst of the fire ..." Ezekial goes on to give details of this
craft, and he writes, "I heard also the noise of the wings of the living
creatures that touched one another and the noise of the wheels over
against them, and the noise of a great rushing." He also gives precise
details for the construction of what can only be described as a space
communications centre including, if you like, an astronaut's headquarters, although the materials prescribed are primitive.

Moses and the Israelites were guided out of Egypt by "a pillar of
cloud by day" and by night "a pillar of fire", which *might* be
interpreted as a description of a rocket. And what of the warning
to Moses in Exodus XIX, 11–12: "Be ready against the third day,
for the third day the Lord will come down in the sight of all people
upon Mount Sinai. And thou shalt set bounds unto the people round
about, saying, Take heed of yourselves, that ye go not up into the
mount, or touch the border of it; whosoever toucheth the mount shall
surely be put to death." Confronted with a modern Apollo spacecraft
and today's strangely attired astronauts a primitive non-technological
people would no doubt be equally inarticulate in describing facts.

As for unseen worlds beyond dimensional or other barriers, even
our own sophisticated scientists, who can safely put men on the
moon and bring them back to earth, can be caught out—and that
excludes psychic phenomena. Radio astronomy, for example, is still
a relatively new science, and almost every day the giant radio tele-
scopes throughout the world are discovering new radio stars which
can be heard but not seen. Even more sensational is that very recent
discovery of what are popularly known as "black holes" in space.
These are simply old stars which, on reaching the closing stages of
their useful "burn out", collapse inwards upon themselves and
create a localized gravitational field (a "kink" in space-time) so
intense that not even light or radio waves can escape. Undetectable
to any instrument devised by man, they have nevertheless existed
for millions and perhaps billions of years. What else, then, lies
around the corner still awaiting discovery and still conforming to
what we regard as natural physical laws?

Talk of another "plane" of existence is generally meaningless, for
a plane has only two dimensions, namely length and breadth but no

thickness, and the denizens of such a world would be as insubstantial as the images on the smooth surface of a cinema screen. We ourselves live in a universe of four dimensions (if not more) of which three are spatial and the fourth is time. We can measure all four (time being measured by a clock) but physically we are only capable of perceiving three. To think of the fourth dimension as a kind of complete universe in itself is an error. A dimension is simply a line or a direction which is totally independent of any other dimension—that is, it must be at right angles to all other dimensions.

For a trans-dimensional cosmos to exist which would be in any way comparable with our own an additional four dimensions would be required, not overlapping with ours, and each new dimension extended at right angles to all others. Such a concept defies the human imagination, although it can be expressed mathematically. This would mean that an adjacent trans-dimensional cosmos, undetectable to human science, would at least need to occupy dimensions five, six, seven and eight, if such exist—but who knows? There are too many mysteries in our own universe which need unravelling first, in particular those of the mind and the human spirit. That they will eventually be seen to obey natural laws is beyond doubt, but as yet we do not know those laws. Meanwhile, we use our imaginations in more familiar materialistic channels.

Professor John Taylor, who holds the chair of mathematics at King's College, University of London, discusses in his recent book, *Black Holes: The End of the Universe?*,* the evidence of ancient records—Sumerian, Tibetan and Indian—suggesting that spacecraft from other worlds have visited earth many times in the past and made contact with mankind. He also notes many pointers in today's attitudes towards a general disenchantment with science.

"There is a greater interest everywhere," he writes, "in anti-scientific activities, as evinced by the general hippy and drop-out culture of the last decade, with its bizarre music, resort to drugs and great interest in the literature of fantasy. A world inhabited by Hobbits, with their dislike of machines more complicated than a forge-bellows or a hand-loom, and by dwarves, elves, wizards and terrible creatures of the dark, has more appeal to many of the younger generation than one in which the atoms wend their certain way to unleash ever greater power for man over his surroundings ...

"Fantasy may even take so great a control that strange objects and visitors from outer space are seen and, in extreme cases, com-

* Published by Souvenir Press. Price, £2·50.

municated with. Unidentified flying objects are still of great popular interest. An alternative fantasy is the world beyond the senses, of the 'psi' faculty—telepathy, telekinesis, precognition and other powers of the mind. This activity merges into witchcraft, which is still practised by a surprisingly large number of educated people in the world ...

"We are naturally led to ask what produces this increasing revolt against science and the life of reason. There would, in fact, appear to be a general cause for this. We live in a world which is certainly incomprehensible. We ask how and why we are here, what was the beginning of it all, what will its end be, what is time or space, and many other impossible questions.

"If we keep our eyes closed and our heads down and refuse to worry about these whys and wherefores of our existence we can usually muddle through. But once we look up and notice how strange our world really is then we very soon find ourselves drowning in a sea of ideas, conjectures, wild surmises and beliefs. Each of these pulls us towards a different island of hope and assurance like so much flotsam and jetsam. Many of us acquiesce and establish ourselves on the best island of faith we can find. Some of us try to struggle on, but often glance with envy at those who have swallowed the carrot of a particular set of beliefs."

Not everyone would go all the way with these views, but what is undeniable is the trend to reject technology for technology's sake. A fragment of moonrock may be priceless, but it does nothing to assuage famine and starvation. Nor must it be assumed that everything defined as "anti-scientific" is necessarily fantasy. The world does not begin and end with a ruler and a clock, and to believe that it does is a fantasy in itself. In the long run, are disappearing men and green children any stranger than black holes in space?

Index

NOTES ON AUTHORS

Michael Blee was educated as a scientist and has since worked as a teacher, a musician and a journalist. In the last capacity he has specialized in scientific and technological topics which he has often found every bit as strange and menacing as any supernatural phenomena.

Douglas Collier, novelist, journalist, and for a time editor of a weekly publication in Calcutta. He has been interested in the occult since his days in India, where several adepts were among his friends.

Patrick Duggan, writer and actor. On leaving school he joined the Dublin Gate Theatre Company, and appeared in the original production of Brendan Behan's *The Quare Fellow*. His books include *The Travelling People* and *The Golden Horseshoe*. Like so many Irishmen he has always been fascinated by the mystical and the occult.

Andrew Ewart, author and Fleet Street Editor, has made contact with many weird and mysterious happenings during his long newspaper career. He has written two remarkable case-books on evil: *The World's Wickedest Men* and *The World's Wickedest Women*.

Ian Fellowes Gordon: born in New York, only reached his Scottish homeland at the age of fifteen. Served for nine years in the British regular army. Now works with the BBC World Service in London, and has written ten books. His interest in the weird and occult commenced while serving with the spirit-worshipping Kachin irregular levies in the jungles of Northeastern Burma.

Michael and Mollie Hardwick are one of the world's busiest and most versatile husband and wife literary teams. Together and separately they have written some forty books. They were responsible for the BBC series "Mystery Playhouse" and "Tales of Mystery and Suspense".

Doddy Hay has been teacher and tail-gunner, regular officer and irregular broadcaster, county cricketer and RAF rugger blue, Cresta rider and international sky diver, syndicated journalist and test parachutist, full-time author and part-time unskilled labourer. Despite the rugged outdoor image, he says he does not so much believe in ghosts as "knows" that they exist.

Charles Eric Maine, though professionally an industrial journalist and editor, is also the author of twenty-five books, fiction and non-fiction, some of which have been translated into eight languages, including Japanese, Hebrew and Greek. He has made a study of the occult, and has drawn upon this source for a number of his science-fiction works.

Ronald Seth was seconded to Special Operations Executive in 1942 and parachuted into Estonia to carry out sabotage and organize resistance. Post-war, he became a full-time writer, specializing in the history, organization and administration of espionage, and in naval and military history for the general reader. Throughout his life he has had unlooked-for psychic experiences, and has come to accept that in some as yet unexplained way other worlds interpenetrate our own.

Clare Smythe is an industrial journalist, a reader for motion-picture companies, a feature-writer and a former editor of children's books. Her family lived in the up-country districts of Kenya, and she early became inured to the reality of African magic.

Rosemary Timperley, teacher, journalist and novelist, has always been interested in the supernatural. She has edited five books of ghost stories.

James Wentworth-Day, author, editor, royal biographer, broadcaster, historian and sportsman. Among his multifarious activities he has had an abiding interest in the weird and the supernatural, and is recognized as being an authority on hauntings in East Anglia and elsewhere.

Lawrence Wilson has written books and articles on a wide variety of subjects (including history, topography, literature and psychology) but, as well as the factual, has always been most interested in the non-rational side of life which is covered by this volume.

ACKNOWLEDGEMENTS

The editor expresses his acknowledgements to publishers for their courtesy in permitting condensations from the following books:

Rider and Company, *A Search in Secret India* by Paul Brunton, *A Search in Secret Egypt* by Paul Brunton, *Twenty Years as a Ghost Hunter* by Elliot O'Donnell; Martin Secker and Warburg Ltd., *Come Into My World* and *The Animals Came in One by One* by Buster Lloyd-Jones; Souvenir Press Ltd., *Unfinished Symphonies: Voices from Beyond* by Rosemary Brown; Hutchinson and Company (Publishers) Ltd. and Doubleday and Company Inc., *The Search for Bridey Murphy* by Morey Bernstein.

He also expresses his gratitude to Ian MacHorton and Henry Maule for permitting condensation of *Safer than a Known Way* (Odhams).